Inside Civil Procedure

What Matters and Why

Inside
Civil Procedure
What Matters and Why

Second Edition

Howard M. Erichson
Professor of Law
Fordham University School of Law

Wolters Kluwer
Law & Business

Copyright © 2012 CCH Incorporated.

Published by Wolters Kluwer Law & Business in New York.

Wolters Kluwer Law & Business serves customers worldwide with
CCH, Aspen Publishers, and Kluwer Law International products.
(www.wolterskluwerlb.com)

To contact Customer Service, e-mail customer.service@wolterskluwer.com,
call 1-800-234-1660, fax 1-800-901-9075, or mail correspondence to:

Wolters Kluwer Law & Business
Attn: Order Department
PO Box 990
Frederick, MD 21705

Printed in the United States of America.

1 2 3 4 5 6 7 8 9 0

ISBN 978-1-4548-1097-1

Library of Congress Cataloging-in-Publication Data

Erichson, Howard M.
    Inside civil procedure : what matters and why / Howard M. Erichson.—2nd ed.
        p. cm.—(The inside series)
    Includes bibliographical references and index.
    ISBN 978-1-4548-1097-1 (alk. paper) 1. Civil procedure—United States—
Outlines, syllabi, etc. 2. Pleading—United States—Outlines, syllabi, etc. I. Title.

    KF8841.E75 2012
    347.73'5—dc23
                                        2012016219

About Wolters Kluwer Law & Business

Wolters Kluwer Law & Business is a leading global provider of intelligent information and digital solutions for legal and business professionals in key specialty areas, and respected educational resources for professors and law students. Wolters Kluwer Law & Business connects legal and business professionals as well as those in the education market with timely, specialized authoritative content and information-enabled solutions to support success through productivity, accuracy and mobility.

Serving customers worldwide, Wolters Kluwer Law & Business products include those under the Aspen Publishers, CCH, Kluwer Law International, Loislaw, Best Case, ftwilliam.com and MediRegs family of products.

CCH products have been a trusted resource since 1913, and are highly regarded resources for legal, securities, antitrust and trade regulation, government contracting, banking, pension, payroll, employment and labor, and healthcare reimbursement and compliance professionals.

Aspen Publishers products provide essential information to attorneys, business professionals and law students. Written by preeminent authorities, the product line offers analytical and practical information in a range of specialty practice areas from securities law and intellectual property to mergers and acquisitions and pension/benefits. Aspen's trusted legal education resources provide professors and students with high-quality, up-to-date and effective resources for successful instruction and study in all areas of the law.

Kluwer Law International products provide the global business community with reliable international legal information in English. Legal practitioners, corporate counsel and business executives around the world rely on Kluwer Law journals, looseleafs, books, and electronic products for comprehensive information in many areas of international legal practice.

Loislaw is a comprehensive online legal research product providing legal content to law firm practitioners of various specializations. Loislaw provides attorneys with the ability to quickly and efficiently find the necessary legal information they need, when and where they need it, by facilitating access to primary law as well as state-specific law, records, forms and treatises.

Best Case Solutions is the leading bankruptcy software product to the bankruptcy industry. It provides software and workflow tools to flawlessly streamline petition preparation and the electronic filing process, while timely incorporating ever-changing court requirements.

ftwilliam.com offers employee benefits professionals the highest quality plan documents (retirement, welfare and non-qualified) and government forms (5500/PBGC, 1099 and IRS) software at highly competitive prices.

MediRegs products provide integrated health care compliance content and software solutions for professionals in healthcare, higher education and life sciences, including professionals in accounting, law and consulting.

Wolters Kluwer Law & Business, a division of Wolters Kluwer, is headquartered in New York. Wolters Kluwer is a market-leading global information services company focused on professionals.

For Sara Ann, Danny and Jake

Summary of Contents

Contents

Preface

Some students love civil procedure. Most don't. Not everybody finds it easy to master topics like personal jurisdiction or res judicata, which—let's face it—strike some people as technical, dry, and unintuitive. I've taught civil procedure long enough to know that not everybody *gets* it. This book is devoted to helping you get it.

The key to learning civil procedure is to get inside it. Procedural rules and doctrines that at first seem incomprehensible finally make sense when you understand what they're trying to do, how they're used in practice, and how they fit into the bigger picture. I suppose you could try to memorize rules without really understanding how they work or how they fit into the overall system, but why would you? It's not going to accomplish what your civil procedure professor expects of you, and it's certainly not going to give you what you need in order to serve clients in the real world of litigation.

This book explains the major topics in civil procedure. You won't find endless citations of cases and law review articles on each topic. You won't find every exception to every twist of every nuance. Nor will you find details that you'll simply look up when you're in practice. I'm not going to tell you, for example, the time limit for responding to a request for admissions in federal court. All right, 30 days.

What you will find are clear explanations and a host of features designed to help you master the material. The Overview at the beginning of each chapter positions the material in that chapter within the field of civil procedure. The Frequently Asked Questions (FAQs) give straight answers to questions that commonly pop up in a civil procedure course, and clear up common mistakes and misconceptions. Sidebars add color and offer insights, study tips, and practice pointers. For a number of topics, you'll find a step-by-step Analysis that demonstrates how you might apply the material. The Summary feature near the end of each chapter gives you a quick and easy guide to the most basic points covered in that chapter. And the Connections feature at the end of each chapter helps you fit the points made in that chapter with the other topics in civil procedure. By the end of each chapter, you should have a clear understanding of not only how the procedural rules and doctrines work, but also how the pieces of the puzzle fit together.

The Second Edition builds on the success of the first edition and updates the book from beginning to end. The past few years have seen numerous amendments to the Federal Rules of Civil Procedure and to the federal jurisdiction and venue statutes, as well as a number of Supreme Court decisions on civil procedure issues. The summary judgment rule has been thoroughly revised. Congress altered the statutes governing venue, venue transfer, and subject matter jurisdiction. Most significantly, the Supreme Court's sudden interest in procedural topics has led to big decisions on personal jurisdiction, subject matter jurisdiction, the *Erie* doctrine, and class actions. All of these recent cases are addressed in the new edition.

For most law students, the course on civil procedure feels different from other first-year courses such as contracts, torts, property, and criminal law. Other courses focus on substantive law, the rights and duties that the law establishes, whereas procedure is all about the process for resolving disputes that arise under those substantive rights and duties. But don't make the mistake of viewing procedure as secondary or insignificant. Process matters. Any lawyer will tell you that the outcome of a case often depends on its procedural path. As Representative John Dingell said during a House subcommittee hearing, "I'll let you write the substance . . . and you let me write the procedure, and I'll screw you every time."[1] Procedural rules affect the likelihood of achieving just outcomes. And process matters for its own sake. We're talking, after all, about nothing less than our system of justice. Treating participants fairly and taking the resolution of disputes seriously rank among the most important things we do in a civilized society.

This book focuses primarily on procedure in the federal courts, because that's what most law school civil procedure courses emphasize, and because much procedure in the United States, even in state courts, follows the model of the federal rules. Unless noted otherwise, the specific rules cited are Federal Rules of Civil Procedure, but you'll find important state variations mentioned throughout the book.

As you learn about each topic, think about how you will *use* these procedures as a lawyer. To serve your clients well in an adversary system of justice, you need to understand the strategies available under the rules of procedure. Lawyers often compare litigation to a chess game or some sort of ritualized battle. Chess and other games of strategy require players to see all available options, anticipate opponents' moves, and see several moves ahead. Others have compared litigation to theater. Lawsuits involve the presentation of competing stories, and skilled lawyers understand how the rules of procedure create opportunities to present a compelling story based on the evidence. Thinking about the ways in which you can use your procedural knowledge for your clients will greatly enhance your understanding of each topic.

Always look for how each part fits into the whole. You cannot really understand summary judgment, for example, without seeing how it relates to pleadings, discovery, and trial. Although this book necessarily teaches procedural topics one at a time, ultimately you have to understand civil procedure as a seamless web in which each aspect of the litigation process relates to all of the others. But enough metaphors. It's a seamless web, it's a chess game, it's theater, it's ritualized battle. . . . It's civil procedure, and it's time to get down to learning it.

Howard M. Erichson

April 2012

---

[1] Hearing on H.R. 2327, 98th Cong. 312 (1983).

Acknowledgments

I thank Fordham Law School and Seton Hall Law School for their generous support of this project. I thank my research assistants on this book, Lincoln Davis Wilson, Victoria Belyavsky, and Joshua Steinberger, not only for their meticulous work but also for never letting me forget that this book is for law students. Thanks also to research assistants Robert Gonello and Sunila Sreepada who worked primarily on other projects but ably assisted with this book as needed. At Aspen, I thank Carmen Corral-Reid, Richard Mixter, Barbara Roth, and Lisa Wehrle, as well as outside reviewers who offered valuable suggestions. I am indebted, finally, to two groups of people without whom I could not have written this. My colleagues at my own institutions and throughout the field of civil procedure have taught me so much about how to understand this area of law and how to convey it effectively. This book is saturated with their teaching. Finally, my students have been a constant source of challenge and inspiration. Their questions, confusions, ideas, and insights are woven into every page.

Credit is given for the cartoons appearing on page 69 to © Peter C. Vey. The New Yorker Collection. www.cartoonbank.com; on page 120 to Michael Maslin. The New Yorker Collection. www.cartoonbank.com; and on page 231 to Al Ross. The New Yorker Collection. www.cartoonbank.com.

Inside Civil Procedure

What Matters and Why

Subject Matter Jurisdiction

1

A first step in civil procedure is understanding the limits on the power of courts. Suppose a judge in traffic court entered a judgment purporting to  grant a divorce and award child custody—no one would consider the judgment legitimate. Why, exactly? Because the judge's power does not extend to that category of cases. In other words, a traffic court lacks **subject matter jurisdiction** over a family law case. *Federal* courts too have limited subject matter jurisdiction, which is the focus of this chapter. Jurisdiction is about power and the structure of our federal system of government. Federal subject matter jurisdiction delineates the power of the federal courts as a matter of federalism (the division of powers between the federal and state governments) and separation of powers (the division of powers between the legislative, executive, and judicial branches of government). From the lawyer's perspective, jurisdiction is also about strategy. Because lawyers perceive strategic advantages in different courts, jurisdictional doctrines set up a game of forum selection strategy that both plaintiffs and defendants play.

O V E R V I E W

A. INTRODUCTION TO STATE AND FEDERAL COURTS

1. One Nation, Multiple Court Systems
2. Trial and Appellate Courts
3. Federal Subject Matter Jurisdiction

A. Introduction to State and Federal Courts

You cannot start learning jurisdictional doctrine without a clear picture of the judicial framework. Courts in the United States do not constitute a unitary and uniform system, but rather multiple systems of multilayered courts. They include a federal court system and multiple state court systems, and each system comprises layers of trial courts and appellate courts.

(1) One Nation, Multiple Court Systems

Each of the 50 states has its own court system. So do U.S. districts and territories such as the District of Columbia, Puerto Rico, and the U.S. Virgin Islands. The state court systems employ their own judges, and are supported by the taxpayers of each state (except the courts of the District of Columbia, which are funded by the federal government). Some states hold judicial elections to select their judges, while others use an appointment process.

    Each system of state or territorial courts includes courts of limited jurisdiction and courts of general jurisdiction. Courts of **limited jurisdiction** vary from state to state, but may include small claims courts, municipal courts, probate courts, traffic courts, and family courts. What makes them courts of limited jurisdiction is that they are empowered to hear only certain categories of cases. Municipal courts, for example, often handle traffic violations, small claims, and misdemeanors, but would not adjudicate felony criminal cases or civil lawsuits for substantial money damages. Courts of **general jurisdiction**, by contrast, can hear any type of case unless it is specifically excluded from the court's power. The name for the court of general jurisdiction varies from state to state. In Texas, it's the District Court. In Tennessee, it's the Circuit Court. In New York, confusingly, it's called the Supreme Court. A number of states label their court of general jurisdiction the Superior Court, to draw a contrast between courts of general jurisdiction and courts of limited jurisdiction, or inferior courts. By whatever name, every state has at least one court of general jurisdiction.

In addition to the more than 50 state and territorial court systems in the United States, there is an additional court system that includes courts across the entire nation. These are the federal courts—the judicial branch of the U.S. government. The federal courts form the central focus of this book and of most law school civil procedure courses; they also present the stickiest problems of subject matter jurisdiction. At a theoretical level, you might picture a map of the 50 states, each with its own state court system, and floating above it, a map of the entire United States with its system of federal courts. Here in the real world, however, lawyers and litigants experience the state and federal courts as institutions that function side by side, presenting different procedural opportunities depending on the nature of the lawsuit. For many lawyers, the visual image of these multiple court systems is not abstract floating maps, but rather a state courthouse building with a federal courthouse literally across the street. Depending on subject matter jurisdiction, some cases can be filed only in the state court, some only in the federal court, and some in either place.

Foley Square, New York, with state courthouse on the left and federal courthouse on the right.
Photo courtesy of Philip Schatz and the Federal Bar Association SDNY Chapter.

(2) Trial and Appellate Courts

Each of the state and territorial court systems, like the federal court system, comprises layers of trial courts and appellate courts. Cases begin in the trial court and make their way to an appellate court if a dissatisfied party appeals. In rare instances, courts other than trial courts have *original jurisdiction* rather than merely *appellate jurisdiction*.

The three-tiered federal court system includes the U.S. district courts, the U.S. courts of appeals, and the U.S. Supreme Court. With few exceptions, federal cases are filed originally in the district court, and the district judge oversees the pretrial and trial process. There are currently 94 federal districts, each of which has a number of judges. Some states and territories have only a single district, such as the District of Connecticut, the District of Minnesota, and the District of Puerto Rico. Others have multiple districts, such as the Northern, Central, Southern, and Eastern Districts of California.

If a party appeals the judgment of the district court, the appeal goes to the U.S. court of appeals. Judges on the courts of appeals usually decide cases in three-judge panels. The courts of appeals are divided into 13 circuits; you will often hear lawyers refer to them as *circuit courts*. Twelve circuits cover geographically defined areas — the circuits numbered First through Eleventh, plus the District of Columbia Circuit. Appeals from the Southern District of Texas, for example, go to the U.S. Court of Appeals for the Fifth Circuit, which includes Texas and Louisiana. The Federal Circuit does not cover a specific geographical area, but instead hears appeals of patent cases and appeals from certain federal agencies and several specialized federal courts — the Court of International Trade, the Court of Federal Claims, and the Court of Appeals for Veterans.

From these 13 U.S. courts of appeals, losing parties may attempt to take a further appeal to the U.S. Supreme Court. Keep in mind, however, that the Supreme Court hears very few cases each year, so the vast majority of cases end either in the district court or the court of appeals. We'll address the details of appellate jurisdiction in Chapter 10.

Most of the state court systems contain three tiers just like the federal system, although the names vary significantly. We've already seen that some state trial courts use names that make it easy for a novice to confuse them with federal courts, such as the District Courts of Texas, the Circuit Courts of Tennessee, and the Supreme Court of New York. State intermediate courts of appeals, such as California's Court of Appeals or New Jersey's Superior Court Appellate Division, hear appeals from the trial courts. Each state has a high court, often called the state supreme court, although again, New York manages to confuse things by naming its highest court the Court of Appeals. This responsibility may be divided; Texas has a nine-justice Supreme Court for civil cases and a separate nine-judge Court of Criminal Appeals. Some smaller states employ a two-tier system in which appeals go directly from the trial courts to the state's high court.

On questions of state law, there is no higher judicial authority than the state high court. But if a state court case involves a question of *federal* law — for example, if a party argues that a state statute violates the U.S. Constitution — then the U.S. Supreme Court has jurisdiction to hear an appeal from the state high court or whichever state court was the last to hear the case. Thus, most appeals to the Supreme Court come from the federal courts of appeals, but each year the Supreme Court hears a number of cases from the state courts that raise important federal issues.

FEDERAL AND STATE COURT SYSTEMS

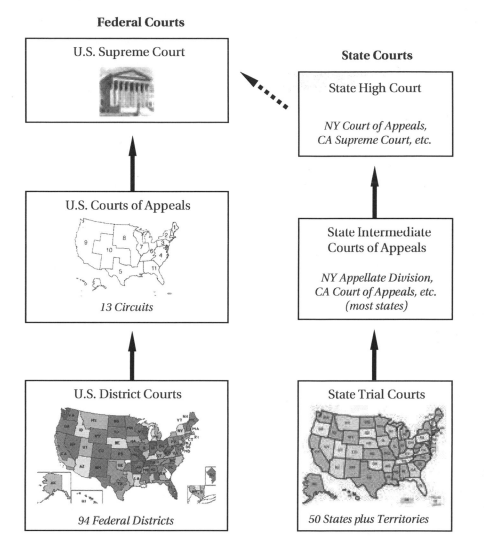

Federal Courts

U.S. Supreme Court

State Courts

State High Court

*NY Court of Appeals,
CA Supreme Court, etc.*

U.S. Courts of Appeals

13 Circuits

State Intermediate
Courts of Appeals

*NY Appellate Division,
CA Court of Appeals, etc.
(most states)*

U.S. District Courts

94 Federal Districts

State Trial Courts

50 States plus Territories

(3) Federal Subject Matter Jurisdiction

Federal courts are courts of limited jurisdiction. This is fundamental, both as a building block in learning civil procedure and as a matter of constitutional law. Federal courts have two attributes, constitutionally speaking, that require constraints on their powers—they're federal, and they're courts. Because they are *federal*, the U.S. courts' powers must be limited to avoid encroaching on the sovereignty of the states, as a matter of **federalism**. Because they are *courts*, their powers must be limited to avoid encroaching on the executive and legislative branches, as a matter of **separation of powers**.

Article III of the Constitution establishes the judicial branch of the federal government and defines the outer limits of the powers of the federal judiciary. According to Article III, Section 2, the judicial power of the United States extends only to certain categories of cases. These categories include "all Cases, in Law and Equity, arising under this Constitution, the Laws of the United States, and Treaties," as well as

"Controversies between two or more States; — between a State and Citizens of another State; — between Citizens of different States; . . . and between a State, or the Citizens thereof, and foreign States, Citizens or Subjects."[1] It also includes cases in which the United States is a party, cases involving ambassadors or consuls, and maritime cases.

Inclusion in Article III, however, does not automatically confer that power on the federal district courts. The Constitution establishes a Supreme Court and declares which categories of cases may fall within federal judicial power, but then leaves it up to Congress to decide whether to create any lower federal courts and, if so, which powers to grant to those courts. Congress promptly created the lower federal courts in the Judiciary Act of 1789 and gave the federal courts original jurisdiction over certain types of cases within the constitutional limits of Article III, including cases between citizens of different states (diversity jurisdiction, which is now codified at 28 U.S.C. §1332). Congress later enacted statutes authorizing the federal courts to hear additional types of cases within the constitutional limits, most significantly the power to hear cases arising under federal law (federal question jurisdiction, which is now codified at 28 U.S.C. §1331).

CONSTITUTIONAL AND STATUTORY GRANTS OF JURISDICTION

U.S. Const., Art. III, §2

28 U.S.C. §1331   28 U.S.C. §1332

Civil procedure professors like to illustrate the relationship between Article III and the jurisdictional statutes with a Venn diagram like the one above. We could clutter up the picture by including dozens of jurisdictional statutes, but you get the idea. The circles represent statutory grants of jurisdiction (such as §1331's grant of federal question jurisdiction and §1332's grant of diversity jurisdiction), which cannot exceed the bounds permitted by Article III of the Constitution. The jurisdictional grants overlap because a case that arises under federal law may also be between citizens of different states.

Most of these statutes grant the federal courts subject matter jurisdiction concurrently with the jurisdiction of the state courts. With **concurrent jurisdiction**, a

---

[1]U.S. Const., art. III, §2.

party can choose to file the case either in state court or in federal court. Some jurisdictional statutes, however, grant the federal courts **exclusive jurisdiction**, which means that such cases may be brought only in federal court.

I know a professor who teaches subject matter jurisdiction by describing an image of two courthouses—a state court and a federal court across the street. The state court has a big sign out front saying "All Welcome," which the federal court does not. The federal courthouse is two stories, and to get up to the courtroom on the second floor, one must either take the escalator (for those with claims arising under federal law) or the rickety old stairs (for those who satisfy the requirements for diversity jurisdiction). I like this image not only because it differentiates between state court general jurisdiction and federal court limited jurisdiction, but also because it conveys a sense of the jurisdictional choices that face litigants. As a lawyer representing a plaintiff, you will have to decide whether to file your client's case in state court or federal court. Often, it will be clear to you that your case cannot be heard in federal court—that you cannot climb either the escalator or the stairs to the courtroom—because the case lacks any basis for federal subject matter jurisdiction. You will file those cases in state court

because federal court is not an option. Other cases, however, will present a basis for federal jurisdiction. Then you'll make the strategic decision whether to file your case in the state court or in the federal court across the street.

One final point before we turn to the legal doctrines governing specific types of subject matter jurisdiction. Subject matter jurisdiction is never waivable. The parties, in other words, cannot simply agree to give a court power over their case if the court's subject matter jurisdiction does not extend to that type of case. Whenever a court realizes that it lacks subject matter jurisdiction, the court *must* dismiss the case even if no party has objected. Even if no one notices the problem until late in the litigation process, dismissal follows as soon as the court realizes that it lacks subject matter jurisdiction. Think about the time bomb aspect of this. There have been cases in which parties spent years litigating the factual and legal issues of the dispute, only to have an appellate court throw the case out of court when it realizes that jurisdiction is missing.

F   A   Q

Q: If the parties waive any objection to subject matter jurisdiction, why shouldn't the court decide the case?

A: In Chapter 2, we'll see that objections to *personal jurisdiction* can be waived by the parties. That's because personal jurisdiction is a right that belongs to the party, so a party may voluntarily submit to a court's personal jurisdiction. And parties may agree to be bound by *arbitration*, which takes a dispute entirely out of the court system, because arbitration is a matter of contract. Subject matter jurisdiction of the courts, by contrast, presents an inherent constraint on the power of an arm of the government, a constraint the Founders purposely imposed. With regard to federal courts, subject matter jurisdiction serves the values of federalism and separation of powers by limiting the judiciary's powers to particular classes of cases that are deemed appropriate for resolution by federal courts.

B. Federal Question Jurisdiction

Unsurprisingly, federal courts have jurisdiction to hear cases that arise under federal law. The general **federal question jurisdiction** statute, 28 U.S.C. §1331, gives the U.S. district courts original jurisdiction over "all civil actions arising under the Constitution, laws, or treaties of the United States." Thus, when plaintiffs sue under federal statutes governing civil rights, securities, antitrust, or other federal laws, they may file their cases in federal court.

What seems surprising from the perspective of the twenty-first century is that the general federal question jurisdiction statute was not enacted until 1875. For the first century of our country's existence, most federal law claims could be brought only in the state courts, and the federal courts were reserved largely for cases between citizens of different states. By expanding federal question jurisdiction in the wake of the Civil War and Reconstruction, Congress ensured the availability of a forum not hostile toward federally created rights.

Originally, the statute granted federal question jurisdiction only in disputes that involved more than a certain dollar amount. By 1980, however, this amount-in-controversy requirement was removed. Currently, federal courts have jurisdiction over cases arising under federal law regardless of the amount at stake.

(1) The Well-Pleaded Complaint Rule

Federal question jurisdiction may appear simple at first glance, but determining which cases fall within its ambit turns out to be complicated. What exactly does it mean for a case to "arise under" federal law? That was the question the Supreme Court addressed in the famous case of *Louisville & Nashville Railroad Co. v. Mottley*.[2]

The Mottleys had received lifetime passes to ride on the railroad. Subsequently, Congress passed a statute prohibiting railroads from issuing lifetime passes. The railroad informed the Mottleys that it would no longer honor their passes. The Mottleys sued the railroad in federal court for breach of contract. The railroad contended that the passes were now illegal, but the Mottleys argued that as a matter of statutory interpretation, the ban on lifetime passes did not apply to previously issued passes, and if it did apply, then it was unconstitutional. The case made its way through the lower courts. When it finally reached the Supreme Court, the Court dismissed the case for lack of subject matter jurisdiction. (Recall that the absence of subject matter jurisdiction requires dismissal no matter how far along a case may be, and even if neither party has objected to the court's jurisdiction.)

---

[2]211 U.S. 149 (1908).

The Mottleys had figured that the federal court had jurisdiction over their claim because it arose under federal law. After all, the dispute occurred because of the federal law banning railroad passes. Moreover, the litigation revolved around two questions—a question of federal statutory interpretation (whether the statute applied to the Mottleys' situation) and a question of federal constitutional law (whether the statute violated the U.S. Constitution). The Supreme Court, however, saw things differently. Even though the outcome depended on questions of federal statutory and constitutional interpretation, at the most basic level the Mottleys' claim was simply a breach of contract claim under state law. The federal issue arose not as part of the Mottleys' claim, but rather as the railroad's *defense* to the breach of contract claim, and the Mottleys' response to that defense.

Federal question jurisdiction, according to the Supreme Court, cannot depend on an anticipated federal defense. For federal question jurisdiction, the claim itself must arise under federal law. Many authorities refer to this notion as the *well-pleaded complaint rule.*

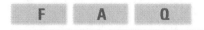

Q: Does the well-pleaded complaint rule have anything to do with whether a complaint is well pleaded?

A: Not really. Federal question jurisdiction does not depend on whether a complaint is "well pleaded" in the sense of verbal clarity or eloquence. Rather, the idea is to suppose that the complaint simply states the basis for the plaintiff's claim, and to ask whether such a complaint—the bare essentials of the claim—would raise the federal issue. The point of the well-pleaded complaint rule is that you cannot premise federal question jurisdiction on an anticipated federal defense or on some issue of federal law that's likely to come up during the litigation. Nor can federal jurisdiction depend on a counterclaim asserted by the defendant. Rather, you must show that the plaintiff's claim itself arises under federal law.

Most of the time, this means that federal question jurisdiction is reserved for cases that are created by federal law. Federal statutes have created numerous causes of action in such areas as antitrust, civil rights, intellectual property, labor, and securities. Under §1331, federal courts have jurisdiction over these claims. Claims created by state law, such as common law claims involving contracts, torts, or property, or claims under a myriad of state statutes, ordinarily do not fall within federal question jurisdiction.

(2) State Law Claim with Federal Issue

The *Mottley* rule gets you most of the way there in terms of understanding federal question jurisdiction. In general, if a claim is created by federal law, then federal question jurisdiction follows, and if a claim is created by state law, then federal question jurisdiction does not follow. But it would be an oversimplification to say that federal question jurisdiction *never* gives jurisdiction over state law claims. Occasionally, state law claims involve federal law so centrally that the federal courts will exercise federal question jurisdiction. Some call it "type two" federal question jurisdiction ("type one" would be claims that are created by federal law, which constitute the overwhelming majority of federal question cases). Federal courts have federal question jurisdiction over state law claims if (1) federal law constitutes an essential element of the pleaded claim, (2) the federal issue is actually disputed and substantial, *and* (3) federal jurisdiction would not interfere significantly with the division of labor between state and federal courts.

Here's how it comes up. A plaintiff sues on a state law claim, such as negligence or breach of contract. But an essential piece of the plaintiff's claim, as pleaded in the complaint, is that the defendant violated some federal law. In one sense, such a case satisfies the *Mottley* requirement that federal law appear in the statement of the claim and not merely as an anticipated defense. But can we really say that a claim "arises under" federal law if, when you get right down to it, it's a state law claim?

A useful case to remember is *Merrell Dow Pharmaceuticals v. Thompson*.[3] The plaintiffs sued Merrell Dow, a drug manufacturer, for injuries that they claimed were caused by the defendant's product. It was a state law tort claim, but the plaintiffs' assertion of negligence was that Merrell Dow breached its duty under the Food, Drug and Cosmetic Act, a federal statute. That statute regulated the drug industry, but it did not create a federal cause of action for private plaintiffs. Therefore, the Supreme Court decided 5-4 that even though the plaintiffs' case relied on federal law for an element of the claim, it did not "arise under" federal law for purposes of federal question jurisdiction.

In contrast to *Merrell Dow*, the Supreme Court upheld this elusive type of jurisdiction in *Grable & Sons Metal Products v. Darue Engineering & Manufacturing*.[4] The IRS had seized property owned by Grable and sold it to Darue. Grable sued under state law to quiet title to the property, alleging that the notice of seizure given by the IRS was defective, and therefore that the sale to Darue was invalid. The complaint was well pleaded in the *Mottley* sense because it required federal law (IRS notice provisions) to assert an element of the claim. Moreover, the federal government had a substantial interest in assuring that IRS notice provisions were interpreted consistently. The federal issue in the case was disputed. Finally, the Court noted that adjudication of the case would not interfere with the state/federal division of labor because the situation would rarely arise.

In light of *Merrell Dow* and *Grable*, it's possible to identify the four conditions listed at the beginning of this section as the test for federal question jurisdiction over a state law claim that raises a federal issue. But remember that most federal question cases involve claims created by federal law; *Grable* represents a pretty uncommon exception.

C. Diversity Jurisdiction

The Framers of the Constitution worried that state courts might favor their own citizens over out-of-staters. This concern led the Framers to authorize federal courts to hear cases between citizens of different states. You might question whether local bias remains as significant a problem as it was when Congress enacted the Judiciary Act of 1789. Indeed, in recent decades some federal judges and others have advocated abolishing diversity jurisdiction. On the other hand, there are still cases—

---

[3]478 U.S. 804 (1986).
[4]545 U.S. 308 (2005).

particularly disputes between a local individual and an out-of-state corporation — in which the out-of-stater feels more comfortable in federal court than in a state court with locally elected judges. In any event, despite calls for its abolition, **diversity jurisdiction** — federal jurisdiction based on diversity of citizenship — has remained a staple of the federal courts ever since their founding.

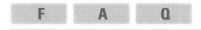

F A Q

Q: The citizenship of the parties has nothing to do with the subject matter of the action, so isn't it misleading to call it *subject matter* jurisdiction?

A: You're right. Probably we should call it something catchy like "jurisdiction over particular categories of actions." Sometimes, a court's subject matter jurisdiction really does depend on the subject matter of the litigation, such as federal question cases in federal court or matrimonial cases in family court. Other times, however, it has nothing to do with the subject of the litigation, such as diversity of citizenship in federal court or dollar limits in small claims court. I won't try to defend the name, but just make sure you stay clear on the distinction between a court's power over categories of actions (subject matter jurisdiction) and a court's territorial power over the parties (personal jurisdiction, addressed in Chapter 2).

For federal diversity jurisdiction, a case must meet two separate requirements. First, the parties must have diverse citizenship as defined in the statute. To apply the diversity requirement, you need to understand the sufficient types of diversity, how to determine citizenship, and how to apply the complete diversity requirement. Second, the amount in controversy must be more than $75,000. To apply the amount-in-controversy requirement, you need to understand how to value the stakes of a lawsuit, as well as the rules concerning whether the stakes of multiple claims can be aggregated.

(1) Types of Diversity

Diversity jurisdiction applies not only to cases between citizens of different states, but also to several other scenarios involving diverse citizenship. Look at the statute, 28 U.S.C. §1332(a), and you'll see that it lists four types of diversity. First and most basically, it grants jurisdiction over cases between citizens of different states (New York plaintiff suing a South Carolina defendant). Second, it covers cases between citizens of a state and citizens of a foreign state (New York plaintiff suing a Brazilian defendant), unless the foreigner is a permanent resident alien who is domiciled in the same state. Third, it includes cases between citizens of different states in which foreign citizens are additional parties (New York plaintiff suing a South Carolina defendant and a Brazilian defendant). Finally, it grants jurisdiction over cases between a foreign state as plaintiff and citizens of a state or of different states (the country Brazil suing a South Carolina defendant).

Notice what this leaves out. There's no diversity jurisdiction over cases between citizens of foreign states. If a Nigerian plaintiff tries to sue a French defendant in a U.S. federal court, the court would not have subject matter jurisdiction based on diversity of citizenship, although the court might have federal question jurisdiction if the case arises under federal law. So don't make the mistake of assuming that any form of diverse citizenship gives rise to federal jurisdiction. "Diversity of citizenship"—like much of civil procedure—is more technical than that, so read the statute carefully before jumping to conclusions.

For diversity jurisdiction, no plaintiff can have the same citizenship as any defendant. We will look at this "complete diversity" requirement in more detail after seeing how citizenship is defined for different types of litigants, but keep the requirement in mind as you think about these various configurations.

Types of Diversity		
Type of Diversity	Statute	Example
Citizens of different states	§1332(a)(1)	NY π v. SC Δ^*
Citizen of state and foreigner	§1332(a)(2)	NY π v. Brazil Δ
Citizens of different states, plus foreigner	§1332(a)(3)	NY π v. SC Δ, Brazil Δ
Foreign state versus citizen of state	§1332(a)(4)	Brazil v. SC Δ

*π = plaintiff; Δ = defendant

(2) Determining Citizenship

Obviously, to determine whether a court has diversity jurisdiction you have to know the citizenship of the parties. Not so obviously, determining a party's citizenship can get complicated.

Individuals. For purposes of diversity jurisdiction, courts determine an individual's citizenship based on domicile. So if you want to be able to analyze diversity jurisdiction, you'd better learn how to determine a person's domicile.

Domicile means a person's home, or more technically, physical presence plus an intent to remain indefinitely. At any given moment, every individual has a single domicile. No one is without domicile, and no one has multiple domiciles. (You can see why this is a useful way to define citizenship for purposes of jurisdiction.) If I own a vacation house in Maine and often travel to New York, but my primary home is in New Jersey, then I'm domiciled in New Jersey. If I leave New Jersey to wander the country for a year, I'm still a New Jersey domiciliary unless and until I take up residence in another state with an indefinite intent to remain there. If I leave New Jersey to take a two-year position in California, but do not intend to remain in California after the job ends, then I'm still a New Jersey domiciliary even while I'm living in California. Even if I never intend to return to New Jersey—"I don't know where I'll end up when I leave California after this job, but I'm never going back to Jersey!"—I'm still a New Jersey domiciliary until the moment when I take up residence somewhere with an indefinite intent to stay there.

There is a subjective aspect to this inquiry because part of the definition of domicile involves what's inside the individual's head. Cases addressing the question of domicile sometimes involve college or graduate school students who have moved out of state for college, and in the battle over federal subject matter jurisdiction, the parties dispute whether the student's domicile has changed to the state where the student attends school. To determine whether the student intends to remain in the new state indefinitely, courts look at things like driver's license and voting registration, as well as the individual's own subjective statement of intent. In the much-publicized litigation over whether Mark Zuckerberg stole the idea for Facebook, a district court ruled in 2007 that Zuckerberg was still domiciled at his parents' house in New York even though he had moved to California. At the time the case was filed, Zuckerberg's intent "was to stay in California for a semester or maybe two to work on Facebook and see how it would go, but then he planned to return to school at Harvard."[5]

Corporations. When the litigant is a corporation, the diversity jurisdiction statute defines citizenship two ways.[6] First, a corporation is considered a citizen of its state of incorporation, which means the state under whose laws the corporation was formed. In addition, a corporation is considered a citizen of the state of its principal place of business. This means that a corporation can have more than one state of citizenship for purposes of diversity jurisdiction. General Motors Corporation, for example, is incorporated in Delaware (like many large U.S. corporations), and has its principal place of business in Detroit, Michigan. For diversity jurisdiction, General Motors is considered a citizen of both Delaware and Michigan. Microsoft Corporation, by contrast, is a Washington corporation with its principal place of business in Redmond, Washington. For diversity jurisdiction, Microsoft is simply a citizen of Washington. If a corporation has been incorporated under the laws of multiple states or countries, it is considered a citizen of each one.

Next question: How do you determine a company's "principal place of business"? Until recently, some courts used a "nerve center" test, focusing on the location of corporate headquarters, while others used a "muscle" test, focusing on where the bulk of the company's day-to-day operations were located. In 2010, the Supreme Court adopted the nerve center test: "We conclude that 'principal place of business' is best read as referring to the place where a corporation's officers direct, control, and coordinate the corporation's activities."[7] In other words, look for the company's main corporate headquarters.

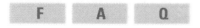

F   A   Q

Q: Can a corporation have more than one principal place of business?

A: No. Section 1332(c) says "principal place" — singular — and means it. Even if a company does extensive business in different states, only one state may be considered its principal place of business for purposes of diversity of citizenship jurisdiction.

---

[5]ConnectU LLC v. Zuckerberg, 482 F. Supp. 2d 3, 31 (D. Mass. 2007).
[6]28 U.S.C. §1332(c).
[7]Hertz Corp. v. Friend, 130 S. Ct. 1181, 1192 (2010).

Unincorporated Associations. Partnerships, labor unions, and other unincorporated associations are treated differently from corporations. For purposes of diversity jurisdiction, such entities are considered citizens of every state in which any member is a citizen. In other words, if partners are citizens of Minnesota, Wisconsin, and Illinois, then the partnership is a citizen of all three states.

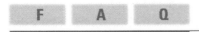

Q: Given the definition of citizenship for unincorporated associations, won't the complete diversity requirement mean that diversity jurisdiction rarely exists for cases involving partnerships or unions with widespread membership?

A: Yes.

(3) Complete Diversity

For jurisdiction based on diversity of citizenship, **complete diversity** is required. In other words, no plaintiff may have the same citizenship as any defendant. As a practical matter, this is a huge limitation on diversity jurisdiction. Lots of cases involve multiple parties, and corporations may have dual citizenship. Therefore, even in cases between citizens of different states, the federal courts often lack diversity jurisdiction because some party on one side of the *v* is a citizen of the same state as some party on the other side of the *v*.

You won't find the complete diversity requirement in the plain language of §1332(a). But for over two centuries—since the Supreme Court's decision in *Strawbridge v. Curtiss*[8]—this is how courts have interpreted the diversity jurisdiction statute. Surprisingly, the Supreme Court has held that the complete diversity requirement applies only to the statute, not to Article III, Section 2 of the Constitution, even though the language is essentially identical. This means that Congress has the constitutional power to enact statutes (like the Class Action Fairness Act, which you'll encounter shortly) that allow diversity jurisdiction based on minimal diversity (any plaintiff's citizenship differs from any defendant's citizenship), even though the standard analysis under §1332(a) requires complete diversity.

Applying the complete diversity requirement is straightforward. Simply look at the citizenship of each of the plaintiffs and see whether any state of citizenship is the same as that of any of the defendants. If a Florida plaintiff sues a Texas defendant and a Florida defendant, then complete diversity is lacking, so there's no diversity jurisdiction. But if a Florida plaintiff sues a Texas defendant and a Louisiana defendant, or if a Florida plaintiff sues two Texas defendants,

Sidebar

DRAWING LITIGATION

When studying or litigating cases with multiple claims or parties, you may find it helpful to visualize the structure by drawing the litigation with an arrow for each claim (rather than simply using a *v.*). The more complex the structure, the more important it becomes to keep track of all the claims and parties. As shorthand, lawyers often use *P* and *D*, or the Greek letters pi (π) and delta (Δ), for plaintiff and defendant.

---

[8]7 U.S. 267 (1806).

then complete diversity exists. Don't forget the dual citizenship of corporations. If a Florida plaintiff sues General Motors (a Delaware corporation with its principal place of business in Michigan), then complete diversity exists. But if a Delaware plaintiff sues General Motors, then complete diversity is lacking.

What if a litigant's citizenship changes during the course of the litigation? For example, an individual may change domicile by moving from one state to another, or a corporation's principal place of business may shift. A long-standing rule, recently reaffirmed by the Supreme Court,[9] holds that the moment for determining citizenship is when the case was filed. Thus, if there's complete diversity at the time of filing, the federal court retains jurisdiction even if one of the parties later changes citizenship.

COMPLETE DIVERSITY:

FL π → TX Δ ↘ LA Δ	FL π ⇉ TX Δ TX Δ	FL π → DE/MI Δ

NO COMPLETE DIVERSITY:

FL π → TX Δ ↘ FL Δ	FL π ⇉ TX Δ TX π	DE π → DE/MI Δ

(4) Amount in Controversy

In addition to the requirement of complete diversity, §1332 imposes an amount-in-controversy requirement. The point is to reserve federal judges for important work. Remember that federal district courts are a limited resource — each judge is appointed by the president and confirmed by the Senate, and these federal judges are vastly outnumbered by state court judges. If a case arises under federal law, the current thinking goes, it makes sense to give litigants the right to have the case decided by a federal judge. But if a case does not arise under federal law, and the basis for jurisdiction is diversity of citizenship, then federal judges should not be burdened with the case unless the stakes are high enough. Currently, for diversity jurisdiction, the amount in controversy must be greater than $75,000.[10] From time to time, Congress amends the statute to increase the amount.

How do you determine the amount in controversy? Usually, it's just a matter of looking at the amount demanded by the plaintiff in the complaint. Complications arise in three situations: (1) when a complaint demands an impossible amount, (2) when a party seeks nonmonetary relief such as an injunction, or (3) when a lawsuit includes multiple claims or parties.

---

[9]Grupo Dataflux v. Atlas Global Group, 541 U.S. 567 (2004).
[10]28 U.S.C. §1332(a).

Plaintiff's Demand. As a starting point, courts generally consider the amount in controversy to be whatever amount the complaint demands. If the complaint demands a specific dollar amount that is at least $75,000.01, then it satisfies the requirement. In some courts, a plaintiff may simply state that "plaintiff demands an amount in excess of $75,000." The question is not whether or how much the plaintiff actually wins, but rather how much the complaint demands. If an Oregon plaintiff sues an Idaho defendant for negligence, demanding $100,000 in damages, then a federal court has subject matter jurisdiction, even if the plaintiff ultimately recovers only $50,000, or even if the plaintiff loses the case.

Relying so heavily on the amount stated in the complaint gives plaintiffs some control over jurisdiction. A plaintiff can avoid diversity jurisdiction by choosing to demand $75,000 or less. Or a plaintiff can create jurisdiction by demanding a higher amount, but bear in mind that plaintiffs risk sanctions if they lack a factual basis for their demand, as we'll see in Chapter 5.

The plaintiff's demand does not control, however, if it appears *to a legal certainty* that the claim is really for less. If the plaintiff *cannot* recover an amount that meets the amount-in-controversy requirement, then the court lacks jurisdiction. For example, if an applicable statute caps the damages at $50,000 or if the lawsuit is to recover on an exact $50,000 debt — but the complaint implausibly demands more than $75,000 — the court will ignore the impossible amount demanded in the complaint and hold the amount-in-controversy requirement unmet.

Nonmonetary Relief. What if the plaintiff seeks injunctive relief rather than money damages? That's more challenging because the court must place a dollar value on ordering the defendant to do (or not to do) something. Some courts have measured the value of the injunction by its monetary value to the plaintiff. Other courts have held that either the value to the plaintiff *or* the cost to the defendant may satisfy the requirement.[11]

Aggregation of Claims. Often, a complaint includes multiple claims or multiple parties. Therefore, you need to know whether amounts can be added up to meet the amount-in-controversy requirement. Courts refer to this as the question of whether the amounts may be *aggregated*. The answer depends on whether you're aggregating the claims of a particular plaintiff against a particular defendant or whether you're aggregating claims involving multiple parties.

A plaintiff may aggregate as many claims as he or she has against a single defendant in order to satisfy the amount. Suppose a plaintiff has a $40,000 negligence claim and a separate $40,000 breach of contract claim against a particular defendant. If the plaintiff joins these two claims in a single lawsuit, then the amount in controversy is $80,000, which exceeds $75,000 and therefore meets the requirement for diversity jurisdiction, even though each claim by itself would be jurisdictionally insufficient.

However, claims by or against multiple parties may not be aggregated for purposes of the amount-in-controversy requirement. If Plaintiff 1 and Plaintiff 2 each have $40,000 breach of contract claims against a defendant, their claims do not satisfy the amount-in-controversy requirement, even if they are joined in a single lawsuit. Similarly, if a plaintiff has claims against multiple defendants, those amounts may not be aggregated. For the amount-in-controversy requirement, *be sure to look at each plaintiff's claims against each defendant.*

---

[11]*See* Olden v. Lafarge Corp., 383 F.3d 495, 503 n.1 (6th Cir. 2004).

AMOUNT-IN-CONTROVERSY REQUIREMENT MET:

AMOUNT-IN-CONTROVERSY REQUIREMENT NOT MET:

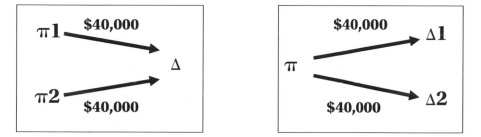

An exception to the no-aggregation rule applies to claims involving a common undivided interest, where multiple parties assert joint rather than individual rights. For example, if co-owners sue to recover property worth $100,000, alleging they own it jointly, their claim would be treated as a single $100,000 claim for purposes of the amount in controversy, rather than as two $50,000 claims. Courts have struggled with whether to extend this "common undivided interest" approach to claims by partnerships and other scenarios. Be aware that some courts may interpret it more broadly than others, but in general, think of this as a relatively infrequent exception to the general rule against aggregating claims by or against multiple parties when determining the amount in controversy.

Q: Why not allow parties to aggregate the amounts of related claims to meet the amount-in-controversy requirement, even if they involve multiple parties?

A: Good question. If the point of the requirement is to protect federal courts from spending time on relatively trivial state law disputes, it's hard to see why a federal court should not adjudicate a dispute involving related claims by or against multiple parties that add up to a significant amount.

(5) Diversity Jurisdiction over Class Actions

Congress expanded federal subject matter jurisdiction over class actions by enacting the Class Action Fairness Act of 2005 (CAFA). In a class action, as we'll see in Chapter 7, a party sues as a representative on behalf of all others who are similarly situated. For diversity jurisdiction over class actions, CAFA eliminates the complete diversity requirement and alters the amount-in-controversy requirement. You will find this newest portion of the diversity jurisdiction statute at 28 U.S.C. §1332(d). CAFA does not affect federal question jurisdiction; under §1331, federal courts can hear class actions that arise under federal law.

Under CAFA, a class action is generally subject to federal jurisdiction as long as it meets minimal diversity and the aggregate amount in controversy exceeds $5 million. Minimal diversity means that at least one member of the class is a citizen of a different state from any defendant.[12] In class actions, it's almost impossible *not* to satisfy minimal diversity, and intentionally so, as the point of the statute was to extend federal jurisdiction to all substantial class actions. Think about it. As long as any two class members are citizens of different states, minimal diversity is met because at least one of the class members must be diverse from a defendant. Similarly, as long as any two defendants are citizens of different states, minimal diversity is satisfied because at least one of them must be diverse from a plaintiff. CAFA spells out a few narrow exceptions, denying diversity jurisdiction in cases where the defendants and many of the plaintiffs are from the same state.[13]

Rather than the usual in-excess-of-$75,000-per-plaintiff requirement, CAFA requires over a $5 million *aggregate* amount in controversy. This means that in a class of hundreds, thousands, or millions of plaintiffs, the amounts of their claims are combined to determine the total amount. For example, if a class action includes 50,000 class members with claims averaging over $100, it meets the requirement. You can appreciate the significance of this provision when you think about how often class actions involve very large numbers of low-value claims. Not many class actions are comprised of individual claims in excess of $75,000, but lots of class actions involve over $5 million in the aggregate.

D. Other Bases for Federal Jurisdiction

In addition to the two dominant bases for federal jurisdiction—federal question and diversity of citizenship—federal courts have several other bases for subject matter jurisdiction. Federal jurisdiction extends to cases in which the United States government is a party,[14] as well as cases involving ambassadors and other public ministers.[15] Federal courts also have subject matter jurisdiction over admiralty and maritime cases.[16]

Congress has enacted dozens of jurisdiction-granting statutes, including bankruptcy,[17] antitrust,[18] intellectual property,[19] and civil rights.[20] Some of these statutes constitute specific applications of the general federal question jurisdiction of §1331 and can be explained mostly as historical remnants that predate the enactment of the general federal question jurisdiction statute. Others, such as the statute on patent and copyright jurisdiction, retain significance because they grant *exclusive* federal

---

[12]28 U.S.C. §1332(d)(2)(A).
[13]28 U.S.C. §1332(d)(3)-(4).
[14]Id. §§1345 (United States as plaintiff), 1346 (United States as defendant).
[15]Id. §§1251(b)(1), 1351.
[16]Id. §1333.
[17]Id. §1334.
[18]Id. §1337 (commerce and antitrust).
[19]Id. §1338 (patent, copyright, and trademark).
[20]Id. §1343.

jurisdiction, allowing the federal courts to be the sole arbiters of these areas of federal law.

For controversies between states, Congress not only granted exclusive federal jurisdiction but made it *original* jurisdiction in the Supreme Court,[21] so unlike other federal court cases that originate in district court, controversies between states go straight to the Supreme Court. In *New Jersey v. New York*,[22] for example, the two states asserted competing claims to a portion of Ellis Island in New York Harbor.

E. Supplemental Jurisdiction

If a federal court has subject matter jurisdiction over a claim — whether federal question, diversity, or some other basis — may the federal court also adjudicate related claims that do not have an independent basis for federal jurisdiction? That's the question of **supplemental jurisdiction**.

(1) Grant of Supplemental Jurisdiction

The federal supplemental jurisdiction statute grants power to the federal district courts to hear additional claims that arise out of the same facts as a claim over which the court has jurisdiction. That statute, 28 U.S.C. §1367, is an important one for you to understand, but you may find its language rather cryptic. The basic grant of supplemental jurisdiction in §1367(a) says that if a federal court has jurisdiction over an action, then the court "shall have supplemental jurisdiction over all other claims that are so related to claims in the action within such original jurisdiction that they form part of the same case or controversy under Article III of the United States Constitution." What's this about "the same case or controversy under Article III"? It makes more sense when you understand that the statute is trying to tell you to refer to the Supreme Court's analysis in *United Mine Workers v. Gibbs*.[23]

In *Gibbs*, the plaintiff Paul Gibbs sued the United Mine Workers union in federal court, asserting two claims. One claim was based on the Labor Management Relations Act, a federal statute. His other claim was a state common law claim for tortious interference with contract. For the labor law claim, the court had federal question jurisdiction. But what about the tort claim? No federal question jurisdiction — the claim did not arise under federal law. No diversity jurisdiction — Gibbs was from Tennessee and the union's membership included Tennessee citizens.

UNITED MINE WORKERS v. GIBBS

**Labor claim
(federal law)**

Gibbs ━━━━━━▶ **UMW**
········▶

**Tort claim
(state law)**

---

[21]Id. §1251(a).
[22]526 U.S. 589 (1999).
[23]383 U.S. 715 (1966).

The Supreme Court decided that it was OK for the state tort claim to tag along with the federal labor claim. Federal court jurisdiction is constrained by Article III of the Constitution, but Article III extends federal judicial power to "cases" arising under federal law, to "controversies" between citizens of different states, and so on. If a related claim forms part of the same "case" or "controversy" as the claim supporting federal jurisdiction, the Supreme Court held, then jurisdiction may extend to the related claim. Because Gibbs's federal claim and state law claim derived from a "common nucleus of operative fact," the Court held that the federal district court had power to adjudicate the state law tort claim along with the federal claim.

When a later case[24] raised questions about whether such jurisdiction was permissible in the absence of legislation, Congress promptly enacted the supplemental jurisdiction statute. The statute ratified the Supreme Court's holding in *Gibbs* by granting federal courts the power to decide related claims, even if they lack an independent jurisdictional basis. In light of the statute's history, you can see that §1367(a)'s grant of supplemental jurisdiction over "claims that are so related . . . that they form part of the same case or controversy under Article III" depends on whether the claims arise out of a "common nucleus of operative fact," as the Court put it in *Gibbs*.

The basic grant of supplemental jurisdiction in §1367(a) does not distinguish between different bases of original jurisdiction or between different types of related claims, so it can work in a wide variety of situations. One is the *Gibbs*-type scenario in which a court has federal question jurisdiction over one claim and supplemental jurisdiction over a related state claim. Another is a federal claim and a related state counterclaim, cross-claim, or third-party claim. (If you haven't studied joinder, which is covered in Chapter 7, don't despair—these supplemental jurisdiction scenarios will make more sense after you've learned about joinder of claims and parties.) Yet another is when the court has diversity jurisdiction over an original claim and a party asserts a related counterclaim, crossclaim, or third-party claim that does not satisfy complete diversity or the amount-in-controversy requirement. As long as the claim arises out of the same facts as the claim over which the court has original jurisdiction, the grant of supplemental jurisdiction applies.

SUPPLEMENTAL JURISDICTION EXAMPLES:

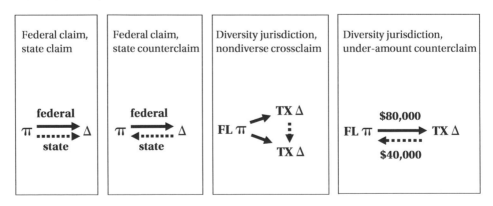

---

[24]Finley v. United States, 490 U.S. 545 (1989).

(2) Constraint on Supplemental Jurisdiction in Diversity Cases

For most law students, the most difficult aspect of supplemental jurisdiction to master is §1367(b)'s rejection of jurisdiction over certain claims in diversity jurisdiction cases. Just as it was hard to understand the §1367(a) grant without knowing *United Mine Workers v. Gibbs*, it's hard to understand the §1367(b) carve-out unless you know *Owen Equipment & Erection Co. v. Kroger*.[25] James Kroger was electrocuted by a crane that was too close to electrical power lines. His widow sued the power company in federal court. The power company asserted a third-party claim against the equipment company that operated the crane. Then, Kroger asserted a negligence claim directly against the equipment company.

OWEN EQUIPMENT v. KROGER

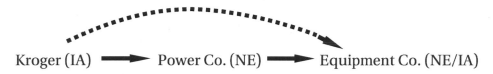

Kroger (IA) ⟶ Power Co. (NE) ⟶ Equipment Co. (NE/IA)

The question was whether the federal court had jurisdiction over Kroger's claim against the equipment company. These were all state law claims, so there was no federal question jurisdiction. Kroger was a citizen of Iowa, and the power company was incorporated in Nebraska with its principal place of business in Nebraska, and the amount in controversy sufficed, so the court had diversity jurisdiction over Kroger's claim against the power company. The equipment company was incorporated in Nebraska with its principal place of business in Iowa. Therefore the court lacked diversity jurisdiction over the power company's third-party claim against the equipment company—both were Nebraska citizens, so complete diversity was lacking. But the court had ancillary (supplemental) jurisdiction over the third-party claim since it arose out of the same occurrence as Kroger's original claim against the power company. Now, what about Kroger's claim directly against the equipment company? That, too, did not meet complete diversity—both Kroger and the equipment company were Iowa citizens. Kroger argued that the court had jurisdiction because her claim against the equipment company arose out of the same facts as her original claim against the power company, over which the court had diversity jurisdiction.

The Supreme Court decided that the federal court lacked jurisdiction over Kroger's claim against the equipment company. This may seem surprising in light of *Gibbs*, but it makes sense if you look at it in terms of the basic requirements of diversity jurisdiction. Suppose Kroger originally brought suit against both the power company and the equipment company—would the court have had jurisdiction? Absolutely not. Kroger and the equipment company were both citizens of Iowa, so complete diversity would be lacking. The Supreme Court reasoned that if Kroger would not have been permitted to file a federal court lawsuit against both the power company and the equipment company, then she should not be allowed to accomplish the same thing by waiting to assert the second claim until after the equipment company was joined as a third-party defendant. The Supreme Court did not want parties to use supplemental jurisdiction as an end run around the statutory constraints on diversity jurisdiction.

---

[25]437 U.S. 365 (1978).

That is precisely the point of §1367(b), which codifies and extends *Kroger*. In diversity cases, supplemental jurisdiction presents the risk that a party may try to get into federal court without meeting the complete diversity and amount-in-controversy requirements. Section 1367(b) therefore carves out certain types of claims and denies supplemental jurisdiction for failure to meet the usual diversity jurisdiction requirements, even if a claim otherwise would have fallen within the jurisdictional grant of §1367(a). Under §1367(b), if the case is in federal court solely because of diversity jurisdiction, then plaintiffs may not use supplemental jurisdiction for claims against additional defendants or third-party defendants. Rather, such claims must independently meet the requirements for diversity jurisdiction—complete diversity and amount in controversy—or have some other independent basis for federal jurisdiction, such as federal question jurisdiction. In addition, it prohibits the use of supplemental jurisdiction in diversity cases for claims by plaintiff-intervenors or required-party plaintiffs; such claims must meet the usual requirements for diversity jurisdiction.

§1367(b) EXAMPLES

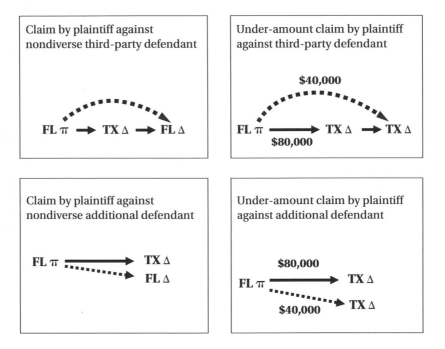

Three warnings about §1367(b): First, remember that it does not grant jurisdiction; it merely takes it away. When analyzing supplemental jurisdiction, your starting point is always the jurisdictional grant of §1367(a). Section 1367(b) carves out certain situations in which supplemental jurisdiction would otherwise have been allowed. Second, it applies *only* in diversity cases. If a case is in federal court on federal question jurisdiction, you do not have to worry about §1367(b). Third, it is a sparsely worded but highly technical statute, so pay attention to its exact terms.

On a careful reading, you'll see that it applies only to claims "by plaintiffs" (not, for example, claims by defendants against third-party defendants). You'll also see that it applies only to claims "against persons made parties under Rule 14, 19, 20, or 24," specific types of joinder that will be covered in Chapter 7. The Supreme Court has interpreted this language quite literally. For example, in a diversity case where an injured girl's claim exceeded $75,000, the Court permitted supplemental jurisdiction over her parents' claims which were under $75,000. Although the girl and her parents were joined under Rule 20, the §1367(b) carve-out did not apply because the parents' claims were not claims by plaintiffs *against* persons joined under Rule 20.[26]

Similarly, in *Exxon Mobil Corp. v. Allapattah Services, Inc.*,[27] the Supreme Court addressed whether a class action could be brought in federal court based on diversity jurisdiction if the class representative met the amount-in-controversy requirement, even if other class members' claims were below the amount. The Court held that when at least one class member meets the amount-in-controversy requirement, the plain language of section 1367 permits supplemental jurisdiction over the claims of the remaining class members. The court made it clear, however, that jurisdiction still required complete diversity between the class representatives and the defendants. The significance of *Allapattah* would have been greater had it not been for the enactment of CAFA, which, as we saw earlier in the chapter, provides an easier path to federal jurisdiction for many class actions.

(3) Discretionary Decline of Jurisdiction

Just because a federal court *can* use supplemental jurisdiction doesn't mean the court *must* use it. When the Supreme Court embraced the idea of supplemental jurisdiction in *United Mine Workers v. Gibbs*, it stated that "pendent jurisdiction is a doctrine of discretion, not of plaintiff's right."[28] Congress included this discretion component in §1367(c), allowing federal courts to decline to exercise supplemental jurisdiction.

Section 1367(c) describes three main circumstances under which a federal court "may decline to exercise supplemental jurisdiction over a claim." It also allows a court to decline supplemental jurisdiction for other "compelling reasons." First, a court may decline jurisdiction if "the claim raises a novel or complex issue of State law." If Paul Gibbs's tort claim had raised a cutting edge issue of state tort law, the federal court might have decided not to exercise jurisdiction over that claim because it would make more sense to allow a state court to decide the issue. The federal court would proceed to hear the federal labor law claim and would dismiss the tort claim so that it could be brought in state court if Gibbs wanted to pursue it.

Second, a court may decline jurisdiction if "the claim substantially predominates over the claim or claims over which the district court has original jurisdiction." Suppose Gibbs's federal labor law claim was limited to statutory damages of a hundred dollars but his tort claim was potentially worth tens of thousands. Under those circumstances, a court might decide that the main event was really the state law claim and might prefer not to treat it as a tag-along with the smaller federal claim.

Third, a court may decline jurisdiction if "the district court has dismissed all claims over which it has original jurisdiction." Suppose that early in the litigation, the court dismissed Gibbs's federal claim on a motion to dismiss for failure to state a claim. At that point, all that would remain is the tort claim over which the court has neither federal question nor diversity jurisdiction. Rather than proceed through

---

[26]Exxon Mobil v. Allapattah, 545 U.S. 546 (2005).
[27]*Id.*
[28]383 U.S. 715, 726 (1966).

discovery and trial purely on the state law claim, the court might decline jurisdiction over the pendent state claim. The plaintiff would then decide whether to pursue the claim in state court.

F. Removal

(1) Removal from State Court to Federal Court

For a defendant, the misery of being sued is compounded by the realization that the plaintiff chose the time and place for the battle. That's where **removal** comes into play. Removal is one of defendants' counterweapons to plaintiffs' forum selection. If the case could have been brought in federal court but the plaintiff chose to file it in state court, the removal statute—28 U.S.C. §1441—gives a defendant the right to switch the case from state court to federal court.

When a case is removed from state court, it goes to the federal district court "for the district and division embracing the place where such action is pending." A case removed from Pennsylvania state court in Philadelphia, for example, would go to the U.S. District Court for the Eastern District of Pennsylvania.

Figuring out whether a defendant may remove a case from state court to federal court largely involves going through the subject matter jurisdiction analysis we've been doing this entire chapter. If the claim arose under federal law, the defendant may remove the case based on federal question jurisdiction. If the parties satisfy complete diversity of citizenship and the amount in controversy exceeds $75,000, the defendant may remove the case based on diversity jurisdiction. If the case is a class action that meets minimal diversity and involves more than $5 million, the defendant may remove the case under CAFA (which includes its own removal provisions).

When a case includes multiple defendants, removal ordinarily requires agreement among all the defendants who have been served.[29] This prevents the confusion that would erupt if removal could split defendants between state and federal court. As a practical matter, this unanimity requirement usually does not create problems because co-defendants often see eye to eye on the question of whether it makes strategic sense to remove a case.

In-State Defendant Exception.   There is one important exception to diversity removal. In-state defendants who are sued in their home state may not remove a case based on diversity jurisdiction. This is what §1441(b) means when it says that a diversity action "may not be removed if any of the parties in interest properly joined and served as defendants is a citizen of the State in which such action is brought."[30] For example, suppose a Florida plaintiff sues a Texas defendant and a Louisiana defendant in Texas state court, and the claims against each defendant exceed $75,000. Although the case meets the standard requirements of diversity jurisdiction, the defendants would not be allowed to remove the case from Texas state court to federal court because a defendant is a Texas citizen. For the same reason, they would not be allowed to remove it if it had been brought in Louisiana state court. But if the case were filed in

---

[29]28 U.S.C. §1446(b)(2).
[30]28 U.S.C. §1441(b)(2).

Florida state court, or indeed any state court besides Texas and Louisiana, then the defendants could remove the case to federal court, invoking diversity of citizenship jurisdiction.

The logic behind §1441(b) is that a defendant should not be worried about unfavorable local bias in the defendant's "home court." Therefore, the defendant should have no need to remove based on diversity jurisdiction, which is intended to provide a federal forum to protect out-of-staters against local bias. That logic sounds reasonable as far as it goes, but note that it creates a double standard. If diversity jurisdiction should be reserved for the protection of out-of-staters, why are plaintiffs allowed to file diversity cases in federal court within their home states? In our example, if the Florida plaintiff files the case in federal court in Florida, the court would have diversity jurisdiction under §1332. But if the defendants try to remove the case to federal court from either a Texas or Louisiana state court, they are barred by the in-state defendant rule of §1441(b). This is one way in which the law favors a plaintiff's autonomy in choosing the forum over a defendant's desire to alter the forum.

Sidebar

REMOVABILITY AND FORUM STRATEGY

Litigants sometimes go to great lengths to secure their forum selection. Plaintiffs who file in state court don't like removal; if they wanted federal court, they would have sued there in the first place. To make a case nonremovable, a plaintiff with potential state and federal claims sometimes forgoes the federal claim to avoid removal based on federal question and supplemental jurisdiction. A plaintiff suing a defendant of diverse citizenship sometimes joins additional parties to ruin complete diversity or joins an in-state defendant to render the case nonremovable. Defendants occasionally remove these cases anyway, arguing that the nondiverse parties or in-state defendants were improperly or fraudulently joined. When the stakes are high and the adversaries' forum selection strategies conflict, these battles over removability—fought out in federal court on the plaintiff's motion to remand—can get pretty intense.

HOME-STATE DEFENDANT

NONREMOVABLE FROM TEXAS OR LOUISIANA STATE COURT:

$$FL\ \pi \longrightarrow \begin{matrix} TX\ \Delta \\ LA\ \Delta \end{matrix}$$

(2) Removal Procedure

The most important thing to remember about removal procedure is this: It's not up to the state court to give permission. *You don't ask permission; you simply remove.* To put it differently, no one makes a *motion* to remove, because a motion means a request that a court order something.

Here's how it works. The defendant files a *notice of removal* in federal court. The details are spelled out in the removal procedure statute, 28 U.S.C. §1446, but the basic point is to notify the federal court of the new case on its docket. Then, the defendant notifies the other parties and the state court to let them know that the case has been removed. The defendant gives the state court a copy of the notice of removal—sometimes awkwardly called a *notice of notice of removal.* Understand what the defendant is saying with that notice of notice of removal: "Dear state court, This case is no longer yours. It's now in federal court. I'm not asking you; I'm telling you. Good-bye. Yours truly, Defendant." Don't use those exact words.

What if the plaintiff disputes the removal of the case, arguing either that the federal court lacks jurisdiction or that the defendant failed to abide by the proper procedure for removal? The plaintiff may *move to remand* the case back to state court. I made a point of emphasizing that a defendant does not make a motion to remove, but if the parties can fight the same fight over a plaintiff's motion to remand, you might wonder what difference it makes. The difference is *where* the motion is made. The plaintiff moves to remand in federal court after the case has been removed. This gives the federal court, not the state court, the power to decide the question of federal subject matter jurisdiction.

Good litigators always stay keenly aware of the time limits that govern each aspect of civil procedure, and removal is no exception. When reading the removal procedure statute, be sure not to ignore §1446(b), which imposes a 30-day time limit for defendants to remove.

There's an interesting twist concerning the timeliness of removal, accounting for the possibility that a case might become removable after the initial pleading. If the original complaint does not meet the requirements for federal question, diversity, or any other basis for federal subject matter jurisdiction, then at that point the defendant cannot remove the case. But suppose the plaintiff amends the complaint to add a federal law claim. Or suppose the plaintiff adds a claim that increases the amount in controversy to over $75,000. Or suppose the plaintiff drops one of the defendants or a co-plaintiff, and the remaining parties are completely diverse. All of a sudden, the case becomes removable. It would be unfair to the defendant to prohibit removal simply because more than 30 days had passed since the initial pleading, since the case was not removable at the outset. So the statute allows a defendant to remove within 30 days of when "it may first be ascertained that the case is one which is or has become removable."[31] To avoid forum changes far into the litigation, however, the statute imposes a one-year time limit on removal based on diversity of citizenship. A recent amendment provides that the one-year time limit does not apply if a plaintiff acted in bad faith to prevent removal.[32]

F   A   Q

Q: If a case is originally nonremovable, can a defendant make it removable by asserting a federal defense or a federal counterclaim?

A: No. Analyze federal question jurisdiction for removal just as you would for original jurisdiction. Although it might seem odd to apply the well-pleaded complaint rule to a situation where the federal issue is not merely anticipated but actually asserted, allowing removal in this situation would give defendants free rein to manipulate federal jurisdiction. If the action is not subject to federal jurisdiction based on the plaintiff's complaint, it cannot be removed.

---

[31] 28 U.S.C. §1446(b)(3).
[32] 28 U.S.C. §1446(c)(1).

(3) Separate Federal and State Claims

What if an action includes some claims over which the federal court possesses jurisdiction, and some over which it does not? Suppose one claim arises under federal law, but another claim arises under state law and satisfies neither diversity jurisdiction nor supplemental jurisdiction. Is the action removable?

Until recently, the removal statute addressed this issue in a bizarre section that appeared to invite federal judges to hear claims over which they had no jurisdiction, which couldn't be right. Thanks to a 2011 amendment, section 1441(c) now makes it clear that a federal court must sever and remand the claims over which it lacks subject matter jurisdiction. In other words, the case may be removed, but the federal court will hear only the claims over which it has original or supplemental jurisdiction, and return the others to the state court.

G. Analyzing Subject Matter Jurisdiction

Let's try to pull this entire chapter together to see how you might analyze whether a federal court has subject matter jurisdiction. Perhaps you represent a potential plaintiff, and you're deciding whether to file suit in state or federal court. Or you represent a defendant who has been sued in state court, and you're deciding whether you have the option of removing the case to federal court. Or you represent a defendant who has been sued in federal court, and you're deciding whether to move to dismiss for lack of jurisdiction. Or maybe you're a judge or law clerk (or even a law student) who's been presented with a question of whether federal jurisdiction exists. Just go step by step through the various bases for federal subject matter jurisdiction, applying the analysis established by the statutes and cases:

Federal Subject Matter Jurisdiction Analysis

I. Federal question jurisdiction: Does the claim "arise under" federal law?
  A. If federal law comes up as an anticipated defense, rather than in the well-pleaded complaint → no federal question jurisdiction. (*Mottley*)
  B. Was the cause of action created by federal law?
    ▪ If yes → federal question jurisdiction.
    ▪ If no → Is there *Grable*-type jurisdiction?
      ▪ federal law forms an essential element of the claim;
      ▪ the federal issue is disputed and substantial; and
      ▪ federal jurisdiction will not interfere with the state/federal division of labor.

II. Diversity jurisdiction
  A. First, determine whether complete diversity exists.
    ▪ For individual citizenship, determine domicile.
    ▪ For corporate citizenship, determine both the state of incorporation and the principal place of business. (*Hertz*)
    ▪ If any plaintiff's citizenship is the same as any defendant's citizenship → no diversity jurisdiction.
  B. Determine the amount in controversy.
    ▪ If $75,000 or less → no diversity jurisdiction.
  C. If complete diversity and amount in controversy over $75,000 → diversity jurisdiction.

D. But in a removal situation, if any defendant is a citizen of the forum state → no diversity removal jurisdiction.

E. If class action → apply either standard diversity jurisdiction analysis or use special analysis under CAFA:
  - If minimal diversity exists and aggregate amount in controversy exceeds $5 million → CAFA jurisdiction, unless exception applies.

III. Other bases of federal jurisdiction
  A. Is the United States a party?
  B. Is it an admiralty or maritime case?
  C. Is there some other applicable federal jurisdictional statute?
    - If yes to any of the above → federal jurisdiction.
  D. Is it a controversy between states?
    - If yes → original jurisdiction in the Supreme Court.

- If any basis succeeds, then the federal court's jurisdiction is proper. Otherwise, the court must dismiss for lack of subject matter jurisdiction.

IV. Supplemental jurisdiction — If the court has subject matter jurisdiction over part of an action, but an additional claim does not meet the usual requirements for federal jurisdiction → analyze supplemental jurisdiction:
  A. Does the additional claim arise out of the same facts as the original? (*Gibbs*)
    - If no → no supplemental jurisdiction.
    - If yes → §1367(a)'s grant applies; proceed with analysis.
  B. Is supplemental jurisdiction over the claim prohibited by §1367(b)?
    - Is federal jurisdiction over the case based solely on diversity?
    - If no → §1367(b) does not apply. If yes →
    - Is the additional claim asserted by a plaintiff against a third-party defendant, a joined defendant, or an intervenor-defendant?
      - If no → §1367(b) does not apply.
      - If yes → the court lacks supplemental jurisdiction over the additional claim.
  C. Will the court decline jurisdiction over the additional claim?
    - Does the claim raise a difficult issue of state law?
    - Does the state law claim substantially predominate?
    - Has the court dismissed the claim over which it had original jurisdiction?
    - Is there some other compelling reason to decline jurisdiction?
      - If yes to any → the court may decline to exercise supplemental jurisdiction.

SUMMARY

- Every state has a court of general jurisdiction, but since federal courts are courts of limited jurisdiction, a federal district court has power over an action only if a constitutional and statutory grant of subject matter jurisdiction applies.

- Some federal jurisdiction is exclusive, but mostly it is concurrent so a party can choose whether to bring an action in state or federal court.

- Federal courts have power over cases arising under federal law, but the federal issue must appear on the face of the well-pleaded complaint.

■ In limited circumstances, federal courts have power over state law claims with embedded federal issues, but only if jurisdiction would not seriously alter the division of labor between federal and state courts.

■ Federal courts have power over cases between citizens of different states, as long as the complete diversity requirement is met and the amount in controversy exceeds $75,000.

■ For diversity jurisdiction, an individual's citizenship is based on domicile, while a corporation's citizenship is its state of incorporation plus its one principal place of business.

■ For diversity jurisdiction, each party must meet the amount-in-controversy requirement; different parties may not add up the amounts of their claims to meet the requirement.

■ If a federal court has jurisdiction over a claim, the court may have supplemental jurisdiction over other claims that arise out of the same facts, but the supplemental jurisdiction statute rejects jurisdiction over certain claims that would undermine the requirements of diversity jurisdiction.

■ When an action is filed in state court but meets the requirements for federal subject matter jurisdiction, a defendant may remove the action to federal court.

CONNECTIONS

Pleadings

In federal court, every complaint must state the basis for the court's subject matter jurisdiction.

Discovery

To determine whether it has subject matter jurisdiction, a court often needs no information beyond the jurisdictional allegations in the pleadings. Sometimes, however, jurisdiction depends on a disputed factual issue such as where an individual is domiciled. In those cases, a court may order limited discovery into the jurisdictional facts.

Joinder

Even if the joinder rules would allow a party to join certain parties or claims in an action, constraints on subject matter jurisdiction may make joinder impossible in federal court. Rule 20 permits joinder of parties, but if the court's jurisdiction depends on diversity of citizenship and one of the parties ruins complete diversity, then the jurisdictional constraint makes joinder impossible. Rule 18 permits joinder of claims, but each claim needs a basis for subject matter jurisdiction. If the claims are related, supplemental jurisdiction may enable joinder of a federal claim with a state claim. If the claims cannot be brought in federal court, then usually a plaintiff can bring the claims together in state court.

Joinder — Class Action

Class actions raise unique jurisdictional issues, and federal subject matter jurisdiction over class actions has swelled in recent years. In *Allapattah*, the Supreme Court permitted supplemental jurisdiction over class claims that fall below the amount-in-controversy requirement. Congress enacted CAFA to expand federal jurisdiction over class actions based on minimal diversity and an aggregate amount in controversy.

Appeal

Even when a case is on appeal, it may be thrown out if the appellate court realizes that subject matter jurisdiction is lacking, which is exactly what occurred in *Mottley*.

Preclusion, Joinder

The *Gibbs* "common nucleus of operative fact" test for supplemental jurisdiction bears a striking resemblance to the transactional test for claim preclusion, as well as the "same transaction or occurrence" tests for compulsory counterclaims, cross-claims, and permissive party joinder. These doctrines work together. Joinder rules and supplemental jurisdiction make it possible for litigants to assert transactionally related claims in the same action, and claim preclusion gives litigants a strong reason to avail themselves of that opportunity.

Personal Jurisdiction

2

Personal jurisdiction addresses the territorial reach of a court's power over the parties. Without jurisdiction over the parties, a court cannot enter

O V E R V I E W

a binding judgment. Suppose you live in Florida and you get into an auto accident in Georgia. If the other driver sues you in Florida, you wouldn't have any serious doubt that you'd be bound by the Florida court's decision since you're a Florida resident. Similarly, if the other driver sues you in Georgia, you would not be surprised that the Georgia court has power over you for this case because the accident occurred in Georgia. But suppose the other driver sues you in Arizona, or for that matter in Bulgaria. If the Arizonan or Bulgarian court purported to exercise power over you despite your lack of connection to those places, you would be understandably annoyed, and you'd be right. That's what *personal jurisdiction* is about. Plaintiffs' lawyers analyze personal jurisdiction to figure out where they can file their clients' lawsuits. Defendants' lawyers analyze it to determine whether they can advise their clients to skip a proceeding with impunity, or less riskily, to move to dismiss the case.

A. DEVELOPMENT OF TERRITORIAL JURISDICTION DOCTRINE

1. *Pennoyer v. Neff*
2. Post-*Pennoyer* Expansion
3. *International Shoe v. Washington*

A. Development of Territorial Jurisdiction Doctrine

Do you get tired of law professors telling you that the only way to understand this or that legal doctrine is by seeing where it came from, and then you slog through century-old cases only to find out later that they have been overruled? Well, here we go. Because sometimes you really do need to look in the rearview mirror, and in civil procedure, nowhere is this truer than when learning personal jurisdiction. The law of personal jurisdiction, as it exists today, makes sense only if you see it as the result of the Supreme Court's partial unraveling of a rigid set of doctrines embodied in one famous case: *Pennoyer v. Neff*.[1]

(1) *Pennoyer v. Neff*

This is the most famous civil procedure case of them all. It's a case that you can bet the most senior partner at the law firm still remembers by name, even if he or she hasn't actually read it since law school. You are about to learn that much of the law stated in

---

[1] 95 U.S. 714 (1877).

Pennoyer has been overturned, so you'd be justified in asking why the case is so famous. There are several answers, but I think the most powerful one is this: *Pennoyer* stands for the principle that a person is not bound by a judgment unless the court properly acquired power over that person. One aspect of this principle is that non-parties are not bound by a judgment, an idea that we examine in Chapter 11 on preclusion. Another aspect of this principle — the central topic of this chapter — is that a court's power is limited by territorial boundaries. A related aspect is that parties must be properly notified about the lawsuit. All three of these ideas are fundamental to an understanding of the power of courts.

Sylvester Pennoyer (1831-1902)

The case started with a simple dispute over legal fees. Attorney John Mitchell sued his former client Marcus Neff for an unpaid fee. Mitchell brought his lawsuit in Oregon state court. Neff did not appear, so the court entered a default judgment against Neff. Apparently Neff had moved to California and did not know about the lawsuit. In order to enforce the judgment — that is, to get his money — Mitchell had the sheriff seize land that Neff owned in Oregon and put it up for sale. At the sheriff's sale, Neff's land was purchased by Mitchell and then sold to Sylvester Pennoyer. Eight years later, along came Neff. Neff sued Pennoyer, demanding his property back. Neff argued that he, rather than Pennoyer, rightfully owned the property because the Oregon court never had power over him, so the court's judgment and the ensuing sheriff's sale were void.

#1 Mitchell → Neff

- Oregon state court
- Claim for unpaid legal fees
- Default Judgment for π
  - ☐ Sheriff's sale of Neff's Oregon land
    - Sold to Pennoyer

#2 Neff → Pennoyer

- Ejectment

The Supreme Court agreed with Neff. The Oregon court in the first case never properly obtained power over Neff. Therefore, Neff was not bound by the judgment and the resulting sheriff's sale was invalid. The Court reached this conclusion based on a rigid understanding of the territorial limits on judicial power. It's worth reading the opinion carefully to see how the Court's language emphasizes power, sovereignty, and territorial boundaries. The Supreme Court divided its analysis into power over property (**in rem jurisdiction**) and power over the person (**in personam jurisdiction**), but both were based almost entirely on territorial boundaries.

In the *Pennoyer* scheme, a state court has power over property within that state, but lacks power over property outside the state. Thus, an Oregon court would have in rem jurisdiction to adjudicate a dispute about the ownership of Oregon property. This case (*Mitchell v. Neff*), however, involved a dispute about unpaid legal fees, which requires in personam jurisdiction, so the Oregon court lacked jurisdiction.

The Supreme Court also accepted a broader application of a court's power over in-state property, beyond disputes about ownership of the property itself. A plaintiff can "attach" the defendant's property. This means that the property is frozen and cannot be sold or otherwise transferred, so that it will be available to the plaintiff in order to enforce the judgment. In the *Pennoyer* scheme, if a plaintiff attaches a defendant's property at the start of a lawsuit, that property can form the basis for the court's power to adjudicate the case. The theory behind such power — known as **quasi-in-rem jurisdiction** — is that the court is merely exercising power over the in-state property because enforcement of the judgment is limited to the value of the attached property. Thus, an Oregon court would have quasi-in-rem jurisdiction to adjudicate a dispute over legal fees if the defendant owned Oregon property and if the plaintiff attached that property. However, for a court to acquire quasi-in-rem jurisdiction, the property must be attached at the outset. In Mitchell's case, Neff's Oregon property was not attached until the conclusion of the proceedings, so the court lacked quasi-in-rem jurisdiction.

Power over the person, in the *Pennoyer* scheme, depends on whether the person was served with process within the state borders. To serve a defendant with process means to give the defendant the summons and complaint in the lawsuit. If Mitchell had served Neff with process in Oregon or if Neff appeared voluntarily to litigate the case, then the Oregon court would have had jurisdiction over Neff. But because Neff was not served in Oregon — indeed, he was not served at all, as the only notice was by publication (one of those fine-print items nobody reads in the newspaper) — the Oregon court lacked in personam jurisdiction.

The *Pennoyer* Court's reasoning might be summed up as follows: (1) A state court has power over persons and property within the state, but no power over persons and property outside the state. (2) A state court obtains power over a person by service of process within the state and obtains power over in-state property by attachment. (3) The Oregon court lacked power in personam because Neff was not personally served with process within the state and lacked power quasi-in-rem because no Oregon property was attached at the outset. (4) Therefore, the Oregon court had no power over Neff in the first case. (5) Because the court in the first case lacked power over Neff, the court in the second case need not give respect to the default judgment or to the sheriff's sale that flowed from it. (6) Therefore, Neff still owns the property.

But Justice Stephen Field, writing for the Supreme Court, decided to take the reasoning one important step further. "Since the adoption of the Fourteenth Amendment to the Federal Constitution," he wrote, "the validity of such judgments may be directly questioned, and their enforcement in the State resisted, on the ground that proceedings in a court of justice to determine the personal rights and obligations of parties over whom that court has no jurisdiction do not constitute due process of law."[2] In other words, *a judgment without personal jurisdiction violates due process.* With this step, Field made *Pennoyer* a case about constitutional rights, and in particular, about a *federal* constitutional limit on the exercise of power by *state* courts. Think about the historical context. The Supreme Court decided *Pennoyer* in 1877, not long after the 1868 ratification of the Fourteenth Amendment, which came on the heels of the Civil War. In that context, concerns about limits on the power of individual states were hardly theoretical.

---

[2] *Pennoyer*, 95 U.S. at 733.

With its decision in *Pennoyer v. Neff*, the Supreme Court set up a federal constitutional limit on the power of state courts, emphasizing the territorial reach of courts' power based on whether persons or property can be found within the state borders. The modern doctrine of personal jurisdiction would emerge from the gradual unraveling of this rigid scheme.

(2) Post-*Pennoyer* Expansion

In its approach to the territorial power of state courts, *Pennoyer* assumed that each state was pretty much separate and that interstate activity was the exception. Wrong. What happened after *Pennoyer*? The automobile was invented. And the airplane. The telephone. Interstate highways. The global economy and global financial markets. The Internet. Google. Facebook.

From a twenty-first-century perspective, it's easy for us to see how irrelevant state boundaries have become in a wide range of business transactions and other human interactions. But this was already becoming clear in the years following *Pennoyer*. For almost 70 years, *Pennoyer* endured as a general theory of the territorial limits of judicial power, but courts found ways to stretch and bend to accommodate changing times.

Consider, for example, the problem of nonresident motorists. If an out-of-state driver enters a state and causes an automobile accident, shouldn't a victim be able to sue the driver in the courts of the state where the accident occurred, even if the driver has returned to his home state? The problem was that *Pennoyer* required in-state service for the court to obtain in personam jurisdiction over the driver. To solve this problem, New Jersey adopted a law that required out-of-state motorists to file a formal document appointing a New Jersey agent for service of process before using New Jersey's highways. The Supreme Court upheld this approach in the 1916 case of *Kane v. New Jersey*.[3] By having motorists appoint an agent, this complied with *Pennoyer*'s requirement of in-state service of process, and it achieved jurisdiction by consent. But what an inconvenient way to go about it!

Massachusetts took this idea a step further, passing a statute that said that by using a Massachusetts highway, a nonresident motorist is deemed to have appointed a state officer as an agent to accept service of process. In 1927, in *Hess v. Pawloski*,[4] the Court approved this as a basis for a Massachusetts court's jurisdiction over a Pennsylvania driver who had gotten into an accident in Massachusetts. The notion that the nonresident motorist had consented to the jurisdiction of the Massachusetts courts was, obviously, pure fiction. But by statutorily "deeming" the driver to have appointed an in-state agent for service, it satisfied the technical requirement of service within the state's borders. Wouldn't it have been easier simply to say that it makes sense to allow a state to protect citizens and regulate the roads by asserting jurisdiction over drivers who use the state's roadways? As long as the *Pennoyer* scheme of jurisdiction held sway, however, such an explanation would not suffice, so instead states used legal fictions to expand personal jurisdiction.

Next, consider the problem of suing a defendant who happens to be out of state when a lawsuit is brought. In the 1940 case of *Milliken v. Meyer*,[5] the plaintiff sued the

---

[3]242 U.S. 160 (1916).
[4]274 U.S. 352 (1927).
[5]311 U.S. 457 (1940).

defendant in Wyoming state court. The defendant was a Wyoming citizen but was in Colorado at the time the suit was brought. The plaintiff had the defendant served with process in Colorado. The defendant argued that the Wyoming court lacked personal jurisdiction over him because *Pennoyer* required in-state service. The Supreme Court, however, upheld personal jurisdiction despite the lack of in-state service, reasoning that implicit in *Pennoyer* was the idea that a state can exercise power over its own citizens.

At some point, would the Supreme Court stop trying to bend and stretch *Pennoyer* and instead adopt a new approach? Yes. The year was 1945, the case was *International Shoe v. Washington*, and it heralded the start of the modern era of personal jurisdiction.

(3) *International Shoe v. Washington*

In *International Shoe v. Washington*,[6] the Supreme Court — while not explicitly overruling *Pennoyer* — articulated a new test for personal jurisdiction. Pretty much everything that followed has been a matter of interpreting the *International Shoe* standard.

The case involved a shoe manufacturer with sales employees working in the state of Washington. The state sued the company in Washington state court to collect money under the state's unemployment compensation statute. International Shoe, which was incorporated in Delaware and headquartered in Missouri, argued that the court lacked personal jurisdiction over it.

The Supreme Court could have analyzed the issue in *Pennoyer* terms, asking whether International Shoe was "present" in Washington or whether it had "consented" to jurisdiction by doing business in Washington. Instead, the Court asked whether the company's *contacts* with Washington justified jurisdiction. In words that are now repeated in virtually every personal jurisdiction case, the Court framed the test in terms of "minimum contacts":

> [D]ue process requires only that in order to subject a defendant to a judgment *in personam*, if he be not present within the territory of the forum, he have certain *minimum contacts* with it such that the maintenance of the suit does not offend "traditional notions of *fair play and substantial justice*."[7]

The Court went on to explain that the demands of due process "may be met by such contacts of the corporation with the state of the forum as make it reasonable, in the context of our federal system of government, to require the corporation to defend the particular suit which is brought there."[8] The analysis, the Court added, includes an "estimate of the inconveniences" the defendant would face in litigating away from home.[9]

Fair play, reasonableness, convenience — are these words found in *Pennoyer*? No, *Pennoyer* was all about sovereignty and territorial boundaries. But times had changed. The clear but rigid *Pennoyer* scheme of personal jurisdiction gave way to a more flexible way to decide whether a court's assertion of personal jurisdiction would violate a defendant's right to due process of law.

---

[6]326 U.S. 310 (1945).
[7]Id. at 316 (quoting Milliken v. Meyer) (emphasis added).
[8]Id. at 317.
[9]Id.

The logic of *International Shoe* is reciprocity: "[T]o the extent that a corporation exercises the privilege of conducting activities within a state, it enjoys the benefits and protection of the laws of that state."[10] If a company or individual gets the benefits of a state, then it should expect to be subject to the power of that state's courts. International Shoe Company got the benefit of having salespeople working in Washington, so it was only fair that it had the burden of being subject to suit in that state's courts for money it owed based on those employees.

In the years since 1945, the Supreme Court and other federal and state courts have explained and refined the *International Shoe* standard as they have decided, in a variety of litigation situations, whether courts had personal jurisdiction over defendants. To show you how you should analyze personal jurisdiction issues, we'll look at a number of these decisions as they relate to each type of territorial jurisdiction, beginning with general jurisdiction.

B. General Jurisdiction

A defendant's contact with a forum state may be so strong that the state's courts have jurisdiction over the defendant for any and all claims, regardless of whether the claims arose out of anything that happened in the state. Suppose someone wants to sue General Motors Corporation. GM is headquartered in Michigan. There is no doubt that the Michigan courts would have power over GM, even if the case is entirely unrelated to Michigan. Similarly, suppose someone wants to sue me (please don't). I'm domiciled in New Jersey. There's no doubt that the New Jersey courts would have power over me, even if the dispute arose elsewhere. That's **general jurisdiction**. The defendant's presence in the state is so solid that the courts of that state have power over the defendant without regard to where the claim arose.

F   A   Q

Q: Doesn't *general jurisdiction* refer to the *subject matter jurisdiction* of certain courts?

A: Yes. Sorry. "General jurisdiction" means one thing in the context of subject matter jurisdiction and something completely different in the context of personal jurisdiction. In subject matter jurisdiction, we say that state trial courts are courts of general jurisdiction because they can hear any type of case, as distinct from courts of *limited jurisdiction*, such as traffic courts, small claims courts, and most important, the federal courts. In personal jurisdiction, general jurisdiction refers to a court's power over a defendant regardless of where the claim arose, as opposed to *specific jurisdiction*, which means the court's power over a defendant for a case that arose out of the defendant's contact with the forum state.

---

[10]Id. at 319.

For an individual, general jurisdiction is based on domicile. The Supreme Court's holding in *Milliken v. Meyer*[11] remains good law. If an individual is domiciled in a state, then the courts of that state have in personam jurisdiction over the person for any claim, regardless of where it may have arisen.

For a corporation, general jurisdiction requires a similarly strong presence in the state. Although *International Shoe* was a case of specific jurisdiction (recall that the dispute involved unemployment fund contributions based on the defendant's employment of workers within the state of Washington), the Supreme Court in that decision endorsed the idea of general jurisdiction over corporations. The Court mentioned "continuous corporate operations within a state . . . so substantial and of such a nature as to justify suit . . . on causes of action arising from dealings entirely distinct from those activities."[12] But how much presence is enough? Certainly, the state of incorporation has general jurisdiction over a corporation. If a company is incorporated in Delaware, for example, then the Delaware courts would have general jurisdiction. Similarly, the state where a company is headquartered has general jurisdiction, as in the example of General Motors and Michigan. The Supreme Court recently explained it this way: "A court may assert general jurisdiction over foreign (sister-state or foreign-country) corporations to hear any and all claims against them when their affiliations with the State are so 'continuous and systematic' as to render them essentially at home in the forum State."[13]

What if a company isn't incorporated or headquartered in the state, but does business there? Is that enough for general jurisdiction? The answer depends on what we mean by "doing business" there. If a company merely buys and sells a lot in a state or sends its employees there regularly to conduct business, that does *not* give the state general jurisdiction over the company. In one case, *Helicopteros Nacionales de Colombia v. Hall*,[14] the defendant had purchased millions of dollars of equipment in Texas, along with other business contacts with the state, but the Supreme Court held that this was insufficient for general jurisdiction. The company could have been subject to personal jurisdiction in Texas for claims that arose out of its contacts with Texas (that would be *specific jurisdiction*), but was not subject to personal jurisdiction in Texas for claims that arose elsewhere. *Helicopteros* was a wrongful death suit involving a helicopter crash in Peru, so it did not arise out of Texas.

General jurisdiction similarly failed in *Goodyear v. Brown*.[15] Two teenagers from North Carolina died in a bus rollover accident in France. Their parents brought a wrongful death lawsuit in North Carolina state court, claiming that a defective tire caused the accident. They sued the companies that had designed and manufactured the tire – Goodyear France, Goodyear Luxembourg, and Goodyear Turkey – as well as the parent company, Goodyear USA. The three foreign subsidiaries moved to dismiss for lack of personal jurisdiction, and the Supreme Court agreed. The North Carolina court lacked specific jurisdiction because the claims did not arise out of contacts with North Carolina, and the court lacked general jurisdiction because the defendants were not "essentially at home" in North Carolina. Unlike Goodyear USA, which did not contest the court's jurisdiction over it, the foreign subsidiaries had no factories, offices or employees in North Carolina.

---

[11]311 U.S. 457 (1940).
[12]*International Shoe*, 326 U.S. at 318.
[13]Goodyear Dunlop Tires Operations, S.A. v. Brown, 131 S. Ct. 2846, 2851 (2011).
[14]466 U.S. 408 (1984).
[15]131 S. Ct. 2846 (2011).

Compare *Helicopteros* and *Goodyear* with *Perkins v. Benguet Consolidated Mining Co.*,[16] in which a company was subject to general jurisdiction of the Ohio courts because for a period of time the company was operating out of an Ohio office where the company's president was located.

The takeaway message of *Helicopteros* and *Perkins* is that for general jurisdiction, the company must have a serious physical presence in the state. A factory or office building with permanent company employees in the state might suffice. Courts often state that for general jurisdiction the contacts must be "continuous and systematic," but they mean something much more substantial than that. Although occasionally courts uphold general jurisdiction over a corporation based on something less than a substantial physical facility in the state, those cases involve claims that are somehow related to the company's contacts with the state. True general jurisdiction — in personam jurisdiction without regard to where the claim arose — requires a very substantial presence in a state.

In the end, general jurisdiction means that for any defendant — whether individual or corporation — there's at least one forum where you *know* the defendant is subject to personal jurisdiction, regardless of where the claim arose. For an individual defendant, it's the state where he or she is domiciled. For a corporate defendant, it's the state where it is incorporated, as well as (if it differs) the state where it is headquartered, plus any other state where its business presence is so substantial (like a factory or office building) that the company is "present" in that state for jurisdictional purposes.

C. Specific Jurisdiction

Whether or not a court would have general jurisdiction over the defendant, the court may have personal jurisdiction for the particular lawsuit because the claim arises out of the defendant's contact with the forum state. In other words, the court may have **specific jurisdiction**. Probably, most of the personal jurisdiction cases you're reading for your civil procedure course are cases involving specific jurisdiction.

The best way to learn about specific jurisdiction is by example — by reading cases. As you read each case, do not merely look for a black-letter statement of the court's holding. Rather, be sure you understand exactly what contacts the defendant had with the forum state, in what way the case arose out of those contacts, and why the court did or did not have jurisdiction based on those contacts.

International Shoe, by modern standards, was a relatively easy case of specific jurisdiction. The defendant employed a number of salespeople in Washington and the dispute arose out of that employment. That, the Supreme Court held, sufficed to meet the requirement of "minimum contacts."

(1) Long-Arm Statutes

The minimum contacts test addresses whether specific jurisdiction over a particular defendant would be constitutional under the Due Process Clause. Before getting to that question, however, a court must ascertain whether it has a statutory basis for asserting jurisdiction over the defendant. Statutes that empower courts to assert

---

[16]342 U.S. 437 (1952).

personal jurisdiction over out-of-state defendants are known as **long-arm statutes**. The idea is that the long arm of the law stretches beyond the state boundaries to reach and grab the defendant.

Some state long-arm statutes list specific bases for personal jurisdiction over out-of-state defendants, such as a contract entered within the state, a tortious act committed within the state, or a tortious act committed elsewhere that caused injury within the state. When analyzing personal jurisdiction in a state with one of these enumerated-act long-arm statutes, the first step is to ascertain whether the defendant fits within the meaning of the statute. If no, then the court lacks jurisdiction. If yes, then the long-arm statute provides a basis for jurisdiction, and the next question is whether the assertion of jurisdiction would be constitutional under the minimum contacts test.

Other state long-arm statutes, rather than enumerating specific bases for jurisdiction, simply state that the courts may assert personal jurisdiction to the full extent permitted by the constitution. Some states with statutes that look like enumerated-act statutes have interpreted their long-arm statutes to reach to the full extent of the constitution. Whether stated explicitly in the statutory language or based on the courts' statutory interpretation, these "sky's the limit" long-arm statutes permit a court to assert personal jurisdiction over any defendant as long as it does not violate due process. When analyzing personal jurisdiction in a state with a long-arm statute that reaches to the full extent of due process, the statutory step in the analysis merges with the constitutional analysis.

(2) Minimum Contacts and Purposeful Availment

Turning to the constitutional test, do not make the mistake of thinking that the **minimum contacts** test is merely about quantity, about somehow counting up the number of contacts a defendant has with the state. A single contact can be enough, if it's a substantial contact and if the claim arises directly from it. That was the lesson of *McGee v. International Life Insurance Co.*,[17] in which a Texas insurance company's sale of an insurance policy to a policyholder in California sufficed to give a California court jurisdiction over the insurance company for a dispute concerning the policy.

The contact, however, must be purposeful. The International Shoe Company purposefully employed persons in Washington. The International Life Insurance Company purposefully mailed an insurance policy to California. Compare that with the facts of *Hanson v. Denckla*,[18] in which a Delaware trustee was responsible for a trust created by Dora Donner, who subsequently moved to Florida. Donner died in Florida, and two of the beneficiaries brought a lawsuit in Florida in which the trustee was a necessary defendant. The Supreme Court held that the Florida court lacked jurisdiction over the Delaware trustee because personal jurisdiction requires "some act by which the defendant *purposefully avails* itself of the privilege of conducting activities within the forum State, thus invoking the benefits and protections of its laws."[19] Donner's move to Florida was a "unilateral activity" by her, not a purposeful act by the trustee.[20]

---

[17]355 U.S. 220 (1957).
[18]357 U.S. 235 (1958).
[19]Id. at 253 (emphasis added).
[20]Id.

Look for that "purposeful availment" language from *Hanson* in nearly every modern personal jurisdiction case, and think about it whenever you analyze a question of specific jurisdiction. More than any other single concept, purposeful availment is the key to understanding specific jurisdiction. The contacts that matter for the minimum contacts test are those in which the defendant knowingly and purposefully does something toward the forum state.

The case that drives home the point about purposeful availment is *World-Wide Volkswagen Corp. v. Woodson.*[21] This is a case in which the Robinson family bought a car in New York and was driving it across the country. While they were passing through Oklahoma, they had an accident in which their car caught fire. They brought a product liability action in Oklahoma state court against multiple defendants, including the automobile dealer from whom they bought the car (Seaway Volkswagen) as well as the regional distributor (World-Wide Volkswagen). Seaway and World-Wide Volkswagen argued that the Oklahoma court lacked personal jurisdiction over them. Seaway sold automobiles in upstate New York; World-Wide Volkswagen was the tri-state distributor for New York, New Jersey, and Connecticut. They had no contacts with Oklahoma, they argued. The plaintiffs argued that the court had specific jurisdiction. The case, according to plaintiffs, arose out of defendants' contact with Oklahoma: the sale of a vehicle that the defendants knew would be used for transportation, and that made its way into Oklahoma and caused harm there.

The Supreme Court agreed with the defendants that the Oklahoma court lacked personal jurisdiction over these two defendants. Picking up on the reasoning of *Hanson v. Denckla*, the Court held that Seaway and World-Wide Volkswagen had not purposefully availed themselves of Oklahoma. They sold a car to customers in New York. They had not made any intentional contact with Oklahoma. The Robinsons' driving to Oklahoma was "unilateral activity" just like Dora Donner's move to Florida in *Hanson*.

World-Wide Volkswagen was a 5-4 decision. A vigorous dissent by Justice Brennan argued that the defendants knowingly sold an inherently mobile product. According to the dissent, it is not unreasonable to hold defendants answerable in Oklahoma for a lawsuit over a product that foreseeably ended up in Oklahoma and caused harm there. Justice Brennan emphasized that personal jurisdiction need not be so restrictive in an era in which modern transportation and communication reduce the inconvenience of litigating in another state. The majority, however, made it clear that state lines still matter, and a court's power over an out-of-state defendant depends on whether the defendant acted purposefully toward the forum state.

Sidebar

THE POLITICS OF PERSONAL JURISDICTION

If you are familiar with the political leanings of Supreme Court Justices, you may notice, as you read the majority and dissenting opinions in closely divided personal jurisdiction cases, that the more "liberal" Justices tend to allow personal jurisdiction while the more "conservative" Justices tend to reject it. What's so *political* about personal jurisdiction? A narrower view of personal jurisdiction gives defendants an edge in civil litigation, while a broader view of jurisdiction favors plaintiffs. Tighter restrictions on personal jurisdiction make it harder for plaintiffs to choose the most favorable forum and may make it inconvenient or expensive for plaintiffs to sue. Much (but certainly not all) litigation pits individual plaintiffs against corporate or government defendants, and pro-plaintiff policies are often described as more liberal, while pro-defendant policies are often considered more pro-business or conservative.

---

[21]444 U.S. 286 (1980).

(3) The Effects Test

In some cases, specific jurisdiction is based on a defendant's out-of-state conduct that causes *effects* in the forum state. *Calder v. Jones*[22] is a good example. Shirley Jones was a well-known singer-actress who lived in California. (If you've ever seen the 1970s TV show *The Partridge Family*, she played the mom.) After the *National Enquirer* tabloid published a story about her, she sued for libel. She brought the lawsuit in California not only against the newspaper, but also against the reporter and editor, both of whom were located in Florida. The Supreme Court upheld California's jurisdiction over the defendants based on the effects of the defendants' conduct, emphasizing that the story "concerned the California activities of a California resident," and that "the article was drawn from California sources, and the brunt of the harm, in terms of both respondent's emotional distress and the injury to her professional reputation, was suffered in California."[23]

Please don't get carried away with the effects test of *Calder*. In some ways, the case is an outlier. Remember that in *World-Wide Volkswagen*, the New York dealer and distributor sold a product that caused effects in Oklahoma, but that was not enough for personal jurisdiction because the defendants had not acted purposefully toward Oklahoma. In *Calder*, by contrast, the reporter and editor knew not only that their paper had a significant circulation in California, but also that Shirley Jones lived in California and would suffer reputational harm there.

(4) Business Relationships

Lots of litigation involves business relationships gone sour. *Burger King v. Rudzewicz*[24] concerned a dispute between the Burger King company and a guy who owned a couple of Burger King franchises in Michigan. Burger King sued Rudzewicz (the franchisee) in Florida. Why Florida? Because that's where Burger King is headquartered. As far as we can tell, Rudzewicz had never set foot in Florida. He had, however, entered into a substantial, long-term business relationship with a company, Burger King, which he knew was headquartered in Florida. The franchise agreement even specified that the contract would be governed by Florida law. That, the Supreme Court ruled, was enough to subject this Michigan businessperson to personal jurisdiction in Florida. The Court emphasized that despite his lack of physical presence in the state, Rudzewicz had purposefully directed his efforts toward a Florida resident, and it was reasonable for Florida to exercise specific personal jurisdiction over him.

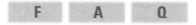

F   A   Q

Q: The Burger King franchise agreement was governed by Florida law, so don't Florida courts automatically have jurisdiction?

A: No. Don't make the mistake of equating *choice of law* and *choice of forum*. Courts often hear cases governed by the law of other states or countries. If Burger King had sued Rudzewicz in Michigan, for example, the Michigan court (which would have

---

[22]465 U.S. 783 (1984). A companion case, *Keeton v. Hustler Magazine*, 465 U.S. 770 (1984), similarly upheld personal jurisdiction based on the effects of a publication in the forum state.
[23]*Calder*, 465 U.S. at 788-789.
[24]471 U.S. 462 (1985).

general jurisdiction over Rudzewicz) would decide the dispute based on Florida contract law. Contracts sometimes include a *consent to jurisdiction clause* or a *forum selection clause*, by which the parties consent to jurisdiction or choose a specific forum, but this franchise agreement simply included a *choice of law clause*. Nonetheless, the Supreme Court considered the choice of law clause a powerful contact with Florida for purposes of determining personal jurisdiction under the minimum contacts test.

Whenever you face a question of personal jurisdiction in a case arising out of a business relationship, ask yourself whether the defendant's relationship to the forum state is comparable to Rudzewicz's relationship to Florida. If so, then there is a strong argument that the court has specific jurisdiction over the defendant.

(5) Stream of Commerce

Here's a common litigation scenario that raises a tough personal jurisdiction issue. A manufacturer in state A sells a product to a company in state B. The company in state B then sells the product to a consumer in state C. If the consumer sues the manufacturer, does state C have personal jurisdiction over the manufacturer? This can involve either wholesaler-distributor-retailer relationships or component-product relationships. Let's make it concrete with two examples:

Example 1: A power drill manufacturer in Ohio sells drills wholesale to a company in Texas that owns a chain of hardware stores throughout the Southwest. The hardware chain sells one of these drills to a consumer in New Mexico. The New Mexico consumer is injured while using the drill and brings a lawsuit in New Mexico against the manufacturer, claiming that the drill was defective. The manufacturer moves to dismiss for lack of personal jurisdiction.

Drill manufacturer (OH) → Hardware store chain (TX) → Consumer (NM)

Example 2: A valve manufacturer in Ohio sells valves to a water heater manufacturer in Pennsylvania, which uses the valves as a component part. The manufacturer sells a water heater to a consumer in Illinois. The water heater explodes, causing injury, and the consumer brings a lawsuit in Illinois against the valve manufacturer, claiming that the valve was defective and caused the explosion. The valve manufacturer moves to dismiss for lack of personal jurisdiction.[25]

Valve manufacturer (OH) → Water heater mfr. (PA) → Consumer (IL)

In each of these two examples, the defendant has no direct contact with the forum state. If the drill manufacturer had sold its product directly into New Mexico or if the valve manufacturer had sold its product directly into Illinois, these would be very easy cases of specific jurisdiction. But instead, these defendants have a more

---

[25]These facts are based on *Gray v. American Radiator & Standard Sanitary Corp.*, 176 N.E.2d 761 (Ill. 1961).

tenuous relationship with the forum states. In each case, the defendant placed its product into the *stream of commerce*, knowing that product was likely to make its way into other states including the forum state. It was foreseeable to the drill manufacturer that its drills could end up with consumers in New Mexico, just as it was foreseeable to the valve manufacturer that its valves could end up inside water heaters in Illinois.

In *Gray v. American Radiator*[26] (which is Example 2), the Illinois Supreme Court held that the Ohio valve manufacturer was subject to specific jurisdiction in Illinois. The court reasoned that the defendant had purposefully placed its valves into the stream of commerce, knowing they could float down that stream into Illinois, so it was reasonable to hold the defendant accountable in the courts of Illinois. The Supreme Court cited *Gray* in dicta in *World-Wide Volkswagen* for the proposition that "[t]he forum State does not exceed its powers under the Due Process Clause if it asserts personal jurisdiction over a corporation that delivers its products into the stream of commerce with the expectation that they will be purchased by consumers in the forum State."[27]

But when the U.S. Supreme Court faced the same question in *Asahi Metal Industry Co. v. Superior Court*,[28] it punted on the key issue. Asahi was a Japanese tire valve manufacturer. It sold valves to Cheng Shin, a Taiwanese tire manufacturer. Cheng Shin tires, with Asahi valves, ended up on Gary Zurcher's motorcycle in California, where Zurcher was injured in a tire-related accident. Zurcher sued a number of defendants including Cheng Shin. Cheng Shin filed a third-party complaint against Asahi (as Chapter 7 explains, this means that Cheng Shin contended that if it was liable to Zurcher, then Asahi should have to pay all or part of the amount). Asahi argued that it was not subject to personal jurisdiction in California. As a stream-of-commerce issue, this is indistinguishable from the examples above, especially Example 2:

Asahi (valve mfr.) (Japan) → Cheng Shin (tire mfr.) (Taiwan) → Motorcycle (CA)

Asahi did not sell the valve directly to California, but Asahi did place its valves in the stream of commerce, and it could foresee that some of its valves would end up in California. Was that enough to meet the minimum contacts test? Or, to put it differently, was that link to California purposeful enough for "purposeful availment"? That's the question the Supreme Court failed to answer in *Asahi* because the Justices split 4-4. Reading the *Asahi* opinions, you'll find, is an exercise in vote counting and frustration. Four Justices (the Brennan opinion) said yes, the minimum contacts test is met when a defendant puts a product into the stream of commerce and can foresee that the product may go to the forum state. Four Justices (the O'Connor opinion) said no, the minimum contacts test requires a more direct link to the forum state than merely placing a product into the stream of commerce elsewhere. And Justice Stevens wrote a concurring opinion that said it's unnecessary to answer that question (although he hinted that "in most circumstances" he would find the minimum contacts test met in a case like this). The whole Court agreed, however, that the minimum

---

[26]176 N.E.2d 761 (Ill. 1961).
[27]*World-Wide Volkswagen*, 444 U.S. at 297-298 (citing Gray v. American Radiator, 176 N.E.2d 761 (Ill. 1961)).
[28]480 U.S. 102 (1987).

contacts test may be met if the defendant, in addition to placing the product in the stream of commerce, did some purposeful act toward the forum state, such as designing its product for the forum state, advertising in the forum state, or establishing service centers there.

Ultimately, the Supreme Court rejected California's personal jurisdiction over Asahi because the exercise of jurisdiction would be unreasonable under the circumstances. Zurcher's claim had settled, and the only remaining claim was Cheng Shin's indemnity claim against Asahi. The Supreme Court Justices could not agree on whether Asahi's placement of its valves in the stream of commerce constituted minimum contacts with California, but they agreed that it made no sense for a California court to adjudicate a Taiwanese company's indemnity claim against a Japanese company that had only indirect contact with California.

When the Supreme Court revisited the stream-of-commerce question in 2011 in *J. McIntyre Machinery v. Nicastro*,[29] everyone expected the Court to resolve the question left open by *Asahi*. Annoyingly, the Court again failed to resolve the matter, leaving the issue ripe for further litigation and a new generation of perplexing civil procedure exam questions. J. McIntyre, a British manufacturer, sold industrial machinery to its Ohio-based U.S. distributer, which in turn sold J. McIntyre machines all over the United States. Robert Nicastro, a scrap metal worker in New Jersey, suffered a serious hand injury while using a J. McIntyre machine. He sued the British manufacturer in New Jersey state court.

Manufacturer (UK) → U.S. Distributer (OH) → Factory (NJ)

The Supreme Court held that New Jersey lacked personal jurisdiction over the British manufacturer. The Court did not, however, embrace any clear rule about stream-of-commerce jurisdiction. A plurality of four Justices emphasized that "[t]he defendant's transmission of goods permits the exercise of jurisdiction only where the defendant can be said to have targeted the forum; as a general rule, it is not enough that the defendant might have predicted that its goods will reach the forum State."[30] Three dissenters would have found specific jurisdiction in New Jersey based on the fact that J. McIntyre actively marketed its products to the United States as a whole.[31] Two Justices felt that J. McIntyre's contacts with New Jersey were too slight to establish personal jurisdiction, but refused to make any "broad pronouncements that refashion basic jurisdictional rules."[32]

(6) Internet Contacts

If interstate highways make *Pennoyer* seem outdated, how about cyberspace? State and national territorial boundaries, already of reduced significance in modern life and the modern economy, become all but invisible in the life and economy of the Internet. Ultimately, however, courts have grappled with cyberspace jurisdiction pretty much as they've grappled with every other boundary-testing type of litigation. That is, they have focused on whether the defendant's contacts with the forum state

---

[29]131 S. Ct. 2780 (2011).
[30]*Id.* at 2788.
[31]*Id.* at 2794 (Ginsburg, J., dissenting).
[32]*Id.* at 2793 (Breyer, J., concurring in the judgment).

are sufficiently substantial and purposeful to justify the state's assertion of judicial power over that defendant.

These cases come in several types, which fall along a spectrum. One type involves the posting of information on a passive website. Ordinarily, a passive website that merely makes information available does not establish personal jurisdiction in each state where that information may be seen (that is, everywhere). At the other end of the spectrum are active websites on which business is actually conducted. Someone in one state (the defendant) runs an Internet-based business. Someone in another state (the plaintiff) conducts business through that website, and then sues the defendant for breach of contract, fraud, or some other claim arising from the transaction. In this scenario, the defendant has acted more purposefully toward the forum state than in the passive-website scenario, so courts are much more inclined to find personal jurisdiction. Finally, there are cases that occupy a middle ground between the passive-website and active-website scenarios. These involve interactive websites that permit an exchange of information. In these cases, personal jurisdiction may depend on the level of interactivity and the commercial nature of the site.

This sliding-scale approach was introduced in *Zippo Manufacturing Co. v. Zippo Dot Com*,[33] and remains the dominant test for Internet-based personal jurisdiction. The Pennsylvania manufacturer of Zippo lighters sued Zippo Dot Com, a California-based Internet news service, for trademark infringement in federal court in Pennsylvania. Even though Zippo Dot Com had no physical presence in Pennsylvania, the court found personal jurisdiction based on the defendant's many Pennsylvania members as well as its contracts with several Pennsylvania Internet service providers.

(7) The Reasonableness Inquiry

In both *Burger King* and *Asahi*, the Supreme Court described personal jurisdiction analysis in two parts. First, are there sufficient purposeful contacts between the defendant and the forum to permit jurisdiction? You can call that the "minimum contacts" or "purposeful availment" inquiry. Second, under the circumstances, would it be reasonable to permit personal jurisdiction in the particular case? You can call that the "fair play and substantial justice" or "reasonableness" inquiry. Remember that in *International Shoe*, the Supreme Court described the due process requirement for personal jurisdiction in terms of whether the defendant has "certain minimum contacts with [the forum state] such that the maintenance of the suit does not offend 'traditional notions of fair play and substantial justice.'"[34] Even if a defendant has purposeful contacts with the forum state, under the circumstances of a particular case it might nonetheless be unreasonable—and therefore unconstitutional under the Due Process Clause—for the court to exercise jurisdiction over the defendant.

The Supreme Court has suggested a multifactor analysis for determining whether personal jurisdiction would be unreasonable. The three dominant factors are the burden on the defendant, the plaintiff's interest, and the forum state's

---

[33]952 F. Supp. 1119 (W.D. Pa. 1997).
[34]*International Shoe*, 326 U.S. at 316 (quoting Milliken v. Meyer).

interest, although some courts balance up to nine different factors. You might break down the essential questions like this:

(1) MINIMUM CONTACTS ("PURPOSEFUL AVAILMENT")

What are the defendant's contacts with the forum state, and did the dispute arise out of those contacts?

Were the defendant's contacts with the forum state purposeful, as opposed to contacts through someone else's unilateral act?

(2) REASONABLENESS ("FAIR PLAY AND SUBSTANTIAL JUSTICE")

How burdensome would it be for the defendant to litigate in the forum state?

How strong is the plaintiff's interest in litigating in the forum state? Is it the plaintiff's home state?

How strong is the forum state's interest in the dispute? Did the dispute arise there, and does it implicate the forum state's policies?

Frankly, having described the Supreme Court's analysis in *International Shoe*, I feel a bit awkward telling you now to separate these two parts of the analysis. In *International Shoe*, "minimum contacts" and "fair play and substantial justice" arrived in a single sentence and seemed to be part of a single idea. The idea was that personal jurisdiction depends on whether the defendant's contacts with the forum state are enough to make it fair and just for the state to exercise power over the defendant. But here we are, a few decades later, talking about "minimum contacts" and "fair play and substantial justice" as separate inquiries. As a lawyer today, you should be prepared to address reasonableness as an independent piece of the personal jurisdiction analysis, but please don't lose sight of how closely it is connected to the question of minimum contacts.

When applying that second step of the analysis, the key case to remember is *Asahi* because in that case, step two—the reasonableness inquiry—proved to be determinative. Recall that in *Asahi*, even though the Court could not agree on whether the defendant met the minimum contacts test, a majority agreed that it would be *unreasonable* for the California court to exercise personal jurisdiction over Asahi. Keep in mind the two reasons why jurisdiction was unreasonable in *Asahi*. One was the international aspect: It's a bigger deal to litigate across the Pacific Ocean and across language barriers than to litigate across state lines. The other was the peculiar procedural posture of the *Asahi* case. By the time the personal jurisdiction issue was being decided, Zurcher (the injured motorcyclist) had settled with the defendants, so the only remaining claim in the case was Cheng Shin's third-party claim against Asahi—a Taiwanese company's indemnity claim against a Japanese company.

Take *Asahi* through the three main questions of the reasonableness inquiry. Defendant's burden? Significant inconvenience for a Japanese company to litigate in another country. Plaintiff's interest? For original plaintiff Zurcher, none, since he already settled. For third-party plaintiff Cheng Shin, no legitimate interest in litigating in California since it's a Taiwanese company asserting a claim against a Japanese company. Forum state's interest? Not much, now that the California plaintiff's claims have been settled and all that remains is the third-party claim. Putting it all together, the Supreme Court saw little sense in allowing the California court to assert personal jurisdiction over Asahi.

Compare that with a case like *Burger King*. Defendant Rudzewicz's burden, while real, did not include crossing international borders or an ocean. Plaintiff Burger King had an interest in litigating in its home state of Florida. And the forum state had an interest in adjudicating a franchise dispute involving a Florida company, especially since the agreement was governed by Florida law. When you analyze the reasonableness of exercising personal jurisdiction, ask yourself whether the case is more like *Asahi* (unreasonable because of international dimension combined with procedural posture in which forum state no longer had any interest) or *Burger King* (reasonable because, despite some burden on the defendant, the plaintiff and forum state had a legitimate interest).

D. Property-Based Jurisdiction

Recall that in the *Pennoyer* world, a court's power over in-state property extended to in rem jurisdiction and quasi-in-rem jurisdiction. *In rem* refers to an action against a *res* (Latin for "thing"). *In rem jurisdiction* refers to power over the thing itself, such as an action to quiet title, which is a lawsuit to determine the ownership of a piece of property. *Quasi-in-rem jurisdiction* refers to power to adjudicate a dispute about something else, but where the court's power is based on attachment of the defendant's in-state property. The theory behind quasi-in-rem jurisdiction was that even though the court was deciding a dispute about something else — a tort claim, breach of contract, or whatever — the court was merely exercising its authority over the attached property.

(1) In Rem Jurisdiction

In rem jurisdiction — pure in rem, such as the action to quiet title — survives. Just as in the days of *Pennoyer*, a plaintiff can bring a case over ownership of property in the courts of the state where the property is located. You may recognize these cases by their captions. They purport to be actions against the property itself, whether real property (land) or other things. The case *United States v. 1,500 Cases More or Less, Tomato Paste*,[35] for example, was an in rem case to determine ownership of — you guessed it — a shipment of tomato paste.

A modern application of in rem jurisdiction concerns Internet domain names. When disputes erupt over domain ownership, the federal Anticybersquatting Consumer Protection Act permits plaintiffs to file actions in rem against the domain names themselves, in the place where the registrar is located. However, plaintiffs may use this in rem option only if the person who registered the domain name is not subject to in personam jurisdiction in the United States.[36] Thus, when Porsche claimed entitlement to Porsche.net, Porsche.com, and other domains, it brought the action in federal court in Virginia because that was the location of the registrar

---

[35]236 F.2d 208 (7th Cir. 1956).
[36]15 U.S.C. §1125(d)(2)(A).

for the domain names.[37] To the extent the dispute involved certain domains registered by a British citizen, Porsche was able to pursue the claims in rem against the domain names. Notice that even though the cybersquatting statute allows in rem jurisdiction, it limits it to situations in which in personam jurisdiction is out of reach, in keeping with the modern preference for in personam proceedings.

(2) Quasi-in-rem Jurisdiction

Unlike in rem jurisdiction, quasi-in-rem jurisdiction is largely a thing of the past. Until 1977, a plaintiff could endow a court with jurisdiction by attaching a defendant's in-state property. Recall that "attachment" refers to the formal process by which a court takes control of a defendant's property, making it impossible for the defendant to transfer that property. With in-state property attached, the court could adjudicate a dispute — even a dispute that had nothing to do with the property that was attached — and if the plaintiff prevailed, the court could enforce the judgment (up to the value of the attached property) by selling the property or simply turning it over to the plaintiff. The classic thing (res) to attach was land, but plaintiffs' lawyers got clever about attaching other forms of property, such as tangible things, bank accounts, and even a debtor. In one famously bizarre case, the plaintiff attached a debt owed to the defendant by serving process on the debtor while the debtor was traveling through the forum state.[38]

But all that quasi-in-rem fun came to an end in 1977 when the Supreme Court decided *Shaffer v. Heitner*.[39] In *Shaffer*, the Court finally acknowledged what smart observers should have understood all along, that a court's assertion of quasi-in-rem jurisdiction is really an assertion of power over the defendant, not merely an assertion of power over the res. With that acknowledgment, the Court declared that attachment of in-state property does not, in itself, give a court power to decide a case. Rather, a court must have personal jurisdiction over the defendant. "The fiction that an assertion of jurisdiction over property is anything but an assertion of jurisdiction over the owner of the property supports an ancient form without substantial modern justification. . . . We therefore conclude that all assertions of state-court jurisdiction must be evaluated according to the standards set forth in *International Shoe* and its progeny."[40]

The Court's decision in *Shaffer* was a big deal. On a purely practical level, it removed from the lawyer's toolbox one useful tool for ensuring the court's power over the defendant in the plaintiff's chosen forum. More significant, in terms of how lawyers and judges think about territorial jurisdiction, *Shaffer* demolished a major piece of the *Pennoyer* system — the idea that territorial power over property sufficed to give a court power over any dispute. *International Shoe* and other cases had altered the *Pennoyer* scheme by *expanding* the jurisdictional reach of courts, but *Shaffer* was the first time the Court had *deprived* courts of jurisdiction that would have been permissible under *Pennoyer*.

It remains possible in some states to use quasi-in-rem jurisdiction, but only as a statutory basis for the court's assertion of power, not as a constitutional basis that dispenses with minimum contacts. Suppose a defendant's contacts with a state

---

[37]Porsche Cars N. Am. v. Porsche.net & Porsche.com, 302 F.3d 248 (4th Cir. 2002).
[38]Harris v. Balk, 198 U.S. 215 (1905).
[39]433 U.S. 186 (1977).
[40]Id. at 212.

suffice constitutionally for jurisdiction in a particular case (keeping in mind that ownership of in-state property counts as a contact), but the state's long-arm statute does not reach the defendant. If the defendant owns in-state property and the state permits attachment as a statutory basis for jurisdiction, then conceivably the court could exercise quasi-in-rem jurisdiction, even after *Shaffer*. But that scenario will rarely arise.

Attachment remains a useful tool in some lawsuits. But nowadays, the purpose of attaching the defendant's property is almost always to secure enforcement of the judgment, not to obtain jurisdiction.

E. Jurisdiction Based on Consent

If a defendant consents to the court's power, then the court has personal jurisdiction over that defendant. That makes sense, doesn't it? The limit on personal jurisdiction is a liberty interest that belongs to the defendant. It's the right not to be subject to the judicial power of an unrelated sovereign. If the defendant does not object to the court's power, then there is no problem.

You can think of consent in two ways. One way is to treat consent as a basis for personal jurisdiction, along with the other bases for personal jurisdiction. If the defendant consents, then the court has personal jurisdiction. Another is to think of personal jurisdiction as a waivable defense. If the defendant consents, then the defendant gives up the right to object that the court lacks personal jurisdiction, even if the defendant otherwise would have had a valid argument that no basis existed for personal jurisdiction.

(1) General Appearance

How does a defendant consent to personal jurisdiction? In theory, a defendant could show up and say "I consent to this court's personal jurisdiction," but that does not happen. The most basic way for a defendant to consent is simply by appearing to litigate the case. If a defendant, without objecting to the court's personal jurisdiction, files an answer or makes a motion, then the defendant has consented to the court's personal jurisdiction by going forward with the litigation. This is called a **general appearance**.

What if the defendant does *not* wish to consent to the court's personal jurisdiction? The defendant has two options.

Option one: default and collateral attack. If the defendant does not appear to litigate, the court will enter a default judgment, as Chapter 8 describes. When the plaintiff tries to enforce that judgment against the defendant, the defendant can object that the first court lacked personal jurisdiction. Defaulting is a risky approach, however, because if the enforcing court finds that the first court had jurisdiction, then the defendant will have lost the chance to dispute the claim on the merits.

Option two: show up and immediately object to the court's personal jurisdiction. Traditionally, this was known as a **special appearance**, in contrast to the general appearance. Ordinarily, if a defendant is present in the state, the plaintiff can serve the defendant with process and thereby give the court personal jurisdiction over the defendant. When a defendant appears *specially*, however, the defendant is showing up solely for the purpose of objecting to the court's personal jurisdiction, and this appearance cannot itself be used to establish personal jurisdiction. Under modern practice, a defendant can object to personal jurisdiction and proceed to litigate the case without thereby consenting to the court's power.

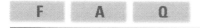

Q: Do courts need personal jurisdiction over plaintiffs?

A: Yes, but ordinarily it's a nonissue. A plaintiff has consented to the court's personal jurisdiction by bringing the lawsuit. Simply by filing the complaint, the plaintiff has made a general appearance, so the plaintiff will be bound by the judgment. Moreover, if the defendant files a counterclaim against the plaintiff, the plaintiff cannot escape the counterclaim by arguing that the court lacks personal jurisdiction. Class actions raise a more difficult question because plaintiff class members may be bound by a judgment even though they have not taken any step to consent to the court's jurisdiction. The Supreme Court addressed the question of personal jurisdiction over class action plaintiffs in *Phillips Petroleum v. Shutts*, 472 U.S. 797 (1985), which we discuss in Chapter 7.

---

(2) Advance Consent

A party can consent in advance to the personal jurisdiction of a court. Sometimes, especially in the business context, parties do this by appointing an agent for service of process in a particular state.

A contract can establish consent to personal jurisdiction. *National Equipment Rental, Ltd. v. Szukhent*[41] provides a straightforward example. The Szukhents were Michigan farmers who leased farm equipment from National Equipment Rental, a New York company. The lease, which was a form contract, stated that the lessees appoint a particular person as their agent for service of process in New York. When the company sued the Szukhents in New York for lease payments, they served the summons and complaint to the named agent, who forwarded them to the Szukhents. The Supreme Court upheld personal jurisdiction in New York. By signing a lease in which they appointed a New York agent for service of process, the Szukhents had consented to personal jurisdiction in New York.

Note that the contract provision in *Szukhent* did not specify that any lawsuit *must* be brought in New York. The company could have sued the Szukhents in Michigan. The contract provision was a *consent-to-jurisdiction clause*. By providing that the Szukhents appointed an agent for service of process, the contract opened up New York as a possible forum and foreclosed any successful objection by the Szukhents to New York's personal jurisdiction over them.

Some contractual clauses go a step further and specify where litigation *must* be brought, if at all. These are called **forum selection clauses** or *choice of forum* clauses. The Supreme Court enforced a forum selection clause in *Carnival Cruise Lines v. Shute*.[42] The cruise contract, which was printed on passengers tickets, stated that any dispute arising out of the cruise must be litigated, if at all, in Florida (where

---

[41]375 U.S. 311 (1964).
[42]499 U.S. 585 (1991).

Carnival Cruise Lines is headquartered). When the plaintiffs filed a slip-and-fall lawsuit against Carnival in a court in the plaintiffs' home state of Washington, Carnival argued that the case must be thrown out based on the forum selection clause. The Supreme Court agreed, holding that the clause was enforceable. Courts may refuse to enforce a forum selection clause if the contract was obtained by fraud or if the chosen forum is illogical or deliberately inconvenient. If Carnival's cruise ticket specified that any lawsuit must be brought in Botswana, just to make it difficult and expensive for any plaintiff to sue, then a court would find the clause unenforceable.

Note the difference between the forum selection clause in *Carnival Cruise* and the consent to jurisdiction clause in *Szukhent*. The forum selection clause eliminated forum options that otherwise would have been available. Without the clause, the Shutes could have filed the case in Florida or several other states, but with the clause, they could sue only in Florida. The consent to jurisdiction clause, by contrast, added a forum option that otherwise would have been unavailable. Without the clause, the equipment company could not have sued the Szukhents in New York, but with the clause, New York courts became an option.

Sidebar

CIVIL PROCEDURE AND CONTRACT DRAFTING

Most civil procedure seems to be aimed at litigators. It's all about where and how lawsuits get litigated. But it turns out to be useful, as well, for lawyers who never intend to see the inside of a courtroom. The contract clauses in *National Equipment Rental v. Szukhent*, *Carnival Cruise Lines v. Shute*, and *Burger King v. Rudzewicz* offer three great examples. If you are negotiating a contract on behalf of your client, you should consider whether it would serve your client's interests to insert a contractual provision that specifies what will happen if a dispute ensues. National Equipment Rental's lawyer included a *consent to jurisdiction clause* to ensure that the company could sue its equipment rental clients in New York. Carnival Cruise's lawyer included a *forum selection clause* to ensure that cruise passengers could sue the company only in Florida. Burger King's lawyer included a *choice of law clause* to ensure that Florida law would govern its franchise agreements. The point is that clients need their lawyers to understand forum selection law, including the law of personal jurisdiction, not only when an actual lawsuit is filed, but also for purposes of business planning and contract drafting.

F. Transient Jurisdiction

In the days of *Pennoyer*, the Supreme Court took it as a given that if a defendant was personally served with process within a state, the state court has jurisdiction over the defendant. It was the one surefire way to get in personam jurisdiction over an individual. Even if the defendant was in the state only for a brief visit, or merely passing through, jurisdiction could be established by handing the defendant a summons and complaint while the defendant was within the state borders. Fast forward to 1959 and the case of *Grace v. MacArthur*,[43] and you have the spectacle of a defendant, on a nonstop flight from Memphis to Dallas, being served with process on the airplane while flying over Arkansas in order to establish personal jurisdiction in Arkansas.

Some lawyers even call it *tag jurisdiction*, as in "tag, you're it." Others call it *transient jurisdiction* because the defendant was served while in the forum state on a transient basis. Some simply call it jurisdiction based on in-state service of process.

---

[43]170 F. Supp. 442 (E.D. Ark. 1959).

After the Supreme Court decided *Shaffer v. Heitner*[44] in 1977, some lawyers wondered whether such jurisdiction remained valid. Recall that the Court in *Shaffer* said that "all assertions of state-court jurisdiction must be evaluated according to the standards set forth in *International Shoe* and its progeny."[45] You can see how people would think that tag jurisdiction was dead. If the *International Shoe* standard means minimum contacts, then how can that test be satisfied if the defendant's only contact with the state is that he happened to step over the state line and someone handed him a summons?

In *Burnham v. Superior Court*,[46] however, the Supreme Court announced that transient jurisdiction is not dead at all. The defendant, from New Jersey, was in California for a brief business trip and also to see his kids (he and his wife were separated). While he was there, his wife had him served with process in a divorce case. The defendant argued that his transient presence in California was not enough to warrant in personam jurisdiction over him. The Supreme Court disagreed, holding that if an individual defendant is served with process within the state, the court has in personam jurisdiction over the defendant.

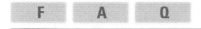

Q: What if the plaintiff gets the defendant into the forum state by force or trickery?

A: If the plaintiff forcibly drags the defendant across the state line, or tricks the defendant into coming by telling her falsely that her sick uncle is dying and she'd better come quickly, then in-state service of process does not establish personal jurisdiction over the defendant. Such cases are rare, but they happen. Also, the defendant has a temporary immunity from service of process when appearing in a state as a party or witness to a judicial proceeding.

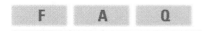

Q: Can a plaintiff establish personal jurisdiction over a corporate defendant by serving an employee of the corporation within the state?

A: Not really. *Burnham* involved personal service on an *individual* defendant, not a *corporate* defendant or other entity. Do not make the mistake of thinking that you can get personal jurisdiction over a corporation just because some corporate employee, or even a corporate officer or director, happens to be found in the forum state. However, if the corporation has authorized someone to be an agent for service of process within a state, then service on that person establishes jurisdiction over the corporation.

---

[44] 433 U.S. 186 (1977).
[45] Id. at 212.
[46] 495 U.S. 604 (1990).

G. Personal Jurisdiction in Federal Court

Personal jurisdiction focuses on state boundaries (or, in international litigation, national boundaries) and the territorial limits on state power. Despite all the changes since *Pennoyer*, that's one thing that has remained constant. But what about federal court? If personal jurisdiction is about limits on state power, do the same restrictions apply to the power of federal courts?

The short answer is yes, mostly. The Federal Rules of Civil Procedure include a provision about the territorial reach of effective service in federal court, Rule 4(k), which as a practical matter makes federal court personal jurisdiction analysis very similar to that in state court. Rule 4(k)(1)(A) states that service of process establishes personal jurisdiction over a defendant "who is subject to the jurisdiction of a court of general jurisdiction in the state where the district court is located." In other words, if the state court would have personal jurisdiction over the defendant, then so does the federal court. (Don't be confused by the multiple uses of "jurisdiction" in the rule. The first "jurisdiction" means personal jurisdiction, but the reference to "general jurisdiction" merely describes the subject matter jurisdiction of the state's general trial court.) So federal court personal jurisdiction analysis begins with Rule 4(k)(1)(A), which asks whether the state court would have jurisdiction, at which point the analysis merges.

Rule 4(k) contains additional provisions, however, which extend personal jurisdiction a bit further in federal court than in state court. Rule 4(k)(1)(B) gives a federal court personal jurisdiction over a defendant "who is a party joined under Rule 14 or 19 and is served within a judicial district of the United States and not more than 100 miles from where the summons was issued." Somewhat embarrassingly known as the *hundred-mile bulge* provision, this rule allows a federal court, in limited circumstances, to exercise personal jurisdiction over a person who can be served with process within 100 miles of the court. Note that the hundred-mile bulge rule does not apply to all defendants; it applies only to those joined as third-party defendants under Rule 14 and those joined as required parties under Rule 19. (We'll look at Rules 14 and 19 in Chapter 7 on joinder.) So don't think that Rule 4(k)(1)(B) gives you an all-purpose get-an-extra-hundred-miles bonus for federal courts. It's much more limited than that. But in its two specific applications — for third-party defendants and for compulsory joinder — it is a small but useful tool for joining certain defendants who are nearby but might otherwise escape the court's power. Although 100 miles may not get you very far in Montana or Texas, in metropolitan areas like New York City or Washington, D.C., it covers an area that crosses state lines and includes multiple federal judicial districts.

Rule 4(k)(1)(C) provides a statutory catchall, stating that service of process gives a federal court personal jurisdiction over a defendant "when authorized by a federal statute." This covers statutes that provide for nationwide personal jurisdiction in federal courts for interpleader (a complex form of joinder explained in Chapter 7), antitrust cases, and a few other types of federal actions.

Then there's Rule 4(k)(2). It's a sensible little rule, but odds are that in your entire career you'll never have an opportunity to use it. It was drafted to cover a tiny potential gap in federal court personal jurisdiction. Suppose a foreign defendant has substantial contacts with the United States, but those contacts are so dispersed that the contacts with each individual state would not suffice to get personal jurisdiction over the defendant in any state court. Rule 4(k)(1)(A) would not provide any federal court with personal jurisdiction over the defendant because that is tied to the power of the states. But if the federal courts are instruments of the U.S. government, shouldn't their power extend to a defendant that meets minimum contacts with the United States as a whole, at least for claims arising under federal law? Rule 4(k)(2) states that "[f]or a claim that arises under federal law, serving a summons or filing a waiver of service establishes personal jurisdiction over a defendant if: (A) the defendant is not subject to jurisdiction in any state's courts of general jurisdiction; and (B) exercising jurisdiction is consistent with the United States Constitution and laws." The rule ensures that whenever a foreign defendant has sufficient contacts with the United States to meet the minimum contacts test, some federal court will be able to assert power over that defendant for purposes of federal law claims.

To challenge personal jurisdiction in federal court, a defendant may assert an objection to personal jurisdiction in the answer or may make a pre-answer motion to dismiss under Rule 12(b)(2) — the motion to dismiss for lack of personal jurisdiction. Often, defendants pair the 12(b)(2) motion with a Rule 12(b)(5) motion to dismiss for insufficient service of process, arguing that service of process failed because it exceeded the court's territorial reach.

H. Notice

(1) The Due Process Requirement of Notice

Territorial power is one part of personal jurisdiction. The other part — equally important — is **notice**. If due process means anything, it means that if a proceeding is going to affect a party's interests, the party should have an *opportunity to be heard*. That opportunity to be heard is meaningless unless the party has been notified about the proceeding.

Sidebar

TWO DUE PROCESS CLAUSES

The constitutional aspect of personal jurisdiction is grounded in the Due Process Clause, which protects persons from deprivation of life, liberty, or property without due process of law. But the Constitution actually contains two Due Process Clauses. The Fifth Amendment (part of the Bill of Rights and best known for the privilege against self-incrimination) prohibits the *federal* government from depriving citizens without due process of law. The Fourteenth Amendment (enacted after the Civil War and best known for the Equal Protection Clause) prohibits the *states* from depriving citizens without due process of law. *Pennoyer, International Shoe*, and most of the other famous personal jurisdiction cases spoke in terms of the Fourteenth Amendment's Due Process Clause because they involved the constitutional limits of *state* court power. In federal court, the relevant constitutional constraint is the similarly worded clause of the Fifth Amendment. Under the Fifth Amendment, the constitutional reach of the federal courts' territorial power extends to any defendant that has minimum contacts with the United States as a whole (this is implicit in Rule 4(k)(2), at least for federal law claims). But because Rule 4(k)(1)(A) links federal court personal jurisdiction to the reach of the state courts, courts rarely need to consider the difference between the two Due Process Clauses when analyzing personal jurisdiction.

In the landmark case of *Mullane v. Central Hanover Bank & Trust Co.*,[47] the Supreme Court explained the due process requirement of notice. Notice, the Court emphasized, is not a mere technicality. The point is to give the affected party a genuine opportunity to be heard. Therefore, notice must be *reasonably calculated* to reach the person: "An elementary and fundamental requirement of due process in any proceeding which is to be accorded finality is notice reasonably calculated, under all the circumstances, to apprise interested parties of the pendency of the action and afford them an opportunity to present their objections."[48] What's reasonably calculated? "The means employed must be such as one desirous of actually informing the absentee might reasonably adopt to accomplish it."[49] I love that description. It's so obvious, and yet on the topic of notice, it would have been easy for the Court to get lost in procedural technicalities.

The Supreme Court reemphasized its *Mullane* holding in 2006. In *Jones v. Flowers*,[50] a state commissioner seized Gary Jones's house after property taxes had gone unpaid. The commissioner attempted to notify Jones twice by certified mail, but each time the letter was returned by the post office marked "unclaimed." Jones never saw the letters because he had moved out of the house when he separated from his wife. When Jones later found out that the state had taken possession of his property and sold it, he brought a lawsuit arguing that the sale violated his right to due process. The Arkansas courts considered the sale valid because the commissioner complied with the notice requirement by sending a certified letter to Jones. But the Supreme Court agreed with Jones. When the letters were returned unclaimed, the commissioner *knew* that Jones had not received them. *Mullane* said that to satisfy the due process notice requirement, you have to do what someone would do who actually wants to inform the person about the proceeding. If you were trying to reach someone and your certified letter came back unclaimed, you would try again or try some other method. The commissioner and the Arkansas courts made the mistake of treating notice as a mere technicality. The Supreme Court took the opportunity to reemphasize that, constitutionally, notice is all about giving the party an opportunity to be heard.

Note what *Mullane* and *Jones* do *not* say. They do not say that due process always requires *actual* notice for a party to be bound by a judgment. What they require is notice reasonably calculated to reach the party. There are circumstances in which personal service is impossible and notice by publication may be constitutionally sufficient, and there are other circumstances in which, for whatever reason, a defendant may not in fact learn about the proceeding. As long as the notice complies with applicable rules and is reasonably calculated to reach the defendant, a judgment may bind the defendant without offending due process.

(2) Service of Process

For a court to have personal jurisdiction over a defendant, the plaintiff must serve the summons and complaint on the defendant. Known as **service of process**, this is the procedure by which the constitutional requirement of notice is met in most cases.

---

[47]339 U.S. 306 (1950).
[48]Id. at 314.
[49]Id. at 315.
[50]547 U.S. 220 (2006).

The *complaint* is the document in which the plaintiff states the claim against the defendant and demands relief. The *summons* is a document issued by the court (it can be prepared by the plaintiff and signed by the clerk of the court) to summon the defendant to appear in court.

Federal court service of process is governed by Rule 4. We've already looked at Rule 4(k), which governs the territorial limits of effective process. Other portions of Rule 4 address the form of the summons and the details of how you go about serving process on various types of defendants. Individuals within the United States, for example, are served under Rule 4(e)(2) by personally delivering a copy of the summons and complaint, or by leaving the summons and complaint at the person's home with someone "of suitable age and discretion" who also lives there. Alternatively, under Rule 4(e)(1), individuals may be served in whatever manner would be allowed under state law. Other provisions describe how to serve corporations, foreigners, minors, and government parties.

Formal service of process, such as personal delivery or the other methods approved by Rule 4, can be costly and time-consuming because it may involve hiring a process server and tracking down the defendant. But the rule suggests a cheaper and easier alternative: *waiver of service*. Rule 4(d) allows a plaintiff to notify the defendant about the action and "request that the defendant waive service of a summons." To make this request, the plaintiff simply sends the defendant a copy of the complaint by first class mail or other reliable means, along with a form that the defendant can return to waive the requirement of formal service. Why, you might ask, would the defendant agree to this? Because Rule 4(d) provides both a carrot and a stick. The carrot: If the defendant agrees to waive formal service of process, the defendant gets extra time to answer the complaint (60 or 90 days instead of the usual 21). The stick: If a U.S. defendant does *not* agree to waive formal service of process, then unless the defendant shows good cause for the failure, the defendant must pay whatever costs the plaintiff incurs serving the defendant.

I. Analyzing Personal Jurisdiction

This chapter has covered a lot of material on personal jurisdiction, including a number of important Supreme Court cases. But it's not enough to know what the cases say. You have to know how to *apply* them. So let's turn to how you might analyze a personal jurisdiction question. Perhaps you represent a plaintiff and are trying to figure out your forum options. For each court you consider, you need to know whether that court would have personal jurisdiction over each defendant. Or perhaps you represent a defendant who has been sued in a particular court, and you need to decide whether to file a motion to dismiss for lack of personal jurisdiction. Either way, you must conduct a personal jurisdiction analysis.

Below, I've outlined one way you might think through the step-by-step analysis of in personam jurisdiction. At various steps, the outline identifies cases and rules on which the step is based. This is not, by any means, the only way to pull this stuff together. Lawyers and judges have various ways of thinking about these questions, and each civil procedure professor teaches it a bit differently. As you read the cases, you may come up with your own way of pulling the material together. What's important is that you have *some* approach in mind that takes you step by step through the analysis.

Personal Jurisdiction Analysis

I. <u>Authorization for assertion of jurisdiction</u> (Does the court's territorial authority for service of process reach this defendant?)
   a. State court
      - Can the defendant be served within the state?
      - If out of state, does the state's long-arm statute extend to this defendant?
         - If the state's long-arm statute extends to the full extent of due process, then this analysis merges with the constitutional analysis in Part II.
   b. Federal court
      - Would the state court have jurisdiction over the defendant? (Rule 4(k)(1)(A))
      - Even if the state court would lack jurisdiction, does the federal court have jurisdiction under the 100-mile bulge provision or other exceptions of Rule 4(k)(1)(B)-(C)?

II. <u>Constitutionality</u> (Does this defendant have sufficient connection with the forum state so that jurisdiction comports with due process?)
   a. <u>General jurisdiction</u>
      i. Individual
         - Was the defendant served with process within the state? (*Burnham*)
         - Is the defendant domiciled in the state? (*Milliken*)
         - Did the defendant consent to jurisdiction?
      ii. Corporation
         - Is the defendant incorporated in the state?
         - Is the defendant headquartered in the state?
         - Is the defendant doing continuous and systematic business in the state that is so substantial that the company can be considered present, focusing on physical facilities within the state? (*Goodyear*)
         - Did the defendant consent to jurisdiction?
   b. <u>Specific jurisdiction</u>
      i. Does the claim arise out of defendant's contacts with the forum state?
      ii. Minimum contacts
         - Did the defendant purposefully direct its actions toward the forum state? Is the contact with the state the result of an act by the defendant, as opposed to someone else's unilateral act? (*Hanson; World-Wide Volkswagen*)
         - Stream of commerce: If the contact is based on placement of a product in the stream of commerce, to what extent did the defendant foresee that its product would reach the forum state, and did the defendant target the forum state? (*Asahi; Nicastro*)
         - Business contacts: If the contact is based on the defendant's business relationship with an in-state company, how substantial are the relationship and the connection with the forum state? (*Burger King*)
         - Effects: If the contact is based on in-state effects, to what extent did the defendant know that its conduct would have effects in the forum state? (*Calder*)
         - Internet: If the contact is via the Internet, to what extent does it involve the active conduct of business, as opposed to a passive informational website? (*Zippo*)
      iii. Reasonableness (Would the exercise of jurisdiction be reasonable under the circumstances?)
         - Consider three main factors (*Asahi*):

      (1) Burden on the defendant

      (2) Interest of the plaintiff

      (3) Interest of the forum state

III. Notice

    a. Service of process (Was service accomplished properly?)

      ■ State court: Did service comply with state rules on service of process?

      ■ Federal court: Did service comply with Rule 4?

        ■ Personal delivery or other service in compliance with rule provisions; or

        ■ Service in compliance with state rules; or

        ■ Waiver of formal service (Rule 4(d)).

    b. Constitutionality (Was the defendant notified in a way that comports with due process?)

      ■ Was notice reasonably calculated to reach the defendant? (*Mullane; Jones*)

SUMMARY

■ For a court to enter a binding judgment, the court must have personal jurisdiction over the parties.

■ Personal jurisdiction is an individual liberty interest protected by the Due Process Clause.

■ For personal jurisdiction, a court needs both constitutional and statutory authority to exercise power over the parties.

■ As a constitutional matter, personal jurisdiction requires that the defendant have "minimum contacts" with the forum state so that the assertion of power does not offend "traditional notions of fair play and substantial justice."

■ The minimum contacts test requires "purposeful availment"; that is, the defendant must have acted purposefully toward the forum state.

■ If a court has general jurisdiction over a person, it has power over the person regardless of whether the claim arose out of contacts with the forum state.

■ A court has general jurisdiction over an individual who is domiciled in the forum state, or who is personally served with process within the state.

■ A court has general jurisdiction over a corporation that is incorporated or headquartered in the forum state, or that has a systematic, continuous, and substantial presence in the state.

■ If a court has specific jurisdiction over a party, then it has power over the person with regard to a claim that arose out of the party's contacts with the forum state.

■ The constitutional test for specific jurisdiction has been elucidated in a series of cases addressing personal jurisdiction based on business relationships with the forum state, effects in the forum state, placing products into the stream of commerce, and other situations.

■ Even if the defendant has minimum contacts with the forum state, a court may reject personal jurisdiction on the grounds that the assertion of jurisdiction would be unreasonable, taking into account the plaintiff's interest, the burden on the defendant, and the forum state's interest.

■ Parties may consent to personal jurisdiction by contract, by appointment of an agent for service of process, or by making a general appearance in court.

■ Due process requires that parties be notified of a proceeding against them, and that the notice be reasonably calculated to reach them.

CONNECTIONS

Subject Matter Jurisdiction

Subject matter jurisdiction and personal jurisdiction share a name; they're both about "juris-diction" (law-telling, from the Latin roots). That's because they both concern limits on the power of courts. But scratch the surface, and you see that they address entirely different sets of issues. Subject matter jurisdiction concerns the power of types of courts over categories of actions, whereas personal jurisdiction involves territorial power over the parties. At a constitutional level, federal subject matter jurisdiction respects federalism and separation of powers. The constraint on personal jurisdiction, by contrast, is an individual due process right based on the territorial limits of state power.

Venue

Venue and personal jurisdiction, in tandem, determine in which states or districts a lawsuit can be filed. For corporate defendants, the link is even more explicit, as the federal venue statute defines corporate "residence" as anywhere the corporation is subject to personal jurisdiction.

Pleadings — Complaint

Unlike federal subject matter jurisdiction, a plaintiff need not allege in the complaint a basis for personal jurisdiction. Rule 8(a)(1) requires a statement of the court's subject matter jurisdiction because without subject matter jurisdiction the court must dismiss the complaint. Because personal jurisdiction may be waived by the defendant, a court cannot know based on the complaint alone whether a dismissal for lack of personal jurisdiction is in order.

Pleadings — Defenses

A defendant must consider personal jurisdiction at the outset of litigation. The defense of lack of personal jurisdiction must be asserted in the answer or in a pre-answer motion, whichever comes first. Otherwise, under Rule 12(h)(1), the objection is waived.

Joinder — Indispensable Parties

Personal jurisdiction plays a role in the analysis of compulsory party joinder under Rule 19. If a party is required under Rule 19(a) but the court lacks personal jurisdiction over that party, then the court must decide under Rule 19(b) whether the case should be dismissed.

Joinder — Interpleader, Impleader

To enable certain useful forms of joinder, the federal courts ease personal jurisdiction restrictions for certain claims. The interpleader statute permits nationwide personal jurisdiction. The bulge provision of Rule 4(k)(1)(B) extends the range of personal jurisdiction over impleaded third-party defendants as well as required parties.

Preclusion

Claim preclusion and issue preclusion describe aspects of the binding effect of a judgment. Personal jurisdiction is a precondition to the binding effect of a judgment. If a court lacks personal jurisdiction over a defendant and the defendant defaults, the defendant is not bound by the judgment. In this sense, *Pennoyer v. Neff*—the mother of all personal jurisdiction cases—is a basic building block of the law of preclusion.

Venue

O V E R V I E W

Where, among those courts, should a lawsuit be heard? Subject matter jurisdiction and personal jurisdiction help determine the choice of forum. But further narrowing of the options may be necessary to assure a convenient and appropriate location for a lawsuit, and that's where **venue** comes into play. In state court, venue ordinarily determines the county or counties where a case may be brought. In federal court, venue determines which district. In addition to examining which venues are permissible, this chapter also looks at the process for transferring a lawsuit from one venue to another. After learning subject matter jurisdiction and personal jurisdiction, with their constitutional foundations and multilayered analyses, you may find venue disappointingly shallow . . . but refreshingly straightforward.

A. Three Hoops

First, let's place venue in context as one of several forum selection doctrines. For a case to be brought in a particular court, that court must have subject matter jurisdiction over the action, must have personal jurisdiction over the parties, and must be a proper venue under applicable federal or state venue rules. Whereas subject matter and personal jurisdiction address the court's power and boast constitutional underpinnings, venue operates on a more mundane level as a statutory constraint on forum choices.

Some students like to understand this by picturing a Venn diagram with three overlapping circles representing subject matter jurisdiction, personal jurisdiction, and venue. If all three circles intersect, the court may hear the case:

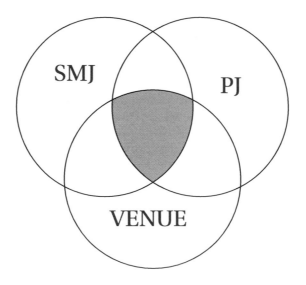

As a lawyer, however, you'll probably find that the three circles feel more like hoops that you have to jump through in order to establish the legitimacy of your chosen forum. Hoop one: In federal court, the plaintiff's complaint or the defendant's notice of removal must state the basis for the court's subject matter jurisdiction. Hoop two: In either state or federal court, if a defendant moves to dismiss for lack of personal jurisdiction, the plaintiff must show the basis for the court's power. Hoop three: If a party objects to venue, the plaintiff will have to show why the chosen venue is proper.

B. Venue in State Court

Venue rules for state courts vary from state to state and are generally regulated by statute. These statutes determine where within a state — which county, parish, or district — cases can be brought. Law school civil procedure courses rarely focus on state court venue, so I'll keep it short.

Often, state venue statutes permit a court to hear a case in the county, parish, or district of the plaintiff's residence, the defendant's residence, where a contract was signed or was to be carried out, or where a substantial part of the events leading to the dispute occurred. Many state venue statutes retain the old common law distinction between local and transitory actions. *Local actions* are those that concern real property, such as lawsuits to determine property ownership, to gain possession of land, or sometimes for trespass. A local action must be brought in the court where the property is located. *Transitory actions* include all other lawsuits and can be brought wherever permitted by the general venue rules as long as the defendant is subject to personal jurisdiction. The notion behind the local-transitory distinction is that a transitory action could have arisen anywhere, whereas a local action, because it involves a specific piece of real property, could have arisen only in one place. Really, it's not a terribly satisfying distinction. Of course, a specific property dispute arises in a specific place. But can't the same be said of automobile accidents, barroom brawls, employment disputes, or a host of other "transitory" actions? Satisfying or not, in most courts, lawsuits involving real property are considered local actions and must be brought in the county, parish, or district where the property is found.

C. Venue in Federal Court

The federal courts are divided into over 90 districts. Venue statutes determine which of those districts are appropriate places for a court to hear a particular case.

```
F        A        Q
```

Q: Is there a single proper venue for each case?

A: No. In many cases, you will see that there are multiple districts where the lawsuit can be brought. It's up to the plaintiff to choose where to file among the permissible venues, and the defendant can decide whether to move to transfer to another proper venue. Some controversies, however, must be brought in a particular district. Under the federal venue statute, for example, if the defendant resides in the same district where all the substantial events occurred, then the suit must be brought in that district.

To figure out which districts are proper venues for a case in federal court, you will usually look at the general federal venue statute, 28 U.S.C. §1391. Keep in the back of your mind, however, that a few types of cases have their own specific venue statutes, such as the interpleader venue statute at §1397.

The three subsections of section 1391(b) spell out in general where venue is proper for a lawsuit or, to use the lawyerly terminology, where venue *may be laid*.

(1) Defendant's Residence

Section 1—that is, 28 U.S.C. §1391(b)(1)—permits a case to be brought in "a judicial district in which any defendant resides, if all defendants are residents of the State in which the district is located." In a lawsuit against one individual, this section is pretty straightforward. The case may be brought in the district where the defendant resides. But in a case involving multiple defendants, section 1 applies only if all defendants reside in the same state. This makes sense, doesn't it? If all the defendants reside in Connecticut, then it's hard for them to complain about venue if the plaintiff files the lawsuit in the District of Connecticut. But if one defendant resides in Connecticut, one in Georgia, and one in Oregon, then it makes more sense to base venue on where the relevant events occurred, rather than on the defendants' residences.

The other twist—and this may be the single most important thing for you to remember about the federal venue statute—is the statute's surprising definition of "reside" for a corporation or other entity. Individuals "reside" where they are domiciled,[1] but the definition of corporate residence is not so intuitive. If you were to look only at §1391(b)(1), you might assume that a corporation resides wherever it is headquartered. Or maybe you would assume that corporate "residence" would be defined just like corporate "citizenship" under the diversity jurisdiction statute, looking at state of incorporation plus principal place of business. But if you assumed that (as countless students have done on civil procedure exams), you would be wrong.

Rather, the venue statute provides that an entity "shall be deemed to reside, if a defendant, in any judicial district in which such defendant is subject to the court's personal jurisdiction. . . . " 28 U.S.C. §1391(c)(2). In other words, if a state has

---

[1] 28 U.S.C. §1391(c)(1).

personal jurisdiction over a corporation, then the corporation is deemed to "reside" in that state for purposes of the venue provision in §1391(b)(1).

If a case involves only a single defendant, and it is a corporation or other entity, then as a practical matter, this definition merges the venue inquiry with the personal jurisdiction inquiry. With a single corporate defendant, if the defendant is subject to personal jurisdiction in a district, then federal venue in that district would be proper under §1391(b)(1).

If a case involves multiple defendants, then to determine venue under §1391(b)(1), take two steps: First, see where each defendant "resides" by figuring out where each individual is domiciled and where each entity is subject to personal jurisdiction. Second, compare to see if there is a state in which all of the defendants are deemed to reside.

Be careful in how you use §1391(c). It does *not* state where venue is proper. All it does is state a definition of "reside." Please do not make the mistake of saying that "§1391(c) establishes that venue is proper in this district because the defendant is subject to personal jurisdiction here." Rather, be precise: "Section 1391(c) establishes that the defendant 'resides' in this district because it is subject to personal jurisdiction here; venue is proper in this district under §1391(b)(1) because all defendants reside here."

(2) Events or Property

Section 2 is the most intuitive part of the venue statute. It permits a case to be brought in "a judicial district in which a substantial part of the events or omissions giving rise to the claim occurred, or a substantial part of property that is the subject of the action is situated." 28 U.S.C. §1391(b)(2).

Many cases invite a straightforward application of section 2. If a dispute involves ownership of a piece of property, then of course venue is proper in the district where the property is located. If a dispute involves an auto accident, then of course venue is proper in the district where the accident occurred.

Often, however, disputes cross state or district borders. If a New Yorker negotiates a contract with a Californian concerning a business in Oklahoma, and a dispute ensues, then section 2 could point to multiple permissible venues, depending on where substantial negotiations and other relevant events occurred. Similarly, if a defective product is sold in New York and causes injury in Oklahoma, section 2 could point to both as appropriate venues.

(3) Fallback Provision

You will never use section 3. OK, it's theoretically possible, but I'm telling you that in your career as a lawyer, it is unlikely that you will ever work on a case in which venue is based on section 3. Here's why. Section 3 — that is, 28 U.S.C. §1391(b)(3) — applies only if there is no proper venue under either section 1 or 2. Section 1391(b)(3) provides that "if there is no district in which an action may otherwise be brought as provided in this section," then the action may be brought in "any judicial district in which any defendant is subject to the court's personal jurisdiction with respect to such claim."

Think about how unlikely it is that "there is no district in which an action may otherwise be brought" under the other two subsections of the venue statute. That would mean that not only do the defendants not reside in the same state, but *none* of the substantial events took place in *any* judicial district within the United States. It applies only in a case where all of the substantial events took place outside the country (yet the plaintiff chose to file in a U.S. court), and the defendants do not reside in the same state (even with the broad definition of "reside" for corporate defendants). If you happen to face that situation, then section 3 allows venue wherever you can get personal jurisdiction.

(4) Waiver

If a defendant does not object to the plaintiff's chosen venue, then the court may go ahead and hear the case. Rule 12(h)(1) provides that the defense of improper venue, like the defense of personal jurisdiction, is waived if not asserted at the outset of the litigation.

(5) Venue upon Removal

Recall from Chapter 1 that a defendant may remove a case from state court to federal court if subject matter jurisdiction exists. When a case is removed, what's the correct federal venue? The removal statute answers the venue question directly by stating that the action may be removed "to the district court of the United States for the district and division embracing the place where such action is pending."[2] In other words, if a defendant removes an action from the New York state court in Manhattan, it goes to the Southern District of New York, regardless of whether §1391 would have permitted that venue.

D. Venue Transfer

Sometimes, it makes sense for a court to transfer a case from one place to another within a judicial system. Within a state court system, a case might be transferred from one county to another. Within the federal court system, a case might be transferred from one district to another, whether within a state (say, from the Southern District of California to the Northern District of California) or between states (from the Southern District of California to the Eastern District of Pennsylvania). This is known as **venue transfer**. The first court is called the *transferor court*, and the second court is called the *transferee court*. As an attorney, if you think your client would be better off in a different venue where the case could have been brought, consider bringing a motion to transfer venue to your preferred location.

---

[2]28 U.S.C. § 1441(a).

"We would like to request a change of venue to an entirely different legal system."

You need to know about three different federal venue transfer statutes. The most basic one — §1404 — deals with cases that are filed in a court that has jurisdiction and where venue is proper, but under circumstances in which it would be more convenient for the case to be heard somewhere else. Another statute — §1406 — deals with cases that are filed in a venue that is *not* proper and permits a court to transfer from the impermissible venue to a permissible venue. Finally, the multidistrict litigation statute — §1407 — deals with situations in which related cases have been filed in multiple federal district courts; it offers a way to bring the cases together so they can be handled more efficiently.

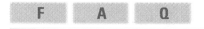

F A Q

Q: Can a case be transferred from a state court to a court in a different state?

A: Not yet. Venue transfer occurs *within* a single judicial system. Cases can be transferred from one federal district court to another because those courts are part of the federal judicial system, just as cases can be transferred from one location to another within a single state's court system. Even if a case is moved from the District of Alaska to the Southern District of Florida, that transfer occurs within the single system of U.S. federal courts. But in the state courts, no mechanism exists (yet) for transferring a case from one state to another. It could happen, though. A proposed statute — the Uniform Transfer of Litigation Act (UTLA) — would enable state courts to transfer cases to other states. So far though, UTLA hasn't gotten much traction.

(1) Transfer from a Proper Forum

The basic federal venue transfer statute, 28 U.S.C. §1404(a), gives federal judges discretion to transfer an action to a more appropriate district: "For the convenience of parties and witnesses, in the interest of justice, a district court may transfer any civil action to any other district or division where it might have been brought or to any district or division to which all parties have consented."

If you are deciding whether a court is likely to grant a motion to transfer venue, look at where the parties are based, where the witnesses reside, where the evidence can be found, and where the relevant events occurred. If the dispute's center of gravity is somewhere other than where the lawsuit was filed, then it may be a good candidate for venue transfer. Keep in mind, however, that venue transfer is highly discretionary. The words of the statute — particularly the key word "may" and the phrase "in the interest of justice" — give the district court plenty of leeway in deciding whether to grant a transfer of venue.

A court may transfer an action to another district "where it might have been brought." This means a district where the court has personal jurisdiction over the defendants and where venue is proper under the applicable federal venue statute. The Supreme Court had interpreted this language to mean that a defendant could not obtain transfer to a different district by waiving its objection to personal jurisdiction in the transferee court,[3] but in 2011 Congress added language to permit transfer to a district "to which all parties have consented."[4]

To see how §1404 venue transfer works — and also to see how venue and venue transfer fit together with subject matter jurisdiction and personal jurisdiction — imagine the following employment discrimination lawsuit:

Example 1: An employee is fired from working at a company's headquarters in Houston, Texas; he believes he was fired because of his race. He then moves to Chicago, Illinois. The company is incorporated in Delaware, has its principal place of business in Texas, and has branches throughout the country including a large office in Chicago. The employee brings an employment discrimination lawsuit against the company in federal court for the Northern District of Illinois, based on the federal employment discrimination statute.

Employee (IL)   ⟶   **Company (DE/TX)**

    ■ Employment discrimination (Title VII)
    ■ N.D. Ill.

To see whether the case was properly filed in the Northern District of Illinois, consider each of the three hoops. First, since the plaintiff filed in federal court, does the court have *subject matter jurisdiction*? Yes, based on federal question jurisdiction. And if the amount in controversy is high enough, then it would satisfy diversity jurisdiction as well since the plaintiff has now become an Illinois domiciliary and the company is a citizen of Delaware and Texas. Second, does the court in Illinois have *personal jurisdiction* over the defendant? Yes, Illinois probably has general

---

[3]Hoffman v. Blaski, 363 U.S. 335 (1960).
[4]28 U.S.C. §1404(a).

jurisdiction over the company based on the presence of its large office in Chicago. Third, is *venue* proper in the Northern District of Illinois? Yes, venue is proper under §1391(b)(1) because the company is deemed to reside in the Northern District of Illinois based on §1391(c)'s special definition of corporate residence for venue. If the company were to move to dismiss for lack of subject matter jurisdiction, lack of personal jurisdiction, or improper venue, the court would deny those motions.

But even though the case was properly filed in the Northern District of Illinois (in the sense of jumping through all three hoops), does it make any sense for the case to be heard there? Not really. The dispute concerns the firing of an employee at the Houston headquarters of a Texas company. The plaintiff has since moved to Chicago, but nearly all of the other witnesses and evidence will be in Houston. Therefore, the company could make a §1404(a) motion to transfer venue to the Southern District of Texas (the federal district that encompasses Houston), and the court would probably grant the motion.

(2) Transfer from an Improper Forum

What if a plaintiff files an action in the wrong venue? One option is for the court to dismiss the action for improper venue. Indeed, Federal Rule of Civil Procedure 12(b)(3) lists improper venue as a defense that can be raised on a motion to dismiss.

But rather than dismiss the case, maybe the judge thinks it makes more sense to transfer the case to a proper venue. That's where the other venue transfer statute, 28 U.S.C. §1406(a), comes into play. Section 1406 lets the court decide whether to transfer or dismiss: "The district court of a district in which is filed a case laying venue in the wrong division or district shall dismiss, or if it be in the interest of justice, transfer such case to any district or division in which it could have been brought." Although the language of §1406 appears to apply only to improper venue, the Supreme Court has interpreted it to allow transfer of a case in which both venue and personal jurisdiction are missing.[5]

Let's modify Example 1 to see how §1406 transfer works:

Example 2: Same employment discrimination lawsuit as in Example 1, except that this time, the employee sues two defendants — the company and the Houston supervisor who was responsible for the firing.

$$\text{Employee (IL)} \longrightarrow \text{Company (DE/TX)}$$
$$\longrightarrow \text{Boss (TX)}$$

■ Employment discrimination (Title VII)
■ N.D. Ill.

As in Example 1, the federal court has subject matter jurisdiction based on federal question jurisdiction and possibly diversity jurisdiction, and the court has personal jurisdiction over the company based on the company's presence in Illinois. But the court lacks personal jurisdiction over the boss (unless, of course, the boss consents to jurisdiction). Under the venue statute, venue would not be proper under §1391(b)(1) because both defendants do not reside in Illinois, nor would venue be

---

[5]Goldlawr, Inc. v. Heiman, 369 U.S. 463 (1962).

proper under §1391(b)(2) because no substantial part of the events took place in Illinois.

Because venue is improper in the Northern District of Illinois, the court could simply dismiss the case. Or, under §1406(a), the court could decide instead to transfer the case to the Southern District of Texas. The Southern District of Texas constitutes a district where the case "could have been brought" because the court would have personal jurisdiction over both defendants and proper venue under both §1391(b)(1) and §1391(b)(2).

Q: Can a case be transferred from state court to federal court, or vice versa?

A: Not exactly. Don't forget that transfer occurs within a single judicial system, rather than between different systems such as the federal courts and the various state courts. As we discussed in Chapter 1, a case may be *removed* from state to federal court based on federal subject matter jurisdiction. But don't call that "transfer"; it's "removal." No mechanism exists for moving a case from federal court to state court, except when a case is improperly removed and the federal court then *remands* the case back to state court.

(3) Venue Transfer and Choice of Law

One interesting twist on venue transfer involves choice of law. As Chapter 4 explores in detail, federal courts in diversity jurisdiction cases apply the same law that would be applied in state court. But different state courts might apply different state law. If a case is transferred from one federal district to a district in a different state, which state law should the federal court apply?

In *Van Dusen v. Barrack*,[6] the Supreme Court held that the transferee court should apply the same law that the transferor court would have applied. That way, when a court is deciding whether to transfer venue, it can focus on the location of the parties and witnesses, rather than worrying about whether transfer would alter the applicable substantive law.

But here's the catch. The *Van Dusen* rule applies only to §1404 venue transfer (transfer from a proper forum), not to §1406 venue transfer (transfer from an improper forum). That makes sense, doesn't it? If a plaintiff chooses a court where jurisdiction and venue are proper, but the court decides to transfer the case to a more convenient location, the substantive law does not change. That's the *Van Dusen* rule. But if the plaintiff filed the case in an improper forum—one where the court lacks personal jurisdiction or where venue is wrong under the venue statute—then the plaintiff should not get the benefit of the substantive law that would be applied in that first court. Rather, after a §1406 transfer, the transferee court treats the case as if it were filed initially in the transferee district.

---

[6]376 U.S. 612 (1964).

(4) Multidistrict Litigation Transfer

The final type of federal venue transfer is multidistrict litigation transfer. **Multidistrict litigation** (MDL), as you can guess from the name, involves situations in which related lawsuits have been filed in multiple federal district courts. The MDL statute, 28 U.S.C. §1407, permits the transfer of multiple cases to a single federal district court for coordinated pretrial handling.

The power to transfer is vested in a seven-judge Judicial Panel on Multidistrict Litigation. The panel not only decides whether it makes sense to transfer the related cases to a single district court, but also decides which court. In some cases, the panel chooses a judge who already is handling some of the cases or whose district is central to the dispute. In other cases, particularly when the dispute is nationwide in scope, the panel seeks out a judge with the expertise and resources to handle such complex litigation.

MDL does not extend through trial. In this sense, it differs markedly from ordinary venue transfer under §1404 or §1406, which send a case completely to another district. The MDL transferee court handles only pretrial matters, and then—at least in theory—remands the cases to their original courts (the transferor courts) when they are ready for trial. I say "in theory" because in reality, many cases never get remanded. Like most litigation, cases in MDL often are resolved before they ever get to trial—by motions to dismiss, by summary judgment, and especially by settlement.

> ### Sidebar
>
> #### MDL TRANSFER AND MASS LITIGATION
>
> Although MDL can be used in any situation involving multiple related cases in different federal district courts, it has become an especially important feature of *mass litigation*. Think of widespread civil rights litigation, product liability litigation concerning widely used products, securities litigation involving numerous investors, and antitrust litigation involving multiple consumers or businesses. In such mass litigation, the lawyers for the various parties know that there will be an MDL, but they often fight over *where* the MDL will be located and which lawyers will serve on the steering committees. If you are interested in this stuff, take a look at the list of currently pending MDLs on the website of the Judicial Panel on Multidistrict Litigation (http://www.jpml.uscourts.gov), which provides a pretty good picture of the hot areas of mass litigation.

E. Forum Non Conveniens

You don't have to know Latin to figure out that *forum non conveniens* means that the forum is not convenient. The doctrine of **forum non conveniens** gives courts a basis to dismiss actions that should more appropriately be brought in a different court.

Forum non conveniens comes into play when the more appropriate forum is an entirely different court system. This basically means two situations: a case filed in state court that ought to be brought in a different state or a case filed in the United States (either state or federal court) that ought to be brought in another country.

Forum non conveniens applies only if the first court has power over the case. As the Supreme Court said in *Gulf Oil Corp. v. Gilbert*, "the doctrine of *forum non conveniens* can never apply if there is absence of jurisdiction or mistake of venue."[7] This is pretty basic. If the court lacks jurisdiction, it should dismiss for

---

[7]330 U.S. 501, 504 (1947).

lack of jurisdiction. If venue is improper, it should dismiss for improper venue (or, in federal court, it can transfer to a proper venue). Forum non conveniens is reserved for the situation where jurisdiction and venue are proper, but nonetheless there is another forum where the case should more appropriately be brought.

To apply the doctrine of forum non conveniens, follow the analysis laid out by the Supreme Court in *Piper Aircraft v. Reyno.*[8] The *Piper Aircraft* case involved the crash of a small plane in the highlands of Scotland. The families of the Scottish victims brought a wrongful death action against the manufacturers of the airplane and the propeller. They filed the suit in California state court, even though the case had nothing to do with California. The defendants removed the case to federal court. The federal court in the Central District of California transferred the case to the Middle District of Pennsylvania because that was where the airplane maker was located, and the propeller maker was in nearby Ohio. But all of this forum maneuvering was merely a lead-up to the big question: Did the case belong in the United States at all? The defendants moved to dismiss on grounds of forum non conveniens, arguing that even though the federal court in Pennsylvania had subject matter jurisdiction, personal jurisdiction, and venue, the case really belonged in Scotland. The Supreme Court agreed that dismissal was warranted because Scotland was a more appropriate forum.

In reaching that decision, the Court in *Piper Aircraft* applied a three-part analysis: (1) adequate alternative forum; (2) private interest factors; and (3) public interest factors.

(1) Adequate Alternative Forum

First, is there an adequate alternative forum? If not, the court must deny the forum non conveniens motion.

The whole point of forum non conveniens is that the case should be brought somewhere else rather than where the plaintiff brought it. If you represent a defendant moving to dismiss on grounds of forum non conveniens, you had better be prepared to state where that somewhere else is and to show that the case truly can be brought there.

One set of questions concerns whether the alternative forum has personal jurisdiction over the defendants and whether the case would be barred there by the statute of limitations. As a practical matter, however, these are rarely a problem. Defendants are nearly always willing to waive personal jurisdiction and statute of limitations defenses in the alternative forum if doing so will persuade the court to grant the dismissal on grounds of forum non conveniens.

Another question concerns the adequacy of the actual legal system in the alternative forum. If the other country's legal processes are underdeveloped or if the system is mired in corruption or other problems, then a court may refuse to grant a forum non conveniens motion.

The fact that the alternative forum may provide less favorable law to the plaintiff does not, in itself, make it an inadequate forum. As the Supreme Court said in *Piper Aircraft*, "the possibility of a change in substantive law should ordinarily not

---

[8]454 U.S. 235 (1981).

be given conclusive or even substantial weight in the forum non conveniens inquiry."[9]

If an adequate alternative forum exists, then the court decides whether to grant the forum non conveniens dismissal based on two sets of factors, addressing private and public interests.

(2) Private Interest Factors

Which forum would be more convenient for the parties and witnesses? Private interest factors include the location of the parties, witnesses, and evidence.

In the *Piper Aircraft* case, the accident site was in Scotland, as were the relatives of the decedents and the witnesses who had trained the pilot and serviced the plane. Potential third-party defendants were in Scotland as well, including the airplane's owners, the airplane charter company, and the pilot's estate. This outweighed the private interest factors that pointed to Pennsylvania, including evidence concerning the manufacture of the airplane.

In general, courts defer to the plaintiff's choice of forum, and disturb it only for good reason. But courts give plaintiff's choice less deference if it is not the plaintiff's home forum. In other words, if a Pennsylvania plaintiff chooses to sue in Pennsylvania, then a court will count plaintiff's desire to litigate at home as a significant private interest factor. But courts treat the value of plaintiff's choice differently when a plaintiff sues away from home, as in *Piper Aircraft*, in which Scottish plaintiffs sought to keep a U.S. forum.

> ### Sidebar
>
> **FORUM NON CONVENIENS AND FORUM SELECTION STRATEGY**
>
> In *Piper Aircraft v. Reyno*, why did the Scottish plaintiffs choose to bring their lawsuit in the United States, and why did the defendants fight so hard to convince the court to reject the plaintiffs' chosen forum? U.S. courts provide a number of perceived advantages to plaintiffs, as compared with the courts of most other countries. These advantages include jury trial, broad discovery, contingent fees, and relatively large awards of compensatory and sometimes punitive damages. Also, U.S. law includes certain legal doctrines favorable to plaintiffs, such as strict liability, although U.S. courts do not necessarily apply their own substantive law to foreign disputes. Because of these features of U.S. courts, foreign plaintiffs often prefer to sue in the United States rather than in the plaintiffs' home countries. The result: Forum non conveniens battles have become a routine aspect of transnational litigation. And as life and business become ever more global, don't expect such battles to end anytime soon.

(3) Public Interest Factors

Which forum has a greater interest in the dispute?
Which forum would offer a more efficient and appropriate use of judicial resources?

In *Piper Aircraft*, the public interest factors pointed both ways. Scotland had a strong interest in the dispute because it involved a local accident with local victims. But the United States and Pennsylvania also had an interest in deterring their own manufacturers from producing defective products. The court, however, had an interest in avoiding the complex choice of law issues that would have been presented if the case were litigated in the United States.

In the end, forum non conveniens leaves the court a fair amount of discretion. The court must balance the various public and private factors to decide whether another forum is clearly more convenient and appropriate.

---

[9]Id. at 247.

SUMMARY

■ Venue statutes limit the choice of permissible forums for a lawsuit.

■ For a court to adjudicate a lawsuit, the court must have subject matter jurisdiction over the action, the court must have personal jurisdiction over the parties, and the venue must be proper under the applicable venue statute.

■ The general federal venue statute permits venue where a defendant resides if all of the defendants reside in the same state. For purposes of this statute, a corporation or other entity is deemed to "reside" wherever it is subject to personal jurisdiction.

■ The general federal venue statute also permits venue where a substantial part of the events occurred or where the property is located.

■ Parties may waive any objection to venue.

■ A federal district court may transfer an action to a different district in the interest of justice and for the convenience of the parties and witnesses, as long as the transferee district is one where venue and jurisdiction are proper or to which the parties consent.

■ If venue is improper in the federal district where an action is filed, the court may either dismiss the action or transfer to a district where venue is proper.

■ The doctrine of forum non conveniens permits a court to dismiss an action, even if jurisdiction and venue are proper, based on the availability of an alternative forum where it makes more sense for the action to be brought.

CONNECTIONS

Personal Jurisdiction

The federal venue statute defines a corporation's residence, for purposes of determining venue, in terms of where the corporation is subject to personal jurisdiction. This means that in a single-defendant case involving a corporate defendant, the personal jurisdiction and venue inquiries merge. Also, in the rare event that §1391(b)(3) of the venue statute applies, it permits venue wherever any defendant is subject to personal jurisdiction.

Pleadings

Venue is a waivable defense under Rule 12(h)(1), so a defendant who objects to venue must assert that objection in the answer or in a pre-answer motion, whichever comes first.

Joinder

Although MDL is technically a type of venue transfer, to the lawyers and litigants it feels a lot like a type of joinder. As a practical matter, MDL pulls large numbers of plaintiffs and defendants together for coordinated discovery, pretrial motions, and settlement negotiations, even without any joinder of claims or parties.

Preclusion

When a court dismisses a case for improper venue, the dismissal is not considered "on the merits" for purposes of claim preclusion. In other words, the plaintiff may refile the action in a proper venue. The point of a dismissal for improper venue is not to eliminate the lawsuit, but rather to insist that the lawsuit be brought in a proper forum.

The *Erie* Doctrine

Suppose you're litigating a common law case and the precedents in the courts of the state go against your client. Can you avoid those unfavorable precedents by litigating in federal court instead of state court? That's the initial question behind the **Erie doctrine**, named for the famous case of *Erie Railroad v. Tompkins.*[1]

The basic answer is no, you cannot avoid state law by litigating in federal court. Unless some specific federal statute or rule applies, the federal court must apply state substantive law. Federal courts apply federal law in matters governed by federal statutes, such as securities, antitrust, and civil rights cases. They apply state law not only in cases under state statutes, but also in common law cases such as contract, tort, or property disputes. Keep in mind that diversity jurisdiction permits many state law claims to be brought in federal court.

It gets more complicated, however. Even though they are bound to follow state substantive law, the federal courts apply their own procedural rules. As a lawyer working in federal court, you have to know how to tell the difference between substance and procedure, which turns out to be trickier than you might expect. This chapter teaches you how to analyze whether federal or state law applies when you are in federal court.

The *Erie* doctrine does not address *horizontal choice of law* (the choice of which state's or which nation's law applies to a case with interstate or international dimensions). Rather, it concerns *vertical choice of law* (the choice between federal and state law in federal court).

---

[1] 304 U.S. 64 (1938).

A. The Basic Doctrine

In one sentence, I can tell you about 90 percent of what a competent attorney needs to know about the *Erie* doctrine.

> On state law claims, federal courts apply state substantive law and federal procedural law.

That's it. As a practical matter, that will take care of you pretty well. But if that sentence covers 90 percent of what lawyers need to know about the *Erie* doctrine, the rest of this chapter addresses the remaining 10 percent, the situations in which it is not obvious whether a federal court will apply federal or state law.

In most cases, it's not hard. Suppose you're litigating a negligence case involving an accident in Memphis, and the case is brought in the federal court for the Western District of Tennessee based on diversity jurisdiction. According to the *Erie* doctrine, the federal court must apply the substantive tort law of Tennessee. So if there are substantive law questions such as the standard of care, the defense of comparative fault, or caps on damages, the court will look to the statutes and common law decisions of Tennessee. But as a federal tribunal, the court will use federal procedural law. For things like pleading requirements, discovery, summary judgment, jury selection, trial processes, and the time limit for filing an appeal, the court will look to the Federal Rules of Civil Procedure and other federal procedural law.

Some situations require a more complex and subtle analysis, however, and these are the cases that civil procedure professors love. To be able to handle these cases, you need to understand the *Erie* doctrine as it has developed through a series of Supreme Court decisions.

B. Development of the *Erie* Doctrine

(1) *Swift* to *Erie*

In 1842, the Supreme Court decided *Swift v. Tyson*,[2] which involved a commercial law dispute in federal court in New York. The federal court had subject matter

---

[2]41 U.S. 1 (1842).

jurisdiction based on diversity of citizenship. The parties disputed an issue of contract law, whether discharge of a debt can be consideration for a contract. The precedents in New York's state courts said no. The question was whether the federal judge was required to follow the New York precedents, as opposed to making up his own mind about the legal issue. Must federal courts apply state common law?

The Rules of Decision Act (RDA), a federal statute that has been around since 1789, seems to answer the question:

> The laws of the several states, except where the Constitution or treaties of the United States or Acts of Congress otherwise require or provide, shall be regarded as rules of decision in civil actions in the courts of the United States, in cases where they apply.[3]

If the "laws of the several states" must be used as the "rules of decision" in federal courts, then doesn't that mean that the federal court in *Swift* must follow the New York precedents about contract law?

Well, no, according to the Supreme Court in *Swift*. The Court held that "laws of the several states" in the RDA meant statutes and regulations, but not general common law. Federal courts, in other words, were not required to follow state court precedents about contract law and tort law. Instead, the federal courts should "ascertain upon general reasoning and legal analogies . . . what is the just rule furnished by the principles of commercial law to govern the case."[4]

The legal theory underlying *Swift* was a notion that judges don't make law, they discover it. The law is the law, and the judge's job in a common law case is to use reasoning and analogies to figure out what the law is. Given that understanding of the common law, it made sense to say that federal judges were free to reject state court precedents since federal judges could use their minds to discover the law just as well as state judges.

A century passes, notions change, and in 1938 the Supreme Court decides *Erie Railroad v. Tompkins*. Remember in Chapter 2 when I said that *Pennoyer v. Neff* was the most famous civil procedure case of them all? I lied. It's *Erie*.

Harry Tompkins was walking alongside a railroad track in Pennsylvania when he was hit by a swinging freight train door. Severely injured, Tompkins filed a lawsuit in federal court against the Erie Railroad, claiming that the railroad was negligent. The railroad argued that Tompkins was a trespasser and that under Pennsylvania common law, the railroad merely owed him a duty to refrain from wanton negligence. The railroad cited Pennsylvania cases, including one from the Pennsylvania Supreme Court, holding that the railroad could be liable only if it engaged in wanton negligence. Tompkins, on the other hand, cited federal court cases holding that the railroad could be liable for ordinary negligence. The case, therefore, turned on an issue of tort law: What level of duty does a railroad owe to a pedestrian along the railroad's right-of-way? The railroad wanted the court to decide this issue according to Pennsylvania law. Tompkins argued that under *Swift*, the federal court was not obligated to follow Pennsylvania's common law decisions.

---

[3]28 U.S.C. §1652.
[4]*Swift*, 41 U.S. at 19.

Erie Railroad Locomotive, 1938
Photo courtesy of the Maywood Station Museum, www.maywoodstation.com

The U.S. Supreme Court, overruling *Swift*, held that the federal court must apply Pennsylvania common law. Bad news for Harry Tompkins. The Court held that the RDA's requirement that federal courts apply the "laws of the several states" includes not only state statutes but also the common law decisions of state courts.

One way to understand *Erie* is as a rejection of the legal theory in *Swift v. Tyson*. In an era of legal realism, it was no longer tenable to believe that law is out there waiting to be discovered. Oliver Wendell Holmes and others had spread the view that law is not discovered, but made. From the legal realist perspective, "law" is not some sort of absolute truth floating in space, but rather a set of rules established by those with power to govern at a particular time and place.

Justice Brandeis's opinion in *Erie* explained the holding largely as a way to avoid favoring of out-of-state litigants. If federal courts do not have to apply state common law, then a litigant might obtain a different result by choosing either federal court or state court. But not every litigant has that choice since federal subject matter jurisdiction is limited. In a common law case (in which there's no federal question jurisdiction), a litigant can choose federal court only if there is diversity jurisdiction. For example, in a tort case like Harry Tompkins', a New York plaintiff could sue a New York defendant only in state court, but a Pennsylvania plaintiff could sue a New York defendant in either state court or federal court. If federal courts are free to ignore state common law, this gives the Pennsylvania plaintiff an advantage relative to the New York plaintiff in a case against a New York defendant.

The Supreme Court could have decided *Erie* simply as a statutory interpretation of the RDA. It could have said that the word "laws" in the RDA includes common law decisions as well as statutes, and left it at that. Instead, Justice Brandeis's opinion suggests that the decision was constitutionally mandated, although he does not make it terribly clear which constitutional provision he has in mind. Constitutionally, the federal courts are limited both as a matter of federalism (respecting the limits of federal government power vis-à-vis the states) and as a matter of separation of powers (respecting the limits of judicial power vis-à-vis the legislative and executive branches). The *Erie* decision keeps the power of the federal courts in check. Understanding the significance of the decision—it not only overruled a settled interpretation of a federal statute, but also rendered precedentially irrelevant a century of federal court common law decisions—Brandeis emphasized the constitutional foundation for limiting federal court power.

F   A   Q

Q: Does *Erie* always require that the federal court apply the substantive law of the state in which the federal court is located?

A: Not exactly. The federal court must follow the *choice of law rules* of the state in which the federal court is located. Often, this means applying the law of that state. But if the case involves a matter that occurred elsewhere, it might mean applying another state's substantive law. The Supreme Court spelled this out in *Klaxon v. Stentor*, 313 U.S. 487 (1941), stating that the federal court must apply whichever substantive law would be applied by the state court where the federal court sits.

The *Erie* case provides a perfect example. Harry Tompkins brought the case in the Southern District of New York, but the court applied Pennsylvania law. Let's state this as precisely as possible in *Klaxon* terms: Tompkins brought his case in the federal court for the Southern District of New York. The federal court in New York was required to apply whatever tort law a New York state court would have applied. A New York state court would have applied Pennsylvania tort law since that's where the accident happened. Therefore, the federal court was required to apply Pennsylvania law.

(2) *Guaranty Trust*

Erie stated that federal courts must apply state substantive law, so the railroad's duty of care was governed by Pennsylvania tort law. But how would the new rule play out in situations where the issue was less substantive than a railroad's duty of care?

In *Guaranty Trust Co. v. York*,[5] a bondholder sued a trustee in federal court for breach of fiduciary duty. Under *Erie*, there was no doubt that the federal court would apply New York law to any issues about fiduciary duties. But what about the statute of limitations? **Statutes of limitations** are laws that limit the time in which a lawsuit can be brought. Depending on the type of case, the statute of limitations may give plaintiffs one year, two years, or longer to assert a claim. In *Guaranty Trust*, the plaintiff brought the claim after the relevant time permitted under New York's statute of limitations had expired. But at the time, federal courts in equity cases (such as breach of fiduciary duty) applied the doctrine of *laches* instead of the statute of limitations. The doctrine of laches is an equitable doctrine that gives a court discretion to decide whether a plaintiff has waited too long to bring a claim. The big question: Should the federal court apply the equitable doctrine of laches or New York's statute of limitations?

The plaintiff argued that the statute of limitations is procedural, and *Erie* and the RDA do not require federal courts to apply state procedural law. Is the statute of limitations "procedural"? To some extent, the statute of limitations advances procedural policies—avoiding stale evidence and controlling the court's docket. But it also advances more substantive policies—disempowering plaintiffs who sit on their rights and, above all, giving repose to potential defendants so that at some point they can stop worrying about liability and get back to their lives and businesses.

---

[5]326 U.S. 99 (1945).

The Supreme Court in *Guaranty Trust* noted the difficulty of labeling rules *substantive* or *procedural*. Instead, the Court focused on whether the rule would determine the outcome of the dispute. The point of diversity jurisdiction, the Court said, was to provide "another tribunal, not another body of law."[6] Therefore, "the outcome of the litigation in the federal court should be substantially the same, so far as legal rules determine the outcome of a litigation, as it would be if tried in a State court."[7] The upshot of the *Guaranty Trust* decision — many call this the **outcome-determinativeness test** — was that if the difference between the federal and state rule would determine the outcome, then the federal court must apply the state rule.

Notice how broadly the Court defined outcome-determinativeness. Is the statute of limitations really outcome-determinative? Even if the court applied the doctrine of laches and allowed the case to go forward, would that have guaranteed a plaintiff victory? Of course not. The plaintiff could still lose on the merits. The statute of limitations is outcome-determinative only in the sense that if the court applied the New York statute of limitations, it guaranteed a plaintiff loss, whereas the doctrine of laches would have given the plaintiff a shot at winning.

The outcome-determinativeness test, unfortunately, was way too simplistic for something as subtle as the distinction between substance and procedure or the balance between federal and state power. This became clear four years after *Guaranty Trust* when the Supreme Court decided a trilogy of cases under the *Erie* doctrine. One case raised the issue of whether a federal court must apply state law to the question of when an action has been "commenced" for purposes of complying with the statute of limitations.[8] The second case asked whether a federal court must apply a state law that stated that in order to sue in the Mississippi courts, a corporation must be registered to do business in Mississippi.[9] The third case asked whether a federal court must apply state law requiring that a plaintiff post a bond in order to file a shareholder derivative suit.[10] You might expect that each of these issues would be the sort of procedural matter that federal courts should decide for themselves. However, applying the test of *Guaranty Trust*, the Supreme Court held in each of the three cases that the rule could determine the outcome and therefore the federal court must apply state law. To put it bluntly, it seemed that, as applied, the *Guaranty Trust* rule meant that *everything* was outcome-determinative.

In *Byrd v. Blue Ridge Rural Electric Cooperative*,[11] however, the Supreme Court acknowledged that there's more to the story than outcome-determinativeness. The *Erie* issue in the case was whether the plaintiff's employment status should be decided by the judge or jury. Byrd, a construction worker, sued Blue Ridge for an injury he sustained on the job. Employees, unlike independent contractors, cannot bring tort suits against their employers for workplace injuries because workers' compensation is their exclusive remedy. Byrd argued that he was an independent

---

[6]Id. at 112.
[7]Id. at 109.
[8]Ragan v. Merchants Transfer, 337 U.S. 530 (1949).
[9]Woods v. Interstate Realty Co., 337 U.S. 535 (1949).
[10]Cohen v. Beneficial Indus. Loan Corp., 337 U.S. 541 (1949).
[11]356 U.S. 525 (1958).

contractor, but Blue Ridge contended that Byrd should be treated as an employee because he was doing the same work as employees. Blue Ridge wanted the judge to decide Byrd's employment status and cited a South Carolina case supporting its view that the issue should be decided by the judge. Under *Erie* and the RDA, Blue Ridge argued, the federal court must do what a South Carolina court would do. Byrd, on the other hand, wanted a jury to decide his employment status, perhaps expecting that a jury would be more sympathetic and more likely to allow him to go forward with his tort suit. He argued that in federal court, the jury should decide the question.

The choice between judge and jury in *Byrd* was arguably outcome-determinative in the *Guaranty Trust* sense, given how broadly that test had been construed. But the Court did not end its analysis there. The Court identified a "countervailing federal interest" in the allocation of power between judge and jury in federal court, especially in light of the Seventh Amendment's affirmation of the role of the federal civil jury. The Court also noted that South Carolina's position of allowing the judge to decide immunity was not "bound up with . . . state-created rights and obligations."[12] Balancing the strong federal interest in the power of the federal jury against the state interest in having the judge decide, the Supreme Court held that the federal court need not follow the South Carolina approach.

Don't rely too heavily on *Byrd*. As a practical matter, its "countervailing federal interests" test has rarely tipped the scales, and the Supreme Court has rarely cited it. But you should at least be aware of the possibility that countervailing federal interests may figure into the choice between federal and state law in federal court.

(3) *Hanna* and Post-*Hanna* Application

If you are going to focus on one case when studying the *Erie* doctrine, make it *Hanna v. Plumer*,[13] the single most important case for understanding how to apply *Erie* (yes, more important than *Erie*). *Erie* got things started, but if you want to know how to apply the doctrine as a lawyer or law student, *Hanna* hands you the analytical keys.

The *Erie* issue in *Hanna* concerned service of process. Hanna sued Plumer, an executor of a decedent's estate, for an auto accident allegedly caused by the decedent's negligence. She brought the case in federal court for the District of Massachusetts based on diversity jurisdiction. Hanna served Plumer with process by leaving a copy of the summons and complaint with Plumer's wife at Plumer's home. Rule 4 of the Federal Rules of Civil Procedure permits service on an individual by leaving a copy of the summons and complaint at the individual's dwelling with a "person of suitable age and discretion."[14] Presumably, Plumer's spouse qualified as a person of suitable age and discretion. Plumer nevertheless argued that service was improper. A Massachusetts statute specified that when serving the executor of an estate, personal delivery was required. Plumer contended that the Massachusetts

---

[12]Id. at 535.
[13]380 U.S. 460 (1965).
[14]Fed. R. Civ. P. 4(e)(2). At the time of the *Hanna* case, this provision was in Rule 4(d)(1).

statute should apply even in federal court, and therefore the case should be dismissed for improper service of process. The conflict between state and federal law in *Hanna* was outcome-determinative, at least in the *Guaranty Trust* sense. If state law applied, then the case would be dismissed for improper service, but if federal law applied, then the case could proceed. The Supreme Court, however, did not simply apply the outcome-determinativeness test.

The Supreme Court decided that the federal court should apply the Federal Rule of Civil Procedure rather than the Massachusetts statute. The Court's *Hanna* decision contains two aspects that are essential to your understanding of the *Erie* doctrine. First, the Court gave instructions on how to handle situations in which state law conflicts with a Federal Rule of Civil Procedure or a federal statute. Second, the Court offered a more sophisticated version of the outcome-determinativeness test. Let's take these one at a time.

Unlike most of the prior cases, the conflict between state and federal law in *Hanna* concerned a Federal Rule of Civil Procedure. Rule 4 stated that service of process could be accomplished by leaving a copy with a person at the defendant's home, which is precisely what the plaintiff did. Massachusetts law required personal service on an executor. But could state law trump the explicit direction of a Federal Rule of Civil Procedure? The Court held that the Federal Rule of Civil Procedure applied notwithstanding the conflict with state law. This was not a matter of the RDA and *Erie*, but rather because of a different statute — the **Rules Enabling Act** (REA).

The REA is the statute by which Congress empowered the Supreme Court to make procedural rules for the federal courts. The statute established a process for rulemaking pursuant to which the original Federal Rules of Civil Procedure were adopted in 1938 and by which the rules have been amended ever since. The REA imposes certain constraints on these rules. First, by definition, they must be "rules of practice and procedure."[15] Second, and related, they "shall not abridge, enlarge or modify any substantive right."[16] Since Rule 4's provision on service of process was a rule of procedure and did not abridge, enlarge, or modify any substantive right, the Court held, it was valid under the REA. Therefore Rule 4, and not the Massachusetts statute, governed service of process in federal court.

That's the most important lesson we learn from *Hanna*. If there is a federal rule directly on point, then that federal rule applies as long as it is valid under the REA. Regardless of conflicting state law, federal courts are obligated to apply validly enacted federal rules of procedure. "When a situation is covered by one of the Federal Rules, the question facing the court is a far cry from typical, relatively unguided *Erie* choice: the court has been instructed to apply the Federal Rule, and can refuse to do so only if [the rule violates the constitution or the REA]."[17] The same logic applies to federal statutes. If Congress has enacted a valid statute — a statute that is not unconstitutional — then federal courts must enforce that statute, regardless of conflicting state law. The Supremacy Clause of the Constitution makes duly enacted federal law "the supreme law of the land."[18] By recognizing that

---

[15]28 U.S.C. §2072(a).
[16]Id. §2072(b).
[17]*Hanna*, 380 U.S. at 471.
[18]U.S. Const. art. VI.

federal courts are bound to uphold legitimately enacted federal rules and statutes, *Hanna* removed a whole set of potential issues from *Erie* and vastly increased the likelihood of applying federal law.

Beyond its treatment of federal rules and statutes, *Hanna* had something else to offer. For situations in which the *Erie*/RDA analysis was unavoidable because there was no federal rule or statute directly on point, *Hanna* introduced a more sophisticated version of the outcome-determinativeness test. As Chief Justice Warren explained, the point of *Erie* was that outcomes in federal and state court should not differ in ways that would make litigants choose one court over another. Warren's majority opinion in *Hanna* famously framed this in terms of the "twin aims" of *Erie*: "The 'outcome-determination' test therefore cannot be read without reference to the twin aims of the *Erie* rule: discouragement of forum-shopping and avoidance of inequitable administration of the laws."[19]

Sidebar

1938

The Supreme Court decided *Erie* in 1938. That same year, the Federal Rules of Civil Procedure went into effect, pursuant to the Rules Enabling Act. Prior to 1938, federal courts did not have their own rules of procedure; previously, under the Conformity Act, federal courts followed state court procedures. It's an astonishing flip-flop in one year, isn't it? In common law cases before 1938, federal courts applied federal substantive law but state procedural law. After 1938, federal courts applied state substantive law but federal procedural law. Now think about the *Hanna* decision upholding the use of a federal rule that conflicted with state law. If federal procedural rules were not insulated from the *Erie* doctrine, then 1938 would have seen the irony of adopting a brand new set of rules while instructing the federal courts to apply state law instead.

HANNA'S TWIN AIMS OF *ERIE*

1. Discourage forum shopping.
2. Avoid inequitable administration of the laws.

Look at Warren's twin aims, and you'll see how closely they are tied to the outcome-determinativeness test of *Guaranty Trust*. What's the best way to discourage forum shopping? Make sure the outcome won't differ from state to federal court. How can we avoid inequitable administration of the laws? Make sure the outcome won't differ from state to federal court. To some extent, then, the twin aims are just another way of saying that if the difference between federal and state law would be outcome-determinative, the court must apply state law. But the twin aims dig deeper than the *Guaranty Trust* version of outcome-determinativeness. They ask whether it's the sort of difference that really matters. Is it the sort of difference that, from the outset, would make a litigant choose one court over another? Is it the sort of difference that would make us worry that litigants receive dissimilar legal treatment in state and federal court?

Take the *Hanna* scenario. State law required personal service of process; federal law permitted leaving a copy at the defendant's home. Under the *Guaranty Trust* version of the outcome-determinativeness test, we would probably conclude that the

---

[19]*Hanna*, 380 U.S. at 468.

difference is outcome-determinative since under state law the case would now be dismissed for improper service. Now apply the twin-aims version of the test. Would either side have chosen a court based on the rules for service of process? Doubt it. Is there anything *inequitable* about requiring personal service in state court but permitting dwelling-place service in federal court? Nope. From the point of view of a litigant filing the case, the service-of-process rule is not outcome-determinative at all. After selecting where to file the case, the plaintiff can simply serve process in compliance with that court's rule.

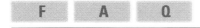

Q: What's so evil about forum shopping?

A: Reading *Hanna*, you get the impression that forum shopping is some sort of crime. But if that's the case, I know plenty of guilty lawyers. And you'll do it, too. When you represent a plaintiff, you're going to select the court that you think will be most advantageous to your client. If you represent a defendant, you'll make decisions about removal and transfer based on whether you think you can obtain a more favorable forum. That's forum shopping. There's nothing wrong with it. One of the reasons we teach you about jurisdiction and venue is so that you'll know what your options are whenever you go on a nice forum-shopping spree. In Chapter 1, a sidebar on forum selection strategy mentioned some of the factors that go into choosing an advantageous court. The point in *Hanna* about avoiding forum shopping is not that lawyers should refrain from choosing the best forum for their clients, but rather that the legal system should set things up so that the choice between federal and state court does not yield substantively different legal norms. Notice, by the way, how limited *Erie* is as a constraint on forum shopping. For vertical forum shopping, *Erie* removes differences in substantive law but has no effect on many other strategic reasons why one might choose federal or state court, such as judges, jury pools, or discovery rules. And *Erie* does nothing to reduce horizontal forum shopping — the choice between one state and another.

You may have figured out by now that the so-called twin aims both say the same thing, only from different angles. The first takes the viewpoint of a litigant choosing between state and federal court. The second takes the viewpoint of a legal system trying to administer equal justice. Both of them make the same point: If the difference between state and federal law matters enough that litigants would choose one court over the other to get a different application of the law, then the federal court must apply state law. Maybe they're identical twins.

Not only do the twin aims avoid the oversimplified *Guaranty Trust* test, they also steer clear of the problematic substance-procedure distinction. When I was a law student learning about *Erie*, my civil procedure professor made us pay 25 cents every time we used the word *substantive* or *procedural*. She would actually walk up the aisle and collect. It was scary. But she got her point across: The line between substance and procedure is often unclear, so we need more subtle ways to understand when a federal court must apply state law.

When you read *Hanna*, don't ignore Justice Harlan's beautiful concurring opinion. He suggested that even though the outcome-determinativeness test went too far in favoring state rules, the majority's approach in *Hanna* "moves too fast and far in the other direction."[20] He cautioned that the majority's forum-shopping rule oversimplified things because "litigants often choose a federal forum merely to obtain what they consider the advantages of the Federal Rules of Civil Procedure or to try their cases before a supposedly more favorable judge."[21] What rule would Harlan apply? "To my mind the proper line of approach in determining whether to apply a state or a federal rule, whether 'substantive' or 'procedural,' is to stay close to basic principles by inquiring if the choice of rule would substantially affect those primary decisions respecting human conduct which our constitutional system leaves to state regulation."[22] In other words, focus on whether the state rule governs human conduct outside the courtroom and the litigation process. It's another way of asking whether the rule is "substantive" rather than "procedural," but the concurrence strives mightily to avoid framing the question with those words. Justice Harlan would have gotten along well with my civil procedure professor.

Hanna transformed *Erie* analysis; indeed, many now call it *Erie-Hanna* analysis. After *Hanna*, federal judges could apply the Federal Rules of Civil Procedure, as well as other federal rules and statutes, with less fear of violating the *Erie* principle. But it's more complicated than that. The straightforward part is that *Hanna* commands federal courts to apply any valid federal rule or statute that is directly on point. Deciding whether a rule or statute is "directly on point," however, leaves a certain amount of leeway. A court eager to apply federal law might stretch to find a federal rule that applies, while a court that prefers state law might construe federal rules narrowly so that they're not directly on point.

In one line of cases, the courts appear to bend over backwards to find a federal rule or statute on point. *Burlington Northern Railroad Co. v. Woods*[23] concerned whether an appellate court must award damages for a frivolous appeal. Under Alabama law, such damages were mandatory, but Rule 38 of the Federal Rules of Appellate Procedure leaves the imposition of sanctions for frivolous appeals to the court's discretion. A plausible approach would have been to insist on the imposition of damages under state law, since that law is not clearly in direct conflict with Rule 38's authorization of sanctions. The Supreme Court, however, found a "direct collision" and therefore held that the federal rule applies. Even if it fell "within the uncertain area between substance and procedure,"[24] the rule was valid under the constitution and the REA, and therefore the federal court must apply it. A year later, *Stewart Organization v. Ricoh Corp.*[25] involved a motion for venue transfer based on a forum selection clause. State law disfavored enforcement of forum selection clauses. The Supreme Court held that the federal court need not apply state law because the federal venue statute, 28 U.S.C. §1404, governed the transfer motion and gave the federal court discretion to take the forum selection clause into account. The Court easily could have found no direct conflict by stating that §1404 sets up

[20]380 U.S. at 476 (Harlan, J., concurring).
[21]Id. at 475.
[22]Id.
[23]480 U.S. 1 (1987).
[24]Id. at 5.
[25]487 U.S. 22 (1988).

a general standard for venue transfer but says nothing specifically about forum selection clauses, but instead the Court found the statute directly on point, and therefore insisted on the application of federal law. *Burlington Northern* and *Stewart Organization* show how far *Hanna* can go if taken to its logical limits by courts looking to apply federal law.

Another line of cases, however, displays much tighter scrutiny of whether a particular federal rule or statute governs. One of these cases, *Walker v. Armco Steel Corp.*,[26] was decided several years before *Burlington Northern* and *Stewart Organization*. *Walker* raised the issue that the Supreme Court had faced in *Ragan v. Merchants Transfer*[27] — when an action is commenced for purposes of the statute of limitations. Rule 3 of the Federal Rules of Civil Procedure states that an action is commenced by filing a complaint. Oklahoma law, by contrast, used service of process to define the commencement of an action for statute of limitations purposes. The plaintiff had filed the complaint within the statute of limitations, but served process after the time period expired. After *Hanna*, you might have expected the Supreme Court to say that Rule 3 governs in federal court because it is a valid procedural rule under the REA. But that's not what the Court did. Instead, the Court reaffirmed its earlier holding in *Ragan* requiring the application of state law. According to the Supreme Court, Rule 3 did not directly apply. Rule 3 states how to commence an action and marks the starting point for procedural time limits in the rules, but the rule does not say anything specifically about the statute of limitations. The Court concluded that "'there being no Federal Rule which cover[s] the point in dispute, *Erie* command[s] the enforcement of state law.'"[28]

It's hard to say exactly what lesson you should learn from *Walker* because its approach seems so different from *Burlington Northern* and *Stewart Organization*. One easy lesson is the power of *stare decisis*; *Ragan* was indistinguishable and the Supreme Court clearly did not want to overrule its precedent. But there's more to *Walker* than that. *Walker* tells you that when you see a conflict between state and federal law, before you assume that some federal rule applies under *Hanna* and the REA, you have to examine closely whether the federal rule (or statute) governs the exact issue on which state law conflicts. Maybe the rule is not *directly* on point, in which case *Hanna* no longer directs application of the federal rule, and you are into the broader analysis under *Erie* and the RDA.

(4) *Gasperini* and *Shady Grove*

When conducting an *Erie* analysis, be sure to consider each issue independently. If federal law and state law diverge on multiple issues, don't assume you're looking for an all-or-nothing answer. Maybe state law should govern one issue but federal law should govern another. That is what happened in *Gasperini v. Center for Humanities*,[29] in which the Supreme Court found a way to accommodate both state and federal interests.

---

[26] 446 U.S. 740 (1980).
[27] 337 U.S. 530 (1949). ·
[28] *Walker*, 446 U.S. at 748 (quoting *Hanna*, 380 U.S. at 470).
[29] 518 U.S. 415 (1996).

In *Gasperini*, a diversity case in federal court in New York, the jury awarded the plaintiff a surprisingly large verdict. The defendant appealed, arguing that the amount of damages was excessive. Under New York law, an appellate court has the power to review the amount of a jury verdict and to order a new trial if the verdict "deviates materially" from a reasonable amount. The federal courts, by contrast, allow a jury verdict to stand unless the amount is so unreasonable that it "shocks the conscience" of the district judge. The federal district court decides whether to grant *remittitur* (a new trial unless the plaintiff accepts a reduced damages award). Unlike New York appellate courts, the federal courts of appeals have no independent power to review the amount of a verdict. Rather, the federal appellate court's power is limited to reviewing the district court's decision for abuse of discretion. The defendant in *Gasperini* argued that the federal court of appeals should act like a New York court and find the damages excessive. The question: Should the federal court of appeals act like a New York state appellate court, reviewing the verdict on a "deviates materially" standard, or should it stick to the federal approach of letting the district judge decide on a "shocks the conscience" standard and then reviewing that decision?

Rather than giving a simple answer, the Supreme Court saw two distinct but intertwined issues. There's the standard for determining whether a damages award is excessive ("deviates materially" vs. "shocks the conscience"), and there's the power of appellate review (independent appellate power to review verdict amount vs. review of trial judge's decision). The first issue, the Supreme Court held, goes to the substantive outcome of the case as an *Erie* matter, and thus the federal court should apply New York's "deviates materially" standard. The second issue, however, concerns the allocation of power between the federal district courts and the federal courts of appeals, and thus the federal court should apply federal "abuse of discretion" appellate review. In this way, the Supreme Court was able to protect the federal interest in setting up the functions and institutional capacities of federal trial courts and appellate courts, while accommodating New York's interest in having a less deferential standard for reviewing excessive jury awards.

The Court's most recent *Erie* case reemphasized that federal courts must follow the Federal Rules even when those rules conflict with state law. *Shady Grove Orthopedic Associates v. Allstate Insurance Co.*[30] concerned a class action for statutory interest. Rule 23 of the Federal Rules of Civil Procedure spells out the requirements for certification of a class action. New York's class action law barred class actions for

---

[30]130 S. Ct. 1431 (2010).

statutory penalties. The question: Could a federal court permit the class action under Rule 23 even if it would be prohibited under New York law?

The *Shady Grove* plurality treated this as a straightforward application of *Hanna*: Is there a federal rule on point? Yes, Rule 23. Is Rule 23 valid under the REA? Yes, because it regulates procedure and it does not alter substantive rights. "The test is not whether the rule affects a litigant's substantive rights; most procedural rules do. What matters is what the rule itself regulates: If it governs only 'the manner and the means' by which the litigants' rights are 'enforced,' it is valid; if it alters 'the rules of decision by which [the] court will adjudicate [those] rights,' it is not."[31]

Shady Grove raises a deeper question, which is whether some state rules should apply in federal court even if they affect federal procedure "because they function as a part of the State's definition of substantive rights and remedies."[32] Suppose the New York rule were embedded in New York's substantive laws concerning statutory penalties rather than in New York's class action law. Suppose it were articulated as a limit on the New York statutory remedy. In that case, would the federal court have to apply the rule as part of New York's substantive law? Justice Scalia's opinion in *Shady Grove* states that the "substantive nature of New York's law, or its substantive purpose, *makes no difference.*"[33] In his view, once the court finds a valid federal rule on point, nothing else matters. The concurring and dissenting Justices, however, would interpret federal rules to avoid conflicting with state substantive law. While the basic steps of *Erie* analysis are reasonably well defined, the different viewpoints in the *Shady Grove* opinions show that fundamental questions remain about *Erie* and the line between substance and procedure.

C. Determining State Law

Because the *Erie* doctrine instructs federal judges to apply state law, we should take a brief detour to see how federal judges determine state law.

First, however, some students wonder how *any* judge can *ever* apply the law of some other government. You have to get used to the idea that courts apply the law of other sovereigns all the time. Federal courts apply state law. State courts apply federal law. Iowa courts apply Texas law. U.S. courts apply French law. It all depends upon what claims are being asserted and application of the court's choice of law rules. Having learned personal jurisdiction, you know that even if a case arose in a particular state and is likely to be governed by that state's law, there may be multiple jurisdictions where the case can be brought. Having learned subject matter jurisdiction, you know that federal question jurisdiction is largely *concurrent* jurisdiction; those cases can be brought either in federal court or state court. And having learned about diversity jurisdiction and supplemental jurisdiction, you know that federal courts often adjudicate state law claims, and therefore must apply state law.

OK, so if a federal judge has to apply state law, how does the judge actually determine what the state law is? In some cases, determining state law is a simple piece of legal research; on the question of New York's statute of limitations, *Guaranty*

---

[31]*Id.* at 1442 (citing and quoting *Mississippi Publishing Corp. v. Murphree*, 326 U.S. 438, 445-46 (1946)).
[32]*Id.* at 1448 (Stephens, J., concurring).
[33]130 S. Ct. at 1444.

Trust may have involved little more than reading the statute. The federal court has the benefit of both sides' briefs on any disputed legal issues.

What if the state law is not so clear or if the parties dispute the correct interpretation? The basic answer is this: State law is whatever the state high court says it is. When applying state law, federal courts must apply the law exactly as they believe the state's high court would do. The federal court therefore looks to see if the state supreme court has decided the issue, and if so, it follows that ruling unless there is very good reason to believe that the state supreme court would no longer decide it the same way. If there is no state supreme court decision on point, then the federal court looks at intermediate appellate decisions from that state, or other sources that the state high court would consider, such as cases from other states, treatises, and policy rationales.

If state law is extremely unclear, such as on a common law issue of first impression, that vacuum gives the federal court wide discretion to determine what the law is. In those situations, it may feel like the federal court is back in the days of *Swift v. Tyson*, "ascertain[ing] upon general reasoning and legal analogies . . . what is the just rule . . . to govern the case."[34] There is supposed to be a difference, however. Under *Swift*, the federal court looked to reasoning and analogies to decide federal general common law, whereas now the federal court's job is to predict what the state's high court would say. As a matter of strategy, however, if your case depends upon a legal argument that's contrary to state appellate court precedents, you may find a federal district court judge slightly more willing to get creative with the law than a state trial court judge whose decision will be reviewed by the state appellate courts.

F A Q

Q: If the federal judge is unsure about state law, why not just ask the state supreme court?

A: Good idea. Some states have *certification* procedures that allow a federal court to certify a question to the state high court in order to resolve a disputed issue of state law. Courts tend to use these procedures sparingly, however. Each additional step in the judicial process, such as sending a legal question to the state court, costs time and money for the litigants and the court systems, so there is always the question of whether the extra input on a legal issue is worth the cost and delay.

D. Applying the *Erie-Hanna* Analysis

Substantive law in federal court may be either federal or state. In cases brought under federal statutes, regulations, or the constitution, federal law supplies the governing substantive standards. Usually these are federal question cases, but they might also include diversity cases that raise some federal issues. In cases brought under state statutes, as well as in common law cases such as contract, tort, and property lawsuits,

---

[34]Swift v. Tyson, 41 U.S. 1, 19 (1842).

state law supplies the governing substantive standards. Usually these are diversity cases, but they also include state law claims in federal court on supplemental jurisdiction or state law claims in which the United States is a party. Regardless of whether it's a federal or state law claim, federal courts generally apply their own *procedures*. In federal court, you can be confident in using the Federal Rules of Civil Procedure as well as federal statutes that govern the litigation process.

The hard part comes when you're in federal court on a state law claim, and you encounter some conflict between how the federal court would handle some issue and how a state court would handle it. Maybe it's not so clear whether the issue is substantive or procedural. And maybe it's not so clear whether any federal rule or statute directly answers the question.

You need an analytical framework for separating the easy questions from the hard ones and for working through the hard ones. Below, I've suggested one way of pulling together the Supreme Court's *Erie* rulings into a usable framework. This is not, of course, the only way to do it, and you may find yourself before a judge (or professor) who would organize things differently. Whether you use the structure below or another one, you should get comfortable with some framework that encompasses the various analytical strands the Supreme Court has identified. And you should get comfortable with it *before* you face a hard *Erie* issue head-on.

Erie-Hanna Analysis

I. Spotting the *Erie* issue

    a. You are in federal court on a state law claim.

    (Probably this is because federal jurisdiction is based on diversity of citizenship, but it could also be a state claim in federal court on supplemental jurisdiction.)

    b. On some issue, you see a conflict between what the federal court would do and what a state court would do in the same situation.

II. Federal rule or statute

    ■ If there is a valid federal rule or statute directly on point, then the court will apply federal law because a federal court must apply any valid federal statute or rule even if it conflicts with state law. (*Hanna*; *Shady Grove*)

    a. Is there a federal rule or statute directly on point?

        i. What is the precise issue on which federal and state law diverge? Find each federal rule or statute that governs that issue, and examine whether it addresses the specific point on which federal and state law differ.

    b. Is the federal rule or statute valid?

        i. For a federal statute, is it constitutional?

        ii. For a federal rule such as a Federal Rule of Civil Procedure, does it comply with the REA? (Under the REA, a valid rule must not abridge, enlarge, or modify any substantive rights.)

III. Federal practice

    a. If there is no valid federal rule or statute directly on point, then you must do the more complete *Erie*/RDA analysis.

    b. How do you know you are in this situation? State law conflicts with a federal practice but not with a specifically enacted valid rule or statute. This scenario can arise several ways:

        i. No applicable federal rule or statute exists (example: *Guaranty Trust*, where federal law was based on the equitable doctrine of laches rather than on any particular rule or statute).

    ii. There is an applicable federal rule or statute, but on closer examination it does not *directly* address the point (example: *Walker*, where Rule 3 defined commencement of the action but did not specifically address the statute of limitations).

    iii. There is an applicable federal rule or statute directly on point, but it is invalid under the constitution or the REA.

  c. *Erie*/RDA analysis

    i. Apply the *Erie*/RDA test to determine whether state or federal law applies.

- Ask the following questions about the point on which state and federal law differ:
  - Is it outcome-determinative? (*Guaranty Trust*)
  - Would applying federal law rather than state law promote forum shopping or inequitable administration of the laws between state and federal court? (*Hanna*)
  - Does the state law affect primary decisions about human conduct? (Harlan's *Hanna* concurrence)
- Based on these questions, if the state law is *not* substantive/outcome-determinative, then the court will apply federal law.
- Based on these questions, if the state law is substantive/outcome-determinative, then the court probably will apply state law, but first may consider the federal and state interests at stake.

    ii. Consider federal and state interests.

- Is there a countervailing federal interest? If so, maybe the court will apply a balancing test to determine whether the federal interest outweighs the state interest. (*Byrd*)
- Is it possible to accommodate both state and federal interests? If so, the court will try to do so. (*Gasperini*)

Let's try running this analysis through an example, using a medical malpractice lawsuit in federal court in a state that has passed legislation to discourage meritless malpractice suits.

Example: New Jersey's legislature passed a statute requiring plaintiffs, when bringing a medical malpractice lawsuit, to file an "affidavit of merit," a certification by another doctor stating that there is a reasonable probability that the defendant's conduct fell outside acceptable professional standards. Suppose a plaintiff brings a medical malpractice case in federal court in New Jersey based on diversity jurisdiction. Does the "affidavit of merit" statute apply in federal court?[35]

First, what's the *Erie* issue in this example? Ordinarily, federal courts do not require an affidavit to be filed in addition to the complaint. The New Jersey state courts, however, require an affidavit of merit in professional liability suits. That's the conflict between federal and state law.

Next, is there a federal rule or statute directly on point? Rule 8(a) states that a complaint need only include "a short and plain statement of the claim showing that the pleader is entitled to relief." Rule 9(b) requires certain claims to be pleaded "with particularity," but does not include malpractice claims. Rules 8 and 9 are clearly valid

---

[35]*See* Chamberlain v. Giampapa, 210 F.3d 154 (3d Cir. 2000).

under the REA and the constitution, but are they directly on point? Do they directly collide with the state law? Not exactly. The affidavit required by state law does not affect the pleadings themselves; it is a separate, additional requirement. In other words, the federal court must follow Rules 8 and 9 concerning the complaint, but nothing in those rules compels the federal court to ignore the state's affidavit-of-merit requirement. Nonuse of the affidavit of merit constitutes a federal practice rather than a requirement of a federal rule or statute.

We therefore turn to the full *Erie*/RDA analysis. Is the state law outcome-determinative? Yes, at least in the *Guaranty Trust* sense. If state law applies, then the case would be dismissed because the plaintiff failed to provide the affidavit. Is it bound up with state-created rights and obligations? Absolutely. The requirement was part of a state tort reform package, driven by concerns that malpractice liability and insurance premiums had gotten out of hand. Is it something over which litigants would forum-shop? Probably, at least in weak cases. Plaintiffs with shaky malpractice claims, who might have trouble obtaining suitable affidavits, would prefer to avoid the requirement by bringing suit in federal court. Inequitable administration of the laws could result from imposing different burdens on plaintiffs, or exposing defendants to different protection from meritless claims, in state and federal court, although arguably these are procedural rather than substantive differences. It is also a close call on Harlan's "primary decisions" standard. On the one hand, the affidavit-of-merit requirement is a procedural requirement for how litigation is conducted. On the other hand, it was driven by substantive concerns about malpractice liability. Overall, a court would likely find the affidavit-of-merit requirement substantive for purposes of the *Erie* analysis because it can determine the outcome, it was driven by substantive state policy concerns, and parties would forum-shop over it.

Is there a countervailing federal interest? The federal courts have an interest in maintaining the integrity of the federal pleading system, which generally allows parties to initiate a lawsuit without producing evidence on the theory that evidence is gathered during the discovery process. The affidavit-of-merit requirement arguably runs counter to this federal approach to pleadings and discovery. It is unlikely, however, that a court would find this federal interest to outweigh the state's clear policy concerning the early dismissal of meritless malpractice lawsuits.

Because no federal rule or statute directly collides with the state law, and because the state law is "substantive" in the *Erie*/RDA sense, a federal court probably would apply the state affidavit-of-merit requirement.

SUMMARY

- The *Erie* doctrine addresses the choice of federal or state law in federal court.

- In cases involving state law claims, federal courts generally apply federal procedural law and state substantive law.

- If a valid federal statute or rule directly addresses an issue, then a federal court must apply that statute or rule.

- If no specific federal statute or rule directly addresses an issue, then a federal court must apply state law as to "substantive" issues.

■ Determining whether state law is "substantive" requires consideration of whether the law would determine the outcome of the dispute, and whether applying different law in federal and state court would be inequitable and would lead to forum shopping.

■ When multiple states are involved, a federal court decides which state's law to apply by applying the choice of law rules of the state in which the federal court is located.

■ When determining state law, federal courts follow the decisions of the state's high court, or decide what that court would do.

CONNECTIONS

Subject Matter Jurisdiction

Erie-Hanna analysis applies to state law claims in federal court. Usually this means diversity cases. But it also can include state law claims in federal court on supplemental jurisdiction or state law claims in which the United States is a party.

Personal Jurisdiction—Service of Process

Hanna involved a conflict between a state statute on service of process, which required personal service on an executor, and Rule 4, which permits service of process by leaving a copy of the summons and complaint at a person's home with a person of suitable age and discretion. The Court held that Rule 4 was a valid Federal Rule of Civil Procedure under the Rules Enabling Act and that federal courts must apply the federal rule.

Discovery

Just three years after *Erie* and the enactment of the Federal Rules of Civil Procedure, the Supreme Court addressed whether federal courts must apply the federal discovery rules in the face of conflicting state law. Specifically, in *Sibbach v. Wilson & Co.*, 312 U.S. 1 (1941), the Court upheld Rule 35 (physical and mental examinations) against a challenge that the rule violated the REA because it abridged substantive rights.

Joinder—Class Actions

In many state law class actions, such as those involving product liability, consumer fraud, or breach of contract, *Erie* imposes an obstacle to class certification in federal court. *Erie* requires the federal court to apply state substantive law to the claims, but if the class members are from multiple states, choice of law rules may dictate that the court apply the law of each plaintiff's home state. This leaves the court in the difficult position of applying, in a nationwide class action, 50 state laws. Faced with this prospect, many courts reject class certification in nationwide state law class actions on the grounds that common questions do not predominate.

Trial

When some federal district courts experimented with trial-by-statistics techniques in asbestos litigation, extrapolating from jury verdicts on sample plaintiffs and applying the results to a large plaintiff group, courts of appeals reversed on the grounds that state law requires individual proof, and under *Erie* the federal courts cannot use trial techniques that fail to respect the substantive requirements of state law.

Appeal

Some states assign powers to their appellate courts that differ from the powers of the federal courts of appeals, presenting *Erie* issues about whether the federal courts must follow the state courts' approach in state law cases. The Supreme Court dealt with this in *Gasperini*, emphasizing the federal interest in allocation of power between district court and court of appeals.

Preclusion

When addressing claim preclusion or issue preclusion based on a federal court judgment in a state law case, *Erie* determines whether the effect of the judgment is governed by state or federal preclusion law. The Supreme Court faced such a case in *Semtek v. Lockheed Martin*, 531 U.S. 497 (2001), addressed in Chapter 11.

Pleadings

5

In every lawsuit, there are at least two sides to the story. That's what makes it a litigated dispute rather than a math problem. **Pleadings** are

O V E R V I E W

where each litigant first gets to tell its side of the story as a formal part of the litigation process.

The plaintiff files a *complaint* setting forth the plaintiff's allegations. The complaint is what officially starts the lawsuit. The defendant then files an *answer* responding to the plaintiff's allegations, or sometimes instead files a *pre-answer motion*. In some cases, the plaintiff files a *reply* to the defendant's answer. By laying out each party's contentions, the pleadings set the framework for the entire litigation. The complaint and answer, taken together, define the boundaries of the litigation by showing which issues are and are not in dispute. The pleadings serve the critical function of notifying each party about the adversary's claims or defenses. Pleadings also give the court the opportunity to decide whether a claim should be dismissed at the outset either for some procedural flaw or because, even taking the plaintiff's factual allegations as true, the claim lacks legal merit.

A. COMPLAINT

1. History
2. Modern Pleading
3. Motions to Dismiss for Failure to State a Claim
4. Inconsistent Pleading

B. HEIGHTENED PLEADING

C. DEFENDANT'S RESPONSE

1. Admissions and Denials
2. Affirmative Defenses
3. Motions to Dismiss and Other Motions on the Pleadings
4. Waiver of Defenses
5. Claims by Defendants

D. REPLY AND OTHER PLEADINGS

E. AMENDMENT

1. Amending the Pleadings
2. Relation Back

F. SANCTIONS AND ETHICAL CONSTRAINTS

A. Complaint

"A short and plain statement" of the claim. That's all that's required, according to modern pleading rules in federal court and most state courts. In historical perspective, it's an easy standard to meet and not a terribly complicated one to understand. Which is why this book has a single chapter on the topic, whereas a century ago you would have taken an entire law school course called Pleadings. The long historical trend has been toward simplification and liberalization of pleading standards, so that cases can be decided on their merits rather than on the technicalities of pleadings. The question of how much detail a complaint requires recently got more complicated, however, due to a couple of Supreme Court cases that signal a shift toward more stringent requirements for the factual allegations that must be included in a complaint.

(1) History

The famous legal historian F.W. Maitland wrote that "the forms of action we have buried, but they still rule us from their graves."[1] If you can understand what he meant, you'll have a firmer grasp of pleading. Modern pleading is not so much a system of its own as it is a reaction to the common law pleading that came before. So it's worth a brief historical detour to figure out what Maitland was talking about.

The next few paragraphs, I have to warn you, will give you an embarrassingly oversimplified account of 800 years of legal development; any historian would be horrified. From about the thirteenth century through the late nineteenth century, common law pleading dominated Anglo-American civil procedure. The legal system was divided into courts of common law and courts of equity, which had different procedures. In the common law courts, pleadings and procedures were linked to a system of *writs*. The writ was what the court issued at the outset of the action, ordering the sheriff to compel the defendant either to appear in court or to satisfy the claim. Every type of claim had its own writ accompanied by its own procedural rules, so the procedures differed depending on the type of claim.

---

[1]F.W. Maitland, The Forms of Action at Common Law 2 (1909).

The categories of liability and their procedures were known as *forms of action*, with names like debt, trespass, replevin, assumpsit, and ejectment. The plaintiff had to file a pleading that showed that the plaintiff's case constituted a cause of action in whichever form of action the plaintiff used. If the plaintiff chose an incorrect form, the case would be thrown out. Over time, the statements required in these pleadings became formulaic.

In response to the plaintiff's pleading, the defendant had several choices. The defendant could *demur*, contending that the plaintiff's pleading does not state a valid legal claim even if the allegations are true. The defendant could make a *dilatory plea*, which focuses on procedural issues such as objections to the court's jurisdiction. The defendant could *traverse*, which means to deny the plaintiff's allegations. Or the defendant could make a *confession and avoidance*, which admits the truth of plaintiff's allegations but pleads something additional as a defense. The idea was to narrow the dispute to a precise issue. By forcing the plaintiff to choose a particular legal theory and set of facts, and by forcing the defendant to choose a response, common law pleading essentially told the parties: First, get your disagreement straight, and then the court will resolve your disagreement. Common law pleading had the virtue of defining neatly the disputed issues. Increasingly, however, the common law pleading system was criticized as unduly rigid and technical.

By the mid-nineteenth century, the flaws of common law pleading had grown significant enough to spur reform. Beginning with New York's Field Code in 1848, states abandoned the common law pleading system and adopted a new approach. This type of pleading is known as *code pleading* because it was enacted by statutory codes, as opposed to judicially developed common law. The codes abolished the forms of action and replaced them with a requirement that complaints plead facts, also known as *fact pleading*. Under code pleading, facts were required to be pleaded at the appropriate level of specificity, called *ultimate facts*. If a pleading stated facts too generally, those allegations were *mere conclusions*. If the pleading was too specific and detailed, those allegations were *mere evidence*. Because of the difficulty identifying what constituted ultimate facts, code pleading developed its own technicalities. While code pleading broke from the rigidity of common law pleading and brought pleadings closer to the actual facts of the case, reformers saw the need to reduce the centrality of pleadings in civil procedure. In the 1930s, the Federal Rules of Civil Procedure ushered in a new era of pleading, breaking away from both common law pleading and code pleading. While the federal courts and most state courts have adopted the new approach to pleading, some states retain code pleading systems.

In 1934, Congress passed the Rules Enabling Act, authorizing the Supreme Court to create rules of procedure for the federal courts. This set in motion the process that would lead to the creation of the Federal Rules of Civil Procedure, which went into effect in 1938. With the federal rules came a new approach to pleading and a new system of procedure that flowed, to a large extent, from the change in pleading.

Just look at the first two rules. In Rule 1, even before the well-known language that states the goal of achieving "the just, speedy, and inexpensive determination of every action," you'll see this language: "These rules govern the procedure in all civil actions and proceedings in the United States district courts. . . ." That may seem obvious for something called the "Federal Rules of Civil Procedure," but the non-obvious part to the mind of 1938 was that the rules established the same pleadings and other procedures for both law and equity.

Now look at Rule 2: "There is one form of action—the civil action." Huh? That hardly looks like a rule of procedure at all. What does it do? Getting back in the mindset of 1938, you can see that it echoed, for the new Federal Rules of Civil

Procedure, the Field Code's abolition of the common law forms of action. If the federal rules rejected the common law pleading system but also broke away from code pleading, what did they put in its place? A simpler approach. In the new system, the point of pleadings is not to reduce the dispute to a single issue. Rather, the pleadings give the parties notice of each other's claims and defenses. The pleadings also provide a basis for motions to dismiss and other procedures to test whether those claims and defenses have enough substance to be allowed to proceed.

(2) Modern Pleading

(a) Federal Rule 8

The **complaint** is the pleading that a plaintiff files to initiate a lawsuit, setting forth the plaintiff's claims against the defendant. For a valid complaint in federal court, Rule 8(a) requires three things: (1) a statement of the basis for jurisdiction, (2) a "short and plain statement of the claim showing that the pleader is entitled to relief," and (3) a demand for judgment. Part two, the statement of the claim, is the heart of the complaint, and that's what we'll focus on. But first, let's understand parts one and three — the jurisdictional statement and the demand for judgment.

Rule 8(a) applies to any "pleading that states a claim for relief." Usually, this means the plaintiff's complaint. But keep in mind that the requirements of Rule 8(a), as well as its pleading standard, apply not only to original claims, but also to counterclaims, crossclaims, and third-party claims. Similarly, the dictates of Rules 8(b) and 8(c) on denials and defenses apply to any pleading that responds to a claim.

Rule 8(a)(1) requires every complaint to include "a short and plain statement of the grounds for the court's jurisdiction." If you think about the limits on federal subject matter jurisdiction from Chapter 1, you'll see why it's important for complaints in federal court to include a jurisdictional statement. Federal courts, by constitution and statute, are courts of limited jurisdiction. If a federal court lacks power to adjudicate a particular case, the court must dismiss, and obviously it is preferable for the court to find this out immediately rather than after having wasted the court's and the litigants' time litigating the dispute in the wrong court. So, for example, if federal jurisdiction is based on diversity of citizenship, the complaint must allege the citizenship of each party and the amount in controversy.

F   A   Q

Q: Rule 8(a)(1) requires a statement of jurisdiction. Does this include personal jurisdiction?

A: No. The rule leaves *jurisdiction* undefined, but courts have held that this means subject matter jurisdiction, not personal jurisdiction. This makes perfect sense because personal jurisdiction, unlike subject matter jurisdiction, may be waived. If the defendant voluntarily appears in the action, then there is no need for the court to dismiss for lack of personal jurisdiction. But if the court lacks subject matter jurisdiction — which may be apparent on the face of the complaint — then the court must dismiss immediately.

Rule 8(a)(3) requires a complaint to include "a demand for the relief sought, which may include relief in the alternative or different types of relief." In other words, whatever it is you're asking for, you have to ask for it. Maybe it's injunctive relief, an order that the defendant do this or refrain from doing that. In a contract case, maybe it's specific performance of the contract. In an intellectual property case, maybe it's an injunction prohibiting the defendant from infringing the plaintiff's patent, trademark, or copyright. Maybe it's a declaratory judgment, declaring the legal rights of the parties. Usually, however, it's a demand for money damages. Rule 8(a) does not require that plaintiffs specify the amount. In some courts, the complaint demands a specific sum of money, while in others, the complaint simply demands fair and reasonable compensation. But every complaint must at least state what kind of relief the plaintiff is seeking.

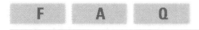

Q: Should a plaintiff always demand as much money as possible?

A: Well, sort of. Some complaints, of course, demand injunctive or declaratory relief rather than money damages. And some courts have local rules that prohibit demanding a specific amount of money. But when permitted, plaintiffs' lawyers often make a demand for judgment at the highest end of the range of money damages that would be plausible in a case. Some think that this increases leverage for settlement discussions. Also, if the defendant defaults, the plaintiff cannot get more than the amount demanded, so it behooves plaintiffs not to undervalue their claims. Keep in mind that Rule 11 and ethical constraints prohibit lawyers from making unsupportable demands. The upshot, if you're formulating a demand for judgment on behalf of a plaintiff: Aim high, but don't aim frivolously.

(b) Statement of the Claim

(i) Notice Pleading

Now let's turn to the heart of the complaint — the statement of the claim. Rule 8(a)(2) requires that the complaint contain a "short and plain statement of the claim showing that the pleader is entitled to relief." This is a bit misleading. The statement doesn't actually have to be short. Or plain. Occasionally a judge will rebuke a party for excessively lengthy or complex pleadings, and a few have actually dismissed complaints for extreme wordiness, but it's rare. In practice you'll find that many complaints are not short and plain at all. A more realistic phrasing of Rule 8(a)(2) might go something like: "a statement of the claim showing that the pleader is entitled to relief, and feel free to keep it short and plain."

The "short and plain" language is important. As part of the new 1938 federal rules, this phrase made it clear that the special requirements of common law pleading and code pleading did not apply. This modern approach is often called **notice pleading**. The name reinforces the concept that the primary function of a complaint is to give the defendant notice of the claim.

To drive home the point that pleadings need not be lengthy or detailed, the rulemakers included official forms illustrating what would constitute an adequate complaint. Form 11, for example, is a sample negligence complaint. In between the allegation of jurisdiction and the demand for judgment, the entire statement of the claim reads as follows:

2. On *date* at *place*, the defendant negligently drove a motor vehicle against the plaintiff.

3. As a result, the plaintiff was physically injured, lost wages or income, suffered physical and mental pain, and incurred medical expenses of $ _____.

This, according to the rulemakers, is a sufficiently detailed complaint under Rule 8(a). It's short, you have to admit. And plain. Rule 84 says that the forms "suffice under these rules and illustrate the simplicity and brevity that these rules contemplate."

But I don't know a single lawyer who would file a complaint that says so little. After all, if you're representing a plaintiff, the complaint is your first opportunity to tell the court your client's side of the story. Even if a barebones complaint satisfies the pleading requirement, good lawyers use the complaint to state a claim that is not merely sufficient, but compelling. The intended audience is not only the court, but also the defendant. If a plaintiff wishes to bring a defendant to the bargaining table, a complaint that tells a powerful story backed up with supporting detail is more likely to do the trick than a complaint that merely notifies the defendant of the claim. On the other hand, lawyers sometimes avoid including too much detail in the complaint because they do not wish to show their cards too early or because they fear boxing themselves into a corner before all the evidence has come to light.

Notice pleading acknowledges that at the start of a lawsuit, the parties may not possess all of the information they need in order to set out their positions in detail. The discovery process can help them get that information during the course of the litigation. At the outset, the pleadings simply set out the basic allegations for each side of the dispute.

A series of Supreme Court cases has fleshed out the pleading standard under the federal rules, but also raised some new questions. In each case, a defendant moved to dismiss the plaintiff's complaint for failure to state a claim, and the courts had to decide whether the complaint's allegations sufficed. In *Conley v. Gibson*,[2] the plaintiffs asserted employment discrimination claims, but their complaint did not specifically spell out what was discriminatory about the defendant's acts. The Supreme Court held that the complaint sufficed, reasoning that "the Federal Rules of Civil Procedure do not require a claimant to set out in detail the facts upon which he bases his claim. To the contrary, all the Rules require is 'a short and plain statement of the claim' that will give the defendant fair notice of what the plaintiff's claim is and the grounds upon which it rests." In *Swierkiewicz v. Sorema*,[3] a plaintiff claimed discrimination based on national origin. After a court dismissed the complaint for failing to allege facts in enough detail to show discrimination, the Supreme Court unanimously reversed, citing *Conley* and Rule 8's notice pleading standard.

(ii) The Plausibility Requirement

The notice pleading standard seemed simple enough until the Supreme Court shook things up with a pair of important cases in 2007 and 2009. In *Bell Atlantic v.*

---

[2]355 U.S. 41 (1957).
[3]534 U.S. 506 (2002).

Twombly[4] and *Ashcroft v. Iqbal*,[5] the Supreme Court announced a requirement of *plausibility* for a complaint to survive a motion to dismiss. In so doing, the Justices made things more difficult for two groups of people—federal court plaintiffs and civil procedure students.

In *Twombly*, two consumers filed an antitrust class action against Verizon, Qwest, and other telephone companies alleging that the companies unilaterally agreed not to compete in each other's territorial market areas for local telephone and Internet business. Under the antitrust law, the defendants could be held liable only if they actually agreed not to compete. Even if the defendants engaged in parallel business conduct and chose not to compete with each other, their conduct would not violate the law unless they actually had an agreement. The complaint alleged numerous ways in which the defendants engaged in parallel business conduct, and "in light of the parallel course of conduct," the complaint alleged that the defendants "have agreed not to compete with one another." The Supreme Court held that the complaint failed to meet the pleading standard of Rule 8 and that the district court should dismiss the complaint for failure to state a claim. Adding the concept of *plausibility* to our pleading vocabulary, the Supreme Court insisted that it was not really requiring a heightened level of pleading: "[W]e do not require heightened fact pleading of specifics, but only enough facts to state a claim to relief that is plausible on its face. Because the plaintiffs here have not nudged their claims across the line from conceivable to plausible, their complaint must be dismissed."[6]

Iqbal concerned a Pakistani Muslim who contended that federal government officials discriminated against him on account of his race, religion and national origin in violation of his constitutional rights when they harshly detained him in the wake of the September 11 attacks. He brought a lawsuit against numerous defendants including Attorney General John Ashcroft and FBI Director Robert Mueller. To establish liability against each defendant, the plaintiff would have to show that the defendant acted with a discriminatory purpose. For the claims against Ashcroft and Mueller, the Supreme Court held that the complaint failed to meet the Rule 8 pleading standard because the allegation of purposeful discrimination was conclusory. "To survive a motion to dismiss," the Court explained, "a complaint must contain sufficient factual matter, accepted as true, to 'state a claim to relief that is plausible on its face.'"[7] The Court emphasized that a plaintiff cannot simply assert conclusions such as "discriminatory purpose" without factual allegations to back up those conclusions. Rule 8 "does not require 'detailed factual allegations,' but it demands more than an unadorned, the-defendant-unlawfully-harmed-me accusation."[8] In other words, a complaint had better not be so "short and plain" that it fails to include factual, nonconclusory allegations to support the essential elements of the claim.

Compared with the cases that came earlier, *Twombly* and *Iqbal* suggest a different attitude about pleading. When the Supreme Court embraced the notice pleading standard in *Conley* and *Swierkiewicz*, it conveyed a permissive attitude: let the plaintiff get the case started and through discovery and possibly trial we will see if the claim has factual substance. The *Twombly* and *Iqbal* opinions, by

---

[4]550 U.S. 544 (2007).
[5]129 S. Ct. 1937 (2009).
[6]*Twombly*, 550 U.S. at 570.
[7]*Iqbal*, 129 S. Ct. at 1949 (quoting *Twombly*, 550 U.S. at 570).
[8]*Id.* (quoting *Twombly*, 550 U.S. at 555).

contrast, convey an attitude of caution: discovery can be really expensive and burdensome, so unless the plaintiff provides enough facts in the complaint to show that the key allegations are plausible, we're not going to let the plaintiffs launch the litigation. The basic standard under Rule 8(a)(2) is still "short and plain"—don't forget Form 11 with its simple allegation of negligence—but the recent cases have shifted the analysis. Complaints do not have to contain a lot of factual detail as long as they state a valid claim, but a plaintiff cannot rely on bare allegations of legal conclusions without alleging the facts on which those conclusions are based.

Remember that Rule 8(a)(2) requires "a short and plain statement of the claim showing that the pleader is entitled to relief." The notice pleading standard emphasized *short and plain*. The Supreme Court's recent cases warn us not to ignore the part about *showing that the pleader is entitled to relief*.

(3) Motions to Dismiss for Failure to State a Claim

To argue to the court that the complaint is insufficient, a defendant makes a **motion to dismiss for failure to state a claim**, under Rule 12(b)(6). This is one of the most important motions for any lawyer to understand, as it is the primary means for challenging the validity of a plaintiff's pleading. The 12(b)(6) motion is the "So what?" motion. It says to the complainant: "So what? Even if what you say is true, that does not give you a valid legal claim." At common law, this was known as a *demurrer*; some state courts retain this terminology. To argue that the complaint was legally insufficient even if everything alleged were true, the defendant would *demur* to the complaint.

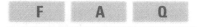

Q: What's the difference between pleadings and evidence?

A: Pleadings are the parties' *allegations*. They lay out the claims and defenses in the case, but they don't *prove* anything. Proof comes later, either as testimony, documents, and physical evidence at trial, or as affidavits and other written evidence in connection with summary judgment or some other motion. To the extent the parties themselves have personal knowledge of the facts, they can testify at trial and such testimony may be used as evidence. But the allegations in the pleadings simply set up the sides of the dispute; they don't count as evidence. Unlike testimony, pleadings ordinarily are not made under oath (but keep in mind that parties and lawyers can be sanctioned for making allegations that lack a factual basis).

(a) Basis for Dismissing Complaint

The Rule 12(b)(6) motion to dismiss was how the defendants challenged the complaints in *Conley, Swierkiewicz, Twombly,* and *Iqbal*. As we just saw, the Supreme Court in *Conley* and *Swierkiewicz* held that those complaints adequately stated their claims, and thus rejected the Rule 12(b)(6) motions. In *Twombly* and *Iqbal*, the Court held that the complaint failed to include sufficient allegations to state a valid claim, and therefore the Rule 12(b)(6) motion should be granted.

There are several ways a complaint may fail, leading to a Rule 12(b)(6) dismissal. First, a complaint may be inadequate because on the facts alleged, it simply does not state a valid legal claim. The pleader, in other words, is not entitled to relief even if the allegations are true.

Example 1: Plaintiff's complaint, in addition to jurisdictional allegations and a demand for damages, includes the following statement of the claim: "Defendant ignored my Facebook friend request. It made me very sad."

In case it's not obvious enough, this is not a legally meritorious claim, at least not under any torts regime I've ever heard of. If the defendant moved to dismiss under Rule 12(b)(6), the court would grant the motion. Second, a complaint may fail because the allegations fail to meet a required element of the claim. For example, if a complaint fails to allege damages or causation as required for a particular type of legal claim, the complaint could be dismissed for failure to state a claim upon which relief could be granted.

Example 2: Recall official Form 11, discussed earlier. Suppose we alter it—deleting only one word—so that the complaint's statement of the claim reads as follows:

2. On *date* at *place*, the defendant drove a motor vehicle against the plaintiff.
3. As a result, plaintiff was physically injured, lost wages or income, suffered physical and mental pain, and incurred medical expenses of $ _____.

The defendant moves to dismiss for failure to state a claim, and this time, the court might grant the motion. Why? Because the complaint fails to meet an essential element of the claim. It alleges that the defendant hit the plaintiff, but does not say whether it was defendant's fault, plaintiff's fault, both, or neither. A court would analyze the motion by considering the elements of a claim of negligence, which it might list as breach of the duty of reasonable care, actual and proximate causation, and damages. The complaint in Example 2 fails to allege breach. Therefore, it fails to state a claim upon which relief can be granted and would be dismissed under Rule 12(b)(6).

The complaint in Example 2 would have survived the motion if it had alleged that defendant drove negligently, or that defendant did not look where he was going, or that defendant was driving over the speed limit, or any of a thousand other possibilities that would have met the element of breach. Under Rule 8(a), there's no magic language that must be uttered, but the complaint must include allegations to meet each required element of the claim. With a valid complaint, if the plaintiff successfully proves each allegation, then the plaintiff would win the case. In Example 2, even if the plaintiff proves every allegation in the complaint, the plaintiff loses because the plaintiff has the burden of proving that the defendant acted negligently.

Modern pleading has escaped many of the technicalities of common law pleading, and the rules no longer require specific words to be uttered, but in one way the basic analytical structure remains. Every legal claim can be reduced to a series of elements that must be pleaded and proved. A complaint, to survive a motion to dismiss, must include allegations that meet each element of the claim, either directly or inferentially.

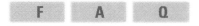

Q: If the plaintiff has no proof to support the claim, shouldn't the case be dismissed?

A: That's what summary judgment is for. Motions to dismiss for failure to state a claim under Rule 12(b)(6) only address the sufficiency of the pleading, not the proof. For purposes of the motion, the court accepts the allegations of the complaint as true. This makes sense from the perspective of the logic of civil procedure under a notice pleading regime. But try explaining it to an actual client who is defending against an adequately pleaded but factually unsupported claim. To the defendant, the denial of a Rule 12(b)(6) motion means the burden of going through discovery and other pretrial litigation, and possibly trial.

Third, a complaint may fail because it alleges only a legal conclusion rather than stating the factual basis for the claim. If a complaint alleges, as its entire statement of the claim, "Defendant is liable to Plaintiff," or "Defendant is liable to Plaintiff for violating section 10(b) of the Securities and Exchange Act of 1934," the complaint would be dismissed for failure to state a claim.

Similarly, the complaint may fail to meet the plausibility test of *Twombly* and *Iqbal*. Even if a complaint gives notice of the basis for the lawsuit and even if it contains allegations about each element of the claim, it may be dismissed if its allegation of an essential element (such as the agreement element in *Twombly* or the purposeful discrimination element in *Iqbal*) is merely conclusory and the complaint does not include enough factual allegations to show why that conclusion is plausible.

Q: Does the complaint set forth the plaintiff's legal theory?

A: The rules do not require that a complaint set forth the plaintiff's legal theory. In other words, if a complaint alleges that the defendant owes plaintiff money based on an enforceable agreement, the complaint does not have to say that it is a claim for *breach of contract.* Or if the complaint alleges that the defendant failed to exercise reasonable care and thereby caused harm to plaintiff, the complaint is not rendered faulty just because it does not use the word *negligence.* If the facts alleged in the complaint make out a valid legal claim, then it does not matter whether the complaint has articulated the legal theory. A "complaint need not pin its claim for relief to a precise legal theory." *Skinner v. Switzer,* 131 S. Ct. 1289, 1296 (2011). Most complaints, however, do specify the legal nature of the claim or claims. Although in theory the plaintiff can trust the court to identify the appropriate legal theory for the claim, in practice, most lawyers believe they strengthen the complaint and diminish the risk of dismissal if they specify what claims they are asserting. Thus, it is common for complaints to be divided into "Count One: Negligence," "Count Two: Strict Liability," and so forth.

(b) Dismissal With or Without Prejudice

When a court grants a motion to dismiss, the court often indicates whether the dismissal is *with prejudice* or *without prejudice*. A dismissal with prejudice precludes the plaintiff from bringing the same claim again. Some courts call this a dismissal *on the merits*, referring to one of the requirements of claim preclusion. A dismissal without prejudice, by contrast, has no claim preclusive effect. If a complaint is dismissed without prejudice, then the plaintiff can try again by filing a new complaint. Courts sometimes refer to this as a dismissal *with leave to amend* or *with leave to replead*.

To understand how courts decide whether a dismissal should be with or without prejudice, use your common sense. In Example 1, the plaintiff has no valid claim. Even if it is true that the defendant saddened the plaintiff by ignoring a Facebook request, that does not give the plaintiff a right to compensation or any other legal relief. As a matter of tort law, this would fall far short of intentional infliction of emotional distress. The problem was not *how* the plaintiff pleaded, but rather that the plaintiff has no legitimate claim. Therefore a court would dismiss with prejudice. In Example 2, by contrast, it is possible that plaintiff has a valid claim but simply failed to plead it adequately. The complaint alleges that the defendant drove a motor vehicle into the plaintiff, but includes no allegation that the defendant failed to exercise reasonable care. It is quite plausible that the plaintiff meant to accuse the defendant of negligence. Maybe the plaintiff's lawyer thought that negligence could be inferred from the allegation that the defendant drove into the plaintiff, or maybe the lawyer just carelessly omitted the negligence allegation from the complaint. But it's also possible that the plaintiff cannot allege negligence because there is no factual basis for the allegation. From the complaint, the court does not know. Most likely, the court would grant the defendant's Rule 12(b)(6) motion to dismiss for failure to state a claim, but would grant it with leave to amend or without prejudice. This way, if the plaintiff does have a factual basis for accusing the defendant of negligence, the plaintiff can file a new complaint that includes the necessary allegations.

What if the court does not say whether a dismissal is with or without prejudice? In federal court, Rule 41(b) states that certain dismissals — lack of jurisdiction, improper venue, and failure to join an indispensable party — are presumed to be without prejudice. This makes sense, doesn't it? If the problem is jurisdiction or venue, then the plaintiff should be free to file the claim in the proper court. If the problem is failure to join a party, then the plaintiff should be able to refile the complaint with the addition of the required party. All other dismissals (including dismissals for failure to state a claim) operate as adjudications upon the merits unless the court specifies otherwise. In other words, unless the court states that the dismissal is *without prejudice* or *with leave to amend* or similar words, then the dismissal is deemed to be with prejudice.

(4) Inconsistent Pleading

May a pleading include allegations that conflict with each other? Under common law pleading, parties were required to choose one set of facts; inconsistent pleadings were not an option. In real life, however, people don't always know exactly what happened, especially at the outset of a lawsuit. Modern pleading systems, recognizing this possibility, permit inconsistent or alternative pleadings. Federal Rule 8(d)(2) permits a party to "set out two or more statements of a claim or defense alternately or hypothetically" and to "state as many separate claims or defenses as it has regardless of consistency." Because of Rule 8(d)(2), a pleading cannot be dismissed simply because it includes allegations that are not consistent with each other.

Ethical and tactical concerns limit the use of inconsistent pleadings. First, as we will see shortly, frivolous pleadings are forbidden. The rules of legal ethics prohibit lawyers from making allegations that have no factual basis, and the rules of procedure empower courts to impose sanctions on lawyers or parties who make such allegations. Thus, even though Rule 8(d)(2) authorizes inconsistent pleadings, such pleadings are permissible only if some factual basis exists for each alternative version of the facts. Second, as a tactical matter, many lawyers prefer the strength of presenting one coherent version of the facts, rather than offering alternative sets of allegations. But keep in mind that at trial a lawyer can present a single coherent theory of the case, even if the pleadings originally included inconsistent allegations.

B. Heightened Pleading

Although as a general rule, notice pleading does not require detail, modern pleading rules require certain things to be pleaded with specificity. Congress has enacted statutes that require heightened pleading in certain types of cases. In both *Twombly* and *Iqbal*, the Supreme Court required enough factual content to nudge the complaints' conclusions "across the line from conceivable to plausible," but the Court insisted that it was not generally requiring "heightened fact pleading of specifics, but only enough facts to state a claim to relief that is plausible on its face."[9]

Fraud. Rule 9(b) requires that "[i]n alleging fraud or mistake, a party must state with particularity the circumstances constituting fraud or mistake." A fraud complaint cannot merely allege that the defendant defrauded the plaintiff by making intentional misrepresentations on which the plaintiff relied. Rather, the complaint must give a more detailed account of the fraud, such as who said what to whom, when and where the representation was made, in what way the representation was false, and how the plaintiff relied on it. Courts have dismissed fraud claims for failure to include sufficient detail about the who, what, when, where, and why of the alleged misrepresentations.

One possible justification for the heightened pleading requirement is that fraud is a powerful and damaging accusation, yet easy to allege. The rule prevents facile accusations of fraud in the absence of supporting facts. But can't the same be said of many other allegations that arise in civil litigation? And isn't there a contrary argument that victims of fraud might be unable to include specific details precisely

---

[9]*Twombly*, 550 U.S. 544, 570 (2007).

because they were defrauded? In any event, the requirement remains under Rule 9(b) that allegations of fraud—whether in a complaint or any other pleading—must be made with particularity, in contrast to the general pleading regime of Rule 8(a).

> ### F   A   Q
>
> **Q: Rule 9(b) requires heightened pleading for "fraud or mistake"—what's the "mistake" part about?**
>
> A: Rule 9(b)'s heightened pleading requirement applies to answers as well as complaints. Fraud and mistake are potential defenses to the enforceability of a contract. The heightened pleading rule protects plaintiffs from facile allegations by defendants that a contract is unenforceable because the contract was fraudulently induced or the product of a mistake. Rather, the rule requires the defendant to offer specific facts in support of those defenses.

Civil Rights. Some courts have attempted to impose a heightened pleading requirement on plaintiffs in civil rights cases, but the Supreme Court has made it clear that unless Rule 9(b) is amended or Congress so legislates, no such requirement exists. In *Leatherman v. Tarrant County,*[10] the plaintiffs sued a municipality and several of its police officers, alleging that the officers violated the plaintiffs' civil rights by killing their dogs and beating an elderly man in connection with a search. The defendants moved to dismiss under Rule 12(b)(6), arguing that the complaint contained insufficient detail to state a claim. The district court granted the motion to dismiss and the circuit court affirmed, reasoning that heightened pleading should be required for such civil rights claims because of the risk of frivolous claims and because the defendants have qualified immunity. The Supreme Court reversed, citing the notice pleading standard of Rule 8(a). If Rule 9(b) ought to include a heightened pleading requirement for civil rights claims, the Court explained, then the proper course would be to amend the rule. Even after *Leatherman,* the judicial impulse to require specificity for civil rights complaints remains, and some courts have found ways to impose the

> **Sidebar**
>
> **STATUTORY PLEADING REQUIREMENTS**
>
> For the most part, federal civil procedure is governed by the rules created by the judiciary's rulemaking committees under the auspices of the Supreme Court. Increasingly, however, Congress has asserted its own power to regulate procedure in the federal courts by enacting statutes. The Private Securities Litigation Reform Act of 1995, for example, imposes heightened pleading requirements on plaintiffs in securities cases. If a plaintiff alleges that a defendant made a material misrepresentation, the complaint must specify which statements were misleading, how they were misleading, and facts showing the requisite state of mind. If the complaint fails to meet these pleading requirements, the action is dismissed.* Such congressional forays into civil procedure are controversial. While they may create greater political accountability for the litigation system, they also have led to accusations of carelessness and undue politicization of procedure.
>
> ---
> *Private Securities Litigation Reform Act, 15 U.S.C. §78u-4(b).

---

[10]507 U.S. 163 (1993).

requirement, such as by requiring plaintiffs to file a detailed reply if a defendant asserts qualified immunity as a defense.

C. Defendant's Response

When a defendant has been served with a complaint, the defendant has a number of options. The defendant can make a responsive pleading, called an **answer**. The answer may include *denials* and *affirmative defenses*. Alternatively, the defendant can make a *pre-answer motion*, such as a motion to dismiss for lack of jurisdiction or for failure to state a claim. In addition to these responses to the plaintiff's complaint, the defendant may assert claims of its own, whether as *counterclaims, cross-claims*, or *third-party claims*.

These responses are not mutually exclusive. Unlike common law pleading, which was more restrictive, modern pleading permits defendants to offer multiple responses to a complaint. A defendant, for example, may object to the court's jurisdiction, argue that the complaint is legally insufficient, deny the truth of the plaintiff's allegations, offer affirmative defenses, and also assert a counterclaim.

(1) Admissions and Denials

Perhaps the most basic response of all is the *denial*. A defendant may answer the complaint by saying that some or all of the plaintiff's allegations are untrue. At common law, this was known as a *traverse*.

A defendant who denies the plaintiff's allegations puts these denials in the defendant's answer. Under Rule 8(b), a responsive pleading admits or denies each of the allegations in the complaint, and asserts the defenses to each claim. The core component of a defendant's answer is a series of statements in which the defendant answers each paragraph of the complaint by stating whether the defendant admits or denies the allegations contained in that paragraph. Any allegation that is not denied is deemed admitted.

In almost any dispute, there's a lot that the parties actually agree about. Maybe they agree that they entered a contract, but they disagree about whether the defendant breached it. Or they agree that the surgeon performed an appendectomy on the patient on a given day at a specific hospital, but they disagree about whether malpractice occurred. Or they agree that on a particular afternoon, their cars collided at a particular intersection, causing damage to both vehicles, but they disagree about whose fault it was. The admissions and denials in the answer clarify these points of agreement and disagreement, so that the litigation can focus on what's really in dispute. If an answer admits some of the complaint's allegations, those allegations are deemed true for purposes of the litigation. The admissions, in other words, take those issues out of the dispute. Facts admitted in the pleadings need not be proved at trial; they are simply accepted as true.

What if the defendant doesn't have enough information to decide whether to admit or deny certain of the plaintiff's allegations? Modern pleading rules don't expect parties to know everything at the outset. Rule 8(b)(5) says that "[a] party that lacks knowledge or information sufficient to form a belief about the truth of an allegation must so state, and the statement has the effect of a denial."

In the answer, the defendant must be careful to respond to each of the complaint's allegations. If you're drafting an answer, and the complaint contains a paragraph that you partly admit and partly deny, you cannot simply deny the whole thing just because part of it is false. These are pleadings, not a true-false quiz. You have to state which parts of the allegation you admit and which parts you deny. In *Zielinski v. Philadelphia Piers, Inc.*,[11] the defendant improperly denied an entire paragraph of the complaint, and the court penalized the defendant by deeming certain facts admitted.

In theory, rather than making *specific denials* of particular allegations, a defendant has the option of making a *general denial*, by which the defendant denies all of the allegations in the complaint. Given the popular perception of litigation as some sort of sport in which the parties fight about everything, you might expect that general denials would be an everyday occurrence. But in reality, it is almost never possible for a party to deny *all* of the adversary's allegations. Does the party really disagree that the plaintiff is in the business of selling furniture? Or that the defendant was driving a blue sedan? Or that the company is incorporated in Delaware and has its principal place of business in Little Rock, Arkansas? Rule 8(b)(3) makes this point by saying that "[a] party that intends in good faith to deny all the allegations of a pleading—including the jurisdictional grounds—may do so by a general denial. A party that does not intend to deny all the allegations must either specifically deny designated allegations or generally deny all except those specifically admitted." In other words, don't make a general denial unless you really mean to deny each and every allegation. Instead, you can make specific denials or you can make a qualified general denial, which denies all of the allegations in the complaint except for those that the defendant specifically admits.

(2) Affirmative Defenses

In the answer, the defendant may assert **affirmative defenses**. You might think of these as "Yes, but . . ." responses. Even if the plaintiff's allegations are true and even if they make out a legally sufficient claim, a defendant may respond that the defendant is not liable because of some additional information that provides a defense. For example, the defendant may assert that the statute of limitations has expired or that the plaintiff has waived the right to assert the claim.

At common law, this was known as *confession and avoidance*, by which the defendant admitted the truth of the plaintiff's allegations but asserted a basis for avoiding liability. Under modern pleading rules, the assertion of an affirmative defense does not require the defendant to "confess" anything. A defendant may deny the plaintiff's allegations or challenge the legal sufficiency of the plaintiff's claim, and additionally assert one or more affirmative defenses. In general, the burden of proving an affirmative defense falls on the defendant. Courts have split on the question of whether the plausibility pleading standard of *Twombly* and *Iqbal* applies to affirmative defenses.

Affirmative defenses are waived if not pleaded, so defense attorneys must think carefully about all possible affirmative defenses before filing an answer. In practice, however, if a party fails to plead an affirmative defense in its original answer, the party often can fix the problem by amending the answer.

Rule 8(c) contains a list of affirmative defenses. It includes assumption of risk, contributory negligence, discharge, duress, failure of consideration, fraud, illegality, license, release, res judicata, statute of frauds, statute of limitations, waiver, and several more. Pay attention to the words the rule contains at the beginning of the

---

[11]139 F. Supp. 408 (E.D. Pa. 1956).

list: "In responding to a pleading, a party must affirmatively state any avoidance or affirmative defense, including . . ." These words tell you that it's not an exhaustive list. So if you represent a defendant, and under the applicable law your client has an affirmative defense, be sure to plead it even if you don't find it on Rule 8(c)'s list. And if you represent a plaintiff and wish to argue that the defendant waived a particular defense because it constitutes an affirmative defense and was not pleaded, don't be deterred by the fact that it's not on the list.

Although the list in Rule 8(c) does not exhaust the possible affirmative defenses, you will find it useful to study the list for two reasons. First, it contains many of the affirmative defenses you are likely to encounter in practice. Second, by seeing what these items have in common, you'll better understand how to analyze whether some other response constitutes an affirmative defense. At first glance, contributory negligence, lack of consideration, res judicata, and statute of limitations may seem about as far apart as any legal doctrines can be. What do they have in common? Each of them involves additional facts pleaded by the defendant that were not part of the plaintiff's pleading (the plaintiff was negligent; there was no quid pro quo for the contract; this claim was already litigated to a final judgment; too much time has expired), and the defendant's assertion that those additional facts undo the plaintiff's claim. In this sense, affirmative defenses differ from denials, which attempt to undo the claim by negating the plaintiff's allegations, and from the defense of failure to state a claim, which asserts that the plaintiff's allegations themselves do not make out a valid basis for granting relief.

(3) Motions to Dismiss and Other Motions on the Pleadings

An answer responds to the substance of a complaint. It constitutes a responsive pleading in the sense that it contains the defendant's answers to the plaintiff's allegations and claims. Answering the complaint imposes a burden on the defendant. It requires time, money, and, depending on the nature of the allegations and whether the defendant can deny them, possible embarrassment. Defendants therefore often look for some basis to ask the court to dispose of the complaint without requiring an answer.

Any defense may be asserted in the answer, but certain defenses may be raised by motion if the pleader so chooses. For the most part, these are motions to dismiss, and they are listed in Rule 12(b). Other motions in response to the pleadings are the motion for a more definite statement, motion to strike, and motion for judgment on the pleadings.

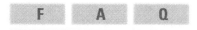

Q: What's a motion?

A: A motion is a request that a court order something. There is no magic list of permissible motions. As a lawyer, if you want the court to order [you name it] — whether it's dismissing the complaint, excluding certain evidence, rescheduling a hearing, compelling production of documents, or anything else you can think of — you make a motion. But please, use the correct verb. *Motion* is the noun; *move* is the verb. In law, you don't *motion* for something; you *move* it. Thus, it would be correct to say either that a defendant *moves* to dismiss or that a defendant *makes a motion* to dismiss, but an embarrassing rookie error to say that a defendant *motions* to dismiss.

(a) Motion to Dismiss

Rule 12(b) lists seven defenses that can be raised by motion rather than in the answer. This useful list tells you what *pre-answer motions* a defendant might make to get a case dismissed. The first five address the choice of forum or the way the defendant was haled into the forum. The sixth is the motion to dismiss for failure to state a claim upon which relief can be granted. The seventh addresses compulsory party joinder.

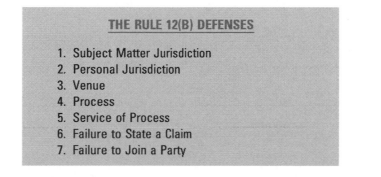

THE RULE 12(B) DEFENSES

1. Subject Matter Jurisdiction
2. Personal Jurisdiction
3. Venue
4. Process
5. Service of Process
6. Failure to State a Claim
7. Failure to Join a Party

Forum and Process. The first three of the Rule 12(b) defenses respond to the complaint by asserting that the action should be thrown out because it is in the wrong place. Rule 12(b)(1) permits a motion to dismiss for lack of subject matter jurisdiction. Although subject matter jurisdiction may be raised by the court on its own, in practice any party who objects to the court's jurisdiction and wants the case dismissed would move to dismiss rather than rely on the court to dismiss sua sponte.

Rules 12(b)(2) and (3) permit motions to dismiss for lack of personal jurisdiction and for improper venue. Unlike subject matter jurisdiction, these matters are waived if not asserted. Therefore, if a defendant objects to the court's personal jurisdiction or venue, the defendant must raise the objection either by a motion under Rule 12(b) or in the answer, whichever comes first.

A defendant also may object to service of the summons and complaint upon the defendant. Specifically, under Rules 12(b)(4) and (5), a defendant may move to dismiss for "insufficient process" or "insufficient service of process." These may sound identical, but here's the difference. Insufficient process means that something was wrong with the summons itself, such as omitting the clerk's signature or misnaming the defendant. Insufficient service of process means that something was wrong with the way in which the summons and complaint were given to the defendant. If service of process was accomplished improperly — either because of a problem with the means of service or because the defendant was served beyond the territorial reach of the court's power — then the court lacks personal jurisdiction over the defendant. For this reason, motions to dismiss under Rule 12(b)(5) often accompany motions to dismiss for lack of personal jurisdiction under Rule 12(b)(2).

Failure to State a Claim. The defendant may *move to dismiss for failure to state a claim upon which relief can be granted.* This important motion, discussed earlier in the chapter, tests the legal sufficiency of the complaint and is used frequently in litigation. At common law it was known as a *demurrer,* and some states retain this name for the device. The defendant, using this terminology, *demurs* to the complaint. Under the federal rules, this is the Rule 12(b)(6) motion, which was used in the *Conley, Leatherman, Swierkiewicz, Twombly,* and *Iqbal* cases. Usually, such a motion argues that even if the plaintiff's allegations are accepted as true, they do not give the plaintiff a right to relief. It says to the plaintiff, "Even if the facts you allege in your complaint are true, you still lose." A variation, relying on Rule 9(b), argues that the complaint fails because it does not plead with particularity.

Failure to Join a Party. If a complaint fails to include a party that the defendant believes is essential to the fair resolution of the litigation, then the defendant may *move to dismiss for failure to join an indispensable party.* In federal court, Rule 12(b)(7) authorizes this motion, and the court's analysis would follow the mandates of Rule 19, which addresses compulsory joinder of parties. Chapter 7 looks at compulsory party joinder, but it's worth mentioning here that the most common way that parties in federal court raise compulsory party joinder is by moving to dismiss under Rule 12(b)(7).

Understanding the Pre-Answer Motions. If you want to understand Rule 12(b) as it relates to pleadings, think about why these particular defenses may be pursued in a pre-answer motion, while denials and other defenses must go in the answer. Rules 12(b)(1)-(5): If the court lacks power or is the wrong forum to adjudicate the case, then it makes no sense for the parties to continue with the litigation process in that forum. The sooner the court dismisses the action, the better. Then, if a party wishes to proceed with the action, that party can go ahead and file the action in a proper forum. Rule 12(b)(6): If the allegations in the complaint are insufficient to state a claim on which the court can grant relief, then going forward would be futile. There's no point to having a responsive pleading, discovery, or trial if, as a legal matter, there is no valid claim to begin with. If the plaintiff has a potentially valid claim, but the complaint is insufficient due to a defect in how it was pleaded, then the court should dismiss the complaint without prejudice. That way, the plaintiff has the opportunity to repair the pleading defect. Either way, it makes sense to resolve the problem or dismiss the action before going forward with the litigation. Rule 12(b)(7): It makes sense to raise compulsory party joinder issues at the outset. If a party is required and joinder is possible, then the plaintiff should join the party. If the party cannot be joined, and if the court decides that dismissal is warranted, then requiring the defendant to submit a responsive pleading before the action is dismissed would accomplish nothing.

By contrast, denials belong in the answer. If the defendant denies the allegations that make up the plaintiff's claim, those factual disputes cannot be resolved on the pleadings. They may be resolved at trial or perhaps on summary judgment. At the pleading stage, what's needed is a simple and clear articulation of what the defendant admits and denies.

(b) Motion for a More Definite Statement

If a complaint is unintelligible or missing critical information, a defendant can seek refinement or explanation. Under the federal rules, the defendant may *move for a more definite statement* under Rule 12(e). In some state courts, the same objective is achieved with a procedural device known as a *bill of particulars*. The motion for a more definite statement can be useful if complaint states a claim but omits basic information that would help the defendant formulate a response. For example, in an action with multiple defendants and multiple claims, if the complaint fails to identify which defendants are charged with which claims, a Rule 12(e) motion could force the plaintiff to connect the dots. On the whole, however, this is not the most useful motion. Because of the notice pleading standard of Rule 8(a), courts generally deny motions that seek greater detail than a short and plain statement. Courts state that the way for a party to get more information about the claims and defenses is through the discovery process, not by asking for more information in the pleadings. Discovery is where parties put flesh on the bones of the pleadings. The point of the motion for a more definite statement is to remedy situations in which a pleading is, as Rule 12(e) puts it, "so vague or ambiguous that a party cannot reasonably be required to frame a responsive pleading."

To understand the infrequency of motions for a more definite statement, imagine yourself representing a defendant who has been served with a poorly drafted complaint. You know that because of the notice pleading standard, the court probably will not grant a Rule 12(e) motion as long as the complaint is comprehensible. If the complaint really is so lacking that you cannot understand it, wouldn't you be better off by moving to dismiss for failure to state a claim under Rule 12(b)(6)? Imagine putting this choice to your client: "The complaint stinks. We can either ask the court to throw out the complaint, or we can ask the court to order the plaintiff to make the complaint stronger. Which do you prefer?"

(c) Motion to Strike

The defendant can move to strike portions of the complaint. In federal court, Rule 12(f) authorizes such motions to strike. Sometimes parties use this device to ask the court to strike irrelevant, redundant, or scandalous matter from their adversary's pleading, but in some cases it is used by defendants as a mini-version of a Rule 12(b)(6) motion, contending that certain aspects of the complaint—a demand for punitive damages, for example—fail to state a legally sufficient claim and therefore ought to be thrown out. It also can be used by plaintiffs to strike insufficient defenses.

(d) Motion for Judgment on the Pleadings

After the pleadings are completed, a party may move for judgment on the pleadings under Rule 12(c). This motion asks the court to decide the case as a matter of law, based solely on what is contained in the pleadings. If made by a defendant, a motion for judgment on the pleadings strongly resembles a Rule 12(b)(6) motion to dismiss for failure to state a claim, except that as a matter of timing, the Rule 12(c) motion comes later, and the court may consider both the complaint and answer. If made by a plaintiff, a motion for judgment on the pleadings points to the admissions in the answer to argue that, as a matter of law, the plaintiff necessarily prevails based on facts established by the pleadings.

(4) Waiver of Defenses

Certain defenses, such as lack of personal jurisdiction, must be asserted at the first opportunity, or they are waived. If a defendant files an answer without filing a pre-answer motion, the defendant must include such defenses in the answer to avoid waiving them. If the defendant files a pre-answer motion such as a motion to dismiss, the motion must include these defenses to avoid waiver. Rules 12(g) and 12(h) spell out which defenses are waived if not asserted at the first opportunity along with other important provisions about when certain defenses may be asserted.

In general, if you make a pre-answer motion, you must include all of your defenses at the same time. Rule 12(g) provides that if you bring any Rule 12 motion (such as a motion to dismiss), you may include any additional Rule 12 defense in the same motion. For example, if you bring a motion to dismiss for improper venue, you may include other defenses such as failure to state a claim upon which relief can be granted. You could call your motion, obviously enough, a "Motion to Dismiss for Improper Venue and Failure to State a Claim." Rule 12(g) not only permits such *consolidation of defenses*, but also requires it, with certain exceptions. If you bring a Rule 12 motion but omit some of the defenses, then you will have lost your opportunity to make a motion based on the omitted defenses, except for failure to state a claim and failure to join an indispensable party.

Rule 12(h)(1) emphasizes that personal jurisdiction, venue, process, and service of process — that is, the defenses contained in Rule 12(b)(2), (3), (4) and (5) — are waived if omitted from the answer or pre-answer motion, whichever comes first. That makes sense, doesn't it? If a defendant chooses to forge ahead with litigation in the plaintiff's chosen forum, either by filing an answer or by making a motion on other grounds, then personal jurisdiction is established by the defendant's general appearance. If the defendant thinks the venue is improper, or that the court's power was asserted improperly because of a problem with the summons or with how or where it was served, then the defendant should raise that objection right away. If the defendant does not raise those objections at the outset, then it makes sense to allow the litigation to proceed in that forum.

Needless to say, you don't want to waive defenses that might be available to your client. At least, you don't want to waive them unintentionally. If you represent a defendant, your client needs you to worry about the risk of waiver under Rule 12(h)(1) as you decide what defenses to assert in your answer or in a motion to dismiss. But if you do mess up and realize your mistake promptly enough, you may be able to fix the problem by amending your answer to include the omitted defense. Under Rule 12(h)(1) a party waives a defense by "(A) omitting it from a motion in the circumstances described in rule 12(g)(2); or (B) failing to either: (i) make it by motion under this rule; or (ii) include it in a responsive pleading or in an amendment allowed by Rule 15(a)(1) as a matter of course."

RULE 12(h) SUMMARY

(1) Defenses that are waived if omitted from pre-answer motion or answer:
- Personal jurisdiction (Rule 12(b)(2))
- Venue (Rule 12(b)(3))
- Process (Rule 12(b)(4))
- Service of process (Rule 12(b)(5))

(2) Defenses that may be raised later by motion or at trial:
- Failure to state a claim (Rule 12(b)(6))
- Indispensable party (Rule 12(b)(7))

(3) Defense that is never waived:
- Jurisdiction (Rule 12(b)(1))

Rule 12(h)(2) addresses the defenses of failure to state a claim upon which relief can be granted (Rule 12(b)(6)) and failure to join an indispensable party (Rule 12(b)(7)). These defenses, if not raised in the pleadings or in a pre-answer motion, may nonetheless be raised in a motion for judgment on the pleadings or may be raised at trial. Ordinarily defendants ought to raise these defenses in a pre-answer motion or in the answer, and the rule imposes some limitation on when these defenses can be raised later on, but the important point of Rule 12(h)(2) is that these two defenses are not waived by their omission from the pre-answer motion or answer. To understand why this makes sense, imagine if the rule were otherwise, and these defenses were waived because a defendant failed to assert them at the first opportunity.

Consider the Rule 12(b)(6) defense—failure to state a claim. If a defendant has a valid defense of failure to state a claim upon which relief can be granted, wouldn't it be nonsensical to say that the defense can be waived? By definition, that defense means that the plaintiff does not have a cognizable legal claim. Waiver of the defense of failure to state a claim would require the court to ignore the substantive merits of the lawsuit. Next, consider the Rule 12(b)(7) defense—failure to join a required party. The idea of compulsory party joinder is that there are some parties without whom it would be unjust to proceed. Sometimes this does not become clear until the litigation is underway. Rule 12(h)(2) ensures that party concerns can be raised later even if omitted from the defendant's answer or pre-answer motion.

Rule 12(h)(3) pertains to subject matter jurisdiction. It says, simply, "If the court determines at any time that it lacks subject-matter jurisdiction, the court must dismiss the action." Rule 12(h)(3) gives procedural form to the fundamental idea, expressed in Chapter 1, that subject matter jurisdiction cannot be waived by the parties. Subject matter jurisdiction goes to the institutional capacity of the court itself. For federal courts, the limits on subject matter jurisdiction protect the constitutional values of separation of powers (making sure that the courts do not encroach on the power of the legislative and executive branches) and federalism (making sure that the federal government does not encroach on the powers of the states). The bottom line: Regardless of whether the defendant makes a Rule 12(b)(1) motion to dismiss for lack of subject matter jurisdiction, and regardless of whether the defendant or any other party objects to subject matter jurisdiction in their pleadings, the court *must* dismiss the case if the court realizes that it lacks subject matter jurisdiction.

(5) Claims by Defendants

In addition to the various responses defendants can make to a complaint—admissions and denials, affirmative defenses, motions to dismiss, and motions to strike or for a more definite statement—there are three types of *claims* defendants can assert when they have been sued: counterclaims, crossclaims, and third-party claims. I'll explain each of these in Chapter 7 when we look at joinder of claims and parties, but a quick definition now will help you understand the full range of options available to a defendant in reaction to plaintiff's pleading.

A **counterclaim** is a claim that the defendant asserts against the plaintiff. Federal Rules 13(a) and 13(b) provide for both compulsory and permissive counterclaims. Be careful not to confuse counterclaims with defenses. A counterclaim is not an assertion that the defendant is *not liable* to the plaintiff; that would be a defense. Rather, a counterclaim is an assertion that the *plaintiff* is liable to the *defendant*; it is a separate claim for relief. Other than the fact that it is asserted by a defendant, a counterclaim is just like a claim asserted in an original complaint and must comply with the pleading requirements of Rule 8(a). That said, you should also know that as a matter of litigation strategy, counterclaims often serve to emphasize the defendant's denials and defenses. For example, in an automobile accident case in which each party accuses the other of running the red light at an intersection, the defendant could deny that she acted negligently, assert the affirmative defense of contributory or comparative

"What better way to express your feelings about that certain someone's suit than to slap him with a massive countersuit?"

negligence, and assert a counterclaim against the plaintiff for the defendant's own injuries and property damage. As a strategic matter, the denial, affirmative defense, and counterclaim—all of which would be included in the defendant's answer—each reemphasize the core message of defendant's responsive pleading: "The accident was plaintiff's fault, not mine."

A **crossclaim** is a claim asserted against a co-party. If a plaintiff sues multiple defendants, for example, a defendant may assert a crossclaim against a co-defendant. Under Rule 13(g), crossclaims are permitted only if they arise out of the same transaction or occurrence as the original claim.

A **third-party claim**, also known as *impleader*, is a device by which a defendant can bring in an additional party (a third-party defendant) and assert that if the defendant is held liable to the plaintiff, then the third-party defendant should be liable to reimburse the defendant for some or all of what the defendant has to pay the plaintiff. Rule 14 makes it clear that third-party claims may be used only for claims such as contribution or indemnification, in which one party must pay another party who was held liable. In a product liability case, for example, if the plaintiff originally sues only the retailer, the retailer may assert a third-party claim for indemnification against the manufacturer of the allegedly defective product.

In Chapter 7, you will learn about these devices as mechanisms for joining additional claims and parties in litigation. Here, we view them as parts of a defendant's overall set of reactions to a plaintiff's complaint. Whereas denials and defenses aim to *avoid* liability, these three devices—counterclaims, crossclaims, and third-party claims—aim to *impose* liability on others or to *shift* potential liability onto other parties. Defendants use

Sidebar

TRANSSUBSTANTIVE PROCEDURE

At common law, each form of action entailed its own rules of pleading and procedure. When Rule 1 of the Federal Rules of Civil Procedure announced that the rules would govern procedure "in all civil actions and proceedings," it marked a fundamental change. The federal rules are *transsubstantive*. That is, the same procedural rules apply across all substantive areas of law. The Federal Rules of Civil Procedure apply to every civil lawsuit in federal court, whether the case involves civil rights, breach of contract, antitrust, or anything else. You've already seen at least one exception, however. Rule 9(b) requires more specific pleading for fraud than for other types of allegations. You'll find other examples of non-transsubstantive procedure. For example, certain civil rights statutes and case law impose burdens of proof that shift from one party to another.

counterclaims to impose liability on the plaintiff; they use crossclaims to impose liability on co-defendants or to shift liability to them; and they use third-party claims to shift liability to parties who had not originally been sued by the plaintiff.

D. Reply and Other Pleadings

Most often, the pleadings consist of a complaint and an answer. Some cases, however, entail additional pleadings. If the defendant asserts a counterclaim in the answer, for example, the plaintiff files a **reply**, which may contain admissions, denials, and defenses just like an answer to an original claim. Under Rule 7(a), the court also has power to order a reply to an answer if the court thinks it would be useful. If a party asserts a crossclaim, then the party against whom it is asserted files an *answer to the crossclaim*. Similarly, if a party is brought in by way of a third-party claim, the party files a *third-party answer*.

E. Amendment

Can a party change its mind about what's in the pleadings? Sometimes, on further reflection, parties would like to edit their complaint or answer. They might wish to delete parts of their pleadings, or maybe there's something they'd like to add. Perhaps through legal research they have learned of an additional claim that they failed to include in the complaint, or a defense that they did not mention in the answer. Maybe the discovery process has turned up factual information that affects the party's factual allegations.

    Amendment of pleadings comes up a lot. Given the dynamic nature of litigation, it should be no surprise that parties' positions on the legal and factual issues in a case may develop during the course of the lawsuit. The pleading rules make amendment a relatively easy process. In complex cases, especially, it is not uncommon to see pleadings with names like "Seventh Amended Complaint" or "Fourth Amended Answer and Counterclaim."

    Remember the basic idea behind notice pleading: Parties are not expected to know everything at the outset of the litigation. The pleading standard of the federal rules generally allows parties to plead their claims and defenses without lots of detail, and increases the chance of deciding cases on the merits rather than on technicalities. The liberal approach of notice pleading was a reaction against the "gotcha!" possibilities of common law pleading. The same reasoning leads to a liberal attitude toward amendment of pleadings.

(1) Amending the Pleadings

Rule 15(a) reflects the modern attitude of liberal amendment of pleading. It addresses *amendment as a matter of course, amendment by consent,* and *amendment by leave of court.* All are easy.

Amendment as a Matter of Course. Often, a party may amend its pleading without asking the court's permission or the other party's consent. Rule 15(a) allows a party to amend its pleading once "as a matter of course" either 21 days after serving it or 21 days after the opposing party's response. This means, first, that a party is free to amend a complaint or answer within 21 days of serving it. The idea is to allow parties to correct their own mistakes promptly. It also means that alternatively a party can amend its complaint or counterclaim within 21 days of receiving the opposing party's answer or a responsive Rule 12 motion. This provides an opportunity to tweak the complaint when the party becomes aware of the adversary's response. Under these circumstances, a party simply files the amended pleading—no special permission needed.

Amendment as a matter of course may be used not only for complaints and other pleadings with claims, but also for answers. Since ordinarily answers don't elicit further responsive pleadings, the time limit for amending an answer cannot be measured by whether a responsive pleading has been served. Therefore, Rule 15(a) states that a party may amend as a matter of course "within 20 days after serving the pleading if a responsive pleading is not allowed and the action is not yet on the trial calendar." In other words, you can amend an answer as a matter of course as long as you do it within 20 days, but not if the case is already scheduled for trial.

Amendment by Consent. Any pleading may be amended if the adverse party consents to the amendment in writing. It's an adversary system, after all, and if the other party does not mind, it's hard to see any reason not to allow amendment.

Amendment by Leave of Court. If it's too late to amend as a matter of course, and if the opposing party won't consent, a party must ask the court's permission to amend a pleading. The party makes a *motion for leave to amend* the pleading. Rule 15(a) instructs that the court "should freely give leave when justice so requires." What a funny way to phrase a rule. It does not simply lay out the standard—"when justice so requires"—for deciding whether to grant a motion for leave to amend. Rather, it encourages judges to grant such motions by adding the words "freely give." It says, in essence: "Go ahead, judge. Grant the motion. Let them amend their pleadings, if it's going to help them get their pleadings right." These are not the forms of action of common law pleading. If amended pleadings will help the court reach a just result in the case, modern pleading rules generally allow parties to make whatever changes they need so that the court can resolve the dispute on the merits.

(2) Relation Back

The hard part about amended pleadings is not really about the pleadings at all, but rather about the statute of limitations. Suppose a party wishes to amend its pleading to assert a new claim against a current party, or to add a claim by or against a new party, but the time for filing the claim has expired under the applicable statute of limitations. Maybe it was carelessness that led to the error or omission in the original pleading, or maybe the party learned of the error or omission from information that came out during the discovery process. The pleader argues that it's simply a matter of amending an existing pleading. The opposing party argues that the limitations period has expired, and therefore the amendment should not be permitted.

That's where the doctrine of **relation back** comes into play. The party seeking to amend the pleading argues that the amended pleading should "relate back" to the date of the original pleading, and therefore does not violate the statute of limitations.

Usually, invocations of the relation back doctrine concern the amendment of a plaintiff's complaint, but the doctrine can apply to defenses as well as counterclaims and other claims for relief.

The timeline for relation back problems always looks like this:

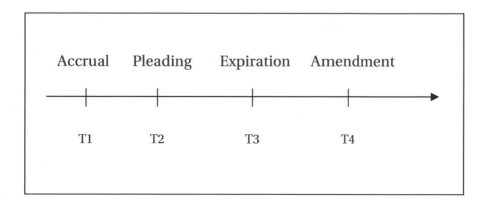

First, an occurrence gives rise to a claim. That's the moment when the claim *accrues*, which we'll call T1. The time limit for filing the claim runs from the date of accrual. If the applicable statute of limitations is two years, the party must file the claim within two years from the accrual date. We'll use T2 for the date when the pleading is filed. After the lawsuit gets started, the limitations period expires. This date—T3—may occur quite soon after the lawsuit begins because plaintiffs sometimes file their cases shortly before time runs out. As the lawsuit proceeds, a party may realize that it should have asserted different claims or named different parties, either in addition to or instead of those that were pleaded. The party, at time T4, seeks to amend its pleading to add a new claim or party. The question: If a claim would be time-barred under the statute of limitations, should a party nonetheless be allowed to amend its pleading to assert that claim, as long as the original pleading was filed within the limitations period?

Imagine the plaintiff arguing with the defendant over whether the court should permit the amendment:

Plaintiff: It's an amended pleading, and courts should *freely give* leave to amend.

Defendant: Yes, but in this case, your amendment is *futile* because your new claim would be dismissed under the statute of limitations. Your claim is untimely because you didn't file it before T3.

Plaintiff: It's not untimely. Even though today is T4, the amendment *relates back* to the complaint I filed on T2. For purposes of the statute of limitations, the court should treat my amended pleading as if it were dated T2.

Defendant: No, your amendment should not be treated as if it were filed on T2 because the claim it raises differs from your original pleading, and the policy behind the statute of limitations is to protect me from stale claims like this one.

A federal court would resolve this argument by referring to Rule 15(c), which states the circumstances under which "[a]n amendment to a pleading relates back to the date of the original pleading." Relation back of a claim is permitted under Rule 15(c)(1)(B) if "the amendment asserts a claim or defense that arose out of the conduct, transaction, or occurrence set out — or attempted to be set out — in the original pleading."

Courts consider whether the original and amended claims are closely enough related so that allowing the amended pleading to relate back would not violate the policies underlying the statute of limitations. The statute of limitations protects defendants from having to defend claims after memories have faded and other evidence has become unavailable. But if the amended pleading closely tracks the original pleading, then the defendant cannot complain of inadequate warning to start gathering the relevant evidence. The statute of limitations also provides *repose* for defendants; after a set period of time, the defendant need not worry about the potential claim hanging over the defendant's head. But if the plaintiff filed the original complaint against the defendant within the statute of limitations, then the defendant can hardly feel relaxed about the situation. Therefore, relation back depends on whether the amended claim arose out of the same underlying occurrence as the original pleading.

The most problematic relation back situations involve amended pleadings that add a new party or change the name of a party. Think about the policies underlying the statute of limitations. To what extent does the relation back doctrine make sense when applied to a party who was not sued within the limitations period and who now may be dragged into a lawsuit by an amended pleading?

Defendant: Your claim against me is time-barred.
Plaintiff: No, it's not, because my amended complaint relates back to my original complaint, which I filed within the statute of limitations.
Defendant: You didn't file any complaint *against me* within the statute. When the limitations period expired, I stopped keeping relevant evidence and started enjoying the repose that I'm entitled to. Just because you filed a lawsuit against *someone else*, that doesn't mean I should lose the protection of the statute of limitations.

This is why courts are much more grudging about applying relation back to amendments that change the name of parties. If you want to amend a pleading to add a new party or change the name of a party, and you need relation back because the limitations period has passed, you will have to show that it was merely a case of mistaken identity and the new party already knew about the lawsuit and knew or should have known that it was the intended target.

Rule 15(c)(1)(C), which governs relation back involving a new party, requires careful attention because it's easy to misunderstand. It lays out three requirements that must be met in order to get the benefit of relation back for an amendment that changes the party against whom a claim asserted. First, the amendment must satisfy Rule 15(c)(1)(B); in other words, it must arise out of the same conduct or occurrence as the original pleading. Second, within the 120-day period for service of process after the original pleading was filed, the new party must have known about the lawsuit so that it will not be at a disadvantage in defending the lawsuit. Third, it must be the case that within the same period, the new party "knew or should have known that the action would have been brought against it, but for a mistake concerning the proper party's identity." In practice, this means that if you failed to join a party within the statute of limitations, you're probably out of luck. You cannot use relation back to add a new party to the lawsuit if the party didn't already know about the lawsuit. Rule 15(c)(1)(C) relation back works best for correcting simple misnomers, where the defendant actually was served with the complaint but the name was slightly incorrect, or for cases in which an amendment replaces a corporate defendant with its corporate parent or subsidiary.

F. Sanctions and Ethical Constraints

Modern pleading rules make pleading relatively easy and do not require a pleader to know everything at the outset of the litigation. But that does not mean that you can say whatever you want. To the contrary. The pleading standard allows a pleader to choose not to include specific legal theories or detailed factual accounts, but whatever the pleader *does* choose to plead must have at least some basis in law and fact.

Rule 11 says that when you sign a pleading, motion, or other paper, or when you file it or present it to the court, you are certifying that it is not frivolous. If a lawyer or party violates this rule by presenting a paper with legally or factually baseless contentions, the court may punish the violator by imposing **sanctions**. It's an important rule, so let's be precise about exactly what it states.

The heart of the rule is 11(b), which explains what is entailed every time a lawyer or party signs or presents a pleading, motion, or other paper. Rule 11(b) states that the lawyer or party "certifies that to the best of the person's knowledge, information, and belief, formed after an inquiry reasonable under the circumstances. . . ." Stop right there. That's the first requirement — "an inquiry reasonable under the circumstances." You may not submit a pleading or other paper without first making a reasonable inquiry into the facts and law. Sometimes, this may require no more than asking appropriate questions to the client to elicit the facts and reviewing essential documents or other evidence. Other times, however, a reasonable inquiry may require more extensive factual investigation or legal research.

Now, what exactly are you certifying, to the best of your knowledge? That's what subsections 11(b)(1) through (4) spell out.

> ### RULE 11(b) SUMMARY
>
> ■ Inquiry reasonable under the circumstances.
> (1) No *improper purpose.*
> (2) Claims and defenses have nonfrivolous *legal basis.*
> (3) Factual allegations have reasonable *factual basis.*
> (4) *Denials* have reasonable factual basis.

Under Rule 11(b)(1), the presenting lawyer or party is certifying that the pleading, motion, or other paper "is not being presented for any improper purpose, such as to harass, cause unnecessary delay, or needlessly increase the cost of litigation." *Any* pleading or motion increases the cost of litigation, of course, and to a party being sued, it always feels like harassment. The point of Rule 11(b)(1) is not to undo the adversary system, but rather to emphasize that pleadings or motions may be presented only if the party actually seeks the relief requested in the pleading or motion, and not if the sole purpose is to harass, embarrass, intimidate, or to make the litigation needlessly burdensome.

Rule 11(b)(2) prohibits *legally* frivolous claims and defenses. The lawyer or party presenting the paper is certifying that "the claims, defenses, and other legal contentions are warranted by existing law or by a nonfrivolous argument for extending, modifying, or reversing existing law or for establishing new law." If you don't have a legal basis to back up your claim, defense, motion, or other legal contention, then you are not allowed to present it. The "inquiry reasonable under the circumstances" requires reasonable legal research if you are unsure of whether the law supports your position. But if you've got a good argument that the law *should* support your position, do not allow Rule 11 to deter you from asserting reasonable, creative legal arguments. The rule's language about "nonfrivolous argument for extending, modifying, or reversing existing law or for establishing new law" is important. Thurgood Marshall was not acting improperly when he argued, as the plaintiff's lawyer in *Brown v. Board of Education*,[12] that racial segregation in education is unconstitutional despite precedent that permitted "separate but equal" schools. One of the dangers of Rule 11, if judges do not respect Rule 11(b)(2)'s protection of reasonable legal arguments, is that sanctions could be used to chill creative lawyering that seeks to move the law forward.

Rules 11(b)(3) and 11(b)(4) prohibit *factually* baseless allegations and denials. Although notice pleading does not expect litigants to have gathered all of their evidence before the lawsuit begins, parties and their lawyers *are* expected not to allege things in their pleadings unless they have evidence to back up their statements or have at least made sufficient inquiry so that they have a basis to expect to find evidentiary support for the allegations. Rule 11(b)(3) concerns factual contentions: "[T]he factual contentions have evidentiary support or, if specifically so identified, will likely have evidentiary support after a reasonable opportunity for further investigation or discovery." Rule 11(b)(4) concerns denials: "[T]he denials of factual contentions are warranted on the evidence or, if specifically so identified, are reasonably based on belief or a lack of information." Remember that under Rule 8, allegations of the complaint are ordinarily deemed admitted unless they are denied in the defendant's answer. This puts significant pressure on defendants to deny the plaintiffs' allegations. But Rule 11 imposes a check on careless denials. Denials must be based on the evidence; if the party lacks information to be able to admit or deny an allegation, the party may say so and treat it as a denial under Rule 8(b), but may not simply deny the opposing party's contentions without a factual basis for doing so.

Notice what Rule 11 does not say. It does not talk about "good faith" or "bad faith." With the exception of Rule 11(b)(1)'s treatment of improper purpose, the

---

[12]347 U.S. 483 (1954).

prohibitions of Rule 11(b) are not about subjective state of mind. The issue is whether the allegations, claims, and defenses have an objectively nonfrivolous basis in fact and law, not whether the person's intentions were good. As some courts have noted, Rule 11 does not contain a "good heart, empty head" defense.

Notice, too, that the requirements of Rule 11 are rather modest. Contentions must have *some* factual and legal basis, but that doesn't mean they all have to be winners. Every day, thousands of plaintiffs and defendants lose cases, but that does not mean that their positions were frivolous. It does not violate Rule 11(b)(2) to assert a claim or defense supported by some legal basis or reasonable argument, even if the position probably will lose because the weight of legal authority falls on the other side. Nor does it violate Rule 11(b)(3) to make allegations that have some factual basis, such as the client's plausible account of the facts, even if the contrary evidence appears stronger. Rule 11, in other words, obligates the lawyer to make a reasonable inquiry and to refrain from making baseless assertions, but it does not obligate the lawyer to serve as judge and jury rather than as the client's advocate.

By the way, don't be confused by Rule 11(d), which declares that Rule 11's requirements do not apply to the discovery process. This does *not* mean that it's OK to make factually baseless or legally frivolous discovery requests, responses, objections, and motions. It's simply a matter of the structure of the civil rules. The discovery rules contain their own provisions concerning certification and sanctions. If you look at Rule 26(g), you'll see that it reads almost exactly like Rule 11, and Rule 37 empowers courts to impose sanctions for discovery violations.

If a lawyer or party violates Rule 11, the court may impose sanctions such as a monetary penalty to be paid to the court, nonmonetary directives, or an order directing the violator to pay the other side's legal fees or expenses. Rule 11(c) empowers the court to impose sanctions on the attorneys, law firms, or parties that bear responsibility for the violation. Although the rule permits sanctions against parties as well as lawyers, Rule 11(c)(5) specifies that "the court must not impose a monetary sanction . . . against a represented party for violating Rule 11(b)(2)." There's logic behind this limitation. For factually baseless allegations (Rule 11(b)(3)) or denials (Rule 11(b)(4)), the client may bear some or all of the responsibility because lawyers often rely in part on their clients' accounts of the facts. Likewise, the client may be wholly or partly responsible for papers submitted for an improper purpose such as harassment (Rule 11(b)(1)). But if a party is represented by a lawyer, then avoiding frivolous *legal* contentions (Rule 11(b)(2)) should be the lawyer's responsibility.

The sanctions provisions of Rule 11 have blown back and forth with the political winds of procedure. A few decades ago, Rule 11 was largely toothless and rarely invoked. The rule was toughened up in 1983, above all by amending Rule 11(c) to state that the court "shall" (rather than "may") impose sanctions for a violation. Over the following decade, courts and lawyers used Rule 11 more aggressively. They used it so much, in fact, that critics charged that Rule 11 motions had become a routine tactical maneuver and fee-shifting device, that lawyers were spending too much time fighting over Rule 11 issues rather than litigating the merits of the case, and that the rule was having a chilling effect on civil rights cases. To address these problems, the rule was amended again in 1993. The word "shall" was changed back to "may," reinstating judicial discretion over whether to impose sanctions. The amendments specified that the sanction "shall be limited to what is sufficient to deter repetition of such conduct or comparable conduct," and made it clear that courts should not automatically impose attorneys' fees as the sanction. If the rule lacked teeth until

1983, perhaps we can say that in 1993, its teeth were filed down because they'd gotten too sharp.

The most intriguing innovation of the 1993 amendments to Rule 11 is the *safe harbor provision* of Rule 11(c)(2). The provision was added to address the concern that Rule 11 motions had become a tactical game in which parties engaged in finger pointing to gain the court's favor and leverage in the litigation. Under the safe harbor provision, a party must *serve* a Rule 11 motion on the other party at least 21 days before the party may *file* the motion with the court. Clever, isn't it? It means that parties cannot go crying to the court every time they think the other side did something baseless. They can write their Rule 11 motion for sanctions, but they can't present it to the court unless they've given the motion to the other party and then given the party an opportunity to withdraw or amend the offending paper.

SUMMARY

■ The pleadings—a complaint, an answer, and, in some cases, a reply—set forth the parties' claims and defenses.

■ A complaint in federal court must state the basis for jurisdiction, a short and plain statement of the claim, and a demand for judgment.

■ Under the notice pleading standard, a complaint must include allegations sufficient to notify the defendant of the basis for the claim and sufficient to show that, if the allegations are proved, the plaintiff would be entitled to relief.

■ A complaint must include sufficient factual allegations to show plausibility.

■ On a motion to dismiss for failure to state a claim, the court assumes that the factual allegations of the complaint are true and asks whether they state a valid claim.

■ Allegations of fraud must be pleaded with particularity.

■ In the answer, a defendant must respond to each allegation by admitting it, denying it, or stating that the defendant lacks sufficient information to admit or deny the allegation.

■ In the answer, a defendant may assert affirmative defenses, which are waived if not asserted.

■ Before submitting an answer, a defendant may raise certain defenses by motion, including lack of jurisdiction and failure to state a claim.

■ The defenses of personal jurisdiction, venue, and service of process are waived if not asserted by the defendant in a pre-answer motion or, if the defendant does not file such a motion, in the answer.

■ A party may amend its pleading once as a matter of course within 21 days after serving it, or within 21 days of the other party's response; or a party may amend its pleading with the adverse party's consent or by leave of court.

■ If the statute of limitations has expired on a claim that a pleader wishes to add by amendment, but would have been timely if asserted in the original pleading, the amendment may be permitted if the claim "relates back" to the original pleading.

■ Lawyers and parties may be sanctioned for pleadings or other papers that contain factually baseless allegations or denials, that contain legally frivolous assertions, or that are put forth for an improper purpose such as delay or harassment.

CONNECTIONS

Subject Matter Jurisdiction

Careful lawyers think about subject matter jurisdiction when crafting their pleadings. If a plaintiff wishes to bring the action in federal court, the complaint must include sufficient allegations of diversity of citizenship, federal law, or other jurisdictional basis. If a plaintiff wishes to avoid federal court — that is, to make the action nonremovable — then the plaintiff can try to craft a complaint that avoids any basis for federal jurisdiction, for example, by omitting claims that arise under federal law or by demanding less than $75,000 if the parties' citizenship is diverse.

Subject Matter Jurisdiction — Waiver

Rule 12(h)(3) gives procedural form to the fundamental notion that subject matter jurisdiction defines the institutional power of the court and therefore can never be waived by the parties.

Personal Jurisdiction — Waiver

Rule 12(h)(1) requires a party to raise the defense of lack personal jurisdiction in a pretrial motion or in the answer, whichever comes first; otherwise, the defense is waived. This is no mere pleading rule, but follows inevitably from the notion that a general appearance functions as consent to jurisdiction. If a party litigates an action without objecting to the court's jurisdiction, the party has made a general appearance and therefore given the court personal jurisdiction.

Joinder

Joinder of claims and parties means, to a large extent, pleading multiple claims, or claims by and against various parties, as part of the same action. If a plaintiff brings multiple claims under Rule 18, the plaintiff includes those claims in a single complaint. If multiple plaintiffs or defendants are joined in an action under Rule 20, a single complaint names all of the parties.

Discovery

Notice pleading assumes litigants don't have all the information at the outset. Discovery assumes the same thing and enables parties to get the information they need to put flesh on the bones of their pleadings. Pleadings are the gateway to discovery in the sense that a plaintiff earns the right to discovery by submitting a complaint sufficient to survive a motion to dismiss.

Claim Preclusion — Same Claim

The pleadings define the scope of the lawsuit, which can be important when determining whether a subsequent is claim precluded.

Claim Preclusion — On the Merits

A dismissal for failure to state a claim may or may not have claim preclusive effect. It depends on whether the dismissal is a judgment on the merits — that is, whether the court dismisses with or without prejudice. Chapter 11 addresses this question in terms of Rule 41(b) and the *Semtek* case.

Discovery

6

As any litigator will tell you, it's about the facts. Don't let a good legal education fool you into thinking that most cases actually turn on ques-

tions of law. Mastery of the law is important, but when representing clients in the real world, mastery of the facts matters just as much and often much more.

Discovery refers to the process by which a party in a lawsuit forces other parties or witnesses to provide information relevant to the case. Understanding the discovery process requires several steps. You need to know how all of the discovery tools work and how they fit into an overall discovery strategy. In addition, you must grasp the scope of discovery. This entails mastering the legal concepts of relevance, privilege, the work product doctrine, and proportionality. Finally, you need to know how discovery disputes are resolved, including motions to compel, motions for protective orders, and sanctions.

A. DISCOVERY TOOLS

1. Disclosures
2. Interrogatories
3. Depositions
4. Production of Documents, Electronically Stored Information, and Things, and Inspection of Land
5. Physical and Mental Examinations
6. Requests for Admission

A. Discovery Tools

Interrogatories. Oral depositions. Written depositions. Document production. E-discovery. Inspection of things and land. Mental and physical examinations. Requests for admission. Disclosures. The discovery rules hand lawyers a toolbox full of powerful tools for extracting information. Learning to use the discovery devices is a lot like learning to wield a wrench, screwdriver, and hammer. Knowing what a wrench is and how it works is only the first step. You also have to develop a sense of when it is the right tool for the job. You can bang a nail into a wall with your wrench, but it's more effective to do it with a hammer. You get the point: If there is certain information you need in order to represent your client in litigation, there may be

Photo by Per Erik Strandberg

multiple discovery tools in your toolbox that could do the job, but the skilled lawyer knows whether a deposition, interrogatory, document request, informal investigation, or some other device is the most efficient and effective way to get the needed information.

As you learn about each of the discovery devices, keep certain distinctions in mind. Can you use the device to get information only from the other parties in the lawsuit or from anyone who has the information? Can you use it on an unlimited basis, constrained only by your client's budget and the proportionality doctrine, or does the rule impose a limit on the number of uses? Can you use it without seeking permission, or do you need leave of court? To the extent the device elicits answers to questions, are the answers provided directly by witnesses or are they filtered through the language of lawyers?

(1) Disclosures

The mandatory disclosure provisions of Federal Rule of Civil Procedure 26(a) differ from all of the other discovery devices. The difference is so basic that a more precise title for this chapter would have been "Disclosures and Discovery." The discovery devices — interrogatories, depositions, and so on — start with a request from the party seeking the information, and the responding party is obligated to provide information in response to the request. The **mandatory disclosure** provisions require parties to disclose certain information to each other without even being asked.

What must be provided in the mandatory initial disclosures? First, each party must disclose the name and contact information of every witness likely to have discoverable information that the disclosing party may use to support its position. Second, each party must provide a description, by category and location, of all documents and electronically stored information that the disclosing party has and may use to support its claims or defenses. Third, a party seeking damages must provide a computation of each category of damages, along with the material on which the computations are based. Fourth, the parties must disclose any applicable liability insurance policies.

The information in the disclosures is not as extensive as that which is available by using discovery tools, but the disclosures provide a starting point. The idea behind Rule 26(a) is that if basic information would be requested and provided as a matter of course in any lawsuit, it is faster and cheaper to make the disclosure automatic rather than to require parties to plow through the request-and-response process of discovery. Even so, the rule was highly controversial when it was first adopted on an experimental basis in 1993. Many lawyers and some judges objected that the whole idea of mandatory disclosures violated the spirit of the adversary system. Several years later, the rule was modified to make it less objectionable to staunch adversarialists. The amendment limited the witness disclosures and document disclosures to evidence that the disclosing party may use. With this change, Rule 26(a) largely avoids forcing a party to disclose at the outset information that harms the party's own position. Of course, the party will have to reveal harmful information if asked about it in interrogatories, at depositions, or by document requests, but at least the party can withhold the damaging information until the adversary asks for it.

Rule 26, in combination with other rules, sets up rather elaborate provisions for the timing of the disclosures. A judge typically issues a scheduling order at a scheduling conference within 90 days after the defendant files the answer and within 120 days after filing the complaint. Before issuing the scheduling order, however, the judge must review the parties' discovery plan. To formulate a discovery plan, the parties hold a discovery conference at least 21 days before the scheduling conference and submit their discovery plan within 14 days after the discovery conference. The mandatory initial disclosures occur either at the discovery conference or within 14 days afterwards. Generally, parties cannot initiate discovery efforts until after they have met at the discovery conference.

In addition to the initial disclosures, Rule 26(a) requires *expert disclosures* and *pretrial disclosures*. These are mandatory disclosures like the initial disclosures of Rule 26(a)(1), but they occur later in the litigation process as the parties are getting ready for trial. Rule 26(a)(2) addresses expert disclosures. If a party plans to use an expert witness at trial, then the party must disclose the identity of that expert to the other parties, along with a written report from the expert stating the expert's opinions, qualifications, and other information. The expert disclosures reduce surprise at trial and give opposing parties the opportunity to prepare for cross-examination or counter-testimony. Pretrial disclosures, addressed in Rule 26(a)(3), occur shortly before trial. Each party provides the others with a list of witnesses the party expects to call at trial, depositions the party plans to present as evidence at trial, and documents, exhibits, and summaries of any other evidence they plan to offer.

(2) Interrogatories

Written questions, written answers. Rule 33 permits each party to serve each other party with a limited number of **interrogatories**, and the responding party must answer in writing and under oath. If the responding party has the answer within its knowledge or control, then it must provide that answer unless it asserts an objection such as irrelevance, privilege, or undue burden.

When thinking about how to use interrogatories, keep in mind who will probably write the answers. Interrogatory answers tend to be drafted by the responding party's attorney. The substance of the answers comes from the responding parties, who are under oath to provide correct answers to the best of their knowledge, but the actual language is usually filtered through the lawyers. Fuzzy questions generate unhelpful responses. Instead, use interrogatories for specific, factual information in the other party's possession. Don't use an interrogatory to ask: "Was your car in good condition at the time of the accident?" Do use an interrogatory to ask: "On what dates in the past five years has your car been serviced, who provided the service, and what services were performed?" Don't ask: "Does your company engage in employment discrimination?" Do ask: "State the number of employees in management positions, by race and gender, from January 1, 2010, to the present." For getting statistical data or similar factual information, interrogatories can't be beat. They are cheap and efficient, they provide written answers to your questions under oath, and the responding party has the opportunity to look things up to provide accurate information. They do not, however, give you an opportunity for follow-up questions as in oral depositions, so you'll get nowhere with interrogatories that leave room for evasive answers.

Sometimes lawyers use interrogatories to ask about the other party's contentions in the case. For example, an interrogatory might say, "Please state all facts upon which you rely to support the allegation in paragraph 5 of the Complaint that defendant acted negligently." These are known as *contention interrogatories*, and they are what Rule 33 is referring to when it says that an "interrogatory is not objectionable merely because it asks for an opinion or contention that relates to fact or the application of law to fact."

Rule 33 limits interrogatories to 25 questions, unless the parties stipulate otherwise or the court orders that the number be changed. In complex cases, it makes sense for parties to agree to a higher number, as interrogatories provide a relatively cheap way for both sides to obtain information. The rule makes it clear that you can't circumvent the limit by breaking each interrogatory into multiple subparts; each discreet subpart counts as one of the 25 interrogatories, regardless of how they are numbered. Interrogatories, unlike some other discovery devices, are limited to the parties in the case. Each party may serve interrogatories on each other party, but to get information from nonparties, you must use other devices such as depositions and document requests.

(3) Depositions

In a **deposition**, an attorney poses questions to a witness and the witness answers those questions under oath. Generally, a court reporter makes a verbatim transcript of the questions and answers; sometimes the deposition is videotaped. Of all the discovery devices, a deposition looks the most like a trial, except that it is not at the courthouse (depositions usually are held in conference rooms at lawyers' offices) and there's no judge (except in rare situations like President Clinton's deposition when he was sued by Paula Jones for sexual harassment).

To depose a witness (who is called the *deponent*), a party serves a *deposition notice*, alerting the deponent and the other parties of the time and place of the deposition. In lawyer speak, you "notice" the deposition. The rules set parameters to avoid making the process too inconvenient for the deponent, but depositions nonetheless can be a burdensome process. At the deposition, the deponent may be represented by a lawyer, who may object to questions. Except for objections on grounds of privilege, however, the lawyer generally may not instruct the deponent not to answer the question. Instead, if the questioner persists with the question under objection, the deponent is expected to answer, and the lawyers may make motions to the court afterwards to sort out whether certain questions were permissible and whether the answers may be used. Rule 30 limits each party to ten depositions, and limits each deposition to one seven-hour day, but like nearly all the details of the discovery rules, these limits can be altered by stipulation or by court order. You may depose a party simply by serving notice of the deposition, but to depose a witness who is not a party to the lawsuit, you need a subpoena to compel the person's attendance at the deposition.

Depositions have several advantages over interrogatories. First, depositions enable you to get answers straight from the horse's mouth, in contrast to interrogatories, which give the opposing lawyer time to phrase each answer in the least damaging way. At a deposition, you ask your question and the witness gives an answer in his or her own words. This does not mean that answers are totally unrehearsed, as deponents commonly meet with lawyers to prepare in advance, but at least it's a less filtered answer than an interrogatory response. A related disadvantage, however, is that unlike interrogatories, depositions do not give deponents the chance to look things up or to double-check information, so interrogatories tend to work better for obtaining hard-to-remember detailed information. Look at any deposition transcript and you will see that one of the most common phrases is "I don't recall."

Second, depositions give you the opportunity to size up the adversary's witnesses, to see how compelling they would be on the witness stand at trial.

Third, at a deposition you can ask follow-up questions. If—make that *when*—the deponent tries to be evasive, you can rephrase your question as necessary until you get the information you seek. When a deponent gives an incomplete response, you can follow up with further questions to nail down the information. You can't do that with interrogatories. When an interrogatory response is evasive or incomplete, you can send another set of interrogatories (if you haven't reached the limit yet), but that's a pretty slow and unsatisfying way to get a complete answer. Fourth, at a deposition you can make on-the-spot decisions about where to go with your questions. A deponent's answers may lead you to fruitful lines of inquiry that you had not thought of.

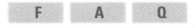

Q: Do lawyers depose every person who has relevant information?

A: No, not even close, for at least three reasons. First, the rules impose a presumptive limit of ten depositions per party. Second, depositions are expensive, so unless the stakes are high, some depositions aren't worth the cost. Third—and this part is obvious to every lawyer but not so obvious to many law students—lawyers generally do not depose their own witnesses. A deposition is a tool for forcing a witness to answer your questions. If you need information from your own client or from a friendly witness, all you need to do is ask. An exception is if your witness may be unavailable for trial—perhaps the witness is ill or will be out of the country during the trial—in which case a deposition offers a way to preserve the witness's testimony for use at trial.

A word about cost. Depositions may be the most powerful pretrial tool for extracting information, but they are also the most expensive. To take a deposition, you need the room, court reporter, and transcripts; each side pays its lawyers for their time; and, depending on the location, there may be lawyer travel expenses as well. In big cases, there may be multiple lawyers for each of multiple parties. I've been at depositions with over a dozen lawyers sitting around a conference table with the deponent and court reporter, some lawyers asking the questions, some defending, and some just there to observe and to ask follow-up questions if necessary. To think of the number of billable hours is painful (at least for the clients). Attorneys planning discovery need to think about the stakes of the case, as well as the importance of the witness, when deciding whether to take a particular deposition.

Frequently, parties need to obtain information from a corporation or other organization but do not know the name of the individual within the company who possesses the relevant knowledge. For a deposition, you need to pose your questions to an actual human being, but what if you don't know which human to ask? You need information about the company's chemical disposal policies, for example, but you do not know the name of the employee who bears that responsibility. This is where Rule 30(b)(6) comes in handy. Rule 30(b)(6) allows you to send a deposition notice to the company describing the topics to be addressed in the deposition, and the company must identify and produce a deponent with the knowledge to speak about those topics. As an alternative, you could use interrogatories to elicit the names of employ-ees with specific responsibilities, and then you could notice the depositions of those individuals. The interrogatory-to-deposition approach is unavailable, however, if the company is not a party, and in any event Rule 30(b)(6) depositions accomplish the same objective somewhat more directly.

When lawyers talk about depositions, they nearly always mean depositions by oral examination, the type of deposition governed by Rule 30. But there's also another type of deposition, found in Rule 31: the deposition by written questions. Depositions by written questions look like a cross between a deposition and an interrogatory. A party delivers the questions to the court reporter, who in turn asks the deponent the questions and makes a verbatim transcript of the answers under oath. This process obviously loses one of the main advantages of depositions, the ability to ask follow-up questions. Rarer than oral depositions, written questions are a way to get basic factual information, especially from nonparties.

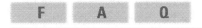

Q: What's an affidavit? Is it part of discovery?

A: An affidavit is simply a sworn written statement. It can be used to indicate the availability of evidence for various purposes during the litigation process, such as to support or oppose a summary judgment motion. Affidavits bear a similarity to interrogatory or deposition responses — both involve statements of fact under oath — but here's the key difference. If you need a sworn statement from your own client or a friendly witness, you just ask. That's an affidavit. If you need a sworn statement from an opposing party or a witness who chooses not to cooperate with you, you need some device that legally obligates the person to provide the information. That's what interrogatories and depositions are for.

(4) Production of Documents, Electronically Stored Information, and Things, and Inspection of Land

Unlike depositions and interrogatories, which involve asking questions and getting answers, Rule 34 requests are all about getting access to stuff. Before turning to documents and data, let's start with tangible things and land. Some disputes involve physical evidence. In an auto accident case, a party may need access to the other party's crumpled vehicle and the opportunity to inspect it with a mechanic. In a pharmaceutical product liability case, it could be a bottle of pills. Rule 34 allows a party to "inspect, copy, test, or sample" items that are in another's "possession, custody, or control." Similarly, some disputes require inspection of property. A party may need to enter the opposing party's factory. Or in a toxic spill case, a party may need to test soil on another's land. Rule 34 provides the discovery tool for "entry onto designated land or other property possessed or controlled by the responding party, so that the requesting party may inspect, measure, survey, photograph, test, or sample the property or any designated object or oper-ation on it."

But mostly, Rule 34 requests are about getting documents and their electronic equivalents. Nearly all litigation involves documentary evidence, although the amount varies widely. Depending on the type of dispute, **document production** may include business records, medical records, e-mails, memos, investigation reports, personnel records, contracts, deeds, or anything else in which information is stored on paper or electronically. The rule describes "any designated documents or electronically stored information — including writings, drawings, graphs, charts, photographs, sound recordings, images, and other data or data compilations — stored in any medium from which information can be obtained."

Some document requests name particular documents that are needed, such as a specific contract. More often, the requests identify categories of documents or subject matter, such as "all documents relating to the proposed joint venture between plaintiff and defendant." The scary thing about drafting document requests is this: Frame your request too narrowly, and you might miss the critical piece of evidence; frame your request too broadly, and you might spend weeks in a warehouse full of useless documents.

Discovery of electronically stored information — or **e-discovery**, as many lawyers call it — unsurprisingly has become a dominant aspect of Rule 34 discovery. Until recently, lawyers simply treated electronic information as "documents" within the rule's meaning. The term "electronically stored information" was added to Rule 34 in 2006 to leave no doubt about the discoverability of electronic information and to establish a basis for several special e-discovery rules. For purposes of discoverability analysis, it usually should make no difference whether information happens to be stored on paper, hard drive, network, CD, backup tape, laptop, handheld device, videotape, audiotape, or any other medium. If information is relevant and nonprivileged, then in general it is discoverable regardless of its format. In fact, plenty of electronic discovery is easier to produce than hardcopy documents. Difficult-to-access forms of electronically stored information, however, are subject to proportionality analysis under Rule 26(b)(2), discussed later in this chapter. That rule specifically mentions that parties may refuse to provide e-discovery if the information is "not reasonably accessible because of undue burden or cost," and gives the court discretion to order discovery from such inaccessible electronic sources upon a showing of good cause.

The discovery rules allow parties to obtain evidence both from other parties and from nonparties, whoever has possession or control of the relevant documents, data, things, or property. For parties, you simply make a Rule 34 request. For nonparties, you use a subpoena under Rule 45 to compel nonparties to produce documents, electronically stored information, or tangible things or to permit the inspection of premises.

(5) Physical and Mental Examinations

A party's physical or mental condition may be an issue in a case. In a personal injury lawsuit, to take the most obvious example, the defendant may wish to determine whether the plaintiff's injuries are as serious as the plaintiff alleges and whether the plaintiff's theory of causation is accurate. While information could also be obtained by requesting medical records and by deposing the plaintiff's physician, a defendant understandably may wish to have the plaintiff examined by a suitably licensed person of the defendant's choosing.

As a discovery tool, Rule 35 **physical and mental examinations** resemble Rule 34 requests for inspection. Instead of inspecting a crumpled car or a pile of documents, you need to inspect a person's body or mind. The rule limits such discovery to cases in which a party's physical or mental condition is "in controversy," which may include cases in which a party's blood type is relevant and disputed. Most people would find document requests less intrusive than being poked and prodded physically by a physician or mentally by a psychologist or some other qualified examiner. Therefore Rule 35 permits physical or mental exams only with a court order based on a showing of good cause. Unlike the other discovery tools, which can be used without making a motion to the court, a party must explain to the judge why a physical or mental examination is needed.

(6) Requests for Admission

If I were the author of this book, I'd put requests for admission in the chapter on pleadings rather than discovery. Wait, I *am* the author of this book. But I'm stuck in this chapter because, well, chronologically the requests are used during the discovery process in litigation, and the federal rules place Rule 36 among the discovery rules (Rules 26-37), and your casebook almost certainly covers this topic in the discovery chapter. So I'll just conform, as long as you promise to remember that the key to understanding requests for admission is to think of them functionally as a kind of pleading like complaints, answers, and replies.

Requests for admissions (or *requests to admit*, as many lawyers say) allow one party to ask another party to admit specific facts, and the responding party must admit, deny, or state exactly why the party cannot truthfully admit or deny. Anything admitted "is conclusively established unless the court, on motion, permits the admission to be withdrawn or amended." Requests to admit, when used effectively, narrow the issues in dispute by establishing certain facts as uncontested. Lawyers often use requests for admission to establish the authenticity of specific documents that may be used as evidence at trial.

Admissions apply only to the case in which they are requested; they may not be used against the party in any other proceeding. In this sense, their function is more limited than other discovery responses, which sometimes may be used as evidence in other cases. In the particular action, however, an admission completely resolves the admitted fact. In this sense, admissions are more conclusive than other discovery responses, which merely constitute evidence and may be refuted with contrary evidence. There is no numerical limit on the use of requests for admission, but they are limited to the actual parties to the action.

F   A   Q

Q: Why can some discovery devices be deployed on nonparties while others can be used only on parties?

A: The parties to a lawsuit are not the only ones with relevant information, so the discovery rules permit using document requests and depositions of nonparties with the use of a subpoena. But some discovery devices are ill suited to use on nonparties. By limiting interrogatories to parties, the rule avoids burdening others with pressure to hire a lawyer to draft responses. Physical and mental exams are uniquely intrusive, and rarely do cases involve the disputed physical or mental condition of someone other than a party or someone in a party's custody or control. Finally, requests to admit, by definition, serve only to define the facts in contention between the actual parties; using them on nonparties would be nonsensical.

B. Planning and Supplementation

(1) Discovery Planning

Now that you know each of the discovery tools, take a moment to think comprehensively about how you will wield them. When representing a client in litigation, how will you conduct your factual investigation? One way to approach discovery planning, I suppose, would be to look at each discovery tool and to decide how to use it in the particular case: What interrogatories should I ask? Whom should I depose? What sort of documents should I request? And so on. Nothing horrible about that approach, but it is *not* the primary way great lawyers think about discovery planning. Great lawyers think about factual investigation more openly and proactively: What information do I need? Who has it? How will I get it?

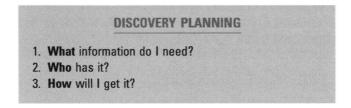

> **DISCOVERY PLANNING**
>
> 1. **What** information do I need?
> 2. **Who** has it?
> 3. **How** will I get it?

What information do I need? To answer the first question, look to the pleadings to understand each party's claims, defenses, and theory of the case, and look to your legal research to understand the elements or factors that bear on each of the claims and defenses. Until you know the claims, defenses, and the applicable law, you don't know what information you need. And until you know what information you need, you are not ready to use investigation and discovery wisely. Some litigators get into the right mindset by envisioning the jury instructions and closing arguments — long before trial — to ensure that they use the discovery process to obtain whatever information they will need at trial.

Who has the information? For each piece of information you need, you cannot get it until you figure out where it might be. Think broadly. Maybe the information is in the possession of another party, a nonparty, your own client, the government, or the public domain. Maybe there are multiple persons or places where you might find the information and you will use a multipronged approach.

Note that the third question is not "How will I try to get it?" but rather "How will I get it?" Because I *will* get it. Given the broad scope of discovery and the powerful tools at your disposal, your expectation should be that if you need a piece of information, somehow you will obtain it. The answer you find may not be one that helps your client's claims or defenses, but you will get an answer. At least, that's the mindset in a case with enough at stake to warrant a thorough factual investigation. You may have to adjust your attitude depending on the stakes of the dispute and your client's budget. When thinking about how to get the information you need, consider not only the formal discovery devices but also informal investigation, such as interviews with witnesses and other factual research. Understanding the strengths and weaknesses of the various discovery tools and other investigation techniques helps you figure out how to get the information most effectively and efficiently.

> ### Sidebar
>
> **INFORMAL INVESTIGATION**
>
> Do not forget that you have lots of ways to get information aside from the discovery devices. Useful sources include your own client, interviews with witnesses, the Internet, newspapers, government documents, private investigators, and any other type of research you can imagine. If a witness is willing to talk to you, there is no rule that says you must take a formal deposition, nor do you have to use a formal document request to get your hands on otherwise available information. (But be careful about talking to other represented parties without their lawyers because that raises ethics issues.) Your whole life, you have been figuring out facts for school, jobs, and life tasks. The good lawyer uses all of those skills of research and investigation, along with the tools in the discovery toolbox, to obtain whatever information is needed in representing a client.

F A Q

Q: Must the discovery devices be used in a specific order?

A: There is no required chronological order for the various discovery tools. With the exception of disclosures, whose timing is set forth in Rule 26(a), the other devices can be used in any combination and in any order. They are a set of available tools, not a series of steps. Many lawyers start with interrogatories to obtain basic information before turning to other devices, as interrogatory responses can provide names of potential deponents and can lead to better-defined document requests. Also, many lawyers obtain documents and e-discovery before taking depositions, because by reviewing the evidence the lawyer determines what questions to ask each deponent.

(2) Supplemental Responses

As a case proceeds, parties may find new information responsive to earlier discovery requests. A party may realize that one of its interrogatory responses was incorrect, for example, or may realize that it failed to produce certain responsive documents or e-discovery. Under Rule 26(e), a "party who has made a disclosure under Rule 26(a) — or who has responded to an interrogatory, request for production, or request for admission — must supplement or correct its disclosure or response," unless the supplemental or corrective information has otherwise been made known to the other parties during discovery.

C. Scope of Discovery

What information is available? Rule 26(b)(1) of the Federal Rules of Civil Procedure sets out the basic scope of discovery, and it is vast: "Parties may obtain discovery regarding any nonprivileged matter that is relevant to any party's claim or defense." In other words, the starting point for thinking about discovery is that if some piece of information is *relevant*, and if it does not fall within a legally recognized *privilege*, then that information is discoverable. As you will see shortly, proportionality and the work product doctrine further limit the scope of discovery, but the basic Rule 26(b)(1) standard — relevant and not privileged — should be your first step when thinking about whether certain information is subject to discovery.

(1) Relevance

The law of evidence defines **relevance** broadly: "having any tendency to make the existence of any fact that is of consequence to the determination of the action more probable or less probable than it would be without the evidence."[1] *Any* tendency. If an item of information is just one tiny piece of the puzzle, it's relevant. If it tends to make one story more plausible than another, it's relevant. If it makes a witness or a document a bit more credible, or a bit less credible, it's relevant. Note that evidence does not have to be direct to be relevant; lots of relevant evidence is circumstantial.

If the definition of relevance is so broad, you might ask, what could possibly make a piece of testimony or other evidence *ir*relevant? The law. Under the substantive law that applies to a dispute, each claim or defense requires certain elements or takes into account certain factors. To be relevant, the evidence must have some bearing, however slight, on facts that have some legal consequence in the matter. In an auto accident negligence lawsuit, for example, one party may wish to find out whether the adversary party is wealthy (both because that information could affect settlement negotiations and because it could affect a jury's perception of the other party), but an interrogatory inquiring into the party's net worth would be rejected as irrelevant because it has no bearing on the material issues in dispute.

Rule 26(b)(1) is one of those rules in which every sentence deserves your close attention (and no, I don't say this about every rule). Take the third sentence, which drives home an important point about the breadth of relevance: "Relevant information need not be admissible at the trial if the discovery appears reasonably calculated to lead to the discovery of admissible evidence." For example, suppose a party seeks discovery from Jones about what Jones heard Smith say about what happened. At trial, that would be considered hearsay. It would be inadmissible. In the discovery process, however, one cannot object to the request on grounds of hearsay (or any other basis of inadmissibility, other than relevance and privilege). One piece of info leads to another. By asking Jones what she heard, the party may get information that will lead to other evidence. As long as the information is relevant and reasonably calculated to lead to usable evidence, it is discoverable. Similarly, the rule allows

---

[1]Fed. R. Evid. 401.

discovery about where to find other evidence or witnesses ("the existence, description, nature, custody, condition, and location of any documents or other tangible things and the identity and location of persons who know of any discoverable matter").

Broad as the scope of discovery is, it used to be even broader. Before 2000, Rule 26(b)(1) permitted discovery "relevant to the subject matter involved in the pending action." Out of concern that the "subject matter" language permitted excessively broad fishing expeditions, the rule was amended to limit the general scope of discovery to information "relevant to any party's claim or defense." That is still a pretty broad standard, but at least it gives courts a basis to deny discovery if a party cannot explain how the information relates to any of the actual claims or defenses in the case. Now, if a party seeks information that is not relevant to any of the claims or defenses, but is somehow relevant to the broad "subject matter" of the dispute, the party may ask the court for permission to take the discovery. Rule 26(b)(1) puts it this way: "For good cause, the court may order discovery of any matter relevant to the subject matter involved in the action." The current rule thus creates a two-tiered relevance inquiry, allowing normal discovery to proceed for information relevant to the claims and defenses, but requiring a court order to obtain more tangential information.

> Relevant to "claim or defense" → Discoverable
> Relevant to "subject matter" → Discoverable with court order

(2) Privilege

Some things are more important than getting the truth. That's the idea behind the law of **privilege**. If the only goal were to find the truth, then all relevant information would be discoverable. The law, however, recognizes the importance of letting us keep some information private. In particular, the law recognizes that the value of certain relationships—such as lawyer-client, doctor-patient, and marriage—depends on the ability to speak candidly within those relationships, which in turn requires that certain communications be protected from compelled disclosure.

Note that privileges are not specific to civil litigation discovery. Privileges are part of the law of evidence, and in the case of the privilege against self-incrimination, a matter of constitutional law. They apply in both criminal and civil proceedings and in both discovery and trial. In this sense, privileges do not necessarily fall within the topic of "discovery" or even within "civil procedure." Nonetheless, to understand the discovery process and its limitations, a basic understanding of evidentiary privileges is essential.

(a) Attorney-Client Privilege

In civil litigation, the privilege that arises most often is the attorney-client privilege. The attorney-client privilege protects confidential communications between a lawyer and a client for purposes of giving or receiving legal advice or services. It protects communications from lawyer to client as well as from client to lawyer. It extends to oral, written, and electronic communications. If a communication is privileged, then neither the client nor the lawyer can be forced to reveal what was said.

The privilege protects *communications*, not the underlying *facts*. If a client in an auto accident case tells his lawyer that he was looking at his cell phone when he got into the crash, neither the client nor the lawyer can be compelled to disclose that conversation because the communication is privileged. But the privilege does not protect the fact itself. When opposing counsel at a deposition or trial asks the client what he was doing when the accident occurred, the client must answer honestly. You should object on grounds of attorney-client privilege whenever someone asks your client, "What did you tell your lawyer about what happened?" But you have no objection on grounds of attorney-client privilege when someone asks your client, "What happened?"

The privilege protects only *confidential* communications. If a client and lawyer have a conversation in a meeting with others present, the privilege does not apply. There is a limited exception for circumstances where the third person is necessary for the lawyer-client relationship, such as a paralegal, a translator, or a client's guardian.

Disclosure outside the lawyer-client relationship waives the privilege. Not only must the communication have been made in confidence to get the benefit of the privilege, the lawyer and client must maintain its confidentiality. If they share the communication with others, then the privilege is lost. As a lawyer, be sure to instruct your clients to maintain the privacy of your communications to avoid inadvertently waiving the privilege.

If you find it surprising how easily the attorney-client privilege can be waived, keep in mind that privileges are obstacles to getting the truth. They run counter to the main thrust of discovery and trial, which is to bring out the evidence to enable the factfinder to make accurate determinations. Blocking access to evidence is worth it, the thinking goes, only for communications in which privacy is essential. If the lawyer and client don't care enough about the confidentiality of a communication to keep it to themselves, then the legal system should not protect it from discovery.

(b) Privilege Against Self-Incrimination

Any American with a television has heard of this one. The Fifth Amendment to the U.S. Constitution says that no person "shall be compelled in any criminal case to be a witness against himself." The privilege against self-incrimination, for obvious reasons, arises in criminal cases more than in civil cases. Even in civil litigation, however, it plays a role. Suppose your client has been accused of killing someone, and faces both a criminal prosecution for homicide and a tort lawsuit for wrongful death. Or think of any other situation that may give rise to both criminal and civil liability, such as fraud, antitrust, physical assault, or driving under the influence. If your client faces possible criminal prosecution, and in the civil litigation is asked in discovery or at trial about what happened, the client could refuse to answer on grounds of the privilege against self-incrimination.

The privilege applies a bit differently in civil cases, however. In criminal cases, the prosecutor is not permitted to comment on the fact that the defendant refused to testify. In civil cases, such comments and adverse inferences are allowed. As a practical matter, this presents a serious downside to invoking the privilege against self-incrimination in civil litigation.

Note that the Fifth Amendment privilege deals only with in*crim*ination, that is, potential criminal liability. The fact that a client faces potential *civil* liability never gets Fifth Amendment protection. Thus, your client who is a defendant in a breach of contract lawsuit cannot refuse to respond to discovery requests on the ground that the information would make it more likely that the client would be held liable for breach of contract. Otherwise, the privilege would be the exception that swallows up the rule! Most civil discovery, after all, involves determinations of civil liability. Litigants in civil cases routinely must produce evidence in discovery that harms their own interests.

(c) Other Privileges

Beyond the attorney-client relationship, several other relationships get the benefit of privileged communications. The law on these varies from one jurisdiction to another. Some of the common privileges are the doctor-patient privilege, the psychotherapist-patient privilege, the clergy-penitent privilege, and the spousal privilege. The doctor-patient privilege is well established, if not quite as firm as the attorney-client privilege. The spousal privilege, by contrast, is not universally accepted, and many states have eliminated the spousal privilege in civil cases.

Q: What about private personal information or sensitive business information?

A: The law does not recognize the mind-your-own-business doctrine. Other than the recognized privileges, there is no general immunity that allows people to refuse to provide information on grounds that it's private. Discovery often requires parties and witnesses to answer questions about confidential business and personal matters. The person may seek a protective order to prohibit disclosure outside of the lawsuit or may object to the discovery if its sole purpose is to embarrass or harass. If information is relevant and not sought for improper purposes, however, then unless it fits within one of the legally recognized privileges, even highly sensitive information is discoverable.

(3) The Work Product Doctrine

Discovery does not entitle a party to steal the other side's work. Lawyers and others create enormous amounts of "work product" for purposes of litigation and trial. Among other things, they produce strategy memos, legal research, factual compilations, and notes from witness interviews, along with piles of e-mails and other correspondence. The **work product doctrine** protects these materials from discovery.

The doctrine traces its roots to the famous 1947 case of *Hickman v. Taylor*.[2] In that case, defense attorney Samuel Fortenbaugh had conducted interviews with surviving crew members of a tugboat that sank. The plaintiff made a discovery request seeking the witness statements that Fortenbaugh had obtained. If discoverability were based solely on relevance and privilege, the statements would have been discoverable. They were highly relevant, and they were not privileged because they involved Fortenbaugh's communications with witnesses rather than with his client. The Supreme Court, however, held that the statements were not discoverable

---

[2]329 U.S. 495 (1947).

because they were Fortenbaugh's work product. It would be "demoralizing," the Court said, for lawyers to be forced to turn over their work product to the other side, and it would discourage lawyers from doing their own work thoroughly and in writing. For years, the doctrine of *Hickman v. Taylor* existed as a common law gloss on the federal discovery rules. Finally, in 1970, the doctrine was modified and added to the Federal Rules of Civil Procedure. Rule 26(b)(3) defines work product and gives it qualified protection.

Rule 26(b)(3) never actually uses the term *work product*, but everybody else does. The rule defines the protected materials as "documents and other tangible things that are prepared in anticipation of litigation or for trial by or for another party or its representative (including the other party's attorney, consultant, surety, indemnitor, insurer, or agent)." Pay attention to three items embedded in this definition. First, the protection applies only to "documents and other tangible things," not to the underlying facts. To use the *Hickman* example, under the work product doctrine a party can object to turning over the witness statements or to describing what each witness said, but the party cannot refuse to answer interrogatories about the facts of the tugboat sinking, even if its knowledge of those facts comes from the witness interviews. Second, the materials must have been "prepared in anticipation of litigation or for trial." This may include materials prepared either before or after an actual lawsuit was filed. The doctrine is all about litigation-related work. It does not protect a client's or a lawyer's documents that were not prepared for litigation purposes (although some of those documents may be covered by the attorney-client privilege). Third, although you may hear people refer to the doctrine as *attorney work product*, the rule explicitly covers litigation materials prepared not only by attorneys, but also by the client or other nonlawyers.

Rule 26(b)(3) grants only qualified protection for work product, not absolute protection. The rule carves out an exception for important information that is otherwise unavailable. Materials that fall within the definition of work product may nonetheless be discoverable if they are "otherwise discoverable under Rule 26(b)(1)" (that is, relevant and not privileged) and if the requesting party "has substantial need for the materials to prepare its case and cannot, without undue hardship, obtain their substantial equivalent by other means." In *Hickman*, the plaintiff did not need Fortenbaugh's work product. Plaintiff's counsel could conduct his own interviews with the crew members; if they declined to cooperate, he could take their depositions. But suppose Fortenbaugh interviewed the sole surviving crew member and the crew member died shortly thereafter. In that case, plaintiff would be entitled to discovery of the crew member's statement because plaintiff has substantial need for the statement and cannot obtain the same information by other means.

Even when the qualified protection of the work product doctrine is overcome by a showing of substantial need, a lawyer's mental impressions are given absolute protection. Rule 26(b)(3) requires the court to "protect against disclosure of the mental impressions, conclusions, opinions, or legal theories of a party's attorney or other representative concerning the litigation." Thus, if Fortenbaugh made marginal notes with his thoughts about the crew member's statement, those notes would be redacted from the copy provided to the other side.

In practice, the work product doctrine often overlaps with the attorney-client privilege. A lawyer's memo to her client about trial strategy would be both privileged and work product. Despite their functional similarity, you should keep the doctrines distinct in your mind. The attorney-client privilege covers communications between lawyer and client. The work product doctrine covers materials prepared for purposes of litigation. Lawyer-client communications for nonlitigation legal services are privileged but not covered by the work product doctrine. Trial preparation materials that are not lawyer-client communications (lawyers' notes, witness interviews, research memos, and so on) receive the qualified protection of the work product doctrine, but not the more absolute protection of the attorney-client privilege. Although some lawyers sloppily refer to the "work product *privilege*," the work product doctrine is not an evidentiary privilege and its protection can be overcome by a showing of substantial need.

Expert Witnesses. Discovery from other parties' expert witnesses is closely related to the work product doctrine because it raises similar concerns about the discoverability of litigation preparation. Earlier, we saw that the Rule 26(a) mandatory disclosures include information about expert witnesses, but what if a party wishes to take an opposing expert's deposition to get more information?

Rule 26(b)(4) draws a sharp distinction between *testifying* and *nontestifying* experts. One may depose any testifying expert, "any person who has been identified as an expert whose opinions may be presented at trial." Rule 26(b)(4) was amended in 2010 to extend work product protection to drafts and other communications between lawyers and expert witnesses, but one can still get discovery of any information that the expert relied on in forming opinions. It is much tougher, however, to get discovery from a nontestifying expert, "an expert who has been retained or specially employed by another party in anticipation of litigation or to prepare for trial and who is not expected to be called as a witness at trial." Who are these nontestifying experts, and why would anyone hire them? They are people with expertise who serve as behind-the-scenes consultants to the parties and their lawyers. Often, they are experts whom a party considered but rejected as testifying expert witnesses because their opinions were not sufficiently helpful to the party to use at trial. The discovery rules permit taking the deposition of a nontestifying expert (or asking about the nontestifying expert's opinions by interrogatories) only in "exceptional circumstances." If it would be practically impossible for the requesting party to obtain facts or opinions on the same subject by other means—for example, if the expert is the only one with expertise on the subject—then the discovery is permissible. Otherwise, the nontestifying expert's opinions are not discoverable.

(4) Proportionality

The burden of discovery should not be disproportionate to its benefit. At the point where the usefulness of certain discovery in the action is outweighed by its expense or difficulty, judges are expected to step in to assert control. How much judges actually do this, and their effectiveness at it, varies from judge to judge, but the rules empower the court to step in when discovery spirals out of control.

Rule 26(b)(2)(C) instructs judges to "limit the frequency or extent of discovery" based on this idea of proportionality. Sometimes this means that information is discoverable only from certain sources, but sometimes it makes information completely nondiscoverable because it just ain't worth it. If "the discovery sought is unreasonably cumulative or duplicative, or can be obtained from some other source that is more convenient, less burdensome, or less expensive," the judge must disallow the unwarranted discovery. Even if information is discoverable, that does not give a party the right to demand the information in an inefficient or repetitive way.

> ### SCOPE OF DISCOVERABLE INFORMATION
>
> ■ Relevant
> ■ Not work product
> ■ Not privileged
> ■ Proportional

The more drastic version of proportionality comes in a subsection of Rule 26(b)(2)(C) that tells the court to limit discovery if "the burden or expense of the proposed discovery outweighs its likely benefit." Based on this subsection, information may be nondiscoverable even if it is relevant and not privileged. Proportionality functions as an important limit on the general scope of discovery announced in Rule 26(b)(1). To do the cost-benefit analysis, the rule tells judges to consider not only the burden of the discovery, but also the amount at stake in the lawsuit and the importance of the discovery in resolving the issues. Hard-to-reach information may not be worth the trouble if the case is small and the information tangential, but if the stakes are high and the hard-to-reach information is key, a court will allow discovery even if it is quite burdensome.

Electronically stored information, because of its sheer volume as well as accessibility issues, raises special problems of proportionality. Rule 26(b)(2)(B), added in 2006, specifies that parties need not provide e-discovery that is "not reasonably accessible." Depending on the technology, inaccessible sources may include certain backup tapes, disaster-recovery systems, and electronic files created on older systems that are incompatible with current technology. With electronically stored information, access is rarely impossible, but it is a matter of cost. If translating data into usable form would be especially difficult or expensive, the rule gives the court the power to decide whether the discovery is worth it. If the producing party shows that the information is not reasonably accessible, the court may nonetheless order discovery if the requesting party shows "good cause."

F   A   Q

Q: Who pays for discovery?

A: Each party generally bears its own legal expenses, such as the cost of having lawyers prepare discovery requests and responses. For depositions, the party taking the deposition pays the costs of conducting the deposition such as hiring the court reporter. For document requests and similar discovery, the producing party ordinarily bears the cost of locating the documents, electronic files, or other information responsive to the request and making it available to the requesting party. In exceptional cases, however, a court may order *cost* *shifting.* That is, the court may shift some or all of the cost to the requesting party, especially if retrieving the information is difficult or expensive. In one well-known case, *Zubulake v. UBS Warburg,** the court shifted 25 percent of the cost of certain difficult-to-access e-discovery to the plaintiff after reviewing a sample of the defendant's e-mail back-up tapes.

D. Discovery Enforcement

Mostly, lawyers handle discovery on their own. The judge is happy to stay out of it. One side requests information; the other side either provides the requested information or objects, or a combination of the two. When there are objections, the lawyers confer with each other to try to work out their differences. If all goes well, initial disclosures are exchanged, interrogatories are asked and answered, documents are requested and produced, depositions are taken, and the judge remains blissfully unaware of all of it until the pretrial conference. But in the imperfect real world of the adversary system, often the lawyers cannot work out their discovery disagreements and need the court's involvement. That is when motions to compel, motions for protective orders, and discovery sanctions come in handy.

(1) Motions to Compel and for Protective Orders

When another party fails to comply with a discovery request, the requesting party may file a **motion to compel**. A motion to compel asks the court to order the other party to provide the discovery. Maybe the responding party objected to certain questions on grounds of relevance, maybe it gave evasive or incomplete responses, or maybe it failed to respond at all. One might move to compel a party to provide required disclosures, to compel a party to answer interrogatories, to compel a deponent to answer particular questions, or to compel a party to produce documents that were not turned over. Depending on why the responding party failed to comply with the initial discovery request, the legal issues raised by a motion to compel might include whether certain discovery is relevant, whether it is privileged or protected by the work product doctrine, or whether it is unduly burdensome. In other words, the dispute might concern any aspect of discoverability or the proper use of the discovery tools. Rule 37 governs motions to compel disclosure or discovery. If the court grants the motion, then the responding party must comply with the court's order or face sanctions. If the court denies the motion, then the responding party need not provide the disputed disclosure or discovery.

The other avenue for discovery disputes to get to court is the motion for a **protective order**. Whereas a motion to compel comes from the requesting party, a motion for a protective order comes from the responding party. A motion for a protective order asks the court to order that certain discovery not be had or to order some other constraint on discovery. Rule 26(c) permits a "party or any person from whom discovery is sought" to move for a protective order.

---

*Zubulake v. UBS Warburg LLC, 217 F.R.D. 309 (S.D.N.Y. 2003) (explaining multifactor test for cost shifting and ordering sampling); Zubulake v. UBS Warburg LLC, 216 F.R.D. 280 (S.D.N.Y. 2003) (allocating cost of restoring backup tapes).

A protective order may forbid certain discovery, such as by ordering that a particular deposition not go forward. It may order that certain topics are off limits or that certain categories of documents need not be produced. As with motions to compel, motions for a protective orders might address any legal issues bearing on discoverability, including relevance, privilege, work product, and proportionality. More generally, Rule 26(c) empowers the court to issue protective orders "to protect a party or person from annoyance, embarrassment, oppression, or undue burden or expense."

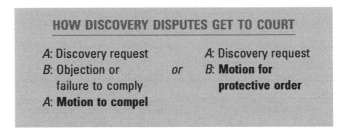

HOW DISCOVERY DISPUTES GET TO COURT

A: Discovery request		A: Discovery request
B: Objection or	*or*	B: **Motion for**
failure to comply		**protective order**
A: **Motion to compel**		

Motions to compel and motions for protective orders require that the movant first attempt to confer in good faith with the other party to try to resolve the dispute without the court's involvement. Both types of motions are common in litigation, but they are intended as a last resort when the parties are unable to resolve their discovery dispute because of a genuine disagreement that they need the court to adjudicate.

In addition to limiting discovery at the behest of the responding party, protective orders can serve another important function — protecting the confidentiality of discovery materials. Even if information is discoverable, the responding party may consider the information highly confidential either for reasons of personal privacy or because it includes trade secrets or other confidential business information. Rule 26(c) includes confidentiality on its list of protective orders, and parties frequently ask courts to order that certain materials, even if subject to discovery, be kept confidential and not be revealed outside of the litigation.

(2) Discovery Sanctions

The discovery enforcement mechanisms — specifically Rule 37 and Rule 26(g) — provide for both minor and major punishments to give teeth to the disclosure and discovery requirements.

If a party fails to disclose required information such as the names of witnesses or descriptions of relevant documents, Rule 37(c) imposes an appropriate punishment: "the party is not allowed to use that information or witness to supply evidence on a motion, at a hearing, or at a trial, unless the failure was substantially justified or is harmless." Recall that the mandatory disclosures of Rule 26(a) require only that parties identify witnesses and documents that the party may use to support its own claims or defenses. Precluding the use of undisclosed witnesses and other information, therefore, creates a strong incentive for parties not to withhold names or information from the required disclosures.

More severe discovery sanctions—listed in Rule 37(b)—are normally reserved for parties who fail to comply with a court order. This rule gives added weight to the motion to compel. When a party responds to interrogatories incompletely or evasively, or makes unwarranted objections to document requests, or refuses to answer certain questions at a deposition, the requesting party may move to compel discovery. If the court grants the motion to compel, and the responding party persists in its noncompliance in violation of the court order, *then* a Rule 37 motion for sanctions would be proper. For parties who disobey a court's order compelling discovery, Rule 37(b) lists punishments for a court to consider imposing: directing that certain facts be taken as established for purposes of the action, prohibiting the disobedient party from making particular assertions or from using certain pieces of evidence, striking pleadings in whole or in part, staying the proceedings, dismissal, default judgment, and contempt of court. Generally, the most severe discovery sanction to impose on a disobedient plaintiff is dismissal (that is, judgment for the defendant), and the most severe discovery sanction to impose on a disobedient defendant is default (that is, judgment for the plaintiff). Courts reserve these extreme sanctions of dismissal and default for the most severe discovery violations. In addition or instead, courts order disobedient parties or their attorneys to pay the other side's attorney's fees caused by the failure to provide discovery.

Although in general the listed sanctions of Rule 37(b) apply only to parties who disobey court orders, certain failures are so basic that the rule allows sanctions even without a motion to compel and subsequent court order. If a party does not show up for a properly noticed deposition or utterly fails to respond to interrogatories or to a document request, Rule 37(d) permits the court to impose most of the listed sanctions.

Another discovery sanctions provision, Rule 26(g), punishes baseless discovery requests, responses, or objections. When you read Rule 26(g), it should look familiar because parts of it are nearly identical to Rule 11, which we addressed in Chapter 5. Rule 26(g) requires attorneys or unrepresented parties to sign "every discovery request, response, or objection." The signature certifies that to the best of the person's knowledge after a reasonable inquiry, the request, response, or objection is legally warranted, not asserted for any improper purpose such as harassment or delay, and is "neither unreasonable nor unduly burdensome or expensive, considering the needs of the case, prior discovery in the case, the amount in controversy, and the importance of the issues at stake in the action." If a request, response, or objection is legally unjustified, asserted for an improper purpose, or unreasonable in violation of Rule 26(g), the rule instructs the court to impose an appropriate sanction.

Sidebar

DISCOVERY IN COMPARATIVE AND INTERNATIONAL PERSPECTIVE

Lawyers from other countries marvel at U.S. discovery. Both in the amount of information available and the extent to which the process is controlled by the parties rather than the court, U.S. procedure contrasts markedly with nearly every other legal system in the world. In many countries, documents may be obtained from other parties only with the intervention of the judge. Pretrial depositions outside the United States are unusual. These differences create tension when foreign litigants face discovery in U.S. courts or when U.S. litigants need another country's assistance in obtaining information abroad. Many countries have signed the Hague Convention on the Taking of Evidence Abroad, which governs discovery in transnational litigation among the signatories.

SUMMARY

- The procedural rules provide tools for obtaining information from parties and witnesses before trial.

- In federal court, certain basic information must be turned over by each side, without the need for a specific request, as mandatory initial disclosures.

- A party may serve interrogatories on other parties to obtain written answers under oath to written questions.

- Depositions allow parties to ask witnesses questions under oath and to obtain transcripts of the questions and answers.

- Parties may require other parties or others to turn over documents and electronically stored information, and to permit inspection of items or land.

- With a court order for good cause, a party may require another party to undergo a physical or mental examination.

- A party may use requests for admissions to require other parties to admit or deny facts.

- In general, the scope of discovery under the federal rules extends to all non-privileged information that is relevant to the claims or defenses.

- Information is not discoverable if it is protected by a recognized privilege such as the attorney-client privilege, the doctor-patient privilege, or the privilege against self-incrimination.

- Information is not discoverable if it is protected by the work product doctrine — that is, if it was prepared for purposes of the litigation — but this protection may be overcome by a showing of substantial need and inability to get the information from other sources.

- Courts may refuse to allow discovery if the request is redundant or unduly burdensome.

- In general, each party bears the cost of responding to legitimate discovery requests, but courts have the power to shift all or some of the cost to the requesting party, particularly if the information is relatively inaccessible.

- Discovery largely proceeds without the court's involvement, but if a responding party fails to provide the requested discovery, the requesting party may move to compel the discovery.

- A party resisting discovery or seeking to limit its use may move for a protective order.

- A court may impose sanctions on a party for failure to comply with a court order compelling discovery or for certain other discovery violations.

CONNECTIONS

Jurisdiction

When threshold questions involve disputed factual issues, courts may allow limited discovery on those issues. For example, discovery may be needed to determine a party's domicile or principal place of business for diversity jurisdiction or to determine contacts with the forum state for purposes of personal jurisdiction.

Pleadings

Because Rule 26(b) defines the scope of discovery in terms of relevance to the claims and defenses, parties can exert some control over the scope of discoverable information by drafting their pleadings broadly or narrowly. By asserting numerous and broad claims or defenses in a complaint or answer, a party expands the amount of available discovery.

Pleadings — Notice Pleading

In the overall procedural scheme embodied in the Federal Rules of Civil Procedure, notice pleading goes hand in hand with broad discovery. Parties are not expected to have all of the information at the outset of the case, but are given the opportunity to obtain that information during the pretrial process.

Pleadings — Motion to Dismiss

Rule 12(b)(6) motions (motion to dismiss for failure to state a claim) function as gatekeepers to discovery. The 12(b)(6) motion is based solely on the complaint and ordinarily decided before parties take discovery, whereas summary judgment is based on the evidence and ordinarily decided after discovery is completed. Thus, from the plaintiff's perspective, getting past 12(b)(6) means access to discovery, which in turn means settlement leverage.

Pleadings — Sanctions

Rule 11 announces its own inapplicability to discovery: "This rule does not apply to disclosures and discovery requests, responses, objections, and motions under Rules 26 through 37." This obviously does *not* mean it is OK to make factually baseless or legally frivolous assertions during discovery. Rather, it simply means that these matters in the discovery context are handled under Rules 26(g) and 37.

Joinder

The rules make it easier to get discovery from parties than from nonparties. If a plaintiff has a potential claim against someone other than the primary defendant but is on the fence about whether to join that person as an additional defendant, discovery considerations may weigh in favor of joinder.

Summary Judgment

A vigorous summary judgment mechanism complements liberal discovery. If a party cannot meet its burden of production despite the broad discovery permitted by the federal rules, summary judgment presumes that the party's position is so weak that it cannot prevail at trial. Summary judgment is rarely appropriate unless the parties have had adequate opportunity for discovery, and courts may defer ruling on summary judgment motions in order to permit additional discovery.

Joinder

In the world of law school hypotheticals, lots of lawsuits involve a single plaintiff suing a single defendant over a single claim. In real life, such

OVERVIEW

lawsuits exist, but they're the exception. Most lawsuits involve multiple claims, multiple parties, or both. Maybe it's as simple as a plaintiff suing a defendant for both fraud and breach of contract or two passengers suing a driver for negligence. Or maybe it's as complex as a class action or other mass lawsuit involving thousands of plaintiffs asserting myriad claims against hundreds of defendants, who in turn assert third-party claims against additional parties and crossclaims against each other.

   To understand when litigants may or must join additional claims or parties, we look to the rules of **joinder**. These rules establish procedural mechanisms for joining more than one claim in a lawsuit (*joinder of claims*), as well as for joining additional parties (*joinder of parties*). As a lawyer, you need to understand both when you *may* join additional claims or parties in a lawsuit (*permissive joinder*) and when you *must* do so (*compulsory joinder*).

A. JOINDER OF CLAIMS

1. Permissive Joinder of Claims
2. Counterclaims
3. Crossclaims

A. Joinder of Claims

(1) Permissive Joinder of Claims

A plaintiff may have more than one claim against a defendant. A wrongfully terminated employee may have claims against the employer for race discrimination, gender discrimination, breach of contract, and other legal violations. These claims, moreover, may have a basis in federal statutes, state statutes, and common law. Similarly, a consumer injured by a defective product may have claims against the manufacturer for negligence, strict liability, breach of warranty, and consumer fraud.

May the plaintiff bring these claims against the defendant in a single lawsuit? Absolutely. A plaintiff may assert multiple claims against a defendant in one complaint. That is what's called **permissive joinder of claims**.

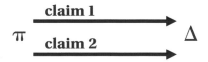

Example 1: An African American woman is fired from her job. She claims that the termination was based not on the quality of her work, but on the fact that she is

African American. She sues her former employer, asserting a statutory claim for employment discrimination as well as a common law claim for breach of her employment contract.

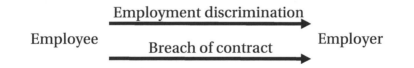

Requiring a plaintiff to choose only a single theory would hearken back to the days of the common law forms of action. Under modern pleading rules, a party may assert claims under each legal doctrine that applies to the party's circumstances. Imagine telling the plaintiff in Example 1 that she can sue for discrimination or breach of contract, but not both. Or telling an injured consumer that she can sue for negligence or breach of warranty, but not both. Maybe it *was* both. Or maybe it was one and not the other, but to determine which, the parties may need the discovery process and a trial.

Given that a plaintiff may have multiple legal theories, it would be incredibly inefficient to require a separate lawsuit for each one. Think how much additional effort would be involved if the product liability plaintiff had to bring separate lawsuits for negligence, strict liability, and so on, or if, in Example 1, the fired employee had to bring separate lawsuits for discrimination and breach of contract. The claims may have independent legal theories, but as a factual matter, most of the evidence will overlap. At every stage — the allegations of the complaint, the information sought during discovery, the proof presented at trial — combining the claims in one lawsuit makes sense.

In each of the examples above, the plaintiff asserts claims that arise out of the same transaction or occurrence. The employment discrimination plaintiff in Example 1 asserts claims that arise out of the employee's termination. The product liability plaintiff asserts claims that arise out of an injury from a particular product. Those are easy cases for permitting joinder of claims because the efficiency is obvious.

What if the claims do *not* arise out of the same transaction or occurrence? Businesses in ongoing relationships may have multiple disputes. A department store, for example, may have many contracts with a clothing supplier for various shipments of merchandise. Suppose one shipment never arrived, and an entirely different shipment, under a different contract, arrived with the wrong merchandise. Although these two breach of contract claims do not arise out of the same transaction or occurrence, the department store may wish to assert both claims as part of a single lawsuit.

Surprisingly, perhaps, the rules permit joinder of claims even if the claims are utterly unrelated. Rule 18(a) says that "[a] party asserting a claim, counterclaim, crossclaim, or third-party claim may join, as independent or alternate claims, as many claims as it has against an opposing party." In all that convoluted language, the one thing it does *not* say—unlike so many other joinder rules—is "arising out of the same transaction or occurrence." Permissive joinder of claims under the federal rules, in other words, is *unlimited*. As long as the plaintiff and defendant are in litigation, the thinking goes, they may as well be allowed to assert whatever claims they have against each other at the same time.

So if you represent a plaintiff with property damage from a neighbor's septic tank overflow, and the neighbor also owes your client money on an unrelated debt, the permissive joinder rule allows your client to file a single complaint asserting both the property damage claim and the debt claim. But you don't have to do so; it's *permissive*. If your client decides to sue the neighbor on both claims, then you and your client will analyze as a matter of strategy and practicality whether to assert the claims together or separately.

(2) Counterclaims

Defendants have claims against plaintiffs, too. In an automobile collision case in which one driver sues another, for example, the defending driver also may have suffered vehicle damage, personal injury, or both. If each blames the other for the accident, a *counterclaim* is all but inevitable. The federal rules provide for permissive counterclaims in Rule 13(b) and compulsory counterclaims in Rule 13(a).

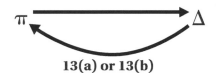

(a) Permissive Counterclaims

A defendant may assert, as a counterclaim, any claim that the defendant has against the plaintiff, even if it is completely unrelated to the plaintiff's claim. Rule 13(b) expressly permits a pleading to "state as a counterclaim against an opposing party any claim that is not compulsory." The logic of **permissive counterclaims** mirrors Rule 18(a)'s unlimited permissive joinder of claims—the plaintiff and defendant are in litigation anyway, so there's some efficiency in letting both of them assert whatever claims they have against each other. But the efficiency is relatively slight since the allegations and evidence may barely overlap, so the rule permits a defendant to choose either to assert the claim as a counterclaim or to file it as a separate lawsuit.

Precisely because they are permissive rather than compulsory, Rule 13(b) counterclaims present a strategic question: If you represent a defendant with a potential claim against the plaintiff, would you prefer to assert it as a counterclaim or in a separate action? Litigators find counterclaims strategically advantageous on the theory that often the best defense is a good offense. Whether trying a case before a jury or showing up at a bargaining table to discuss settlement, it's helpful to have something of your own to assert. On the other hand, counterclaims carry a strategic cost. Whenever you assert a counterclaim, you have allowed the opposing party to choose your forum and timing. If your client has a potential claim that is unrelated to the plaintiff's claim and that would be better asserted in a different court or at a different time, you may choose to forgo the permissive counterclaim and instead file a new action at the time and place you choose.

(b) Compulsory Counterclaims

Rule 13(a) states that "[a] pleading must state as a counterclaim any claim that — at the time of its service — the pleader has against an opposing party if the claim: (A) arises out of the transaction or occurrence that is the subject matter of the opposing party's claim; and (B) does not require adding another party over whom the court cannot acquire jurisdiction." The word *must* is what makes this a rule of **compulsory counterclaims**. If the claim arises out of the same transaction or occurrence, then the defending party must assert it as a counterclaim. But what, exactly, is *compulsory* about it? If the defendant fails to assert the counterclaim, will the court order the defendant to do so because it's compulsory? No. What makes it compulsory is claim preclusion. If the defending party fails to assert the transactionally related claim as a counterclaim, then the party will be precluded from asserting the claim later in a separate suit.

By forcing both plaintiffs and defendants to assert in a single action whatever claims they have against each other arising out of the same transaction, the legal system enhances efficiency, consistency, and finality. The compulsory counterclaim rule protects against the inefficiency of presenting much of the same evidence and relitigating the same factual disputes in two separate lawsuits. It protects against the potential inconsistency of having related claims adjudicated by different decision makers. And it serves the goal of finality by letting the parties know that the adjudication of their action precludes relitigation of claims between the same parties arising out of the same factual situation. These values will resurface in our discussion of preclusion in Chapter 11.

Sidebar

JOINDER AND JURISDICTION

The joinder rules establish *procedural mechanisms* for including multiple claims and parties in a lawsuit. They do not, however, automatically give the court *jurisdiction*. Even if a claim complies with the procedural requirements of the joinder rules, the claim may be dismissed if the court lacks either subject matter jurisdiction over the claim or personal jurisdiction over the added party. Suppose a plaintiff sues a defendant in federal court under federal antitrust law, and the defendant asserts a state law counterclaim for breach of contract. The counterclaim is *procedurally* proper under Rule 13, but the court still needs *jurisdiction*. The court has federal question jurisdiction over the plaintiff's antitrust claim, but not over the counterclaim. If the parties are diverse and the counterclaim meets the amount-in-controversy requirement, then the court has diversity jurisdiction over the counterclaim. Even if the court does not have diversity jurisdiction, if the counterclaim arises out of the same transaction as the antitrust claim (that is, if it's a compulsory counterclaim), then the court may have supplemental jurisdiction over the counterclaim. As you learn the joinder mechanisms and as you use them in practice, don't forget about jurisdiction.

F A Q

Q: Is there compulsory joinder of claims?

A: Yes, although you won't find any Federal Rule of Civil Procedure that says so. As a practical matter, there's compulsory joinder of claims, but it goes by the name of claim preclusion or res judicata. As we'll see in Chapter 11, if a plaintiff chooses not to bring part of her claim in the first lawsuit, then a final judgment on the merits will preclude her from asserting the claim later.

Example 2: Company A complains that company B delivered goods of lower quality than specified in their contract, so company A rejects the goods and refuses to pay for them. Unable to work out their differences amicably, A sues B for breach of contract. B counterclaims for breach of contract based on A's failure to pay.

Breach of contract:
Nonconforming goods

A ⟶ B

Breach of contract:
Nonpayment

In Example 2, B's claim — that A breached the contract by failing to pay for the goods — is a compulsory counterclaim. It arises from the same transaction as the original claim — A's claim that B delivered unsatisfactory goods. Therefore, if B fails to bring its claim as a counterclaim in this action and later files a separate lawsuit against A for this nonpayment, B's claim will be dismissed for failure to bring it as a compulsory counterclaim in the first action.

Rule 13(a)(2)(A) creates a sensible exception to compulsory counterclaims: "[T]he pleader need not state the claim if: when the action was commenced, the claim was the subject of another pending action." So if, in Example 2, B had *already* sued A for nonpayment, and then A filed its suit for unsatisfactory goods, B would not be required to assert the counterclaim in A's lawsuit. By the way, notice that if B had filed the first suit, then A's claim would have been a compulsory counterclaim in B's lawsuit. Therefore, this exception to the compulsory counterclaim rule is unlikely to come up except when the first case was filed in a state court system that does not have compulsory counterclaims.

(3) Crossclaims

Shortly we'll look at joinder of parties and see that many cases involve multiple plaintiffs, multiple defendants, or both. May co-parties assert claims against each other? In other words, to what extent do the rules permit **cross-claims**? Rule 13(g) permits crossclaims as long as they are transactionally related to the claims already asserted in the action: "A pleading may state as a crossclaim any claim by one party against a coparty if the claim arises out of the transaction or occurrence that is the subject matter of the original action or of a counterclaim, or if the claim relates to any property that is the subject matter of the original action."

In the case of co-defendants, crossclaims often involve claims for contribution or indemnification, in which one defendant asserts that if it is held liable to the plaintiff, then the other defendant should have to pay the damages. In a product liability case, for example, if the plaintiff sues both the retailer and the manufacturer of a defectively manufactured product, the retailer may assert a crossclaim against the manufacturer for indemnification. Indeed, Rule 13(g) anticipates exactly such crossclaims by stating that they "may include a claim that the coparty is or may be liable to the crossclaimant for all or part of a claim asserted in the action against the crossclaimant." This type of crossclaim among co-defendants substantively resembles a third-party claim under Rule 14, but procedurally the third-party claim is used to bring in someone who has not already been made a party to the lawsuit.

Sidebar

CROSSCLAIMS AND CONFUSING TERMINOLOGY

The federal rules use *crossclaim* to refer to a claim against a co-party (by a plaintiff against a co-plaintiff, or by a defendant against a co-defendant), and *counterclaim* to refer to a claim by a defendant against a plaintiff (or, more precisely, a claim by a party against whom a claim was asserted, against the party asserting the claim). This book uses the same definitions. But be careful out there, because in some state courts, *crossclaim* or *cross-complaint* refers not only to claims between co-parties, but also to what the federal rules call a counterclaim and, less commonly, to what the federal rules call a third-party claim.

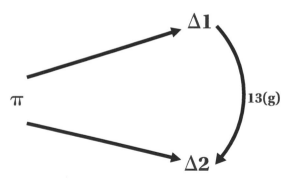

Similarly, co-plaintiffs may assert crossclaims against each other. For example, consider an automobile accident case in which a driver and passenger sue the driver of the other car for their injuries. As discovery proceeds, the passenger decides that the driver of her own car was at fault as well. If the passenger decides to assert a negligence claim against her own driver, she may do so either by bringing a separate lawsuit or by filing a crossclaim against her co-plaintiff in the initial action.

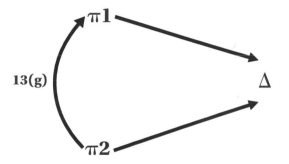

Although a few states make related crossclaims compulsory, just like compulsory counterclaims, the federal rules and most states treat crossclaims as purely permissive. This means that if your client has a potential crossclaim, you and your client must decide whether to assert it as a crossclaim, independently, or not at all. As with permissive joinder of claims and permissive counterclaims, the decision depends on strategy as well as practical considerations such as cost and timing. But with crossclaims, you have to consider an additional strategic layer, the risk that crossclaims may undermine an otherwise united front by the co-parties.

It's easy to understand why courts permit related crossclaims. If the claims arise out of the same transaction or occurrence, or relate to the same property, then resolving those claims in the same action improves efficiency and consistency.

But you should also try to understand the answer to the opposite question, which is why the rules impose greater constraints on crossclaims than on claims or counterclaims. Permissive joinder of claims is unlimited under Rule 18. So are permissive counterclaims under Rule 13(b). A plaintiff and defendant may assert whatever claims they have against each other, even *unrelated* claims. How come co-parties may assert crossclaims only if they arise out of the same transaction? Not only that, but claim preclusion and the compulsory counterclaim rule *require* a plaintiff and defendant to assert claims against each other if they arise out of the same transaction, whereas the crossclaim rule is merely permissive. Why?

The answer takes you beyond the efficiency and consistency rationales for joinder of related claims and into the complexity of the adversary system. Claims and counterclaims between the original plaintiff and defendant may add layers of factual and legal disputes to an action, but they all involve the original adversary relationship between the parties. Crossclaims, on the other hand, create an additional axis of adversariness. Parties who previously were merely co-plaintiffs or co-defendants become, with the assertion of a crossclaim, adversaries as well as allies. This additional layer of complexity explains why crossclaims are treated differently from both original claims and counterclaims. The efficiency gain is thought to outweigh the cost of additional complexity for related crossclaims, but not for unrelated crossclaims.

B. Permissive Party Joinder

So far, we've looked at joinder of *claims* among those who are already parties. We turn now to joinder of *parties*. Under what circumstances may a complaint include multiple plaintiffs or multiple defendants? That is the question of **permissive party joinder**.

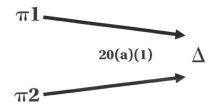

Rule 20(a) makes it relatively easy to join parties, as long as the claims by or against them arise out of the same underlying circumstances. Rule 20(a)(1) explains when multiple plaintiffs may sue together: "Persons may join in one action as plaintiffs if: (A) they assert any right to relief jointly, severally, or in the alternative with respect to or arising out of the same transaction, occurrence, or series of transactions or occurrences; and (B) any question of law or fact common to all plaintiffs will arise in the action."

> **PERMISSIVE PARTY JOINDER UNDER RULE 20(a):**
>
> (A) same transaction, occurrence, or series, *and*
> (B) common question of law or fact

Frankly, if the first part is satisfied, it is almost unimaginable *not* to be able find at least one common question of law or fact, so as a practical matter this boils down to a "same transaction or occurrence" test. But as a lawyer, judge, or law student doing a Rule 20 analysis, you should dutifully take it through both steps by pointing out (1) the transaction or occurrence that gave rise to the claims by or against the various parties, and (2) at least one common question that will arise with regard to each of the parties.

Determining whether claims arise out of the same transaction or occurrence can be trickier than it seems. Courts often describe it as a "logical relationship" test: Are the claims by or against the parties closely enough related that it makes sense to package them together for trial?

One widely cited example is *Mosley v. General Motors Corp.*,[1] in which ten plaintiffs sought to join their employment discrimination claims against General Motors. General Motors *moved to sever*, that is, asked to court to divide the single ten-plaintiff action into ten separate actions. General Motors argued that the plaintiffs did not meet the test under Rule 20 because the plaintiffs' claims were too varied—some claimed race discrimination, while others claimed gender discrimination; some were fired, some were denied promotions, and some were never hired; the plaintiffs worked under different supervisors, and some of them worked in entirely different divisions of the company. The district court agreed with General Motors, and granted the motion to sever. On appeal, however, the circuit court reversed. The court accepted the plaintiffs' argument that even though their claims varied, all of the plaintiffs alleged a companywide policy of discrimination, so they satisfied the test for joinder under Rule 20.

Notice the importance of framing the issue. In *Mosley*, the district court viewed the "transaction or occurrence" as each individual plaintiff's termination, nonhiring, or nonpromotion. The court of appeals, on the other hand, viewed the "transaction or occurrence" as the alleged companywide policy. For the lawyers arguing the severance motion, the battle was over whether the court would view the plaintiffs' claims individually or collectively. Think about the strategic benefit at trial of presenting a string of plaintiffs with similar claims against the company, as opposed to presenting one individual plaintiff's claim which the jury may perceive as sour grapes. It's no wonder the plaintiffs chose to file the claims in a single action, and no wonder the defendant fought so hard to sever them.

---

[1] 497 F.2d 1330 (8th Cir. 1974).

You will see many cases both in law school and in practice that, like *Mosley*, involve permissive joinder of plaintiffs. Civil rights claims often involve multiple similarly aggrieved plaintiffs. Consumer claims often involve multiple consumers suing a company for fraud or other violations. Tort claims often involve multiple injured persons or related persons asserting claims such as loss of consortium.

Rule 20 does not place any cap on the number of parties who can be joined, as long as they satisfy the two-part test, so permissive joinder of plaintiffs can be massive. There have been mass tort cases with tens of thousands of plaintiffs. Although it might seem more practical to pursue such a case as a *class action* rather than by using permissive joinder on a massive scale, class certification is not always possible.

Permissive joinder not only allows multiple plaintiffs to sue together, but also allows plaintiffs to sue multiple defendants, and multidefendant cases are very common. Often, including many employment cases and tort cases, a plaintiff accuses someone of doing something in the course of employment, and names as defendants both the individual and the company for which that individual works. Securities cases often involve claims against a company as well as individual officers and directors. Product liability cases often involve claims against each company in a chain of distribution, such as a manufacturer, distributor, and retailer. Rule 20(a)(2) applies the same test — (A) same transaction, occurrence, or series; and (B) common question of law or fact — to joinder of defendants.

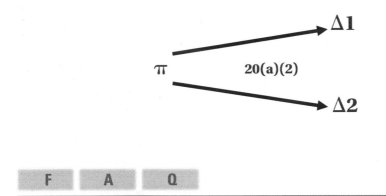

F   A   Q

Q: How does permissive joinder relate to amendment of pleadings?

A: Permissive joinder relates to both original pleadings and amended pleadings. If a plaintiff intends at the outset to sue multiple defendants, or if multiple plaintiffs know at the outset that they wish to sue together, they may do so in the original complaint as long as they satisfy the requirements of Rule 20. To join an additional party after the original pleading, however, necessitates amendment of the pleading. To amend a pleading to add a new party, one must satisfy both Rule 15 for amendment and Rule 20 for joinder.

The two parts of the test for permissive party joinder — same transaction or occurrence and common question of law or fact — echo the standards for a number of other joinder rules. "Transaction or occurrence" is the test for whether a counterclaim is compulsory and whether a crossclaim is permitted. This transactional test ensures a close enough relationship between claims to advance the procedural goals of efficiency, consistency, and finality. With these goals in mind, it should not surprise you that the supplemental jurisdiction statute, 28 U.S.C. §1367, incorporates essentially the same test. Remember the "common nucleus of operative fact" test from *Gibbs v. United Mine Workers*[2] in Chapter 1? It was in *Gibbs* that the Supreme Court declared that under the Federal Rules of Civil Procedure, "the impulse is toward entertaining the broadest possible scope of action consistent with fairness to the parties; joinder of claims, parties and remedies is strongly encouraged."

SAME TRANSACTION OR OCCURRENCE

Rule 13(a) Compulsory counterclaims
Rule 13(g) Crossclaims
Rule 20(a) Permissive party joinder

COMMON QUESTION OF LAW OR FACT

Rule 20(a) Permissive party joinder
Rule 23(a)(2) Class action
Rule 24(b) Permissive intervention
Rule 42(a) Consolidation

The "common question" test is generally easy to satisfy, so the rules use it either as a baseline or in combination with stricter requirements. The rules on consolidation and permissive intervention use it as a baseline; if claims involve at least one common question of law or fact, then a court may use its discretion to decide whether it makes sense to consolidate or to permit intervention. The rules on class actions and permissive party joinder use the "common question" test in combination with stricter requirements to ensure that those procedural mechanisms are used only for closely related matters.

At this point, I should say something about **consolidation**. Although not technically a joinder mechanism, consolidation can have the same practical effect. Rule 42(a) empowers a court to bring multiple cases together for a joint trial or other joint proceedings: "If actions before the court involve a common question of law or fact, the court may: (1) join for hearing or trial any or all matters at issue in the actions; (2) consolidate the actions. . . ." The minimal requirement ("a common question of law or fact") leaves the consolidation decision almost entirely to the court's discretion. A major obstacle to consolidation, however, is that the actions must be pending in the same court. The flipside of consolidation is **separation**. Under 42(b), a court may order *separate trials* of any claims, crossclaims, counterclaims, third-party claims, or even of separate issues, "[f]or convenience, to avoid prejudice, or to expedite and economize." Rule 20(b) reminds the court, in the context of permissive party joinder, that even if a party is properly joined under the rule, the court retains the power to order separate trials. The upshot is that permissive joinder of claims and parties does not always dictate whether the claims will be tried together. Judges have

---

[2]383 U.S. 715 (1966).

significant discretion to consolidate actions that were brought separately or to separate claims that were brought in a single action.

C. Compulsory Party Joinder

The **compulsory party joinder** rule dictates who *must* be joined in an action and empowers the court to order joinder of such a required party. The rule also offers guidelines for determining whether a case should be dismissed if such a required party *cannot* be joined. It's useful to think about compulsory party joinder from both sides. If you represent a plaintiff, you need to know whether you are required to join particular parties. If you represent a defendant, and the plaintiff has not joined someone, you need to know whether you can ask the court to order that the person be joined, or better yet, whether the nonjoinder provides a basis for dismissal.

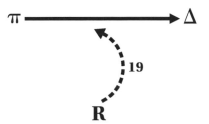

Rule 19 establishes a two-step process for analyzing compulsory party joinder. The first question is whether a person must be joined. Lawyers and judges often refer to this as a question of whether the absent person is a *required party* or *necessary party* under Rule 19(a). If so, the court may order that the person be joined. Suppose, however, that the person is a required party under Rule 19(a), but cannot be joined because of the court's jurisdictional limits. Then, the question is whether the person is so critical to the lawsuit that, in the person's absence, the lawsuit should be dismissed. Lawyers and judges often refer to this second question as whether the absent person is an *indispensable party* under Rule 19(b). Neither the word *necessary* nor *indispensable* appears in the current federal rule, but some people still use the older terminology as shorthand for the two steps in the compulsory party joinder analysis.

Keep in mind that compulsory party joinder under the federal rules is very narrow. When students make mistakes about compulsory party joinder, they almost always err on the side of breadth, so be careful not to read Rule 19 too expansively. I doubt you will enjoy reading Rule 19 — one of the densest and most convoluted federal rules — but do read it well, particularly Rule 19(a), because a close examination will show you just how tight it is.

(1) Required Parties

Rule 19(a) defines "persons required to be joined if feasible" and instructs the court to order their joinder: "If a person has not been joined as required, the court must order that the person be made a party." A required party, depending on the circumstances, may be aligned as a plaintiff or as a defendant. Required parties are those who are so inextricably linked to the case that their absence could create real problems.

Example 3: Employees A and B work for the same company and seek the same promotion, which is a single position that can be given to only one of them. Their employment contracts dictate that promotion is based on seniority, but they disagree about the application of the seniority rule. Employee A claims that she is entitled to the promotion, but the company asserts that it is obligated to give the promotion to employee B. A sues the employer, seeking injunctive relief to obtain the promotion. The employer moves for an order that employee B be joined as a required party under Rule 19(a).

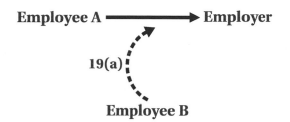

The rule spells out three circumstances under which a person will be deemed a required party. These three provisions often overlap, but they are analytically distinct, and you must apply each one on its own. Example 3 presents a situation in which the absent party arguably satisfies all three (but as long as *one* is satisfied, the person is a required party).

Rule 19(a)(1)(A) requires joinder if "in that person's absence, the court cannot accord complete relief among existing parties." In Example 3, because employee A seeks injunctive relief and the promotion is a single position that cannot be held by both A and B, employee A cannot get complete relief unless B is bound by a ruling that the promotion belongs to A.

Rule 19(a)(1)(B)(i) requires joinder if "that person claims an interest relating to the subject of the action and is so situated that disposing of the action in the person's absence may: as a practical matter impair or impede the person's ability to protect the interest." In Example 3, employee B certainly claims an interest relating to the subject of the action—the promotion. And as a practical matter, the action may impair B's ability to protect that interest, because if the court rules that A is entitled to the promotion, there is a significant risk that the company will remove B from the position. In one case, individual members of a Native American tribe sued for a declaration that a state cigarette tax that affected merchants on American Indian reservations violated the Indian Commerce Clause of the Constitution. The tribe itself, however, was not named as a party. The court of appeals ruled that the tribe was a required party because the disposition of the action would affect the legally protected interest of the tribe.[3]

---

[3]Wilbur v. Locke, 423 F.3d 1101, 1111-1115 (9th Cir. 2005).

Rule 19(a)(1)(B)(ii) requires joinder if "that person claims an interest relating to the subject of the action and is so situated that disposing of the action in the person's absence may . . . leave an existing party subject to a substantial risk of incurring double, multiple, or otherwise inconsistent obligations because of the interest." In Example 3, suppose the case goes forward without joining B, and the court orders the employer to give A the job. B was not a party to the lawsuit, so B is not legally bound by the judgment. B brings a separate lawsuit and obtains a judgment ordering the employer to give the position to B, not A. The two judgments would place the employer in an untenable position. One judge has ordered the employer to give the position to A, and another judge court has ordered the employer to give the position to B. In the language of Rule 19(a)(1)(B)(ii), disposing of the action in B's absence would leave the employer subject to a substantial risk of inconsistent obligations.

Compare the relatively uncommon setup of Example 3, in which the parties' positions are truly intertwined, with the more common situations in which related claims are brought by or against multiple parties:

Example 4: Employees A and B are fired from the same company, and both blame the termination on the same allegedly discriminatory policy. A sues the employer for employment discrimination.

In Example 4, if A and B *choose* to file a lawsuit together, that's their prerogative. Under Rule 20(a), A and B may use *permissive joinder* because their claims arise out of the same transaction or occurrence (the allegedly discriminatory policy), and involve at least one common question of law or fact (whether the employer's policy was illegal). But *must* A and B sue together? In other words, is B a *required party*? Absolutely not. Take it through the Rule 19(a) analysis step by step:

19(a)(1)(A): Is B needed in order to accord complete relief *among those already parties*? No. As between the employer and A, their dispute can be completely resolved whether or not B is a party.

19(a)(1)(B)(i): Will A's lawsuit impair B's interests? No. Whatever happens in A's lawsuit, B remains free to bring a separate action against the employer.

19(a)(1)(B)(ii): Is B needed to prevent a risk of inconsistent obligations? No. Even if they bring separate lawsuits and A wins and B loses, that's not what the rule means by *inconsistent obligations*. "Inconsistent obligations" means the untenable situation presented by Example 3, in which a party may be ordered to do *X* and also ordered to do *not X*. Here, even if A and B obtain different outcomes, the employer can reinstate and pay damages to A and can say goodbye to B — nothing *inconsistent* about that.

The analysis would be the same in the vast majority of situations in which multiple plaintiffs have claims against a defendant that arise out of the same transaction or occurrence. Multiple victims injured by a defendant's negligence are *not* required parties in each other's lawsuits. Nor are multiple consumers defrauded by a business, or multiple investors who lost money on securities based on an issuer's misrepresentation, or multiple victims of a civil rights violation, and so on. *May* they bring their claims in a single action against the defendant? Sure. That's permissive joinder under Rule 20. *Must* they bring their claims together? No, that's up to them.

Example 5: A patient suffers injury after receiving a surgical implant. The patient blames both the surgeon, accusing him of malpractice, and the manufacturer of the implant, accusing it of producing a defective product. The patient brings a product liability lawsuit against the manufacturer. Rather than joining the surgeon as a defendant in that action, the patient files a separate lawsuit against the surgeon for medical malpractice. In the product liability action, the manufacturer moves to dismiss for failure to join an indispensable party.

Example 5 is based on the Supreme Court case of *Temple v. Synthes Corp.*[4] In that case, the district court and court of appeals both held that the surgeon was a required party under Rule 19, and even went a step further and dismissed the action, finding the surgeon indispensable. The Supreme Court emphatically disagreed. The Court stated plainly that the surgeon was *not* a required party under Rule 19(a). Indeed, as if to put an exclamation point on it, the Court decided the case by granting certiorari and summarily reversing in a unanimous per curiam opinion, which means that the Justices found this one so easy that they didn't even need to hear oral argument! To understand why it was so obvious to the Court that the surgeon was not a required party, take it through the Rule 19(a) steps:

19(a)(1)(A): Is the surgeon needed in order to accord complete relief among those already parties? No. The manufacturer may argue that the injury was the surgeon's fault, so the plaintiff cannot get "complete relief" unless the surgeon is joined as a defendant. But that's not the point. The rule talks about complete relief *among those already parties.* As between the plaintiff and manufacturer, their product liability dispute can be completely resolved whether or not the surgeon is a party. Either the manufacturer is liable or not. The manufacturer also may argue that the surgeon is required because he knows what happened in the operating room. But a person can be subpoenaed to testify as a *witness* even if not a party to the case. The surgeon may be a critical witness in the product liability case, but that does not mean he is a required *party.*

19(a)(1)(B)(i): Will the lawsuit impair the surgeon's interests? No. Whatever happens in the product liability lawsuit, the surgeon remains free to assert any defenses against a potential malpractice claim. The manufacturer may argue that the surgeon's interests will be impaired if the jury in this action decides that the implant was not defective and the injury was the surgeon's fault. But remember that as long as the surgeon is not a party, he is not legally bound by the judgment.

19(a)(1)(B)(ii): Is the surgeon needed to prevent a risk of inconsistent obligations? No. The manufacturer may argue that if the plaintiff brings two separate lawsuits, one jury may blame the injury entirely on the surgeon and another jury may blame it entirely on the manufacturer, and that would be "inconsistent." But again, remember what the rule means by *inconsistent obligations*—the type of incompatible orders presented by Example 3.

The rule of *Temple v. Synthes* is clear: *Joint tortfeasors are not required parties. May* the plaintiff bring the product liability claim against the manufacturer and the

---

[4]498 U.S. 5 (1990).

malpractice claim against the surgeon in a single action? Yes, as permissive party joinder; the claims arise out of the same occurrence (the surgical implantation). *Must* the plaintiff sue both defendants together? No, that's up to the plaintiff. And, as with Example 4, the analysis would be the same in most situations in which a plaintiff has claims against multiple potential defendants arising out of the same transaction or occurrence.

(2) Indispensable Parties

If a court finds that a person is a required party, the court may order that the person be joined. But what happens when a required party *cannot* be joined? That's what Rule 19(b) addresses.

There are two reasons why it might be impossible to join a required party in federal court: *personal jurisdiction* and *subject matter jurisdiction*. If the absent person is beyond the court's reach as a matter of personal jurisdiction, then the court is powerless to order that he or she be joined. Recall from Chapter 2 that the hundred-mile bulge provision of Rule 4(k)(1)(B) expands a federal court's jurisdictional reach for joining parties under Rule 19. But if a party cannot be served within 100 miles of the court and otherwise is not subject to the court's personal jurisdiction, then joinder is impossible. Similarly, if subject matter jurisdiction is based on diversity of citizenship and joinder of the party would destroy complete diversity, then the court cannot order that the party be joined.

The absent party is needed under the Rule 19(a) analysis, but cannot be joined because of the jurisdictional barrier. In this situation of "We must, but we can't," the court's choices are to go forward without the required party or to dismiss the action. Rule 19(b) instructs the court to "determine whether, in equity and good conscience, the action should proceed among the existing parties or should be dismissed." It forces the judge to make a hard decision: Under the circumstances, would it be better to go forward with the case to do at least *some* justice, or would it be so unjust to proceed in the party's absence that it's better not to adjudicate at all?

Rule 19(b) lists four factors for the court to consider: (1) To what extent might a judgment be prejudicial to the parties or to the absent person? (2) To what extent can relief be shaped to avoid prejudice? For example, if the court can minimize the prejudicial impact by awarding money damages rather than injunctive relief, then dismissal may be unwarranted. (3) Would a judgment rendered in the person's absence be adequate? If the judgment would not provide the relief sought, then it may make little sense to proceed with the action in the person's absence. (4) Would the plaintiff have an adequate remedy if the action is dismissed? Dismissal may be the right option if the plaintiff can bring the action in a different forum. If the obstacle to joinder was diversity jurisdiction, can all of the parties be joined in state court? If the obstacle was personal jurisdiction, can all of the parties be joined in a different state? If so, then the court may dismiss so that all of the required parties may be joined in a single action elsewhere. As the Supreme Court explained in *Provident Tradesmens Bank & Trust Co. v. Patterson,*[5] one goal of Rule 19 is "the interest of the courts and the public in complete, consistent, and efficient settlement of controversies."

As a practical matter, it's the possibility of dismissal that usually brings compulsory party joinder into play. Some defendants actually want an additional party joined, but think about it — wouldn't most defendants rather get the case dismissed?

You will need to conduct a compulsory party joinder analysis if you represent a plaintiff deciding whether you must join a party or if you represent a defendant deciding whether you're able to make a viable motion for joinder or a motion to dismiss for failure to join a party. Either way, when you are trying to figure out whether an absent party is required, indispensable, or neither, here's how your analysis might go:

Sidebar

WHAT MAKES COMPULSORY JOINDER "COMPULSORY"?

Lawyers often refer to compulsory counterclaims and compulsory party joinder, but rarely think about the difference in what actually makes them *compulsory*. There are at least three ways to make joinder compulsory. First and most simply, a court can *order* joinder. That's the approach of Rule 19(a) for joinder of required parties. Violation of a court order is punishable as contempt, so there's an implicit threat behind such an order. Second, a court can *dismiss* an action for failure to join. That's the approach of Rule 19(b) and the Rule 12(b)(7) motion to dismiss for failure to join an indispensable party. Third, failure to join can result in *preclusion*. That's the approach of compulsory counterclaims under Rule 13(a), as well as claim preclusion.

Compulsory Party Joinder Analysis

I. First, determine whether the absentee is a *required party*. (Rule 19(a))
- 19(a)(1)(A): If the case proceeds without the person, is *complete relief impossible* among those already parties?
- 19(a)(1)(B)(i): If the case proceeds without the person, would a judgment impair the *absentee's interests*?
- 19(a)(1)(B)(ii): If the case proceeds without the person, is there a substantial risk of *inconsistent obligations*?
- ☐ If the answer to these three questions is no, then the person need not be joined.
- ☐ If the answer to any of them is yes, then the person is a required party and must be joined if feasible →

II. If the absentee is required, then proceed to determine whether joinder is *feasible*.
- Does the court have *personal jurisdiction* over the person? Apply the jurisdictional analysis from Chapter 2. Keep in mind the extended reach of federal courts over Rule 19 parties pursuant to Rule 4(k)(1)(B).
- Would the court retain *subject matter jurisdiction* if the person were joined? Apply the diversity jurisdiction analysis from Chapter 1 to determine whether joinder would destroy complete diversity.

- ☐ If the answer to both of these questions is yes, then joinder is feasible, and the party must be joined.
- ☐ If the answer to either of them is no, then joinder is not feasible, and the party may not be joined. The court then must decide what to do →

---

[5]390 U.S. 102, 111 (1968).

III. If the party cannot be joined, then proceed to determine whether the action should be dismissed. (Rule 19(b))
  ☐ In the interests of justice and equity, does it make more sense to proceed without the absentee, or not to proceed at all?
  ☐ Four factors:
    ▪ Extent of prejudice to parties and absentee.
    ▪ Possibility of minimizing prejudice.
    ▪ Whether judgment would be adequate.
    ▪ Whether plaintiff would have remedy if dismissed.

D. Third-Party Claims

When a defendant gets sued, the most predictable response is some version of "I'm not liable." That's the stuff of denials, affirmative defenses, motions to dismiss, motions for summary judgment, and trial. But there's another extremely common response that may not be quite as obvious to the uninitiated: "If I am liable, then this other person should have to pay for all or part of my liability." That's what **third-party claims** are all about.

With a third-party claim, a defendant joins a new party—the *third-party defendant*—and asserts a claim against that party for indemnification or contribution in case the defendant is held liable to the original plaintiff. As Rule 14 puts it, a "defending party may, as third-party plaintiff, serve a summons and complaint on a nonparty who is or may be liable to it for all or part of the claim against it." You will often hear lawyers, judges, and professors refer to this as *impleader*—the defendant *impleads* the third-party defendant.

Courts reject third-party claims if they do not involve some sort of secondary or derivative liability. One district judge explained this point particularly well: "In other words, a third party claim is not appropriate where the [defendant] says, in effect, 'It was him, not me.' Such a claim is viable only where a [defendant] says, in effect, 'If I am liable to plaintiff, then my liability is only technical or secondary or partial, and the third party defendant is derivatively liable and must reimburse me for all or part . . . of anything I must pay plaintiff.'"[6] Indeed, a third-party claim does not establish a claim by the original plaintiff against the third-party defendant. The plaintiff may decide to amend the complaint to add a related claim directly against the third-party defendant, but unless the plaintiff does so, the third-party claim runs strictly between the defendant/third-party plaintiff and the third-party defendant.

---

[6]Watergate Landmark Condominiums Unit Owners' Ass'n v. Wiss, Janey, Elstner Assocs., 117 F.R.D. 576, 578 (E.D. Va. 1987).

F   A   Q

Q: By asserting a third-party claim, does a defendant admit liability on the underlying claim?

A: No. A third-party claim does not require the defendant to admit liability on the underlying claim. The third-party claim is conditional: "*If* I'm liable, then the third-party defendant is required to reimburse me for all or part of my liability."

Third-party claims are similar to counterclaims and crossclaims. Representing a defendant seeking ways to shift some or all of the ultimate liability, you may consider all three. If you can place some of the responsibility on the plaintiff, such as under a comparative fault statute, you would consider filing a *counterclaim*. If the plaintiff sued multiple defendants and a co-defendant may be liable to your client for indemnification or contribution, then you would consider filing a *crossclaim*. And if your client has a potential claim for indemnification or contribution against someone who has not been joined in the lawsuit, then you would consider filing a *third-party claim*. But whereas counterclaims and crossclaims involve only joinder of claims, the third-party claim constitutes a type of *party joinder* because it adds a new party to the litigation.

E. Intervention

Intervention is the procedural mechanism by which someone seeks to become a party to an action that has already commenced. Although the plaintiff did not join the person as a plaintiff or as a defendant, the person desires to be part of the lawsuit and therefore *intervenes* in the action.

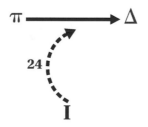

One way to think about intervention is as a counterpoint to compulsory party joinder. In each situation, there is someone who could have been a party to the litigation but who was not joined. The difference is that with required parties, it's the defendant who drags the outsider into the litigation, whereas with intervention, it's the outsider who wants to jump in. Who in their right mind would *want* to jump into ongoing litigation? Isn't litigation something people (with the possible exception of the plaintiff) try to avoid? As the great Judge Learned Hand once commented, "I must say that, as a litigant, I should dread a lawsuit beyond almost anything else short of sickness and death."[7] Mostly, outsiders to a lawsuit would want to jump in only if they have some substantial interest that may be harmed by the outcome of the litigation and they cannot trust any of the current parties to protect their interest.

(1) Intervention of Right

Rule 24 divides intervention into **intervention of right** and **permissive intervention**. If a would-be intervenor satisfies the requirements for *intervention of right* under Rule 24(a), then a court must allow the party to intervene. Rule 24(a), in other words, gives the would-be intervenor a *right* to intervene in the action. *Permissive intervention*, by contrast, is discretionary. If the would-be intervenor satisfies Rule 24(b), then it is up to the court whether to *permit* the party to intervene.

Rule 24(a) lists two bases for the right to intervene. First, if a federal statute grants the right to intervene, then of course the court must allow intervention in accordance with the terms of the statute. Second and more important, the rule grants a right to intervene when the applicant "claims an interest relating to the property or transaction that is the subject of the action, and is so situated that disposing of the action may as a practical matter impair or impede the movant's ability to protect its interest, unless existing parties adequately represent that interest." This language—"so situated that disposing of the action may as a practical matter impair or impede the movant's ability to protect its interest"— should sound familiar. It tracks almost exactly the language of Rule 19(a)(1)(B)(i) defining one type of required party. The logic is related: For Rule 19, it's an outsider to the litigation whose interest is at stake and who therefore must be joined if feasible. For Rule 24, it's an outsider to the litigation whose interest is at stake and who therefore must be allowed to intervene.

Courts usefully describe Rule 24(a)(2) as establishing a three-part test: (a) an interest in the action, (b) a risk that the action may impair or impede that interest, and (c) no current party who adequately protects that interest.

INTERVENTION OF RIGHT UNDER RULE 24(A)

(1) Conferred by statute, *or*
(2) Three-part test under Rule 24(a)(2):
    (a) legally protectable interest
    (b) may be impaired or impeded
    (c) not adequately represented

The intervenor's interest must be a *legally protectable interest*—often but not always an economic interest—and not merely a moral or political concern about the issues in the lawsuit. The test for whether the interest may be impaired or impeded is pragmatic rather than legalistic, as emphasized by the inclusion of the words "as a

---

[7]3 Lectures on Legal Topics, Association of the Bar of the City of New York 106 (1926).

practical matter." Determining whether the current parties adequately represent the interests of the would-be intervenor requires a realistic assessment of the interests of the parties. Often, it is helpful to think about what sort of settlement might satisfy each party and whether such a settlement would adequately protect the interests of the party applying to intervene. In an environmental lawsuit by the Sierra Club against the secretary of agriculture, for example, two timber trade associations intervened under Rule 24(a) to protect the interests of the trade association members, because the lawsuit could affect their economic interests, and neither the environmental group nor the government adequately protected the interests of the timber industry.[8]

(2) Permissive Intervention

Let's be precise about the use of the word *permissive*. *Permissive intervention* uses the word in a different sense from permissive counterclaims, permissive joinder of claims, and permissive party joinder. In each of those instances, *permissive* refers to a party's discretionary decision. A permissive counterclaim is one that the defending party *may*, but need not, assert. Permissive joinder refers to claims or parties that the pleader *may*, but need not, join. In this sense of the word, *all* intervention should be considered "permissive." There's no such thing as *compulsory* intervention under the federal rules, a point emphasized by the Supreme Court in *Martin v. Wilks*.[9] Unless a statute dictates otherwise,[10] the decision whether to intervene is up to the potential intervenor. The distinction between Rules 24(b) and 24(a) is not between permissive and *compulsory*, but rather between permissive and *of right*. Whereas Rule 24(a) describes when a person *has a right* to intervene, Rule 24(b) describes when a *court may permit* intervention at the court's discretion.

Under Rule 24(b), a court may permit a person to intervene in an action when an applicant "has a claim or defense that shares with the main action a common question of law or fact." This requirement — at least one common question of law or fact — echoes Rule 42(a)'s requirement for consolidation. Both permissive intervention and consolidation set up this bare minimum requirement and then leave the court wide discretion to decide whether it would make sense to consolidate or to let another party join the action by intervening.

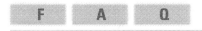

F A Q

Q: Why would someone choose to intervene rather than participate as amicus curiae?

A: Amicus curiae ("friend of the court") is a status that allows a nonparty, with the court's permission, to offer input on the issues in a case by submitting briefs and sometimes by oral argument. When a nonparty wishes to provide input on a legal issue, filing an amicus brief often suffices. Participation as amicus, however, does not make someone a *party* to the

---

[8]Sierra Club v. Espy, 18 F.3d 1202 (5th Cir. 1994).
[9]490 U.S. 755 (1989).
[10]*See, e.g.,* Civil Rights Act of 1991, 42 U.S.C. ?2000e-2(n)(1).

action. Parties enjoy procedural opportunities unavailable to nonparties, such as taking discovery, making motions, presenting evidence at trial, and filing an appeal. To participate fully in the action, one must become a party, and for someone who has not been joined by the parties, intervention is the ticket.

(3) Timeliness

Interestingly, Rule 24 does not specify the time limit for applying to intervene, which is noteworthy in a set of procedural rules that contains dozens of ultra-specific time limits complete with rules on precisely how to compute the number of days. Instead, Rules 24(a) and 24(b) each begin with "On timely motion . . ."

Applications to intervene may be denied for being *untimely*. Rather than stating a certain number of days, the rule requires a more fact-specific inquiry to determine timeliness. That is because the situations for intervention vary so widely. When did the intervenor first learn about the lawsuit? When should the intervenor have realized that its interests were at stake? When did it become clear that the existing parties would not adequately protect the intervenor's interests? The upshot is that it can be difficult to analyze whether an application is timely, but if you represent a potential intervenor, make sure you file the application promptly once you realize that intervention is warranted.

F. Interpleader

Please do not confuse this topic with *impleader*, which is another name for third-party claims under Rule 14. This is *interpleader*, a more obscure joinder mechanism, but one that can prove extremely useful in the right situation. Although you'll encounter interpleader pretty rarely, it's worth learning not only for the occasion when the procedure actually comes in handy, but also because it highlights the limitations of other joinder devices.

Interpleader is an action brought by a stakeholder against multiple claimants. It is used in the following situation: Someone (the stakeholder) is holding something (the stake) that others (the claimants) claim. Maybe it's an insurance company holding the proceeds of an insurance policy and facing multiple persons claiming to be the beneficiary. Maybe it's a parking garage holding an automobile that has multiple persons claiming to be the owner. The stakeholder needs to know whether it must give the stake to one of the claimants, and if so, to whom. Interpleader provides the procedural mechanism by which the stakeholder can bring an action against the claimants and thereby obtain a judgment that will be binding on all of them.

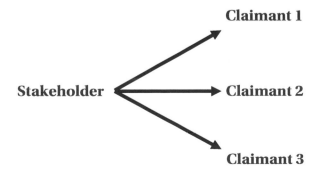

Without interpleader, a stakeholder might find itself subject to multiple liability or inconsistent obligations. Fundamentally, the problem flows from the principle that nonparties are not bound by a judgment. If claimant 1 sues the stakeholder and prevails, it remains possible that claimants 2 and 3 will sue the stakeholder later for the same thing. Compulsory party joinder under Rule 19 offers one solution to this problem, but for some stakeholders that option is too reactive and uncertain. Interpleader allows the stakeholder to take the situation into its own hands to obtain a judicial resolution. A concrete example may help.

Example 6: Acme Life Insurance Co. wrote a $500,000 life insurance policy on the life of Ms. Farrell. The policy named "my husband" as the beneficiary. Farrell died, and now two people have submitted claims. One is Farrell's ex-husband, H1, who was married to Farrell when she bought the insurance policy. The other is Farrell's new husband, H2, whom she married a year ago.

Acme knows that it owes $500,000, but it does not know to whom. It's the perfect occasion to use interpleader. Interpleader would be permissible even if Acme itself had a claim to keep the money, such as an argument that the insurance policy was void for nonpayment of premiums. Whether or not the stakeholder claims an interest, interpleader allows a court to resolve the claims of competing claimants.

To see why no option other than interpleader fully resolves Acme's problem, let's run through the other procedural possibilities. Suppose H1 sues Acme and wins a judgment. Can the insurance company simply pay the money to H1, relying on the judgment? Not comfortably. H2 could file his own suit against Acme demanding payment of the life insurance proceeds.

#1 H1 → Acme Insurance Co.

    ■ Judgment for π — $500,000

#2 H2 → Acme Insurance Co.

Imagine an exchange between the parties when Acme, having satisfied the judgment in case #1, receives H2's complaint in case #2:

Acme:	Sorry, H2, you're too late. We just paid the proceeds to H1.
H2:	That's your problem. I'm entitled to $500,000 under the policy.
Acme:	No, you're not. The court decided that H1 was the beneficiary.
H2:	I was not a party, so I'm not bound by what that court determined. Now, I'm asking *this* court to determine that *I'm* the rightful beneficiary.

H2 is right, of course. A nonparty is not bound by a judgment, so Acme remains vulnerable to being ordered in case #2 to pay $500,000 to H2, even though Acme was already ordered in case #1 to pay $500,000 to H1.

How about impleader as a solution? If H1 sues Acme, can Acme file a third-party claim to bring in H2? No, that approach obviously won't work. To assert a third-party claim under Rule 14, Acme would have to contend that if it is liable to H1, then H2 must reimburse Acme for all or part of that liability, which would be nonsensical under these circumstances.

A better option might be compulsory party joinder under Rule 19. If H1 sues Acme, Acme could move to have H2 joined as a required party or could make a Rule

12(b)(7) motion to dismiss for failure to join H2. The Rule 19 motion *might* solve the problem. Thinking about the compulsory party joinder analysis, H2 undoubtedly would qualify as a required party, especially under Rule 19(a)(1)(B)(ii). As long as H2's joinder would not present problems of personal jurisdiction or subject matter jurisdiction, the court would order that H2 be joined, and this would resolve Acme's problem because the court could render a decision that would bind Acme, H1, and H2. But what if the court lacked jurisdiction to join H2? Then, under Rule 19(b), the court would decide whether to proceed or to dismiss. To Acme, both of those options are unsatisfactory. Acme doesn't want a dismissal; it wants a *binding resolution* in an action that includes both H1 and H2.

Interpleader allows Acme to take control of the situation. Acme can commence an interpleader action against H1 and H2, seeking a binding judgment from the court on who is the rightful beneficiary under the insurance policy.

Even if the action began with H1's filing a lawsuit against Acme for the insurance proceeds, Acme could commence the interpleader action by bringing an interpleader counterclaim against H1 and joining H2 as an additional claimant.

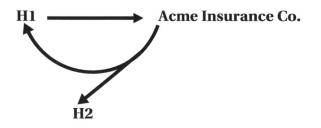

Interpleader does not work as an all-purpose tool for potential defendants who want to preempt multiplaintiff litigation. Imagine a company that knows it's facing a large number of potential lawsuits. It may seem like a clever idea for the company to commence a huge interpleader action against all of the potential plaintiffs. The strategic advantage would be to eliminate plaintiffs' power to choose the forum or to bring multiple individual lawsuits. When a party tried this tactic in a bus accident case, however, the Supreme Court stated that interpleader cannot be used as a general aggregation mechanism to bring together claims in mass litigation.[11]

Federal law establishes two types of interpleader: *rule interpleader* and *statutory interpleader.* Both offer the same procedural mechanism—an action by a

---

[11]State Farm Fire & Casualty Co. v. Tashire, 386 U.S. 523 (1967).

stakeholder against multiple claimants — but statutory interpleader alters the provisions on jurisdiction and venue to facilitate gathering all the claimants in a single forum.

(1) Rule Interpleader

Rule interpleader refers to interpleader pursuant to Rule 22 of the Federal Rules of Civil Procedure. The numerical placement gives it away as a joinder rule just like its neighbors Rules 20 (permissive party joinder), 23 (class actions), and 24 (intervention). Rule 22 simply establishes a procedural mechanism for interpleader in federal court. It does not alter the requirements of subject matter jurisdiction, personal jurisdiction, and venue. When you represent a stakeholder facing multiple inconsistent claims, you could use rule interpleader in federal court if there is a basis for federal subject matter jurisdiction, if the chosen court has personal jurisdiction over each of the claimants, and if venue is proper under the usual venue rules of 28 U.S.C. §1391.

Unless the underlying claims arise under federal law, subject matter jurisdiction for rule interpleader ordinarily depends on diversity jurisdiction under 28 U.S.C. §1332, which requires that the stakeholder's citizenship be diverse from the claimants and that the amount in controversy exceed $75,000.

(2) Statutory Interpleader

Interpleader's goal is to enable stakeholders to obtain a resolution of the competing claims of inconsistent claimants to an asset. For that resolution to carry finality, the stakeholder needs to make sure that all of the claimants are joined in the action. But any lawyer seeking to join multiple claimants in a single action knows that even if the joinder is procedurally proper under the applicable joinder mechanism, two major obstacles stand in the way — subject matter jurisdiction and personal jurisdiction.

Returning to Example 6, in which Acme Insurance needs to know whether to pay the life insurance proceeds to H1 or H2, let's look at jurisdiction. Acme is a Delaware corporation with its principal place of business in Connecticut. H1 is a Texas domiciliary, and H2 is a Connecticut domiciliary. H2 lacks minimum contacts with Texas, and H1 lacks minimum contacts with Connecticut.

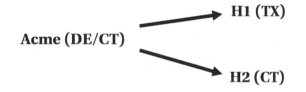

You see Acme's problem. Under the usual personal jurisdiction analysis, Acme cannot join both H1 and H2 in either Texas or Connecticut, or perhaps anywhere else. And under standard subject matter jurisdiction analysis, Acme cannot get into federal court anywhere; there's no federal question jurisdiction over these state law claims, and complete diversity is lacking because both Acme and H2 are citizens of Connecticut.

Statutory interpleader to the rescue! First, the federal interpleader statute, 28 U.S.C. §1335, alters the requirements for federal subject matter jurisdiction. It lowers the amount-in-controversy requirement from over $75,000 to $500, and instead of requiring complete diversity between plaintiffs and defendants, it requires only minimal diversity among the claimants themselves. Acme's interpleader would have federal subject matter jurisdiction because the amount is at least $500 and at least one claimant is of diverse citizenship from at least one other. Second, another provision of the statute, 28 U.S.C. §2361, grants nationwide personal jurisdiction for statutory interpleader. Acme could bring the interpleader action in federal court in either Texas or Connecticut, and the court would have personal jurisdiction over both H1 and H2, even if one lacks minimum contacts with the state. Third, the statute's venue provision, 28 U.S.C. §1397, permits a statutory interpleader action to be brought in any district where at least one claimant resides, so Acme could choose either Texas or Connecticut.

By reducing the jurisdictional obstacles, statutory interpleader tries to make good on the promise of the interpleader device—to allow a stakeholder to obtain a resolution that will bind all of the known claimants in one fell swoop.

Q: If statutory interpleader lowers the obstacles, why would a stakeholder ever use rule interpleader?

A: It's correct that statutory interpleader generally offers greater benefits to a stakeholder by making it easier to drag all of the claimants into a single forum. Sometimes, however, the special provisions of statutory interpleader are unnecessary because jurisdiction and venue are satisfied under the usual rules. Moreover, one particular set of circumstances renders *statutory* interpleader unavailable but leaves *rule* interpleader working fine. It's when the amount in controversy exceeds $75,000 and all of the claimants are citizens of the same state but diverse from the stakeholder (in Example 6, suppose H1 and H2 are both Texan, and Acme is still a Delaware corporation with its principal place of business in Connecticut). In that situation, no minimal diversity exists among the claimants, but there is complete diversity in the usual §1332 sense. Yes, I admit that this little twist probably interests civil procedure professors more than any normal person.

G. Class Actions

In most law schools, the details of class action procedure are taught in advanced courses on complex litigation. In the basic civil procedure course, some professors ignore class actions altogether while others teach class actions in some depth. In this book, I won't get into all the nitty-gritty of class actions, but I will try to cover the topics that are most likely to come up in civil procedure classes.

(1) A Different Kind of Joinder

This chapter has looked at a number of joinder devices that bring multiple parties together in a single lawsuit — permissive party joinder, compulsory party joinder, impleader, intervention, and interpleader. Each involves a different structure and arises in a different situation, but so far, they all have this in common: Every party is included by name.

Class actions work differently. A **class action** is *representative litigation*. In a class action, a party sues on behalf of herself and on behalf of all others who are similarly situated. She may not know who the class members are or just how many of them are out there, but she is their representative. The class members may have no interest in pursuing their claims, indeed they may be totally unaware that they even have claims, but if they are part of the defined class in a certified class action, then their claims are represented by the named class representative and class counsel. When a class action reaches judgment, the judgment is binding on all the class members as long as they were adequately represented.

$$\pi \; [\textbf{class}] \longrightarrow \Delta$$

Class actions, in other words, run contrary to all our usual notions of autonomy, consent, and participation in civil procedure. Why would the law allow such a crazy thing? Three answers: efficiency, consistency, and empowerment. When huge numbers of claimants share essentially the same claim, a class action can resolve the dispute much more efficiently than individual litigation or even nonclass mass joinder. Class actions also yield more consistent results than individual litigation because all class members are bound by the outcome of a single lawsuit. Consistency matters in cases involving money damages, but it is especially crucial in cases involving common injunctive relief.

Finally, class actions empower plaintiffs to pursue claims that are not worth pursuing individually but are worth pursuing in the aggregate. Suppose a cell phone company with a million customers imposes $5 of illegal extra charges on each customer's monthly bill. Over the course of a year, that's a $60 million violation! But probably not a single customer would sue because it would cost much more to litigate than the $60 that each plaintiff has at stake. The class action device enables a lawyer and a class representative to pursue the claims on behalf of all of the customers. Even if none of the class members really care about their monetary recovery, the class action creates a mechanism for enforcing the law and furthering the policies of disgorgement and deterrence.

Because class actions bind persons who may not have participated in the litigation, the law imposes a number of special procedures to protect the interests of class members. First, a case does not proceed as a class action unless the court certifies the class. Second, the court has the power to appoint the lawyer for the class and the court has power over the class counsel's fees. Third, settlement of a class action requires court approval. Fourth, in most money damages cases, class members get notice and have the right to opt out of the class action. Fifth, a class action is binding on the class members only if they were adequately represented.

(2) Rule 23(a) Prerequisites

Filing a class action complaint does not create a class action; it merely creates a "putative class action" that the plaintiff hopes will be certified. The only thing that creates a class action is **class certification**. When a party moves to certify the class, the judge must decide whether the case meets the class certification requirements of Rules 23(a) and 23(b).

For class certification, a class action must meet all four of the prerequisites stated in Rule 23(a): numerosity, commonality, typicality, and adequate representation. In addition, class certification requires that the class action meet the requirements of at least one of the class action categories identified in Rule 23(b).

Numerosity. If the number of class members is not too large, then the parties can simply join together in a single lawsuit under the permissive joinder rule. Rule 23(a)(1) therefore requires that the number of class members be so large than joinder is impracticable. Courts emphasize that no magic number exists; numerosity requires case-by-case determination. In general, classes in the hundreds usually meet the numerosity requirement, and classes below 40 rarely meet the requirement. Really big class actions sometimes involve millions of class members; in the big cases, nobody disputes numerosity.

Commonality. Rule 23(a)(2) requires common questions of law or fact. We saw a similar requirement for permissive joinder under Rule 20. Lawyers used to consider Rule 23's commonality requirement pretty easy to meet, but in 2011, the Supreme Court took commonality to a new level in *Wal-Mart Stores v. Dukes*.[12] Rejecting a gender discrimination class action against Wal-Mart, the Court emphasized that the claims were not unified enough: "Their claims must depend upon a common contention—for example, the assertion of discriminatory bias on the part of the same supervisor. That common contention, moreover, must be of such a nature that it is capable of classwide resolution—which means that determination of its truth or falsity will resolve an issue that is central to the validity of each one of the claims in one stroke."[13] A party seeking class certification must show that there is "some glue" holding the claims together.[14]

Typicality. For the class representative to sue on behalf of the entire group of similarly situated plaintiffs, the representative's situation must be like that of the rest of the class. Rule 23(a)(3) therefore requires that the named party's claim be typical of the

---

Sidebar

DEFENDANT CLASS ACTIONS

The vast majority of class actions involve classes of plaintiffs. The class action rule, however, also permits actions against a class of defendants. (Look at the language "sue or be sued" in the first sentence of Rule 23.) For example, if a plaintiff files a civil rights action to reform the prison system in Texas and wants each of the hundreds of prison wardens to be bound by the judgment, the plaintiff might ask the court to certify a class of wardens as defendants in the action. Forcing an unwilling defendant to be an adequate class representative doesn't make much sense except in special situations such as where a trade organization has a preexisting duty to represent the interests of the group, so you won't see defendant class actions very often. Defendant class actions—weird in theory, rare in practice.

---

[12]131 S. Ct. 2541 (2011).
[13]*Id.* at 2551.
[14]*Id.* at 2552.

class. Although some variation may exist within the class, the class representative should not be an outlier.

Adequacy of Representation. This is the most fundamental requirement of them all. Rule 23(a)(4) requires, for class certification, that the class representative will adequately represent the interests of the entire class. Courts rarely worry about the class representative's skills or knowledge or ability to handle the litigation because, as a practical matter, class representatives often function as figureheads while the lawyers for the class actually handle the litigation. Courts do worry, however, about whether the class representatives have any conflicts of interest that prevent them from being adequate representatives. In this way, the adequacy requirement becomes another means of ensuring that the class is cohesive enough to justify a class action.

The adequacy requirement transcends Rule 23. Without adequate representation, a class action would violate the constitutional guarantee of due process. In the landmark case of *Hansberry v. Lee,*[15] the Supreme Court held that a class action judgment can bind the members of the class, but only if they were adequately represented.

In class actions, the issue of adequate representation comes up in different ways at different times. First, for class certification, the court must find under Rule 23(a)(4) that the class will be adequately represented. Second, when appointing class counsel under Rule 23(g), the court must ensure that the lawyer will adequately represent the class. Third, the court has an ongoing responsibility to ensure that the class is adequately represented throughout the proceedings, and has the power to modify the class certification decision or to remove class counsel if necessary. Fourth—and this is the one that raises the most vexing issues—after the conclusion of a class action, class members occasionally argue that they are not bound by the judgment or settlement on the grounds that they were not adequately represented.

(3) Rule 23(b) Categories

For class certification, the court must find not only that the class meets all four of the Rule 23(a) prerequisites, but also that it fits into at least one of the Rule 23(b) categories. These categories are a kind of shorthand for lawyers who handle class actions, so you might hear a lawyer say, "Hey, the court certified my b3 class action yesterday."

Sidebar

APPEALS FROM CLASS CERTIFICATION DECISIONS

The court's decision on class certification often looms as the single most important ruling in a case. If the court grants class certification, it creates massive litigation and places enormous pressure on the defendant to settle. If the court denies class certification, in theory the lawsuit proceeds as a nonclass action, but in reality the denial often amounts to a death knell for the litigation. Either way, the party on the losing side of the class certification motion usually would love to appeal the decision before proceeding with the case. In general, only final judgments are appealable, as discussed in Chapter 10. Grants or denials of class certification are interlocutory rulings rather than final judgments, and thus would not be appealable under the final judgment rule. But because class certification is such a critical moment in the case, Rule 23(f) permits interlocutory appeals of class certification rulings at the discretion of the court of appeals.

---

[15]311 U.S. 32 (1940).

The categories are significant not only for class certification, but also because different procedural requirements attach to them. In particular, Rule 23(b)(3) class actions have a stringent notice requirement and give class members the right to opt out, while (b)(1) and (b)(2) class actions do not permit opt-outs and carry a more flexible notice provision. Because they do not allow opt-outs, class actions under Rule 23(b)(1) and 23(b)(2) are sometimes called *mandatory class actions*, in contrast to Rule 23(b)(3)'s *opt-out class actions.*

(a) Rule 23(b)(1) Class Actions

Rule 23(b)(1) actually includes two subcategories of class actions, (b)(1)(A) and (b)(1)(B). The main thing they have in common is that their language and logic strongly resemble the compulsory party joinder analysis of Rule 19(a).

Rule 23(b)(1)(A) permits class certification if individual adjudications would create a risk of "incompatible standards of conduct" for the defendant. For example, suppose a company has issued a bond that is owned by thousands of investors, and an investor sues the company for a declaratory judgment that the bond may be converted to common stock. It would make no sense to address that issue individually, because if the bond is convertible to common stock, then it must be so for all of the investors. Without a class action, the company might face inconsistent rulings and would not know how it should treat the security. The 23(b)(1)(A) class action permits a single adjudication or settlement that applies to all of the investors who own that security.

Rule 23(b)(1)(B) permits class certification if individual adjudications might impair the ability of other class members to protect their own interests. The typical (b)(1)(B) class action involves a limited fund. For example, suppose a large number of individuals have claims to money that is held in a trust. The maximum amount available for all of the claims is the amount in the trust. As a practical matter, individual adjudications for some of the claimants would limit the amount of money for the remaining claimants and might even exhaust all of the available funds. The 23(b)(1)(B) class action permits a single adjudication or settlement that attempts to deal fairly and consistently with all of the claimants.

"Limited fund class actions" under Rule 23(b)(1)(B) were once considered a useful device for sorting out claims of money damages when the parties doubted the defendant's ability to pay the entirety of the claims. In 1999, however, the Supreme Court in *Ortiz v. Fibreboard Corp.*[16] imposed strict requirements for limited fund class actions, emphasizing that they may be certified only if the fund is clearly inadequate and the entire fund is applied to paying the claims.

(b) Rule 23(b)(2) Class Actions

Some class actions seek injunctive or declaratory relief rather than money damages. Most notably, civil rights class actions often have sought prison reform, school desegregation, voting rights enforcement, changes in hiring practices, and other types of institutional reform. If a court orders such injunctive relief, the remedy applies to all members of the class. Rule 23(b)(2) permits certification of a class action when the defendant has acted with respect to the entire class so that injunctive or declaratory relief "is appropriate respecting the class as a whole."

---

[16]527 U.S. 815 (1999).

In a Rule 23(b)(2) class action, can class members get money damages in addition to an injunctive or declaratory remedy? For example, in an employment discrimination class action certified under Rule 23(b)(2), can the class members get back pay as well as reform of the defendant's employment practices? Some courts have allowed 23(b)(2) class certification with monetary claims as long as the class seeks predominantly injunctive or declaratory relief. In the *Wal-Mart* employment discrimination class action, however, the Supreme Court held that Rule 23(b)(2) class certification was impermissible because the claims for back pay were not "incidental" to the claims for injunctive relief.[17]

(c) Rule 23(b)(3) Class Actions

Last but not least, Rule 23(b)(3) permits a class action if common questions predominate and if the court finds that a class action is the superior way to adjudicate the controversy. When you hear about a class action in the news—or when you receive a class action notice or a class settlement notice—usually it's a (b)(3) class action. For the most part, class actions for money damages—whether they involve antitrust, securities, product liability, consumer fraud, or other claims—are handled under Rule 23(b)(3).

Because money damages class actions seem less necessary than class actions under (b)(1) and (b)(2), Rule 23(b)(3) adds the two requirements that define this category: *predominance* and *superiority*. First, the court must find that "questions of law or fact common to class members predominate over any questions affecting only individual members." Common questions often involve the defendant's conduct and classwide defenses, while individual questions often relate to individual causation and damages as well as individual defenses such as comparative fault.

Second, the court must find that "a class action is superior to other available methods for fairly and efficiently adjudicating the controversy." The rule spells out factors for courts to consider when deciding whether a class action is superior. One important factor is "the class members' interests in individually controlling" their cases. If each claim involves high enough stakes that individual class members might pursue the claims themselves, a court is less likely to find superiority, in contrast to cases where each claim is too small to make an economically viable individual lawsuit. The rule also instructs courts to consider "the likely difficulties in managing a class action." If the

> ### Sidebar
>
> **MASS TORT LITIGATION**
>
> In recent years, some of the biggest and best-known examples of multiparty litigation have involved mass torts. Some arise from mass disasters such as air crashes or terrorist attacks, some involve toxic spills and environmental damage, and some arise from exposure to widespread products such as asbestos, tobacco, and pharmaceuticals. You might think that enormous litigation would always be certified as class actions. You would be wrong. Although a few courts have permitted mass tort class actions, most have rejected them on the grounds that personal injury claims are too individualized for class treatment. But just because class certification is denied, don't be fooled into thinking that mass torts proceed as truly individual cases. Even without a class action, lawyers sometimes represent hundreds or thousands of clients, and they sometimes negotiate mass aggregate settlements to resolve the disputes. In nonclass mass litigation, courts use consolidation and multidistrict litigation (a type of venue transfer explained in Chapter 3) to handle related cases together.

---

[17]*Wal-Mart Stores v. Dukes*, 131 S. Ct. 2541, 2545 (2011).

court cannot see how it will be able to manage the case if it gets to trial, then the court may reject class certification.

The predominance and superiority inquiries often overlap. If the class action would require the court to apply the laws of different states to different class members, for example, the court may find that the various laws are individual issues and thus reject predominance, and the court may also find that applying the various laws would be unmanageable and thus a class action is not superior. Similarly, if the class action would require individualized determinations of causation, the court may find that common issues do not predominate, and also find that the individual causation analysis makes the class action an inferior way to handle the dispute.

Remember that unlike (b)(1) and (b)(2) class actions, Rule 23(b)(3) class actions give class members the right to exclude themselves from the class. When you hear people refer to an "opt-out class action," they are talking about a (b)(3) class action.

(4) Jurisdiction in Class Actions

(a) Subject Matter Jurisdiction

When does a federal court have subject matter jurisdiction to hear a class action? To what extent does jurisdiction in class actions differ from the analysis described in Chapter 1 for non-class action cases?

For federal question jurisdiction, the analysis is identical to nonclass cases. Plenty of class actions arise under federal law — securities, antitrust, and civil rights are three major examples — and for those cases federal courts possess subject matter jurisdiction under the federal question jurisdiction statute, 28 U.S.C. §1331.

For diversity jurisdiction, class actions make things more interesting. Whose citizenship counts for purposes of diversity? And does the amount-in-controversy requirement apply to each individual class member? For basic diversity jurisdiction under 28 U.S.C. §1332(a), courts look only at the citizenship of the named class representatives, not every single class member.[18] In a nationwide class action against a New York defendant, as long as none of the named class representatives are citizens of New York, the complete diversity requirement is satisfied, even if many of the class members are New York citizens. For basic diversity jurisdiction under §1332(a), at least one class representative must individually meet the $75,000 amount-in-controversy requirement. If other class members do not meet the requirement, the court may exercise supplemental jurisdiction over those claims.[19]

More important, Congress passed a statute in 2005 that dramatically expanded federal court jurisdiction over class actions. The Class Action Fairness Act (CAFA), discussed in Chapter 1, permits federal jurisdiction over class actions based on minimal diversity (rather than the usual complete diversity requirement) and over a $5 million aggregate amount in controversy (rather than over $75,000 for each individual). Even if they do not satisfy the requirements of either federal question jurisdiction or basic diversity jurisdiction, most large-scale multistate class actions may now be brought in (or removed to) federal court.

---

[18]Supreme Tribe of Ben-Hur v. Cauble, 255 U.S. 356 (1921).
[19]Exxon Mobil Corp. v. Allapattah Servs., Inc., 545 U.S. 546 (2005).

(b) Personal Jurisdiction

The analysis for personal jurisdiction over defendants in class actions is the same as in any other case. But what about personal jurisdiction over the members of a plaintiff class? If you have studied personal jurisdiction, this should seem like a really odd question. In Chapter 2, personal jurisdiction over plaintiffs was never a concern because by filing the action a plaintiff consents to the court's jurisdiction. That's why every personal jurisdiction case you can think of—*Pennoyer, International Shoe, Worldwide Volkswagen,* and so on—addresses the court's power over a defendant. When you think about it, however, members of a class action bear a certain resemblance to ordinary defendants. We're not talking about the named class representatives or class members who individually choose to intervene in the action, but rather about the vast majority of the class—the *absent class members.* They did not choose the forum and did not even choose to bring the action, but the court purports to enter a judgment that binds them. Personal jurisdiction, simply, is the question of whether the court has power to enter a judgment that is binding on a particular person.

The Supreme Court addressed the question of personal jurisdiction over absent class members in *Phillips Petroleum v. Shutts.*[20] The Court reasoned that class members are similar but not identical to ordinary defendants for purposes of jurisdiction. Therefore the Court held that the minimum contacts test does not apply. Rather, a court may enter a judgment that binds absent class members as long as certain due process requirements are met: notice and an opportunity to be heard, the right to opt out (at least for money damages class actions), and, of course, adequate representation. This ruling enables courts to resolve nationwide class actions without worrying about whether every class member has minimum contacts with the state.

(5) Class Action Settlements

Class action settlements require court approval. Outside of class actions, settlements usually require only the parties' agreement. A settlement is simply a contract in which the plaintiff agrees to drop the lawsuit and release any claims against the defendant in exchange for the defendant's agreement to pay a sum of money or provide some other remedy. Settlements need a judge's approval only in special situations such as when one of the parties is a minor or mentally incompetent to consent to the settlement. That's the way you should think of class action settlements: Some of the parties are unable to consent to the settlement because they are not there. The absent class members will be bound by a settlement even though they did not agree to it. Therefore, the class action rule gives the judge the responsibility to protect the interests of absent class members in a settlement.

Rule 23(e) requires that the court hold a hearing to determine whether the proposed settlement is "fair, reasonable, and adequate." Class members must get reasonable notice of the proposed settlement, and they may voice any objections. When the court approves a proposed class action settlement, that outcome becomes a judgment of the court. An approved class action settlement is binding on all of the parties, including absent class members.

In some cases, the parties negotiate a classwide settlement even before seeking class certification. These are known as *settlement class actions* or *settlement-only class*

---

[20]472 U.S. 797 (1985).

actions. The parties ask the court to certify a class action solely for purposes of the settlement they already negotiated. Simultaneously, they ask the court to approve the class settlement they negotiated but only if the class is certified. Settlement class actions arise when a defendant faces widespread potential liability and seeks to dispose of the entire dispute with a single massive settlement. The defendant may be willing to pay a large amount of money to settle the dispute, but only if the settlement truly resolves the whole thing. Settling cases one by one cannot bring that sort of finality, but a class action settlement can. Two settlement class actions reached the Supreme Court in the late 1990s, both arising out of gargantuan asbestos litigation. *Amchem Products v. Windsor*[21] presented a Rule 23(b)(3) opt-out settlement class action, and *Ortiz v. Fibreboard Corp.*[22] presented a Rule 23(b)(1)(B) limited fund settlement class action. In each case, the Court found that the proposed class actions failed to meet the requirements of Rule 23, but the Court did not reject the idea of settlement class actions. The Supreme Court expressed concerns about the fact that plaintiffs' lawyers lack leverage when negotiating a settlement class action (since the class action has not yet been certified, the plaintiffs' lawyer cannot make a realistic threat of taking the class action to trial). Nonetheless, a court may approve a settlement class action as long as it finds the settlement fair under Rule 23(e) *and* finds that the class meets the requirements of Rule 23(a) and 23(b) for class certification.

SUMMARY

- In a single lawsuit, a party may join as many claims as the party has against an opposing party, even if the claims are unrelated.

- A defending party may assert any counterclaim it has against the opposing party, even if it is unrelated to the original complaint.

- If a counterclaim arises out of the same transaction or occurrence as the original claim, it is a compulsory counterclaim and is waived if not a sserted.

- A party may assert a crossclaim against a co-party if it arises out of the same transaction or occurrence as the original action.

- Multiple plaintiffs may join their claims in a single lawsuit, or may sue multiple defendants in a single lawsuit, if the claims share a common question and arise out of the same transaction, occurrence, or series.

- Compulsory party joinder is uncommon, but occasionally a nonparty's position is so strongly intertwined with an action that a court will order that the nonparty be joined pursuant to the compulsory party joinder rule.

- If a nonparty must be joined pursuant to the compulsory party joinder rule, but cannot be joined because of jurisdictional constraints, then the court must decide whether to dismiss the action or to go forward despite the party's absence.

- A defendant may bring in another party as a third-party defendant if the third party may be liable to the defendant for indemnification or contribution.

---

[21]521 U.S. 591 (1997).
[22]527 U.S. 815 (1999).

- A nonparty may intervene in an action as of right if it has an interest in the action that may be impaired and if none of the present parties will adequately protect the nonparty's interest.

- When a holder of disputed property desires an adjudication of which claimants, if any, are entitled to the property, the stakeholder may use interpleader to join all of the claimants in a single proceeding, and the federal interpleader statute facilitates such joinder by relaxing the requirements for subject matter jurisdiction, personal jurisdiction, and venue.

- In a class action, a representative party or parties pursue claims on behalf of themselves and all others similarly situated.

- For class certification, a class action must meet the four prerequisites of numerosity, commonality, typicality, and adequate representation, and in addition must fit within one of the categories in the class action rule.

- For a money damages class action, class certification also requires that common issues predominate over individual issues and that a class action be the superior method for resolving the dispute.

- In money damages class actions, class members receive notice and the right to opt out of the class action.

- A class action settlement is binding only if the court approves it.

CONNECTIONS

Subject Matter Jurisdiction, Personal Jurisdiction

In a Rule 12(b)(7) motion to dismiss for failure to join a required party, a critical step is establishing that the court lacks either subject matter jurisdiction or personal jurisdiction. Unlike the usual motion to dismiss for lack of jurisdiction, in this context the movant must show that the court lacks jurisdiction over the *absent* party.

Subject Matter Jurisdiction, Personal Jurisdiction, Venue

Both rule interpleader and statutory interpleader provide a procedural mechanism for a stakeholder to join multiple claimants, but the statutory version facilitates joinder by removing the three main obstacles to finding a single forum where all parties may be bound. It alters the diversity of citizenship requirement and lowers the amount-in-controversy requirement for subject matter jurisdiction, extends personal jurisdiction nationwide, and eases venue restrictions.

Supplemental Jurisdiction, Claim Preclusion

It's no coincidence that the "same transaction or occurrence" tests for compulsory counterclaims, crossclaims, and permissive party joinder resemble the

standard for supplemental jurisdiction and the transactional test for claim preclusion. Together, they enable and encourage litigants to assert all transactionally related claims in the same action.

Personal Jurisdiction — Bulge Rule

The rule on service of process favors certain types of joinder. Specifically, Rule
4(k)(1)(B)'s hundred-mile bulge provision expands a federal court's reach to
bring in third-party defendants under Rule 14 or required parties under Rule 19.

Personal Jurisdiction

The court's power to bind absent class members in a certified class action presents a strange twist on personal jurisdiction analysis. As the Supreme Court
explained in *Phillips Petroleum v. Shutts*, plaintiff class members are similar
to defendants in that they are bound by a judgment even if they did not choose
to participate in the action, but they differ enough from defendants that due
process does not require the usual minimum contacts analysis.

Discovery

Although depositions and document production can be obtained from nonparties by using a subpoena, it's easier to get discovery from a party. Interrogatories
may be used only on parties. When deciding whether to join parties under Rule
20 or other joinder devices, the discovery advantage gives one tactical reason to
favor joinder.

Trial

Party joinder complicates the trial process because multiple parties need to
present openings and closings, introduce evidence, cross-examine witnesses,
make objections, and so forth. The judge has wide discretion to order separate
trials, even if the parties and claims are properly joined under the joinder rules.

Appeals

Because so much depends upon the grant or denial of class certification, Rule
23(f) carves out a class action exception to the usual final judgment rule for
appealability.

Claim Preclusion

The compulsory counterclaim rule operates by precluding a party from later
asserting a claim that should have been asserted as a counterclaim. Compulsory
counterclaims therefore must be understood in part as a type of claims joinder
and in part as a type of claim preclusion.

Preclusion — Parties Bound

Don't get so caught up in the details of the joinder rules that you forget what
party joinder is all about. Ultimately, it's all about who will be bound by a judgment. The main reason to join a party is to obtain a judgment that will bind that
person. Compulsory party joinder and interpleader are driven by concerns over
whether the essential parties will be bound by the judgment, and class actions
are the great exception to the rule that nonparties are not bound by a judgment.

Summary Judgment and Pretrial Adjudication

8

At a jury trial, each party presents its evidence and the jury decides who wins. But what if it is clear even before trial that there is only one way

O V E R V I E W

a reasonable jury could decide? The jury's job is to determine the disputed facts and apply the law to those facts, taking into account burdens of proof. What if, based on the applicable law and the evidence in the case, one side simply cannot meet its burden of proof or has proved its case so thoroughly and indisputably that no reasonable person could disagree? *Summary judgment* gives the judge the power to decide such a lopsided case before the case gets to trial. To master summary judgment, you must understand burdens of proof — the *burden of persuasion* and the *burden of production* — as well as the concept of judgment as a matter of law.

Summary judgment is the most important of several types of pretrial adjudication. Together, the pretrial adjudication mechanisms keep litigation moving forward toward trial while weeding out cases that need not get there. The threat of *involuntary dismissal* or *default judgment* forces the parties to press forward. Meanwhile, *voluntary dismissal* and especially summary judgment ensure that the actions that reach trial involve genuine disputes that require a factfinder's attention.

A. SUMMARY JUDGMENT

1. The Summary Judgment Standard
2. Summary Judgment Motion Practice
3. Partial Summary Judgment

B. VOLUNTARY DISMISSAL

C. INVOLUNTARY DISMISSAL

D. DEFAULT

E. RECAP: TYPES OF PRETRIAL ADJUDICATION

A. Summary Judgment

Summary judgment allows a court to decide a case before trial based on a determination, as a matter of law, that only one side could reasonably prevail. Do not underestimate the importance of summary judgment in litigation practice. The motion is frequently made and granted often enough to make parties take it seriously. In certain cases where jury sympathy or confusion may play a role, lawyers think of summary judgment as the moment when a case is won or lost. For the party pursuing summary judgment, the opportunity to end the case favorably without the cost and uncertainty of trial is a happy prospect. For the other party, summary judgment presents the unpleasant risk of losing before even getting the chance to present evidence (and to cross-examine the adversary's witnesses) at trial.

F   A   Q

Q: Is summary judgment ever used in nonjury cases?

A: Yes, but it is a much bigger deal in jury cases than in bench trial cases. In an action that would be tried without a jury, a judge's decision to grant summary judgment matters but is not a power grab. It matters because it shortens the time frame to adjudication and deprives the parties of the chance to present live evidence at trial. In a jury case, however, summary judgment does not merely shorten the time frame or alter the process; it replaces the decision maker, with the judge deciding the case as a matter of law rather than allowing the jury to decide it as a matter of fact.

(1) The Summary Judgment Standard

Rule 56 of the Federal Rules of Civil Procedure states the standard for granting summary judgment:

> The court shall grant summary judgment if the movant shows that there is no genuine dispute as to any material fact and the movant is entitled to judgment as a matter of law.

The standard stated in Rule 56 raises as many questions as it answers. What does it mean that a party is entitled to "judgment as a matter of law"? The movant has to "show" such entitlement, but what exactly is required for such a showing? Above all, what does it mean for there to be "no genuine dispute as to any material fact"?

"no genuine dispute as to any material fact"

Because summary judgment is all about burden of proof, the analysis depends mightily on whether it's a motion by a plaintiff or by a defendant, since plaintiffs generally bear the burden of proof at trial.

For a plaintiff to win summary judgment, the plaintiff must be able to establish every element of the claim and show that if the case were to go to trial, no reasonable jury could find for the defendant. For example, suppose a plaintiff sues a defendant for payment of a debt and moves for summary judgment. The plaintiff attaches to the motion a copy of the promissory note plus an excerpt from defendant's deposition transcript in which the defendant admitted that he has not paid. Unless the defendant offers some basis for finding the agreement unenforceable or presents some evidence that he in fact paid the amount owed, the court will grant summary judgment to the plaintiff. In the language of Rule 56, there is "no genuine dispute as to any material fact" because the material facts (whether the defendant owes the money and whether he paid it) are undisputed. Or, to be more precise, even if the defendant purports to dispute those facts, the dispute is not *genuine* unless defendant presents enough evidence to contradict the plaintiff's evidence of an unpaid debt.

For a defendant to win summary judgment, the defendant must show that the plaintiff does not have sufficient evidence to raise a genuine dispute as to any element of the claim. In one sense, this is easy—the defendant need only show plaintiff's failure as to a single element of the claim. Think about it this way: On a claim whose required elements are duty, breach, causation, and damages, the plaintiff loses if the plaintiff cannot prove that the defendant breached a duty, *or* if the plaintiff cannot prove that the defendant's breach caused the plaintiff's harm, *or* if the plaintiff cannot prove any damages.

But in another sense, showing the lack of a genuine dispute is quite hard—the defendant must show that the plaintiff's evidence is so utterly lacking that no reasonable jury could find for the plaintiff on that element of the claim. Courts deciding summary judgment cases often talk about viewing the evidence "in the light most favorable to the nonmoving party." This means that if each side has enough evidence to support its version of the facts, the court's job on summary judgment is not to weigh the credibility of the conflicting stories. Even if a plaintiff's only supporting evidence is the plaintiff's own testimony (as shown by an affidavit or deposition transcript), summary judgment is improper unless no reasonable factfinder could believe the plaintiff's version.

The Supreme Court explained the summary judgment standard in *Celotex Corp. v. Catrett*.[1] Catrett brought a wrongful death suit against manufacturers of

---

[1]477 U.S. 317 (1986).

asbestos-containing products, claiming that her husband died because of exposure to asbestos. Celotex argued that there was no evidence that Mr. Catrett was exposed to Celotex asbestos; in other words, even if he died because of asbestos exposure, it could have been another company's product. Celotex moved for summary judgment and attached a copy of an interrogatory that asked the plaintiff to identify any evidence that her husband was exposed to Celotex asbestos and plaintiff's response that failed to name any witnesses or other evidence. The plaintiff argued that the defendant had not proved that Mr. Catrett was *not* exposed to Celotex asbestos, and therefore there was a genuine dispute of material fact.

The big question for the Supreme Court in *Celotex* was whether a defendant, to win summary judgment, must present evidence to negate an element of plaintiff's claim, or whether a defendant can win summary judgment merely by showing that the plaintiff herself lacks evidence to support the element. Did Celotex have to present evidence to exclude the possibility that Mr. Catrett was exposed to their asbestos? The Court decided that the defendant need only point out the plaintiff's lack of evidence:

> In our view, the plain language of Rule 56[] mandates the entry of summary judgment, after adequate time for discovery and upon motion, against a party who fails to make a showing sufficient to establish the existence of an essential element to that party's case, and on which that party will bear the burden of proof at trial. In such a situation, there can be no "genuine issue as to any material fact," since a complete failure of proof concerning an essential element of the nonmoving party's case necessarily renders all other facts immaterial.[2]

That's because the plaintiff bears a **burden of production**, the burden of producing enough evidence so that a reasonable jury *could* find in the plaintiff's favor.

F   A   Q

Q: Do plaintiffs ever win summary judgment?

A: Yes, but lawyers tend to think of summary judgment as a defendant's tool. Since plaintiffs bear the burden of proving each element of their claims, it's easier for defendants to get summary judgment. A defendant need only show the plaintiff's lack of evidence as to any one element, whereas a plaintiff needs to establish every element. But Rule 56 explicitly permits motions by both claiming parties and defending parties, and plaintiffs do win summary judgment in certain types of cases. Some cases, for example, involve unambiguous contract liability (such as an unpaid enforceable debt), undisputed facts of blatant negligence (such as a driver looking for something in the glove compartment and rear-ending another vehicle), or other clear-cut liability.

---

[2]*Celotex*, 477 U.S. at 317.

(2) Summary Judgment Motion Practice

Now that we've covered the standard for granting summary judgment, let's talk about how the motion happens. The party moving for summary judgment must file the motion with the court and serve the motion on the other parties. What gets filed and served ordinarily includes three parts. The *notice of motion* takes only about a page and simply notifies the court and the other parties that the movant seeks summary judgment. The *memorandum of law*, a.k.a. the brief, contains the legal argument in favor of granting the motion. Along with the motion and brief, the moving party nearly always includes *attachments*, pieces of evidence to show why the court should grant the motion. The nonmoving party responds with a memorandum of law in opposition to summary judgment, plus attachments to show why summary judgment should not be granted. The moving party may submit a reply brief, and the court may hold a hearing for oral argument on the motion.

Be sure you understand what the attachments do. First of all, what exactly gets attached? Attachments may include affidavits (sworn written statements from witnesses), interrogatory responses, excerpts from deposition transcripts, copies of documents, or pretty much anything else to convince the judge to grant or deny summary judgment. In *Celotex*, for example, the asbestos company moving for summary judgment attached a copy of the interrogatory responses in which the plaintiff failed to identify any evidence of exposure to the company's asbestos products. The plaintiff, in her response to the summary judgment motion, attached a letter from her husband's former employer, a letter from an insurance company, and a transcript of her husband's deposition from an earlier workers' compensation case. With these attachments, she sought to convince the court that she had enough evidence of her husband's exposure to the company's asbestos to meet her burden of production.

The role of attachments clues you in to the difference between summary judgment and motions at the pleadings stage. Unlike a Rule 12(b)(6) motion to dismiss for failure to state a claim or a Rule 12(c) motion for judgment on the pleadings, summary judgment looks at *evidence*. The motion to dismiss or motion for judgment on the pleadings says to the judge, "The other party has not stated a legally valid claim (or defense). Just look at the pleadings and you'll see that we have to win." A summary judgment motion says to the judge, "The other party does not have the evidence to establish its claim (or defense). Just look at the evidence and you'll see that we have to win."

The attachments also reflect the difference between summary judgment and trial. On a summary judgment motion, unlike trial, witnesses do not testify in court. Witness testimony may figure prominently in the summary judgment decision, but it gets to the judge by way of affidavits or deposition transcripts attached to the motion or response. Similarly, documents are not "admitted into evidence" on a summary judgment motion. Rather, they are included as attachments to the motion or response. A summary judgment motion, in other words, gives everything to the judge on a paper record.

If the party opposing the motion needs more time for discovery or to obtain affidavits, the party may ask the court to postpone ruling on the summary judgment motion. Rule 56(d) gives the court flexibility about how to handle such situations, but the basic idea is that a court may defer ruling on a summary judgment motion if the nonmoving party shows that it has been pursuing discovery diligently but needs more time to obtain evidence in opposition to the motion.

Q: May summary judgment be granted before discovery is completed?.

A: Rule 56 does not prohibit the use of summary judgment before discovery is finished, or even before discovery has begun. But the Supreme Court in *Celotex* spoke of summary judgment "after adequate time for discovery," and judges do not like to grant summary judgment before the nonmoving party has had enough opportunity to gather information. In rare cases, the facts may be so clear that even without discovery a court can decide there is no genuine dispute. But as a general matter, think of summary judgment as a post-discovery motion, in contrast to the motion to dismiss for failure to state a claim, which normally precedes discovery.

A party responding to a summary judgment motion has one additional weapon to consider — the *cross-motion for summary judgment*. If a defendant moves for summary judgment, the plaintiff might cross-move. That is, the plaintiff might say to the judge, "Not only should you deny the defendant's motion, but you should grant summary judgment for me." Cross-motions are not unique to summary judgment. Anytime a party responds to another party's motion, it might make a motion of its own if it has sufficient legal and factual basis for doing so. Strategically, cross-motions have much in common with counterclaims, which we encountered in Chapter 5. Cross-motions for summary judgment present the possibility that the judge may decide the case *either way* as a matter of law.

(3) Partial Summary Judgment

Summary judgment need not resolve the entire case. Often, it narrows the issues in dispute. If certain parts of claims or defenses are established or rejected clearly enough to meet the summary judgment standard, the court may grant *partial summary judgment* on those issues.

There are two basic versions of partial summary judgment. First, Rule 56(a) states that a party moving for summary judgment should identify "each claim or defense — or the part of each claim or defense — on which summary judgment is sought." When a plaintiff sues a defendant for both compensatory and punitive damages, for example, the defendant might seek summary judgment as to punitive damages. If the defendant can show that the plaintiff lacks evidence from which a reasonable jury could find a basis for punitive damages under applicable law, then the court should grant partial summary judgment for the defendant. The case would move forward to trial on the compensatory damages claim. Similarly, if a fired employee has sued her employer for race and gender discrimination, the court might grant summary judgment rejecting the sex discrimination claim based on lack of evidence, but allowing the race discrimination claim to proceed.

Second, summary judgment may reduce the number of factual issues for trial, even if it does not fully resolve any claims. Rule 56(g) instructs judges that if the court does not fully grant summary judgment, the court may determine that certain facts have been established. In a case involving a crash of two bicyclists, for example, a judge might determine that a material dispute exists concerning whether the defendant was negligent, but that no genuine dispute exists concerning whether the plaintiff's broken arm was caused by the crash. By determining some of the material facts at the summary judgment stage, the court streamlines the case for trial. Similarly, the evidence at the summary judgment stage may establish clearly that the defendant is liable to the plaintiff, yet the extent of plaintiff's damages may be disputed. In that situation, the judge should grant summary judgment on liability. At trial, the court would instruct the jury that the defendant is liable to the plaintiff, the parties would present evidence only on the extent of plaintiff's harm, and the jury would render a verdict on the amount of damages.

B. Voluntary Dismissal

In addition to summary judgment, several other procedural devices end cases before trial. These include voluntary dismissal, involuntary dismissal, and default.

Voluntary dismissal means exactly what it says. The plaintiff voluntarily dismisses the lawsuit. Why would a plaintiff want to drop the suit? Often, it's because the parties have negotiated a settlement. When parties settle, the defendant agrees to pay money or provide some other benefit in exchange for the plaintiff's agreement to drop the lawsuit and release the claims. Sometimes, voluntary dismissal occurs because the plaintiff (or the plaintiff's lawyer) realizes that the claim lacks merit. This realization may come from legal research or factual discovery, or may be prompted by a Rule 11 motion from the defendant. Recall from Chapter 5 that when a party is served with a Rule 11 motion for sanctions, the party has 21 days (the "safe harbor" period) to correct the problem before the motion is filed with the court. For a plaintiff who has brought a factually baseless or legally frivolous claim, the way to correct the problem is a voluntary dismissal. Finally, voluntary dismissal sometimes occurs as part of forum selection strategy when a plaintiff realizes that a different court would be more favorable, but judges frown on such "judge shopping."

If a party no longer wishes to pursue a claim, you'd expect the procedural rules to permit the party to drop the lawsuit without much fuss, and you'd be right. Rule 41(a), which governs voluntary dismissals, strikes a delicate balance. It makes it easy for plaintiffs to drop their claims for any reason, but it tries to limit plaintiffs' ability to use dismissal for strategic gamesmanship. Without even asking the court's permission, a party may voluntarily dismiss an action if all of the parties agree and sign a "stipulation of dismissal," or if the opposing party has not yet served an answer or a summary judgment motion. If the parties have not all stipulated to the dismissal, and the opposing party has already either answered or moved for summary judgment, then a party may ask the court for permission to dismiss. This makes it easy for plaintiffs to drop their claims early on, but more difficult for a plaintiff to avoid an adverse adjudication by dropping a lawsuit when the writing is on the wall that the plaintiff is about to lose.

When a party voluntarily dismisses a lawsuit, can the party later file the same claim? To put it in the language of res judicata, addressed in Chapter 11, do courts treat voluntary dismissals as judgments on the merits for purposes of claim preclusion? Rule 41 declares that the first voluntary dismissal is without prejudice. That is, a plaintiff may voluntarily dismiss a claim once and file the same claim a second time without a problem. However, if the plaintiff decides to voluntarily dismiss his case a second time, the second dismissal is with prejudice, precluding the party from bring-ing the claim a third time. The message is clear: If you've decided to drop your case, fine, but don't play games.

C. Involuntary Dismissal

You have already encountered **involuntary dismissals** of various sorts. There's the Rule 12(b)(6) motion to dismiss for failure to state a claim. And don't forget all the other pre-answer motions to dismiss listed in Rule 12(b), including lack of subject matter jurisdiction, lack of personal jurisdiction, improper venue, insufficient process, improper service of process, and failure to join an indispensable party. You have also encountered the possibility of dismissal as a sanction for egregious conduct under Rule 11 or for discovery abuse under Rule 37. All of these are "invol-untary" dismissals in the sense that the dismissed party does not voluntarily relin-quish the claim, but instead gets thrown out unwillingly. In this chapter, we complete our look at pretrial dismissals by turning to Rule 41(b), which addresses involuntary dismissals for failure to prosecute or for noncompliance with rules or orders.

If a plaintiff wishes to pursue a claim, the plaintiff must move forward at a reasonable pace. It would be unfair to the defendant and to the court for a plaintiff to file a complaint and then to sit on it, leaving the defendant with a lawsuit hanging over her head and leaving the court with an extra case on its docket. After the plaintiff files a complaint and the defendant answers, the plaintiff should move forward with discovery and preparation for trial. When plaintiffs fail to move forward, the court may dismiss for **failure to prosecute**. Don't be thrown off by the word *prosecute*; although it often refers to the state's role in criminal cases, it also denotes what plaintiffs do in civil cases. Rule 41(b) also permits a defendant to move for dismissal if the plaintiff fails to comply with a court order or with the rules of civil procedure.

When you look at Rule 41(b), don't ignore the second sentence. It explains the impact of involuntary dismissals and contrasts starkly with the treatment of voluntary dismissals under Rule 41(a). Here's what the sentence says: "Unless the dismissal order states otherwise, a dismissal under this subdivision (b) and any dismissal not under this rule—except one for lack of jurisdiction, improper venue, or failure to join a party under Rule 19—operates as an adjudication on the merits." Notice that it addresses *every* type of involuntary dismissal: dismissals "under this subdivision" (failure to prosecute and noncompliance), plus dismissals "not under this rule" (all other involuntary dismissals, such as those under Rule 12(b) or Rule 37). With a few exceptions, the rule states that every involuntary dismissal "operates as an adjudication on the merits." This language links the rule to the idea that judgments "on the merits" have claim preclusive effect. In other words, if a claim is involuntarily dismissed, then Rule 41(b) says that in general the claim cannot be brought again.

Rather than apply the "on the merits" approach to every involuntary dismissal, Rule 41(b) offers several exceptions. If the case is dismissed for "lack of jurisdiction, improper venue, or failure to join a party," then it does not constitute an adjudica-tion on the merits. Each exception makes perfect sense. After a dismissal for lack of federal subject matter jurisdiction, the plaintiff should be free to refile the case in state court. After a dismissal for lack of personal jurisdiction or improper venue, the plaintiff should be free to refile the case in a court with jurisdiction and where venue is proper. And after a dismissal for failure to join a required party, the plaintiff should be free to refile the case if the plaintiff is able to join the missing party. The other exception is found in the words "[u]nless the dismissal order states otherwise." This signals the court to state whether the dismissal is "without prejudice." Rule 41(b) operates as a default setting. If the court orders dismissal (other than for jurisdiction, venue, or indispensable party) and does not state whether the dismissal is with or without prejudice, then the rule treats the dismissal as an adjudication on the merits.

D. Default

Failure to prosecute is when the plaintiff fails to move forward with the lawsuit. The penalty, under Rule 41(b), is precisely what plaintiffs fear — dismissal with prejudice. But what if the opposite happens? What if a *defendant* fails to move forward? Suppose the deadline for answering passes and the defendant has neither filed an answer nor made any pre-answer motion. Dismissal obviously won't do as a solution. Dismissal of the lawsuit is what defendants *want*. Rather, the legal system's response to the defendant's failure is to grant judgment in favor of the plaintiff. In other words, **default**.

Default occurs when the defendant fails to answer or otherwise respond to the complaint. As you know from Chapter 5, a defendant has several options when responding to the complaint. The defendant may file an *answer*, admitting or denying each allegation in the complaint. Alternatively, the defendant may file a *pre-answer motion* such as a Rule 12(b) motion to dismiss or a Rule 12(e) motion for a more definite statement. What the defendant may not do, however, is ignore the complaint and do nothing, tempting as that may be. If a defendant fails to respond to the complaint within the time limits established by Rule 12(a), then the defendant risks losing by default.

Under Rule 55, default involves a two-step process. First, the court clerk "enters" the default, which is basically an administrative notation that the defendant has failed to plead or otherwise defend. After the entry of default, the plaintiff requests a *default judgment* by applying either to the court clerk or to the judge. The clerk enters the default judgment, at the plaintiff's request, only if the amount of damages is "a sum certain or a sum that can be made certain by computation." For example, if the defendant defaults in a lawsuit on a $100,000 debt, the clerk may enter default judgment in the amount of $100,000 (or, more realistically, a specific higher amount after computing the interest). Most claims, however, are not for a "sum certain," and the plaintiff must apply to the judge for a default judgment. The court may hold a hearing to determine the amount of damages. At such a hearing, the defendant may not contest whether liability will be imposed, but does have the opportunity to argue that the plaintiff's damages are less than what the plaintiff requested.

Speaking of damages, you should be aware of an interesting strategic option created by a difference between default judgments and all other judgments. Rule 54(c) provides: "A default judgment must not differ in kind from, or exceed in amount, what is demanded in the pleadings. Every other final judgment should grant the relief to which the party is entitled, even if the party has not demanded that relief in its pleadings." This means that if a jury finds that a plaintiff's claim is worth $100,000, it should award that amount even if the complaint only demanded $50,000. If the defendant defaults, however, the default judgment may not exceed the $50,000 demanded in the complaint. To a smart defendant, default may be an appealing option in such a case. It depends on the strength of plaintiff's case for liability and how clear it is that the verdict at trial would exceed the amount sought in the pleading. Of course, a smart plaintiff should never put the defendant in the strategic position of being able to elect smaller damages by defaulting. Therefore, when plaintiffs specify the relief sought in their complaint, they ordinarily demand an amount at the high end, keeping in mind Rule 11's requirement that the amount have a reasonable factual and legal basis.

What about justice? When setting up a procedural system that tries to reach just results (remember Rule 1?), default raises the concern that cases may be decided on technicalities rather than on the merits. The big fear is that a defendant might fail to respond because the defendant never actually knew about the lawsuit. Rule 55 addresses this concern by permitting a court to "set aside" a default when justice requires. Rule 55(c) permits the court to "set aside an entry of default for good cause," and if default judgment has already been entered, the court may "set aside a default judgment under Rule 60(b)." In Chapter 11, you will learn that in general courts are quite stingy about setting aside judgments under Rule 60(b), but a major exception is cases involving default judgments against defendants who did not receive actual notice of the lawsuit or who had some other sound explanation for why they failed to respond to the complaint.

With the expectation that courts will exercise discretion to set aside unfair defaults, the default procedure aims to dispose of cases in which default judgment makes sense. In some of these cases, the defendant really does not contest liability and therefore offers no defense. In others, the defendant makes a strategic choice not to litigate the merits, either to take advantage of a surprisingly low demand in the complaint or to contest the personal jurisdiction of the court by collateral attack. Or maybe the defendant simply fails to answer for no good reason. By punishing the nonresponsive defendant, the default procedure puts pressure on defendants to respond to the complaint within the established time limits.

E. Recap: Types of Pretrial Adjudication

This chapter has addressed several of the ways in which cases reach judgment before they reach trial. Specifically, it has covered summary judgment, voluntary dismissal, involuntary dismissal for failure to prosecute or for noncompliance with rules or orders, and default judgment. But you know that these are not the only types of pretrial adjudication, as you have already encountered a host of other ways in which litigation may be resolved by the court before trial.

To put the various forms of pretrial adjudication in context, you might find it useful to see them all together, grouped in procedural categories. The following table lists most of the ways in which cases are adjudicated before trial in federal civil procedure. The table notes the applicable Federal Rule of Civil Procedure, as well as the chapter in which each topic is addressed in this book.

Pretrial Adjudication

Procedural Device/Basis	FRCP	Ch.
❖ **Adjudication on the pleadings**		
➤ Pre-answer motion to dismiss	12(b)	5
■ Lack of subject matter jurisdiction	12(b)(1)	1
■ Lack of personal jurisdiction	12(b)(2)	2
■ Improper venue	12(b)(3)	3
■ Insufficient process	12(b)(4)	1
■ Insufficient service of process	12(b)(5)	1
■ Failure to state a claim	12(b)(6)	5
■ Failure to join a party	12(b)(7); 19	7
■ Forum non conveniens		3
➤ Motion for judgment on the pleadings	12(c)	5
❖ **Summary judgment**	56	8
❖ **Voluntary dismissal**	41(a)	8
❖ **Involuntary dismissal**		
➤ Failure to prosecute	41(b)	8
➤ Noncompliance with rule or order	41(b)	8
❖ **Default judgment**	55	8
❖ **Adjudication as punishment**		
➤ Default or dismissal as sanction for baseless assertions	11	5
➤ Default or dismissal as discovery sanction	37	6

SUMMARY

■ Summary judgment permits a court to enter judgment on a claim without a trial.

■ To win summary judgment, the moving party must show that there is no genuine dispute as to any material fact, and that the moving party is entitled to judgment as a matter of law.

- A party may win summary judgment by showing that the opposing party bears the burden of production on an issue and that the opposing party has failed to produce sufficient evidence for a reasonable factfinder to find in its favor.

- A court may grant partial summary judgment on liability, even if the amount of damages remains to be determined at trial.

- A plaintiff may voluntarily dismiss an action if the opposing party has not yet served an answer or summary judgment motion, or with the permission of the other parties or the court.

- The court may dismiss an action for failure to prosecute or for failure to comply with a court order.

- The court may enter a default judgment against a defending party if that party fails to file a responsive pleading or motion.

CONNECTIONS

Pleadings

The pleading regime of Rule 8(a) makes it relatively easy for plaintiffs to initiate claims and the discovery rules provide plenty of opportunity to gather information. When the Supreme Court in *Celotex* called summary judgment "an integral part of the Federal Rules as a whole," it meant that therefore summary judgment is needed to dispose of claims that prove to be unfounded.

Pleadings — Motion to Dismiss

Summary judgment bears a certain resemblance to Rule 12(b)(6) dismissals for failure to state a claim, as both can be used to throw out claims that have no reasonable chance of prevailing on the merits. Indeed, Rule 12 specifically mentions the possibility of a court converting a 12(b)(6) motion into a summary judgment motion if the parties present matters outside the pleadings. The essential difference between the two is that the 12(b)(6) motion looks only at the allegations in the complaint, whereas the summary judgment motion may look at the evidence presented as attachments to the motion and response.

Discovery

Summary judgment presupposes the existence of discovery rules that permit the parties to gather the evidence they need to support their claims and defenses, which explains why courts generally avoid granting summary judgment before the parties have completed discovery.

Trial

It's not incidental, or merely of chronological significance, that summary judgment is *pretrial* adjudication. The point of summary judgment is to avoid trial.

The expense and uncertainty of trial are the main reasons why parties seek summary judgment, and also why courts are not averse to granting it in appropriate cases.

Trial — Seventh Amendment

When a court grants summary judgment in a case that would have gone to a jury trial, the court shuts down the jury's power to decide the case. In this sense, summary judgment impinges on the Seventh Amendment right to a jury trial. Courts have rejected the argument that summary judgment is unconstitutional, but when considering summary judgment motions, many judges are sensitive to the implications of adjudicating a case as a matter of law rather than letting it go to the jury.

Trial — Judgment as a Matter of Law

At trial, parties may move for "judgment as a matter of law" under Rule 50. Courts often state that there is no difference between the legal standards of Rule 56 and Rule 50. The difference is in the timing and procedure. Summary judgment occurs before trial and looks at the paper record in the attachments. Judgment as a matter of law occurs at trial and looks at the evidence presented at trial.

Preclusion — Claim Preclusion

The significance of a dismissal depends on whether the plaintiff is free to refile the claim. Rules 41(a) and 41(b) include directions about the effect of voluntary and involuntary dismissals by noting when the dismissals are "with prejudice," *i.e.*, adjudications "on the merits."

Trial

9

Trial is what nonlawyers imagine lawyers spend their time doing. Trial happens a lot in movies and television legal dramas. In the real world, trial

represents only one segment of the litigation process—a very important segment, but a surprisingly uncommon one. Of all the civil cases filed in federal courts, only about 2 percent reach trial. Most cases are settled out of court, dropped by the plaintiff, or resolved before trial by summary judgment or other procedures. But even though the vast majority of cases are resolved without trials, the U.S. legal system is designed around the trial as the main event of the litigation process. Every lawyer, therefore, must understand how trials work, and every successful litigator must be prepared to take cases to trial with skill and vigor.

This chapter does not teach you how to be a trial lawyer, nor does any basic civil procedure course. Most law schools offer a separate course on trial practice where you can learn the skills of direct and cross-examination, opening statements and closing arguments, and evidentiary foundations and objections. Any good trial lawyer will tell you that the only way to perfect those skills is through lots of observation and experience. This chapter does something less thrilling. It explains certain aspects of civil procedure that relate to how trials proceed. In particular, it covers the constitutional right to a jury trial, certain rules governing jury selection, the basic contours of the trial process, and the power struggle between judge and jury as played out on motions for judgment as a matter of law or motions for a new trial.

A. Jury Trial

In the United States, we are so accustomed to the civil jury that it is easy to forget what a unique and peculiarly American institution it is. Instead of charging a government bureaucrat with the responsibility for determining the facts, we grab a representative sample of ordinary citizens and give them the power—and the civic duty—to decide the case. In other countries, civil jury trials are virtually non-existent. Some countries use juries or other forms of lay participation in *criminal* cases, where concerns about government overreaching run strong, but *civil* cases around the world are nearly always decided by the judge. Even in England—the historic source of the jury trial—civil juries have largely been abandoned except in a few categories of cases.

Not all trials involve juries. In a bench trial, the judge plays the role of both factfinder and legal decision maker. Later in the chapter, we'll look at certain procedural aspects of bench trials, but we begin with the jury and the contours of the Seventh Amendment right to a jury trial.

Photo courtesy of Ron Chapple/Getty Images

(1) The Jury

In a jury trial, the jury and the judge play different roles. The judge runs the trial process, makes all legal rulings, decides what evidence is admissible, and instructs the jury on the law. The jury determines the facts and applies the law to those facts.

The jury hears the witnesses' testimony and sees the documentary or physical evidence presented by both sides. In some courts, jurors are allowed to submit questions for the judge to ask witnesses, but mostly, the jury sits and listens to the testimony as elicited by the lawyers' questions on direct and cross-examination. Much trial time can be taken up with evidentiary issues and other motions, some of which must be discussed outside the jury's presence. It is not uncommon for jurors to have the frustrating experience of being shuttled in and out of the courtroom and spending much of their time waiting for something to happen.

Traditionally juries had 12 members, but these days juries range in size from 6 to 12. In a federal case, the jury's decision must be unanimous unless the parties agree otherwise. Some states, on the other hand, do not require unanimity.

(2) Right to a Jury Trial

The Constitutional Jury Right. The constitution enshrines the jury right in two separate provisions of the Bill of Rights. The Sixth Amendment establishes the right to a jury trial in criminal cases, along with other protections for criminal defendants. The Seventh Amendment preserves the right to a jury trial in certain civil cases. *Preserve* may seem like a strange verb for a constitutional right, but it comes straight from the constitution: "In Suits at common law, where the value in controversy shall exceed twenty dollars, the right of trial by jury shall be preserved. . . ." Unlike most of the Bill of Rights, the Seventh Amendment explicitly preserves a right as it already existed in the common law courts of England and the fledgling United States. It is the language of compromise, reflecting some uncertainty among the Framers about the necessity of juries in civil cases.

Because of the backward-looking nature of the Seventh Amendment, the constitutional right to a jury trial in federal court depends on history. Here's the basic rule: A party in a federal civil case has a right to a jury trial if the same case would have been tried by a jury in 1791, the year the Seventh Amendment was ratified.

To understand the right to a jury trial in the twenty-first century, therefore, you need a bit of eighteenth-century Anglo-American legal history. In 1791 and for a long time before and after, courts were divided into courts of *equity* (also known as *chancery*) and courts of *law* (also known as *common law* courts), as you may recall from the short history of pleadings in Chapter 5. Common law courts had juries. Equity courts did not. Therefore, under the Seventh Amendment, if a case would have fallen within the jurisdiction of the common law courts in the eighteenth century, then the parties have a constitutional right to a jury. The common law courts had jurisdiction over certain categories of cases, including most cases for money damages. Other categories of cases, most notably those seeking injunctive relief, went to the equity courts.

Based on the historical test, you will often find it easy to determine whether a party has a right to a jury trial. A tort claim or breach of contract claim for money damages, for example, carries a right to a jury trial. Those cases would have been heard in the common law courts in 1791. By contrast, a claim for an injunction prohibiting certain conduct by the defendant or a claim seeking specific performance of a contract does not carry a right to a jury trial; it would be heard solely by the judge because in 1791 those claims would have been decided in the courts of equity. Other cases are trickier. For example, although replevin (demanding recovery of goods taken unlawfully from the plaintiff's possession) looks a lot like a form of injunctive relief, historically it was a common law action and therefore it carries a right to a jury trial. For a lawyer handling a particular type of claim, basic legal research often provides the answer about whether the jury right attaches based on the historical test.

The historical test, however, only goes so far. Stuff has happened in the centuries since the Seventh Amendment was ratified, and many types of current claims had not even been imagined in 1791. How does the Seventh Amendment apply to a cause of action that was created after the Seventh Amendment's adoption? The Supreme Court addressed this question in *Chauffeurs Local 391 v. Terry*.[1] The plaintiff, a labor union member, sued the union for a breach of the union's duty to fairly represent the union member. The plaintiff wanted a jury trial, and the question was whether the Seventh Amendment provided a right to a jury trial in the case. The simple historical test could not answer the questions because a claim for a union's breach of the duty of fair representation had not been invented at the time the Seventh Amendment was adopted. At that time, labor unions didn't even exist!

The Supreme Court, acknowledging this limitation of the historical test, described a two-pronged analysis for applying the Seventh Amendment to more recent types of claims. First, the Court said, look for a historical analog to the claim. In other words, find the type of eighteenth-century claim that most closely resembles the claim in the case. In the *Terry* case, the parties disputed whether the union member's claim more closely resembled a legal malpractice claim (which would have been heard in the common law courts with a jury) or a fiduciary duty claim against a trustee (which would have been heard in the equity courts without a jury). Second, the Court said, look at the remedy sought. In *Terry*, the plaintiff sought compensatory damages, and therefore the Court held that the union member's claim resembled a case at common law, and that the Seventh Amendment therefore provided a right to a jury trial. The Court emphasized that the remedy sought often provides the determining factor under the Seventh Amendment.

In another case, *Markman v. Westview Instruments*,[2] the Supreme Court considered the practical abilities and limitations of juries in deciding whether a particular issue in patent litigation would be determined by the judge or jury. This pragmatic analysis arose, however, only because the Court found that the historical test gave no clear answer. Although occasionally the comparative skills of judges and juries may come into play, generally the Seventh Amendment revolves around the historical test.

What if a case involves both common law and equitable issues? Suppose the plaintiff alleges wrongdoing by the defendant and demands both an injunction against the wrongful conduct and monetary compensation for the damages it has caused. Or suppose the plaintiff asserts a common law claim and the defendant

---

[1] 494 U.S. 558 (1990).
[2] 517 U.S. 370 (1996).

responds with an equitable counterclaim. The Seventh Amendment right to a jury for the common law claims must be protected, but neither party has a right to a jury on the equitable claims. In such a case, generally the jury decides all of the legal claims first, and then the remaining equitable claims are decided by the judge, applying any applicable facts already determined by the jury.

The Seventh Amendment applies only to the federal courts, not state courts. As a matter of constitutional law, many provisions of the Bill of Rights have been applied to the states by "incorporating" those rights into the Due Process Clause of the Fourteenth Amendment, but the Supreme Court has treated the Seventh Amendment differently, applying it to the federal courts alone. Nearly every state, however, has an analogous state constitutional provision for a civil jury right, many of them applying historical tests along the lines of the Seventh Amendment.

Statutes. Keep in mind that even if the Seventh Amendment does not provide a right to a jury trial for a particular type of claim, the legislature can create a statutory jury right. Therefore, when thinking about whether parties have a jury right, do not forget to look at the statute if it is a statutory claim. For example, Congress has established a jury right for certain employment discrimination claims.[3]

The Federal Rules of Civil Procedure. The Seventh Amendment and certain statutes provide a right to a jury trial, but they do not spell out how a party should assert that right. That's where Rule 38 comes into play.

The most important things to know about Rule 38 are the related concepts of *demand* and *waiver*. If a party wants to have a jury, the party must demand it within the time limit set by the rule. A party demands a jury trial by "serving the other parties with a written demand — which may be included in a pleading," and filing the demand with the court. Parties often make jury demands by including a prominent statement on the first page of their complaint or answer. The statement usually consists of something creative and poignant, like "PLAINTIFF DEMANDS TRIAL BY JURY."

The jury right belongs to any party. Although as a strategic matter plaintiffs often prefer juries, this is by no means universally true, and both plaintiffs and defendants have the right to demand a jury trial. If the plaintiff demands a jury, assuming it is a case in which the jury right applies, it will be a jury trial. If the defendant demands a jury, again assuming the jury right applies, it will be a jury trial. The parties do not have to agree. As long as any party properly demands a jury trial, that party's right will be respected, even if every other party would prefer a bench trial.

The corollary to the *demand* requirement is the doctrine of *waiver*. Like many other constitutional rights, the right to trial by jury is waivable. If a party does not demand a jury, that party loses the right to a jury trial. As Rule 38 puts it, "A party waives a jury trial unless its demand is properly served and filed." Therefore, if neither party requests a jury, the trial will be a bench trial, even if the right to a jury trial would have been available under a statute or the Seventh Amendment. In any action where the constitution or a statute provides the right to a jury trial, the lawyers must consider the tactical question of whether they would prefer a jury trial or bench trial.

---

[3]Civil Rights Act of 1991, 42 U.S.C. §1981a(c)(1).

(3) Jury Selection

The jury selection process serves multiple, sometimes competing, goals. First, the process aims to provide the court with a representative jury, or at least a jury that is drawn from a representative sample of the population in the court's district. Second, the process aims to give litigants some assurance of protection from biased jurors. Third, the process aims to provide the jurors themselves with an opportunity to exercise civic responsibility by participating in the judicial process.

As a first step, the court summons citizens to appear for jury duty. The group of people from whom the jury will be selected, known as the *jury venire*, is then narrowed until the jury is finally seated for a particular trial. During this narrowing process, the judge or lawyers ask the potential jurors questions to elicit bias or other reasons why a person might be unable to decide the case fairly. (And some potential jurors try to get out of jury service by explaining to the judge why their personal or work obligations make it impossible for them to serve.) This questioning process is known as *voir dire* — French for "to see to say," as in "let's see what these potential jurors are going to say." Courts vary in how they conduct this process. In some, the judge does most of the questioning, while in others, lawyers have more leeway to ask their own questions.

During the voir dire process, the court excuses potential jurors who might be unable to listen fairly to the evidence and decide the case based on their independent, unbiased judgment. For example, jurors who have personal relationships with the litigants or who have had personal experiences that might prejudice them about the case are generally excused.

Litigants have the right to challenge particular jurors, either for good reason or no reason at all. They may make *challenges for cause*, in which a party argues that a particular juror should be excused because the juror would be unable to decide the case fairly. In addition, each side may make several *peremptory challenges*, in which the party gets rid of a particular juror without offering any reason. A federal statute limits each party in a federal court civil case to three peremptory challenges,[4] in contrast to challenges for cause, which are unlimited. The idea is to give each litigant greater confidence in the fairness of the jury by excluding the specific jurors about whom each side feels most uncomfortable.

The Supreme Court has addressed constitutional questions about peremptory challenges, declaring that peremptory challenges on the basis of race or gender are unconstitutional as violations of the Equal Protection Clause.[5] If a party believes the other party has used a peremptory challenge to exclude a juror

---

[4]28 U.S.C. §1870.
[5]J.E.B. v. Alabama, 511 U.S. 127 (1994) (gender); Edmonson v. Leesville Concrete Co., 500 U.S. 614 (1991) (race); *see also* Batson v. Kentucky, 476 U.S. 79 (1986) (rejecting race-based peremptory challenges in criminal trials).

based on race or gender, the party may object and the court may require the party using the challenges to show that their challenge is not based on race or gender. Think about what a strange scene this can create. On the one hand, peremptory challenges are, by definition, *not* challenges for cause; the whole point is to give each side the right to exclude certain jurors without having to offer a good reason. But on the other hand, could the justice system condone a process that would exclude some citizens from the right to participate in jury service based on their race or gender?

B. Trial Process

(1) The Course of a Trial

To understand procedural issues such as motions for judgment as a matter of law, you need to know the basic chronology of a trial. Here's a brief description of standard trial proceedings, but keep in mind that the details vary from court to court and from case to case.

After jury selection is completed (if it's a jury trial), the parties present their case to the judge and jury. First, the lawyer for each side makes an *opening statement* describing the case and setting the stage for the evidence that will follow. Following these opening statements, the plaintiff presents witnesses and other evidence. Each witness, after taking an oath to testify truthfully, answers questions on *direct examination* from the lawyer who called the witness. Opposing counsel then has the opportunity to ask the witness questions on *cross-examination*. After completion of the plaintiff's case, the defendant presents the case in opposition. During the questioning of witnesses and the presentation of documentary and other evidence, the lawyers may *object* to certain questions or to the admissibility of certain evidence. Common objections include hearsay, relevance, and privilege. The judge rules on each objection to decide whether the evidence will be admitted. After both sides have presented their evidence, the lawyers give *closing arguments* summing up the case and explaining why their client should prevail.

At that point, the judge instructs the jury on the law to be applied in the case. These *jury instructions*, also known as the *jury charge*, explain the substantive law that the jurors must apply in reaching their decision. Many jurisdictions have *pattern jury instructions* available to judges either as the exact instructions to use or as a starting point for writing instructions in a particular case. The exact language of jury instructions becomes a point of contention in some cases, with lawyers for each side presenting the judge with the version they hope the court will adopt. Jury instructions provide fertile ground for appeals, too, as a losing party may blame the loss on a jury charge that the party argued was erroneous. Finally, the jurors return to the jury room to deliberate in private, discussing the evidence until they reach a verdict.

(2) Verdicts

(a) Burden of Persuasion

When the judge instructs the jury, the judge must be clear about the **burden of persuasion**: Who has it, and how strong is it? Without knowing the burden of persuasion, the jury would lack a critical piece of analytical guidance.

Who bears the burden? The plaintiff, mostly. Defendants generally have the burden to prove affirmative defenses. Certain types of claims, including many claims of discrimination, involve burden shifting in which the plaintiff bears the initial burden of establishing a prima facie case, but then the burden shifts to the defendant. But as a general matter, the plaintiff bears the burden of persuasion in civil cases. The real question for the jury, in other words, is not "What happened?" but rather "Did the plaintiff prove the case?"

How strong is the burden? The plaintiff must establish each element of the claim by a *preponderance of the evidence*. In other words, the jury decides whether the fact is more likely than not. Some lawyers describe it as a 51 percent standard, although mathematically speaking, it would be more accurate to call it something like 50.000001 percent. To meet the preponderance standard, the jury merely has to find the fact a tiny bit more likely than not. In a breach of contract case, for example, if the jury decides that probably the defendant breached the contract, then the plaintiff prevails. If the jury decides that probably the defendant did not breach the contract, then the defendant prevails. If the jury cannot decide — if the evidence for each side is so equal that the jurors are in perfect equipoise on the matter — then the defendant prevails because the plaintiff had the burden of persuasion.

The preponderance standard in civil cases contrasts starkly with the standard in criminal cases. In criminal cases, the prosecution has the burden of proving its case *beyond a reasonable doubt*, a high burden intended to make it difficult to convict the innocent. Civil lawsuits are different. The plaintiff in a civil case need not remove doubt, but need only convince the jurors that the plaintiff's version of the facts is more likely than the defendant's version. Whereas criminal justice policy strongly favors protecting defendants from wrongful convictions, civil justice policy does not reflect any consensus that the system should systematically favor either plaintiffs or defendants.

In certain types of proceedings, you will encounter an in-between burden of persuasion known as *clear and convincing evidence*. Falling somewhere between the high burden of "beyond a reasonable doubt" and the lower burden of "preponderance of the evidence," the clear and convincing evidence standard often applies in quasi-criminal proceedings such as attorney disciplinary matters. In many states, punitive damages must be established by clear and convincing evidence.

(b) Forms of Verdicts

The most basic form of verdict, the **general verdict**, simply asks the jury to decide who wins and how much. The jury either returns a verdict for the defendant or a verdict for the plaintiff in the amount of X dollars. In addition to the general verdict, Rule 49 gives courts two alternative forms of verdicts: the special verdict and the general verdict with questions.

The **special verdict** does not ask the jury to state which party should prevail, but instead asks the jury to answer specific factual questions. The judge then enters judgment for the appropriate party based on the answers given by the jury. For example, a special verdict form in a negligence case might begin with "Do you find by a preponderance of the evidence that the defendant failed to exercise reasonable care?" If the jury answers yes to the first question, then the form would instruct the jury to answer similar questions about proximate causation, damages, and any other essential issues. The more complex the case, the more useful courts find the special verdict. Although a special verdict can guide the jury through the elements of a single claim, special verdicts provide structure in cases involving numerous claims and parties. By asking the jury to render its verdict in the form of answers to specific questions, the court is able to sort out liability on varied legal claims, damages of multiple plaintiffs, responsibility of multiple defendants, and other individualized issues that could easily get lost in a jury's deliberations over a general verdict.

The third type of verdict is basically a combination of the first two. With a *general verdict with answers to written questions*, also known as a *general verdict with interrogatories*, the jury renders a verdict stating which party prevails, just like a general verdict, but in addition the jury answers specific questions presented by the court. This type of verdict gives the court a tool for making sure the jury understood what it was doing and followed the court's instructions.

Here's the problem: Sometimes the jury's answers demonstrate that the jury did *not* understand what it was doing or did *not* follow the court's instructions. When a court uses a general verdict with interrogatories, there is always the risk that the jury's verdict will be inconsistent with the jury's answers to the specific questions. In that event, the court has several options. If the answers are consistent with one another but not with the verdict, the court may enter judgment according to the answers notwithstanding the verdict, may send the case back to the jury for further consideration, or may even order a new trial. If the answers are inconsistent with one another and one or more is inconsistent with the verdict, then the court will either return the jury for further consideration or order a new trial. Some courts view it as a downside of general verdicts with answers — and, to a lesser extent, special verdicts — that these forms of verdicts have the potential to highlight jury confusion. There's something appealing about a simple general verdict by which the jury does its job and announces the result. Of course, jurors could be equally confused in a case with a general verdict; the difference is that the judge would never know about it.

(3) Bench Trials

Bench trials — trials without juries — occur under two circumstances. First, when there is no right to a jury trial, the judge does it alone. Second, even if the lawsuit is one that entails a right to a jury, when no party makes a timely jury demand the judge does it alone.

To a large extent, bench trials proceed just like jury trials. Each side presents its case in open court, with opening statements, witnesses, and closing arguments. The witnesses testify under oath through direct and cross-examination. Lawyers assert objections and the court rules on the admissibility of evidence. In the end, the factfinder assesses the evidence and decides the case by applying the law to the facts in light of the burden of persuasion. The salient difference between bench and jury trials — that the factfinder is a judge rather than a jury — does not alter the basic function of the trial.

It does affect the feel of the trial, however, both in terms of how lawyers conduct themselves and the efficiency of the process. Jury trials bring out a certain theatricality by some trial lawyers; bench trials tend to be more subdued and businesslike. Bench trials tend to treat the rules of evidence with somewhat less formality than jury trials, and bench trials avoid the need to spend time ushering the jury in and out of the courtroom out of concern about what the jury may and may not hear.

One important difference between jury and bench trials comes at the end of the trial. A jury announces its decision by rendering a verdict. As discussed above, there are several forms of verdicts, but the most basic — the general verdict — is completely opaque. With a general verdict, the jury declares who prevails but does not explain its reasoning. A special verdict or general verdict with answers to written questions obligates the jury to answer specific questions about the case, but even there, the jury does not have to explain its logic or which evidence it considered credible. By contrast, a judge in a bench trial must state his or her *findings of fact* and *conclusions of law*. As Rule 52 puts it, "the court must find the facts specially and state its conclusions of law separately." The judge may state these findings and conclusions on the record in court after the close of the evidence or may put them in writing in the decision.

The transparency of a bench trial decision — as contrasted with the opacity of a general verdict — makes a bench trial decision both less powerful and more powerful than a jury verdict. A judge's decision is more vulnerable to reversal on appeal. An appeals court may reverse a trial judge's factual findings if they are "clearly erroneous." That's a high standard, but not impossible. Jury verdicts, by contrast, are largely immune from appellate review. But a bench trial decision carries the potential to be more powerful than a jury's general verdict because of issue preclusion. Issue preclusion, discussed in Chapter 11, permits courts in later proceedings to use certain factual determinations reached in an earlier case. General verdicts make it difficult in some cases to figure out precisely what issues the jury determined, but judicial findings of fact are explicit (like special verdicts), making it easier to use those findings in other cases.

Q: Is there a constitutional right to a bench trial?

A: No. Jury trials get special treatment under the U.S. Constitution. Under the Seventh Amendment, parties have a constitutional right to a jury trial in certain types of cases. By contrast, if a case falls outside the parameters of the Seventh Amendment, no party has a constitutional right to insist that there *not* be a jury. This explains why Congress may enact statutes that extend the jury right beyond what is protected by the Seventh Amendment.

Bench trials naturally skip the entire jury selection process, including issues of peremptory challenges and excusals for cause. The rough equivalent to jury selection is the assignment of the judge. The judicial assignment process varies among courts. An assigned judge must *recuse* herself from any proceeding in which her impartiality may reasonably be questioned,[6] or if the judge has expressed an opinion on the case or has a financial interest.[7] Parties may move to disqualify a judge under such circumstances. California's code of civil procedure permits each party one "peremptory" challenge to the judge, but only if the party alleges that the judge is biased.[8]

---

[6]28 U.S.C. §455(a).
[7]28 U.S.C. §455(b).
[8]Cal. Civ. Proc. Code §170.6.

C. Judgment as a Matter of Law and New Trial

(1) Judgment as a Matter of Law

What if the evidence at trial is so lopsided that only one party can reasonably prevail? That's where Rule 50 comes into play — the *motion for judgment as a matter of law* and the *renewed motion for judgment as a matter of law*. Older cases use the terms *directed verdict* and *judgment notwithstanding the verdict* (or *j.n.o.v.*). You should get comfortable with both sets of terms because earlier cases and some state courts use the older terminology, as do plenty of lawyers and judges.

Judgment as a matter of law shifts some of the jury's authority to the judge. In a jury trial, the judge and jury have different jobs. The job of ruling on questions of law belongs to the judge. The job of resolving disputed facts and applying the law to those facts belongs to the jury. Whenever a judge grants judgment as a matter of law, the judge is taking the decision-making authority away from the jury. The justification is that the jury may decide the case within the bounds of reason, but juries are not empowered to decide civil cases without regard to the evidence and the applicable law. If the evidence is so clear that there is only one way a reasonable jury could decide, then judgment as a matter of law may be appropriate.

The standard for granting judgment as a matter of law is just like summary judgment. When a plaintiff or defendant moves for judgment as a matter of law, the court must look at the evidence in the light most favorable to the nonmoving party. This means drawing all reasonable inferences and resolving credibility disputes in favor of the nonmoving party. If, by believing certain witnesses and disbelieving others, a jury could reasonably find in favor of the nonmoving party, then the court must deny the motion for judgment as a matter of law.

Motion and Renewed Motion (or Directed Verdict and J.N.O.V.). Judgment as a matter of law can occur before or after the jury has rendered a verdict. It's important to be aware of the procedural details that relate to this difference in timing.

Before the verdict, this device is what used to be known as *directed verdict*. Historically the name came from the notion that the court was directing the jury to render a verdict in favor of a certain party, but the Federal Rules of Civil Procedure discard the terminology of directing a verdict and instead call it *judgment as a matter of law*. Rule 50(a) states that a party may move for judgment as a matter of law "at any time before the case is submitted to the jury," but also makes it clear that judgment as a matter of law may be granted only after the nonmoving party has been fully heard on the relevant issue. Therefore, the timing to move for judgment as a matter of law depends on whether the movant is a plaintiff or a defendant. For a plaintiff, judgment as a matter of law ordinarily must wait until the close of all the evidence because the court doesn't know whether the defendant should lose until the defendant has had an opportunity to present its evidence. For a defendant, however, judgment as a matter of law can occur either at the close of all the evidence or at the close of the plaintiff's case. Once the plaintiff has had a full opportunity to present his case, the defendant can argue that the plaintiff has failed to meet his burden.

If the court grants judgment as a matter of law, then the judge sends the jurors home. Thanks for your time, goodbye. The jury never gets the chance to render a verdict, which must be pretty frustrating for jurors who have just spent however many hours or days listening to the evidence. That's one big difference between

Rule 50 (judgment as a matter of law) and Rule 56 (summary judgment). Just like summary judgment, judgment as a matter of law takes the decision away from the jury. But at the Rule 56 stage, the jury is just an idea; by granting summary judgment the court ensures that no actual jury will be empaneled for the case. At the Rule 50 stage, the case is at trial. There's an actual group of jurors sitting in the jury box in the courtroom, and they've listened to the evidence. Although as a matter of procedural theory, Rule 56 and Rule 50 motions function almost identically, the fact that Rule 50 motions occur during trial puts an exclamation point on the judicial assertion of power.

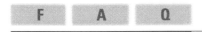

Q: If a case is so lopsided that a party wins judgment as a matter of law, why did the case even get to trial? Shouldn't that party have won summary judgment before trial?

A: Although the legal standard for granting judgment as a matter of law under Rule 50 mirrors the standard for summary judgment under Rule 56, the difference in timing explains why some of these cases reach trial. At the summary judgment stage, a party may have met its burden of production by attaching an affidavit or other evidence that suggested a witness would testify a certain way, but at the actual trial, the witness's testimony may have differed or perhaps the witness never showed up. Also, in a questionable case, some judges might decline to grant summary judgment to see how the evidence will develop at trial, but on a Rule 50 motion, the evidence has already been presented so there is nothing left to see.

After the jury has rendered a verdict, the losing party may ask the judge to take the decision away from the jury and decide it the opposite way, arguing that based on the evidence and the applicable law, no reasonable jury could have decided the way this jury did. This is what traditionally has been called *judgment notwithstanding the verdict*, usually abbreviated *j.n.o.v.* (the abbreviation comes from *judgment non obstante veredicto*, Latin for "notwithstanding the verdict"). Rule 50(b) calls it the *renewed motion for judgment as a matter of law*.

Rule 50(a)	Rule 50(b)
Motion for judgment as a matter of law (directed verdict)	Renewed motion for judgment as a matter of law (j.n.o.v., or judgment notwithstanding the verdict)

The "renewed motion" terminology helps you remember a critical procedural detail about Rule 50(b). Using the traditional terms, a party cannot move for j.n.o.v. unless that party previously moved for a directed verdict. In Rule 50 terms, a party obviously cannot *renew* a motion for judgment as a matter of law unless that party previously made such a motion. In other words, if a party thinks that the other side's evidence is so weak or the case is so clear that it can be decided only one way, the party may not wait until after the jury verdict to make this argument.

You might wonder why a judge would ever grant a renewed motion for judgment as a matter of law. After all, if the case was so clear-cut based on the evidence at trial, wouldn't the judge have granted the original motion for judgment as a matter of law? Logically, it seems impossible that a court would deny the motion for judgment as a matter of law at the close of all the evidence, but then grant the very same motion after the jury has rendered its verdict. Moreover, to whatever extent judges worry about jurors' annoyance at a directed verdict, just imagine how jurors feel about being told — *after* deliberating and rendering their verdict — that their service was for naught because the judge thinks their decision was irrational! Yet despite all this, judges sometimes deny (or defer decision on) motions for judgment as a matter of law at the close of the evidence and then grant the renewed motion after the jury verdict. Why?

The first reason is straightforward psychology and political science. If the judge thinks it's so clear which party should win the case, the judge may think this will be equally obvious to the jury. Judges prefer to let jurors do their job. As long as the jury gets it "right," it obviates any need for the judge to grant judgment as a matter of law, and everybody's happy (except the losing party, that is).

The second reason is more subtle but equally important as a matter of civil procedure. Suppose a judge grants a motion for judgment as a matter of law at the close of the evidence. The judge sends the jury home without rendering a verdict, and the court enters judgment in favor of the moving party. Now, suppose the losing party appeals, and the appellate court reverses the grant of judgment as a matter of law. What happens next? Since the jury never had the opportunity to render a verdict, the entire case must be retried. By contrast, suppose the judge does *not* grant the motion for judgment as a matter of law at the close of the evidence and lets the jury render a decision. If the jury decides "incorrectly," and the judge therefore grants the renewed motion for judgment as a matter of law, and that judgment is reversed on appeal, then what happens next? The trial court can simply reinstate the original jury verdict. Unlike in the first scenario, no new trial is required. It's counterintuitive, but judges understand that the more efficient approach may be to deny a deserving Rule 50(a) motion and instead to grant the Rule 50(b) renewed motion if necessary.

(2) New Trial

A trial may have problems serious enough that the court cannot allow the result to stand, but the circumstances do not warrant granting judgment as a matter of law for one party or the other. In such cases, the court may order a **new trial**. Just as it sounds, it means "let's have a do-over." If you're a tennis player, it's a let.

What constitutes a permissible basis for a new trial? Rule 59 spells out the procedure for new trial motions in federal court, but the rule is pretty cryptic about what are adequate grounds, stating only that a court may grant a new trial on whatever grounds have traditionally been permitted. The case law, however, makes it clear that new trials can be granted in response to two types of trial flaws — process problems and outcome problems.

Process problems, to justify a new trial, must be serious enough to raise serious questions about the fairness of the proceedings. For example, the judge's instructions to the jury may have been an erroneous interpretation of the law, or important evidence may have been erroneously admitted or excluded. Or a lawyer may have engaged in misconduct such as an improper closing argument. Or perhaps the jurors themselves engaged in misconduct that raises questions about their objectivity and independence. If a judge believes that allowing the trial result to stand would be unjust in light of the error in the conduct of the trial, then the judge has the discretion to order a new trial.

Outcome problems, as a basis for new trial motions, tend to go hand in hand with motions for judgment as a matter of law. Courts say that a new trial may be granted if the jury verdict is "against the weight of the evidence." Some courts emphasize the high standard by using the phrase "against the *great* weight of the evidence." Judges have wide discretion when deciding whether to grant a new trial. It's a judgment call. But the trial judge may not simply substitute her own judgment for that of the jury. The question is not what the judge would have decided had she been a juror. Rather, the question is whether the jury's decision was so clearly contrary to the evidence that the verdict cannot stand.

OK, then how does the new trial standard differ from granting a renewed motion for judgment as a matter of law (j.n.o.v.)? The harsher the impact, the higher the standard. New trial takes away the verdict and lets the parties try again, whereas j.n.o.v. takes away the verdict and hands it to the other side! To grant j.n.o.v., the judge must determine that no reasonable jury could have reached the result the jury reached. It's a direct assault on the jury's rationality. The new trial standard is a bit softer. For a new trial, the judge disagrees strongly with the jury, but cannot say that *no* reasonable jury could have gone there. For example, suppose the judge finds the defendants' witnesses highly credible and finds the plaintiff's witnesses not credible because of their conflicting accounts, tentative delivery, or other credibility problems. A jury *could* rationally find for the plaintiff *if* the jury believed the plaintiffs' witnesses, but the judge is strongly convinced that a verdict for the plaintiff would be a miscarriage of justice. The judge could not grant judgment as a matter of law because on that motion the judge must view the evidence in the light most favorable to the nonmoving party. But at least some courts would consider this a proper basis for granting a new trial.

Judges also use the power to grant new trials as a way to lower the amount of damages awarded by the jury. Here's how. When a judge finds the amount of damages awarded by the jury irrationally high, the judge may order a conditional new trial, telling the plaintiff that there will be a new trial unless the plaintiff accepts a reduced amount of damages. For example, if the jury awarded $300,000 and the judge thinks that a reasonable amount, based on the evidence, must fall in the range of $50,000 to $100,000, then the judge might inform the plaintiff that the judge will grant a new trial unless the plaintiff accepts $100,000 in damages. Judges should not simply substitute their measure of damages for the jury's; courts sometimes state that the judge should alter the damages only if the amount "shocks the conscience." Known as *remittitur*, this type of conditional new trial order is permitted in both federal and state courts.

Turn remittitur upside-down and you get *additur*, which allows a judge to address damages that are irrationally low. Some state courts permit additur, but for the federal courts, the Supreme Court has declared additur unconstitutional as a violation of the Seventh Amendment. You might wonder about the logic of permitting remittitur but prohibiting additur, a difference that tilts the field in favor of defendants on the question of damages. Remember the historical test for applying the Seventh Amendment right to a jury trial? The Supreme Court's logic about additur and remittitur, in part, was that remittitur was permitted in 1791. Some historians have raised questions about this account, but for now, federal courts may use remittitur to lower damages but may not use additur to raise them.

Rule 50 and Rule 59 motions often go hand in hand. When a losing party believes the jury's verdict was unsupported by the evidence, the party may make a Rule 50(b) renewed motion for judgment as a matter of law, and in the alternative, a Rule 59 motion for a new trial. Naturally, the losing party's first choice is to win judgment as a matter of law, the next-best option is to get a new trial, and the worst option is to let the verdict stand. By renewing a Rule 50 motion and moving in the alternative for a new trial, the party is trying to say to the judge, "We think the facts and law in this case so clearly support our position that no rational jury could have found otherwise, and therefore we think you should grant judgment as a matter of law for us. But even if you're unwilling to go that far, the evidence weighs so heavily in our favor that you should find the jury's verdict to be against the weight of the evidence and therefore grant a new trial." The trial judge must decide the renewed motion for judgment as a matter of law before the new trial motion. If the court denies the Rule 50 motion, then the court must decide the new trial motion. Even if the court grants judgment as a matter of law, Rule 50(c) asks the judge to provide a conditional ruling on the new trial motion. That way, in case the judgment is reversed on appeal, the court knows whether to reinstate the original jury verdict or to remand for a new trial.

Not all trials involve juries. In a bench trial, the judge plays the role of both factfinder and legal decision maker. Later in the chapter, well look at certain procedural aspects of bench trials, but we begin with the jury and the contours of the Seventh Amendment right to a jury trial.

SUMMARY

- At trial, the parties present their evidence in open court and the judge or jury determines the outcome.

- In a jury trial, the judge rules on issues of law and the jury determines the facts; in a bench trial, the judge serves both functions.

- For federal court civil actions, the Seventh Amendment preserves the right to a jury trial as it existed in 1791, which generally means that common law claims include a right to a jury trial while equitable claims do not.

- If a case includes a right to a jury trial, any party may demand a jury. If no party demands a jury, then the trial proceeds without a jury.

- In the selection of jurors, parties may use challenges for cause as well as peremptory challenges.

- Peremptory challenges on the basis of race or gender violate the Equal Protection Clause.

- A court may have a jury render a general verdict, a special verdict (a written finding on each issue of fact), or a general verdict with answers to written questions.

- If a party fails to meet its burden of production at trial, the court may enter judgment as a matter of law against that party upon a determination that no reasonable jury could find in that party's favor.

■ If a court does not grant a party's motion for judgment as a matter of law, the party may renew the motion after trial.

■ A court may order a new trial if there has been a serious flaw in the trial procedure or if the verdict is against the great weight of the evidence.

CONNECTIONS

Pleadings

The pleadings set up the framework of the claims and defenses that the parties intend to prove at trial. Shortly before trial, the court may hold a final pretrial conference to formulate a trial plan, and a final pretrial order issued after such a conference supersedes the pleadings by setting out the issues to be resolved at trial. Pleadings also may be amended at trial to conform to the evidence at trial.

Discovery

In theory, the point of discovery is to provide parties with the evidence they need at trial. In reality, most cases never get to trial, and the information obtained in discovery drives settlement negotiations. But skilled lawyers always think about trial when planning discovery. Imagining the jury instructions is one way to get a handle on exactly what must be proved for each claim or defense, and thus to see clearly what information you need to gather.

Joinder — Class Action

For a class action under Rule 23(b)(3), a court must decide whether a class action would be a superior way to adjudicate the controversy. In making this determination, judges consider the manageability of a trial, and class action lawyers sometimes present detailed trial plans as part of their motion for class certification.

Summary Judgment

What makes summary judgment attractive is that it avoids the expense and uncertainty of trial, particularly a jury trial. That's also what makes summary judgment somewhat controversial. Summary judgment under Rule 56 has a lot in common with Rule 50 motions for judgment as a matter of law: Both Rule 56 and Rule 50 allow a judge to take the decision away from the jury based on a determination that no reasonable jury could find otherwise.

Appeal

The standard of review depends in part on whether there was a bench trial or jury trial. After a bench trial, the appellate court applies a "clearly erroneous" standard when reviewing the trial judge's findings of fact. After a jury trial, the appellate court does not directly review the jury's findings, but may review them indirectly by considering appeals from the trial judge's legal rulings including the grant or denial of judgment as a matter of law or new trial.

Preclusion

Issue preclusion affects trials in two ways. First and most directly, if an issue has already been determined in a prior case and if issue preclusion applies, then the issue will not be relitigated and no evidence need be presented on that issue at a subsequent trial. Second, if an issue in a trial might bear importantly on other cases — such as a defendant's liability in a dispute involving numerous potential claimants — then the risk of future issue preclusion raises the stakes and thus may raise the intensity with which the parties litigate that issue in the first trial.

Appeals

10

Judges are human (though you may encounter a few who don't like to admit it). And humans make mistakes. By allowing disappointed litigants to

OVERVIEW

seek review from a higher authority, the appeals process creates an opportunity for the judicial system to correct its own errors. In addition to error correction, appeals permit greater uniformity in interpretation of the law.

To understand how appeals fit into the justice system, you need to know the jurisdictional reach of appellate courts and how appellate judges review trial court decisions. Civil procedure courses vary in the extent to which they cover appeals, but many professors include at least the topics of *appealability* and *standards of review*. **Appealability** concerns when an appeal may be taken and what may be appealed. The federal courts of appeals generally hear appeals only from final judgments; litigants may not run to the appellate court every time they don't like the trial judge's decisions during the litigation. But the final judgment rule admits of numerous exceptions, and the skilled litigator always knows which decisions may be appealed immediately and which decisions cannot be appealed until the trial court's work is finished. The closely related idea of *reviewability* addresses which issues may be presented to the appellate court. **Standards of review** concern how deferentially the appellate court must treat the trial judge's decisions. On legal questions, appellate judges give no deference whatsoever, but on factual questions and discretionary decisions, appellate judges are more hesitant to reverse decisions of the trial court. Knowing the standards of review not only makes you a more effective appellate advocate, but is also indispensable for understanding appellate decisions you read as a law student or lawyer.

A. THE APPELLATE COURTS

B. SUPREME COURT JURISDICTION

C. APPEALABILITY AND REVIEWABILITY

1. Who May Appeal: Adversity and Standing
2. When May Decisions Be Appealed: Appealability
3. What May Be Appealed: Reviewability

D. STANDARDS OF REVIEW

A. The Appellate Courts

In Chapter 1, we introduced the various federal and state courts and their relationships as a matter of subject matter jurisdiction. This chapter focuses on the road from trial court to appellate court. We will look briefly at the jurisdiction of the U.S. Supreme Court, but because nearly all federal cases that are appealed end in the U.S. courts of appeals, that is where we will focus most of our attention.

Each state has its own rules, statutes, and constitutional provisions concerning the structure and powers of its appellate courts. Recall that most state court systems contain three tiers like the federal courts, but some smaller states have only a trial court and a high court, while other systems are structured with even more tiers and divisions. Losing litigants in most state courts have a right to appeal. Taking the appeal even higher to the state's high court (such as the California Supreme Court or the New York Court of Appeals) generally is not a matter of right. Rather, the highest court of the state ordinarily has the power to select which appeals to hear. Some states allow exceptions for particularly important types of appeals (in the criminal area, for example, many states allow automatic appeals to the state high court in death penalty cases) or for appeals in which a judge dissented at the intermediate appellate level.

In the federal court system, each court of appeals hears appeals from the district courts within its circuit. For example, the U.S. Court of Appeals for the Second Circuit hears appeals from the U.S. district courts within New York, Connecticut, and Vermont. One exception is the Federal Circuit, which does not cover a particular geographic area but instead hears nationwide appeals in cases involving patents, international trade, veterans' claims, and certain other specialized categories of cases. The jurisdiction of the U.S. courts of appeals is governed largely by statute but constrained by Article III of the constitution, which states the outer limits of federal court jurisdiction. Sections 1291 and 1292 of Title 28 of the U.S. Code spell out the final judgment rule for appealability to the U.S. courts of appeals and certain exceptions to the final judgment rule, which we will consider in detail later in this chapter.

The U.S. Supreme Court's jurisdiction comes from both the constitution and federal statutes. Before turning to the specific aspects of the Supreme Court's authority or to the detailed explanation of the final judgment rule for the U.S. courts of appeals, let's use the chart shown in Figure 10.1 to get the big picture. I've used a solid line for appeals as of right from the trial court to the court of appeals. Appeals to the Supreme Court or to the state high courts are shown with a dotted line to reflect that most such appeals are subject to the discretion of the high court. Finally, appeals to the U.S. Supreme Court from state courts are not only up to the discretion of the Supreme Court, but also limited to issues of federal law. The multiple dotted lines from state to federal reflect that appeals to the Supreme Court need not come from the state high court, but come from whichever state court was the final court within the state system to address the issue.

Appellate courts normally hear appeals in multi-judge panels, unlike trial courts where, with rare exceptions, a single judge handles the case. The U.S. courts of appeals use three-judge panels, as do some state appellate courts. The total number of court of appeals judges within each circuit ranges from 6 in the First Circuit to 29 in the enormous Ninth Circuit, which encompasses California and much of the western United States. In extraordinary cases, the court of appeals judges within a circuit may vote to hold a rehearing *en banc*, which means that the entire group of judges reconsiders the appeal after the original decision by the three-judge appellate panel.

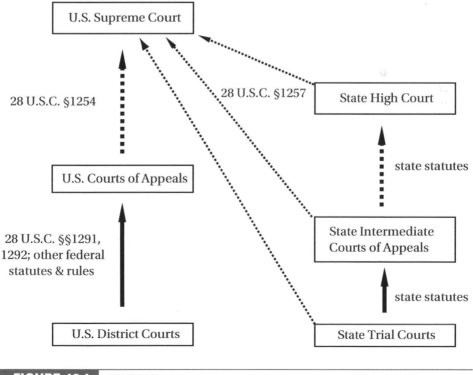

FIGURE 10.1 APPEALS

State supreme courts often have five, seven, or nine justices (or judges, depending on the state's terminology) who decide each case *en banc*. The New York Court of Appeals has seven judges, the California Supreme Court has seven justices, and the Texas Supreme Court has nine justices. The U.S. Supreme Court, of course, has nine Justices, whom any self-respecting law student should know by name and judicial orientation. For obvious reasons, odd numbers are preferred; even numbers can lead to ties. In the Supreme Court, if one or more Justices recuse themselves from a case because of conflicts of interest, the Court hears the case with fewer than nine Justices and may reach a 4-4 or even 3-3 tie. When a tie occurs, the judgment below is affirmed, but the Court issues no opinion and the affirmance has no precedential value.

B. Supreme Court Jurisdiction

The Supreme Court chooses which appeals to hear, granting only a small percentage of the thousands of *petitions for certiorari* filed each year by litigants vying for the Court's attention. The Justices decide whether to grant the petition — that is, whether to permit the appeal — based primarily on whether it presents an important legal issue that needs to be resolved.

The U.S. Supreme Court hears appeals from both federal and state courts, but with one huge difference. On questions of state law, the highest authority is the top court of that state, and the U.S. Supreme Court has no authority to tell the state courts how they should interpret their own state law. Appeals from state courts to the U.S. Supreme Court, therefore, are limited to questions of federal law. Under 28 U.S.C. §1257, if a state court case raises a federal law issue, a party may seek Supreme Court review. For example, in a New Jersey state court medical malpractice case, the losing party may appeal from the trial court to the Appellate Division of the New Jersey Superior Court, raising whatever issues of state or federal law the party considers significant. After the appellate court decides the case, the losing party might try to appeal to the New Jersey Supreme Court, and if that court grants certification to hear the case, the parties can raise state and federal issues. But if a party then wishes to appeal to the U.S. Supreme Court, the appellant may not ask the U.S. Supreme Court to reexamine the New Jersey Supreme Court's interpretation of New Jersey common law tort doctrines, New Jersey statutes, or New Jersey's constitution. The appellant could, however, ask the U.S. Supreme Court to determine whether New Jersey law, as applied by the state courts, violates the U.S. Constitution or some other aspect of federal law.

Appeals under §1257 need not come from the state high court. Rather, the statute permits appeal of a final judgment from the highest state court in which a decision could be had. In the example above, if the case went all the way to the New Jersey Supreme Court, then any appeal to the U.S. Supreme Court would wait until after the state supreme court had decided the case. But if the New Jersey Supreme Court declined to hear the case, then the Appellate Division would have been the highest state court in which a decision could be had. If state law does not provide an appeal for a particular proceeding, then the trial court may be the highest state court in which a decision could be had. In such circumstances, §1257 permits a party to seek certiorari in the U.S. Supreme Court directly from the intermediate state appellate court or even from a state trial court.

Most Supreme Court appeals, however, arise from the U.S. courts of appeals. Under 28 U.S.C. §1254, cases from the courts of appeals may be reviewed by the Supreme Court either by "writ of certiorari granted upon the petition of any party to any civil or criminal case, before or after rendition of judgment or decree" or "certification at any time by a court of appeals of any question of law in any civil or criminal case as to which instructions are desired, and upon such certification the Supreme Court may give binding instructions or require the entire record to be sent up for decision of the entire matter in controversy."

C. Appealability and Reviewability

You may be surprised to learn that there is no constitutional right to appeal a civil case. As a matter of statute and judicial decision making, the federal court system permits certain appeals, and in general a losing party has the right to seek review at least once. To understand the right to appeal, lawyers must familiarize themselves with several doctrines that constrain the *who*, *when*,

and *what* of appeals. We turn now to these three important aspects of the law governing appeals, focusing on appeals from the federal district courts to the courts of appeals:

1. *Who* may appeal — the topics of adversity and standing
2. *When* may decisions be appealed — the final judgment rule and its exceptions
3. *What* may be appealed — the topics of waiver and harmless error

(1) Who May Appeal: Adversity and Standing

To appeal, a party must have lost. This is the requirement of *adversity* or *aggrievedness*. It sounds like an obvious point. After all, why would a winning party even *want* to appeal? But it turns out that winning and losing are not always so simple.

Suppose a plaintiff wins a judgment but the relief granted by the court differs from what the plaintiff requested in the complaint. Perhaps the damages are lower than the plaintiff sought, or the plaintiff was denied injunctive relief in addition to damages, or the court awarded compensatory but not punitive damages. Even though the plaintiff "won" the lawsuit, the plaintiff may appeal the denial of the requested remedy. As a strategic matter, the plaintiff may decide that an appeal is not worth the risk and expense if the relief awarded was satisfactory, but as a legal matter, the plaintiff would have the right to appeal. Similarly, in a case involving multiple claims, the plaintiff may succeed on some claims but lose on others, and both the plaintiff and defendant could consider appealing the aspects of the case on which the other side prevailed.

Frequently, both sides emerge dissatisfied with the outcome of a case because no one entirely got what they wanted. You should not be surprised, therefore, to encounter *cross-appeals*, in which opposing parties appeal the judgment on different grounds.

Here's what does *not* count as adversity: dissatisfaction with the court's reasoning. If a defendant prevails and the plaintiff is awarded nothing, but the defendant dislikes the court's opinion because the defendant believes it creates a bad precedent for the defendant in future cases, the defendant has no right to appeal. A party appeals from the *judgment*, not from the opinion. Similarly, if a plaintiff sues under multiple legal theories and obtains the full relief requested, the plaintiff cannot appeal simply because the court awarded the relief pursuant to one theory rather than the other. One interesting exception helps to explain the rule. In a case for fraud and breach of contract, an insurer won full damages under the breach of contract theory, but its fraud claim was rejected. Because the defendant was going bankrupt and bankruptcy law made it easier for the insurer to recover damages for fraud than for breach of contract, the insurer was permitted to appeal the denial of its fraud claim.[1] To establish adversity for purposes of bringing an appeal, a party must show that it did not obtain the result it sought.

Nonparties ordinarily lack standing to appeal. Outsiders may be unhappy about the outcome of a case and their personal interests may be affected, but they have no right to appeal the judgment if they were not actually parties to the lawsuit. A nonparty may ask the court's permission to participate as *amicus curiae*—"friend of the court"—which allows the nonparty to submit a brief and possibly to participate in oral argument, but it does not give a party standing to file the appeal. If a nonparty wishes to become a party for purposes of bringing an appeal, it may apply to intervene under Rule 24. In a class action, however, even though class members are not parties in the usual sense unless they choose to intervene in the action, a class member who objects to a settlement may appeal from the court's approval of that settlement.

(2) When May Decisions Be Appealed: Appealability

(a) The Final Judgment Rule

Only final judgments may be appealed—that's the general rule. Master it, then get ready for a slew of exceptions and alternatives.

Start with the statutory grant of jurisdiction to the U.S. courts of appeals in 28 U.S.C. §1291: "The courts of appeals . . . shall have jurisdiction of appeals from all final decisions of the district courts of the United States. . . ." Key word—*final*. What counts as a final decision? According to the Supreme Court, it means "one which ends the litigation on the merits and leaves nothing for the court to do but execute the judgment."[2] During the trial court process, judges make plenty of **interlocutory** rulings—decisions along the way—but these do not constitute final judgments.

---

[1]*See* Aetna Cas. & Surety Co. v. Cunningham, 224 F.2d 478 (5th Cir. 1955).
[2]Caitlin v. United States, 324 U.S. 229, 233 (1945).

To be sure you're clear on what constitutes a final judgment within the meaning of §1291, run through the following examples. The question for each is whether the court's decision is *final* or merely *interlocutory*:

Final vs. Interlocutory	
(1) Case goes to trial and court enters judgment based on the jury verdict, with no posttrial motions pending.	Final
(2) Court grants motion to compel discovery.	Interlocutory
(3) Court denies motion to compel discovery.	Interlocutory
(4) Court grants motion for summary judgment on all claims.	Final
(5) Court denies motion for summary judgment.	Interlocutory
(6) Court grants motion to dismiss for failure to state a claim.	Final
(7) Court denies motion to dismiss for failure to state a claim.	Interlocutory

You get the idea. If the case is still going on at the trial court level, it does not constitute a final judgment for purposes of appealability. Certain types of rulings, such as discovery motions, are interlocutory regardless of which way the court rules. Other types of rulings, such as motions to dismiss or for summary judgment, may be final judgments if granted, but interlocutory if denied.

Note that in every one of these examples, one of the parties is unhappy about the court's decision and possibly anxious to get it reversed. In the last example, the defendant may be utterly convinced that the trial court erred in denying the Rule 12(b)(6) motion and deeply annoyed at having to go forward with litigating what the defendant believes is a meritless case. But at that point, there is no final judgment. Denial of the motion to dismiss means that the defendant must file an answer and the litigation continues. After the completion of the case, if the defendant loses, *then* the defendant may raise the issue on appeal and argue that the trial court erred in failing to grant the motion to dismiss.

That last point is important. The final judgment rule does not prevent parties from raising on appeal all sorts of issues that may have come up during the litigation. On appeal, a losing party may argue that the trial court made erroneous rulings about pleadings, discovery, pretrial motions, admissibility of evidence, or other interlocutory decisions. The fact that those trial court decisions are *interlocutory* does not insulate them from review; it simply means that they cannot be reviewed immediately but instead their review must wait until after the case has reached a final judgment. Interestingly, however, a denial of summary judgment is not appealable after a full trial, because the trial record supersedes the record that existed at the time of the summary judgment motion.[3]

---

[3]Ortiz v. Jordan, 131 S. Ct. 884, 888-89 (2011).

Why does the federal court system (as well as many of the state courts) impose the final judgment rule? Why not permit parties to appeal decisions along the way, if they believe those decisions were important and erroneous? Mostly, it's about efficiency. If parties routinely could seek review of interlocutory decisions, it might extend litigation and raise costs as parties go repeatedly up to the appellate court in a series of piecemeal appeals. Moreover, if routine interlocutory appeals were allowed, the appellate courts would have to decide numerous issues unnecessarily, as parties lose battles even if they later will win the war. Suppose a trial court denies a plaintiff access to certain discovery. If interlocutory appeal were permitted, the plaintiff might seek appellate review of the discovery decision, imposing substantial delay and cost on both parties and the courts. But the plaintiff might win the case even without the discovery, in which case the appeal would be pointless. By forcing parties to wait until the case concludes and then allowing the losing party to raise whatever points of error the party considers most important, the court system avoids the cost and delay associated with piecemeal and unnecessary appeals.

There is another perspective, however. When a trial judge makes a serious error, there's something to say for reversing the error as expeditiously as possible. If a trial court erroneously denies a motion to dismiss, justice and efficiency arguably are better served by a prompt reversal, rather than forcing the parties to slog through the entire litigation only to find on appeal that the action should have been dismissed at the outset. Also, most cases settle before reaching a final judgment, so as a practical matter many trial court decisions are unappealable. Because of these concerns, some state courts strike a different balance from the federal courts, permitting interlocutory appeals more liberally. In New York, for example, parties may appeal not only from a final judgment, but also from an order that "involves some part of the merits" or "affects a substantial right."[4]

(b) Exceptions to the Final Judgment Rule

If it were absolute, the final judgment rule would be way too harsh. Sometimes parties need appellate review of interlocutory decisions and forcing them to wait would be untenable. Congress, federal rulemakers, and the courts therefore have carved out certain exceptions to the final judgment rule of appealability. Litigators know that in these circumstances, they can seek review of adverse decisions without awaiting the final judgment.

Injunctive Relief. Again, we start with the statutory grant of authority to the courts of appeals. Section 1292(a) of Title 28 gives the courts of appeals jurisdiction over interlocutory orders by district courts "granting, continuing, modifying, refusing or dissolving injunctions, or refusing to dissolve or modify injunctions." Injunctions — orders that tell parties what they must or must not do — have an immediacy that differs from money damages. Imagine a lawsuit to stop the defendant from running his ice cream shop based on a noncompete agreement that the parties dispute. If the court grants injunctive relief, the defendant must stop operating his business. If the court denies injunctive relief, the plaintiff must face business competition possibly in violation of the agreement. Even if the grant or denial of injunctive relief is interlocutory — perhaps the lawsuit seeks money damages as well and

---

[4]N.Y. Civ. Prac. L. & R. §5701.

"And don't go whining to some higher court."

that issue has not been resolved—the impact of the injunction decision on the parties is so immediate and tangible that interlocutory appeal is permitted.

Certified Interlocutory Appeal. Section 1292(b) builds some flexibility into the final judgment rule by allowing a district judge to certify that an important issue needs to be resolved by the appellate court right away. When the district judge makes an interlocutory order, the judge may state in writing that the order "involves a controlling question of law as to which there is substantial ground for difference of opinion and that an immediate appeal from the order may materially advance the ultimate termination of the litigation." Notice the three requirements embedded in that sentence. First, the interlocutory order must involve a controlling question of law. Second, there must be substantial basis for disagreement about that question of law. Third, the district judge must believe that immediate appellate review would help bring the lawsuit to a close.

Certified Interlocutory Appeals Under §1292(b)

District Court	Court of Appeals
(1) "controlling question of law" (2) "substantial ground for difference of opinion" (3) "immediate appeal . . . may materially advance the ultimate termination"	discretion to accept appeal certified by district court

Section 1292(b) works well in lawsuits with claims or defenses based on novel legal theories. If a plaintiff brings a claim based on a legal theory that no one has ever tried before, the district judge might think the claim questionable but nonetheless deny defendant's motion to dismiss for failure to state a claim. The district judge knows that ultimately the appellate courts will have to decide on the legal viability of the plaintiff's claim. Rather than go through discovery and trial without the benefit of the appellate court's input, the district judge would prefer to allow the parties to take an immediate appeal of the Rule 12(b)(6) decision before going forward.

Even if the district judge certifies an issue for interlocutory appeal under §1292(b), the court of appeals gets to decide whether to accept it. As the statute puts it, the court of appeals "may thereupon, in its discretion, permit an appeal to be taken from such order."

Interlocutory appeals under §1292(b) occur infrequently. According to some studies, the district courts certify only a few hundred interlocutory appeals each year, and the courts of appeals accept less than half of those. Think about what's required for one of these appeals to happen. A federal district judge—a member of a group not known for smallness of ego—must state that his decision on a crucial issue may well be wrong. Then the court of appeals judges—members of a group not known for happiness about burgeoning appellate dockets—must state that yes, it would like extra work, thank you very much. It is understandable that both the district and circuit judges reserve these appeals for special cases. But despite their rarity, certified interlocutory appeals carry a disproportionate impact because they tend to occur in important cases on the most interesting and controversial issues.

Collateral Order Doctrine. The final judgment rule works pretty well in most situations when a trial court's erroneous decision can be repaired by altering the outcome of the case. But what if the trial court's erroneous decision affects an important right aside from—*collateral* to—the outcome of the lawsuit itself? The collateral order doctrine allows parties to appeal certain decisions that would be effectively unreviewable on appeal. For the collateral order doctrine to apply, the decision must (1) conclusively determine the disputed question, (2) resolve an important issue completely separate from the merits of the action, and (3) be effectively unreviewable on appeal from a final judgment. A judge-made doctrine, it allows appellate courts to treat certain nonfinal decisions as though they were final for purposes of appeal.

> ### COLLATERAL ORDER DOCTRINE
>
> (1) conclusive determination
> (2) important issue separate from merits
> (3) effectively unreviewable after final judgment

Suppose a judge orders a party to submit to a blood test in discovery. The party objects that the court erroneously treated it as a Rule 34 request for inspection and thus failed to make any finding of good cause as required in Rule 35 for physical exams, and that the court failed to take into account the party's frail physical condition, which makes it dangerous for her to give a blood sample. May the party appeal the court's decision? The order is interlocutory so it cannot be appealed as a final judgment. But imagine telling this litigant that she can appeal the order after the case has reached a final judgment. She'd say: "How sweet that you'll let me appeal *later*, but right *now* I don't want my blood taken, I don't want my health endangered, I don't want to get poked with that needle. What's the appellate court going to do later—*unpoke* me? I want the appellate court to reverse this erroneous order *before* I get poked." Be sure you understand how her argument would invoke the three elements of the collateral order doctrine. First, the court's order conclusively determined whether the party must provide the blood sample. Second, the party's right not to be involuntarily poked with needles (a legal question for the court to resolve) is separate from the merits of the lawsuit. Third, the decision is effectively unreviewable on appeal because by then the party will already have submitted to the blood test. Whether a court would accept the application of the collateral order doctrine to allow interlocutory appeal in this case might depend on whether the court considered the blood test a significant enough intrusion to justify special treatment for purposes of appealability.

The classic application of the collateral order doctrine is to the issue of sovereign immunity. In civil rights cases, government officials have qualified immunity. Courts have made it clear that such immunity not only protects officials from being held liable, it also protects officials from the burdens of trial. Suppose a civil rights defendant moves for summary judgment based on qualified immunity and the court denies the motion. The defendant would like to appeal the court's rejection of the immunity defense, but the denial of summary judgment constitutes an interlocutory order, not a final judgment. Using the collateral order doctrine, the defendant would argue that his immunity from trial exists apart from his immunity from liability, and that this right is effectively unreviewable after final judgment because he would already have been forced to endure the trial process.

Class Certification. In class actions, many lawyers consider the single most important moment to be the court's decision on class certification. A grant of class certification propels an enormous litigation forward and places massive settlement pressure on the defendant. A denial of class certification often sounds a death knell for the litigation. Either way, the court's decision on the motion for class certification matters profoundly to both sides. But it's interlocutory. If the court grants class certification, the case does not end; it proceeds as a class action. If the court denies class certification, the case does not end; at least in theory, it proceeds as an individual action. Until recently, class certification decisions therefore remained unappealable until after a final judgment. To avoid the harshness of the final judgment rule as applied to class certification, litigants and judges often used either §1292(b) interlocutory appeals or the writ of mandamus to obtain review of class certification decisions.

In 1998, the Supreme Court adopted an amendment to the class action rule to permit interlocutory appeals of class certification decisions at the discretion of the court of appeals. Rule 23(f) says that a court of appeals may permit, in its discretion, an appeal of a class action certification decision if it is made within ten days of the ruling.

F   A   Q

Q: How can a mere Federal Rule of Civil Procedure alter the jurisdiction of the U.S. courts of appeals?

A: In general, the rules of civil procedure cannot alter the jurisdictional reach of the courts, which is a matter of constitutional and statutory authority. With regard to interlocutory appeals, however, Congress explicitly left open the possibility of expanding such appeals through the rulemaking process. *See* 28 U.S.C. §1292(e). The rulemakers had solid statutory authority, therefore, when they amended Rule 23 to permit appeal of class certification decisions.

Partial Final Judgment. Litigation often includes multiple claims, multiple parties, or both. Chapter 7 discusses the rules that permit numerous claims or parties to be joined in a single action. Now, think about how joinder alters appealability. Suppose a case is completely finished with regard to one of those claims or one of those parties, even if other parts of the case remain to be decided. May a party seek appeal of that decision, even though the entire action has not concluded? On the one hand, the decision is interlocutory because the case is still going on. On the other hand, it feels a lot like a final judgment because, at least with regard to that particular claim or party, nothing else remains to be done.

Federal Rule of Civil Procedure 54(b) resolves this conundrum by permitting a district court to enter a final judgment as to a particular claim or party. Rule 54(b) says that when there are multiple claims or parties, "the court may direct entry of a final judgment as to one or more, but fewer than all, claims or parties only if the court expressly determines that there is no just reason for delay." Unless the judge does this explicitly, however, a decision as to each claim or party is interlocutory until the whole case is resolved. To be clear about it, judges ordinarily use the exact language of the rule. Thus, if the judge grants a motion to dismiss or summary judgment as to a particular claim or party, and if the judge thinks that it makes sense to permit the appeal right away, the judge's order would say something like, "Finding no just reason for delay, the court directs that final judgment be entered as to . . . ."

Consider the three scenarios diagrammed in Figure 10.2 in which Rule 54(b) might come into play. In Example 1, the plaintiff sues two defendants (recall that Rule 20 allows joinder of parties if the claims arise out of the same transaction or occurrence), and the plaintiff prevails against the second defendant while the case against the first defendant is still pending. Perhaps the court grants summary judgment for the plaintiff against Defendant 2, finding no genuine dispute as to either liability or damages, but needs a trial to determine whether Defendant 1 is liable as well. Because the claim against Defendant 2 has been fully resolved, the court could choose to enter a final judgment against Defendant 2, which would permit Defendant 2 to appeal without waiting for Defendant 1's trial to conclude.

In Example 2, two plaintiffs sue a defendant and the defendant prevails against one of them, perhaps on a Rule 12(b)(6) motion to dismiss for failure to state a claim. Because the claim by Plaintiff 2 has been fully resolved, the court could choose to enter a final judgment against Plaintiff 2, which would permit Plaintiff 2 to appeal the 12(b)(6) dismissal without waiting for Plaintiff 1's claim to conclude.

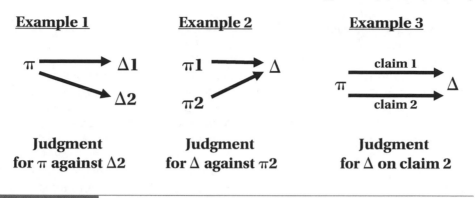

FIGURE 10.2 PARTIAL FINAL JUDGMENT

In Example 3, the plaintiff asserted two claims against the defendant (recall that Rule 18 allows unlimited joinder of claims between plaintiff and defendant, even if they are unrelated), and the court has adjudicated claim 2 in favor of the defendant. If the claims are related, then most likely the court would not enter final judgment until both claims were fully resolved. If the claims are quite distinct, however, the court could choose enter final judgment as to claim 2, which would permit the plaintiff to appeal that decision without waiting for the rest of the case to finish. Just as it can apply in cases with multiple claims by a plaintiff against a defendant, Rule 54(b) also applies to counterclaims, cross-claims, and third-party claims.

Q: Does Rule 54(b) create an exception to the final judgment rule?

A: Not exactly. Not in the way that §§1292(a) and 1292(b) do. Rather than carving out an *exception* to the final judgment rule, Rule 54(b) empowers the district court to enter a *final judgment* that is appealable under the ordinary operation of §1291. Then why did I include Rule 54(b) in the portion of this chapter called "Exceptions to the Final Judgment Rule"? Because in practice, when you wish to take an appeal from a decision but the action is still pending in the district court, you should think functionally about all potential avenues to the court of appeals.

Mandamus. The writ of mandamus, one of the old "prerogative writs," dates back about 700 years in English legal history. In Latin, *mandamus* means "we command," and that is exactly what the writ does—it allows an appellate court to command a government official to perform a mandatory duty. What does this have to do with appeals? Remember that government officials include lower court judges. When a trial judge fails to correctly perform a judicial duty, a superior court can use the writ of mandamus to force the judge to apply the law correctly.

Mandamus is not an *appeal* from the trial court to the appellate court. Rather, the applicant brings a separate proceeding directly in the appellate court asking the court to grant a writ of mandamus. Technically, the mandamus proceeding is brought against the government official. That explains why the caption of a mandamus opinion includes the name of the trial court or the judge. Remember the personal jurisdiction case of *World-Wide Volkswagen v. Woodson?*[5] Woodson was the Oklahoma trial court judge who denied World-Wide's motion to dismiss for lack of personal jurisdiction. World-Wide could not appeal the decision because it was interlocutory. Instead, World-Wide brought a separate proceeding in the appellate court asking the court to compel Judge Woodson to dismiss the case against it for lack of personal jurisdiction. Do not be fooled. Although the new proceeding names the judge as the respondent, the positions are still argued by the parties to the underlying litigation.

Courts insist that parties may use the writ of mandamus only in exceptional circumstances, when standard procedures do not suffice. In appropriate cases, however, parties find mandamus useful as an end-run around the final judgment rule. When a party wishes to appeal an interlocutory decision but cannot find a basis for an interlocutory appeal, sometimes the only way to get the appellate court's attention is to bring a separate proceeding asking the appellate court to order the trial court to do its duty.

(3) What May Be Appealed: Reviewability

Not every trial court error may be raised on appeal, and not every raised error leads to reversal. Even if an appellant has standing to appeal, and even if the appeal is from a final judgment (or fits into an exception to the final judgment rule), and even if the appellant is correct that the trial judge made an error, that does not necessarily mean the appeals court will reverse the trial court decision. To warrant appellate attention the error must be *reviewable*, and to warrant reversal the error must not have been *harmless*.

(a) Waiver

In general, a party may not raise an issue on appeal unless the party raised that issue at the trial court level. If a trial lawyer has objections to the trial judge's decisions, the lawyer should point out those concerns promptly. If the lawyer waits until after the trial judge has completed her work, and then on appeal accuses the trial judge of various errors, the trial judge is deprived of the opportunity to correct the problems. Also, if a lawyer believes his client will probably lose at trial, and the trial judge makes an erroneous decision along the way, the lawyer should not be allowed to keep that error in his pocket to obtain reversal on appeal rather than objecting to the error at the trial court level. Therefore, if an appellant seeks to raise issues on appeal that were not raised in the trial court, the appellate court ordinarily will refuse to hear those arguments on the ground that the issues were waived.

Remember that effective litigators always think several moves ahead. Because of the doctrine of waiver, skilled trial lawyers never lose sight of the possibility that they will need to raise issues on appeal, and they are careful to *preserve* errors for appeal by making the proper objections during the pretrial and trial process. When a trial court makes a decision adverse to your client and you believe the court erred, you should object for two reasons: first, to persuade the trial judge to change course, and second,

---

[5]444 U.S. 286 (1980).

to preserve the issue for appeal in case your effort to persuade the trial judge fails. This explains why trial lawyers sometimes make what appear to be futile motions or objections during pretrial or trial. Even if the trial judge has made it clear that she will reject the lawyer's argument, the lawyer hopes for a better result on appeal and must raise the objection to avoid waiving it.

Recall from Chapter 5 that Rules 12(g) and (h) spell out certain provisions on waiver of defenses. Under Rule 12(h)(1), a defendant waives the defenses of personal jurisdiction, venue, summons, and service of process unless the defendant raises those defenses at the outset of the case — in the answer or a pre-answer motion, whichever comes first. Naturally, the waiver of those defenses persists into the appeals process. If a defendant fails to raise its objection to personal jurisdiction or venue on a timely basis, then the defendant cannot raise those issues on appeal or otherwise. But waiver on appeal goes much further. Think of nearly any decision a trial judge might make during the pretrial or trial process — setting a discovery cutoff date, bifurcating the trial, admitting or excluding certain evidence, instructing the jury. If a party believes the judge got it wrong, but fails to raise that objection in the trial court, then the appeals court will refuse to hear about it.

Courts allow certain exceptions to the general rule that issues are waived if not raised below. Some courts permit parties to raise arguments on appeal if the arguments stem from a change in the law that occurred after the judgment. Also, if the trial court mistake was *plain error*, appellate courts may permit a party to raise the point on appeal even if it was not raised explicitly in the trial court. The Federal Rules of Civil Procedure mention "plain error" only once — in the rule on jury instructions. Under Rule 51(d), if parties wish to raise arguments on appeal concerning errors in the jury instructions, they ordinarily must have made timely objections, but even if the party did not properly preserve the issue by objecting, a court "may consider a plain error in the instructions . . . if the error affects substantial rights."

(b) Harmless Error

Causation matters. In torts, if a driver behaves negligently but does not hurt anyone, no private plaintiff has a claim. Similarly, if a trial judge makes an error but the error causes no harm, then an appellate court will not reverse the judgment. It's **harmless error**.

Suppose in a case for money damages the trial court, over the plaintiff's objection, instructed the jury incorrectly on how to calculate the amount of damages. The jury then reached a verdict for the defendant finding no liability, and the court entered judgment accordingly. If the plaintiff were to appeal, the plaintiff would meet the requirement of adversity (the trial court entered judgment for the defendant), appealability (it was a final judgment), and reviewability at least in the sense of nonwaiver (plaintiff objected to the court's instruction). But as a basis for reversal, plaintiff's argument about the trial court's erroneous instruction would fall flat. On the question of whether the defendant was liable at all to the plaintiff, the court's error about how to calculate damages is beside the point.

The harmless error doctrine is not absolute. Despite the general principle that errors should lead to reversal only if they may have altered the outcome, some errors impinge on rights that are too fundamental to yield to the harmless error doctrine. One appeals court, for example, held that a trial court's erroneous failure to strike a juror for cause must lead to reversal, even if exclusion would have made no difference. As that court put it, "[d]enial of the right to an unbiased tribunal is one of those trial errors that is not excused by being shown to have been harmless. . . ."[6]

D. Standards of Review

To get reversed, how wrong must the trial court be? Some errors are more egregious than others. Suppose a decision was a close call, but the appellate court happens to disagree with the trial court—should the appellate court reverse the trial court's decision? That depends on how much deference the appellate court gives to the trial judge's decisions. In other words, it depends on what *standard of review* the appeals court applies.

De Novo. The primary function of appellate courts is to review the legal decisions of the trial court to ensure that the law was properly interpreted and applied. Appellate courts possess higher authority to decide the law; they develop expertise in legal decision making; they have more time to consider the briefs and to write careful opinion; and, because they have authority over multiple trial courts, they can ensure greater uniformity in legal application. Therefore, on questions of law, appellate courts give zero deference to the trial judge's decisions. Rather, appellate courts review a trial court's legal rulings *de novo*, which means that the appellate judges take a fresh look at each legal issue and decide it for themselves. Suppose the appellate judges think that a legal issue in the case was very close, but they decide—just barely—that the trial judge decided it the wrong way. Under the de novo standard of review, the appellate court will apply its own interpretation of the law rather than defer to the trial judge's interpretation.

Clear Error. Facts are a different story. With regard to factual findings in a specific case, we don't worry about uniformity across different courts. Nor do we assume that appellate judges have greater expertise than trial judges at figuring out the facts. On the contrary, trial judges gain experience at hearing factual evidence, while appellate judges spend more time reading briefs and analyzing legal nuances. And in any specific case, the trial judge—not the appellate judges—actually heard the witnesses. Thus, when trial judges make findings of fact, appellate courts defer to those findings unless they are *clearly erroneous*. In bench trials, Rule 52 requires the district court to state the court's findings of fact and conclusions of law, and it goes on to declare the standard of review: "Findings of fact, whether based on oral or other evidence, must not be set aside unless clearly erroneous, and the reviewing court must give due regard to the trial court's opportunity to judge the witnesses' credibility."

The Supreme Court has explained that "clearly erroneous" means that even if some evidence supports the finding, the reviewing court based on the entirety of the record is left with the definite and firm conviction that a mistake has been committed.[7] The idea is not for the appellate court to substitute its judgment for that of the trial court (in sharp contrast to the de novo review applied to legal rulings), but rather for the appellate court to step in to correct errors only when the trial court clearly got it wrong.

---

[6]Thompson v. Altheimer & Gray, 248 F.3d 621 (7th Cir. 2003).
[7]United States v. United States Gypsum Co., 333 U.S. 364, 395 (1948).

Abuse of Discretion. As we have seen throughout this book, trial judges make numerous discretionary decisions—decisions that the law permits but does not compel—and these include some of the most important decisions during the litigation process. These include Rule 11 sanctions, leave to amend pleadings, consolidation or separation of trials, venue transfer, proportionality decisions in discovery, new trial, and a host of other procedural rulings. You can spot the discretionary decisions by the language in the rules and statutes—words like "may" or "when justice so requires" or "for good cause." When an appellant seeks review of a trial court's discretionary decision, the appellate court will reverse only for *abuse of discretion*. In other words, the appellate court defers to the trial judge's decision unless the decision falls outside the scope of what a reasonable judge could have done under the circumstances.

Review of Jury Decisions. What about factfinding by a jury? As you would expect, jury verdicts get even greater protection than judicial findings of fact. An appellate court does not review a jury's determinations. A losing party cannot appeal on the ground that the jury got it wrong. Instead, the appeal must focus on what the *judge* did or did not do.

This is how, as a practical matter, jury verdicts get reviewed on appeal: A party moves for judgment as a matter of law at trial, which the court denies. The jury finds against that party. The party then renews the motion for judgment as a matter of law, or in the alternative for a new trial, which the court denies. On appeal, the party does not simply argue that the *jury* got it wrong. Rather, the party argues that the *judge* got it wrong by denying the Rule 50 motion for judgment as a matter of law or the Rule 59 motion for a new trial. The argument that the court erred by denying judgment as a matter of law requires the appellant to argue that no reasonable jury could have found as the jury did. The argument that the court erred by denying a new trial requires the appellant to argue that the jury's verdict was against the great weight of the evidence.

> ### Sidebar
>
> **APPELLATE ADVOCACY**
>
> Writing appellate briefs and presenting oral arguments requires thorough command of the factual record, careful legal research and analysis, and the ability to frame an argument with clarity, eloquence, and concision. Compared with other lawyering skills such as client counseling, negotiation, and trial advocacy, you may find that appellate advocacy is the one skill set for which standard law school classes actually prepare you (let that give you some comfort the next time you get called on in class). Beyond the classroom, many law students find moot court a fantastic way to develop the skills required for effective appellate advocacy.

It's tough to win such an appeal. As to the Rule 50 denial, the appellate court reviews the denial de novo because whether to grant judgment as a matter of law is a legal decision, but the underlying question is whether *any* reasonable jury could have reached the same conclusion. Thus, in reviewing the denial of judgment as a matter of law, the court of appeals does not ask whether the jury was correct but only whether any reasonable jury could have found that way—an extremely deferential standard, even more so than the clearly erroneous standard applied to judicial factfinding. As to the Rule 59 denial, the underlying question is whether the verdict was against the great weight of the evidence, but the appellate court reviews the decision for abuse of discretion. Thus, the jury's verdict is doubly protected—first by the high standard for a trial judge to grant a new trial, and second by the deferential review of the trial court's discretionary decision to deny a new trial.

SUMMARY

■ The U.S. Supreme Court may grant certiorari to hear appeals from the federal courts of appeals, or from a state court if the appeal raises a federal issue.

■ The U.S. courts of appeals have jurisdiction over final judgments from the U.S. district courts, as well as over narrow categories of interlocutory appeals.

■ Interlocutory appeals are permitted from decisions granting or denying injunctive relief.

■ Interlocutory appeals are permitted at the discretion of both the district court and the court of appeals if the district court certifies that the appeal involves a controlling question of law on which there is serious grounds for debate.

■ The collateral order doctrine permits appeals from decisions that resolve an important issue completely separate from the merits of the action and that would be effectively unreviewable on appeal from a final judgment.

■ Interlocutory appeals regarding class certification are permitted at the appellate court's discretion.

■ In general, parties may appeal a ruling only if they objected to the ruling in the trial court.

■ When reviewing decisions of law, appellate courts make their own legal determinations without any deference to the trial court's rulings.

■ When reviewing trial court determinations of fact, appellate courts reverse only if the trial court determination was clearly erroneous.

■ When reviewing trial court discretionary rulings, appellate courts reverse only for abuse of discretion.

CONNECTIONS

Subject Matter Jurisdiction

Unlike other issues, which are reviewable on appeal only if the party raised the issue in the trial court, subject matter jurisdiction may be raised on appeal even if no one previously raised it. This is because parties cannot waive subject matter jurisdiction. Recall that in *Louisville & Nashville Railroad Co. v. Mottley*,[8] the Supreme Court dismissed the Mottleys' case for lack of federal question jurisdiction even though neither the parties nor the trial court had raised any question about jurisdiction.

---

[8]211 U.S. 149 (1908).

Erie

The case of *Gasperini v. Center for Humanities*[9] involved the *Erie* doctrine's intersection with standards of review and the role of appellate courts. The Supreme Court decided that although New York's substantive standard for review of damage awards must apply in federal court, the federal courts need not follow the same division of labor that the New York state courts assign to their trial and appellate courts. *Gasperini* serves as a useful reminder that the roles of appellate courts vary from one jurisdiction to another.

Trial

When thinking about the difference between bench trials and jury trials, bear in mind that bench trials yield findings of fact that are reviewable on a clearly erroneous standard, whereas jury trials yield jury verdicts that are largely unreviewable except by way of attacking the judge's denial of new trial or judgment as a matter of law, or the judge's legal decisions along the way such as jury instructions or admissibility of evidence.

Preclusion

Claim preclusion and issue preclusion apply only to final judgments, so the question arises whether a judgment is "final" if an appeal is still pending. The federal courts treat decisions as final for purposes of preclusion even though the case is on appeal. Some state courts, however, do not treat a decision as final for purposes of claim preclusion and issue preclusion until the appeal has concluded. The important point is that the requirement of a final judgment for preclusion need not mean the same thing as the final judgment rule of appealability embodied in 28 U.S.C. §1291, because the two final judgment rules serve different functions.

---

[9]518 U.S. 415 (1996).

Preclusion

11

Preclusion doctrines are all about the binding effect of a judgment. After a case has been decided and a court has entered judgment, sup-

OVERVIEW

pose one of the parties tries to bring another lawsuit relating to the same situation, hoping for a better result. Or suppose another suit raises some issue that was decided in the first case. To what extent are parties permitted to relitigate claims or issues? These questions are addressed by the law of judgments, and in particular by the doctrines of claim preclusion and issue preclusion.

These doctrines matter whenever litigation involves more than one related lawsuit. If a prior suit addressed any of the claims or issues in your client's case, you need to know whether any of the parties are precluded from bringing claims, asserting defenses, or litigating particular issues. If yours is the first lawsuit, you need to understand what effect a judgment will have on potential future litigation.

A. TWO KINDS OF PRECLUSION

B. CLAIM PRECLUSION

1. Same Claim
2. Same Parties
3. Valid and Final Judgment
4. "On the Merits"

A. Two Kinds of Preclusion

First, be sure you understand the difference between claim preclusion and issue preclusion. In some cases the two go hand in hand, but it is critical that you see how they serve different functions. **Claim preclusion** (a.k.a. *res judicata*) addresses whether parties are prohibited from asserting a claim because they already received a judgment on the same claim. **Issue preclusion** (a.k.a. *collateral estoppel*) addresses whether parties are prohibited from litigating a particular issue that was decided in a prior lawsuit. A simple example will introduce the difference between the two doctrines.

Example 1: A sues B for property damage to her car, alleging that B negligently caused a collision. B denies that he was negligent. A jury renders a general verdict in favor of A for $20,000, and the court enters judgment. A files a second lawsuit against B based on the same collision, this time seeking damages for personal injury.

#1   A → B
- Auto accident
- Negligence claim — property damage
- Judgment for A — $20,000

#2   A → B
- Same auto accident
- Negligence claim — personal injury

In case #2, B will argue that A has already had a lawsuit about this collision and should not be allowed to bring another one. That's *claim preclusion.* B wants to preclude A from relitigating the claim. In most jurisdictions, B's claim preclusion argument would succeed, and A's claim would be dismissed. In a few jurisdictions, however, courts would treat the personal injury suit as a different claim from property damage and would allow the case to go forward. In that event, if B again denies negligence, A would argue that they already litigated the issue of negligence and it was determined that B negligently caused the collision, so the court in case #2 should take negligence as conclusively established. That's *issue preclusion.* A wants to preclude B from relitigating the issue of negligence.

B. Claim Preclusion

The idea of claim preclusion is that a plaintiff gets one bite at the apple. If a party asserted a claim and a court entered judgment on it, the party may not bring the same claim again. It's a thing decided. Or to say it in Latin, it's *res judicata*.

In reading cases on claim preclusion, you may encounter the words *merger* and *bar*. If the plaintiff wins the first suit but comes back for more, claim preclusion tells the plaintiff: "You brought your claim, you won, now that's enough." That's what courts used to call *merger*. The idea is that the entire claim merges into the judgment for the plaintiff. If, instead, the plaintiff loses the first suit and then tries again, claim preclusion tells the plaintiff: "You brought your claim, you lost, now go away." That's what courts used to call *bar*. The judgment against the plaintiff bars the plaintiff from reasserting the losing claim. As you can probably tell, the distinction between merger and bar makes no real difference; claim preclusion applies equally whether the plaintiff won or lost.

The doctrine of claim preclusion can be pretty well summed up in one sentence: A valid, final judgment on the merits precludes relitigation of the same claim between the same parties. Simple, huh? The problem is that the sentence contains at least four pieces that take some real effort to understand. Picture the sentence like this:

> A **valid, final judgment on the merits** precludes relitigation of the **same claim** between the **same parties**.

Before you're ready to apply the doctrine of claim preclusion, you have to be able to answer four questions about the underlined terms:

1. How do courts decide whether lawsuits present the *same claim*, and in particular, to what extent are related but nonidentical claims treated as the same?
2. How do courts decide whether lawsuits involve the *same parties*, and in particular, to what extent are related but nonidentical parties treated as the same?
3. What makes a judgment *valid* and *final*?
4. Which types of decisions count as *on the merits*?

Each of these questions has been the subject of extensive case law and commentary, and the answers vary somewhat among jurisdictions.

(1) Same Claim

Just because A sued B in the past, that obviously does not mean A can never sue B again on any claim. If it's a different claim, then there is no problem. Claim preclusion only prevents relitigation of the same claim. But how exactly do we know what's the same claim? What if the second lawsuit asserts a different legal theory, or adds new factual allegations, or seeks a different remedy?

States have adopted various tests for determining whether the claim in the second lawsuit is the same as the claim in the first lawsuit. The *same evidence test* focuses on whether the same evidence could be used to prove each of the claims. The *primary rights test* asks whether the same rights are involved in the two actions.

The majority approach and the modern trend, however, is to apply a broad *transactional test*. According to the influential Restatement (Second) of Judgments §24, a claim is precluded by a prior judgment if the actions arise out of the same underlying transaction or series of transactions. The federal courts and most state courts apply tests along these lines. The transactional test tends to further the goals of claim preclusion — efficiency, consistency, finality — by encouraging joinder of related claims. If parties know that they will be precluded from bringing other lawsuits later, then they are likely to think carefully about all of their potential claims when they file their initial actions.

To apply the transactional test, resist the law student temptation to think about lawsuits in legal terms. Do not focus on what legal theories the complaint invokes (strict liability, breach of contract, antitrust, and so on). Don't focus, either, on what remedies the complaint demands (damages, injunctive relief, and so on). Instead, ask what the case was actually about. What was alleged to have happened that gave rise to the dispute? Maybe it was a business deal, or a motorcycle accident, or an employment termination. The transaction test asks whether the claim asserted in the second lawsuit arose out of the same underlying factual situation as the first. If so, then it's the same claim for purposes of claim preclusion.

The transactional test casts a wide net. It makes claim preclusion a powerful tool for defendants to get claims dismissed in the second case. More significant, it creates a huge incentive for a plaintiff to join all related claims in a single lawsuit. If you represent a plaintiff and you are deciding what claims to include in the complaint, claim preclusion tells you that you cannot "split the claim" and pursue it in multiple lawsuits. You could not, for example, split theories by bringing a breach of contract claim first and a promissory estoppel claim later based on the same promise. Nor could you split claims for different remedies by bringing separate actions for money damages and for specific performance. Thus, in Example 1, a court applying the transactional test would dismiss A's personal injury claim in #2, holding that it is claim precluded because it arises out of the same occurrence as the property damage claim that was adjudicated in #1. If A's injury was significant, you can imagine A's dismay at never getting to assert the personal injury claim (and A's lawyer should not be too surprised when a malpractice complaint arrives). But claim preclusion leaves little room for sympathy. It is irrelevant that A did not assert the personal injury claim in #1 because claim preclusion covers not only those claims that were actually asserted, but also those that *could* have been asserted and that are deemed to be part of the same claim. The point of claim preclusion is *finality.* Next time, A's lawyer should remember that all of the client's claims for relief arising out of the occurrence must be asserted, if ever, in the first lawsuit.

(2) Same Parties

Claim preclusion applies to claims between the same parties. If A sues B and a court enters judgment on A's claim, then A is precluded from reasserting the same claim against B. Claim preclusion does not prevent a different plaintiff from asserting a claim against B, even if it arises out of the same event. Nor does it prevent A from asserting a claim against a different defendant.

First, consider why claim preclusion cannot prohibit a new plaintiff from asserting a claim, and why this constraint is a matter of constitutional due process. Let's vary Example 1 by supposing the accident involves three cars:

Example 2: A three-car collision occurs among drivers A, B, and C. A sues B for negligence, and the court enters judgment. Subsequently, C sues B for negligence in the same collision.

#1   A → B
   ■ Auto accident
   ■ Negligence claim
   ■ Judgment for A or B

#2   C → B
   ■ Same auto accident
   ■ Negligence claim

If B were to assert a claim preclusion argument ("We already had a lawsuit about this, and the court entered judgment, so go away."), C's response would be irrefutable: "*I* haven't had a lawsuit about this. *You* and A did."

One way to think about this is that B's claim preclusion argument fails to meet two of the basic claim preclusion requirements. It fails to meet the *same parties* requirement, because C was not a party to the first action. And it fails to meet the *same claim* requirement, because even though the claims arise out of the same event, different plaintiffs necessarily possess different claims.

The other way to think about this is more fundamental and ultimately much more important to your understanding. C cannot be bound by judgment #1 because C was not a party to the case. As a due process matter, if C was not made a party to case #1, then the court never had the power to enter a binding judgment against C. At this point, if you're thinking this sounds like personal jurisdiction, and especially if you hear echoes of *Pennoyer v. Neff*, that's good. Part of personal jurisdiction is the idea that a court lacks the power to bind someone by judgment unless he or she is properly made a party to the case through service of process or otherwise.

The *same parties* requirement is not only about the principle that you can't bind a nonparty. It also means claim preclusion does not prohibit a party from suing a different defendant. Consider the three-car collision again:

Example 3: A three-car collision occurs among drivers A, B, and C. A sues B for negligence, and the court enters judgment. Subsequently, A sues C for negligence in the same collision.

#1   A → B
- Auto accident
- Negligence claim
- Judgment for A or B

#2   A → C
- Same auto accident
- Negligence claim

If C were to assert a claim preclusion argument against A ("You already had a lawsuit about this."), A would respond: "I had a lawsuit against *B*, but not against *you*." For claim preclusion to apply, the claims must be between the same parties. A's claim against C in case #2 is not precluded because the claim is not between the same parties as the claim in case #1.

Up to this point, the *same parties* requirement seems pretty straightforward. It gets messier when we add the notion of **privity**. Some nonparties are deemed to be represented by parties. A "successor in interest" (such as someone who purchases an ongoing business), for example, is bound by the outcomes of its predecessor's litigation. Similarly, a person is bound by a judgment in a case brought on his behalf by a guardian or other legal representative. With the added twist of privity, our single-sentence recitation of claim preclusion could sensibly be revised: A valid, final judgment on the merits precludes relitigation of the same claim between the same parties *or their privies*. But conceptualizing privity as an extension of *same party* keeps it in proper perspective.

You'll find that most definitions of privity are circular to the point of uselessness. Rather than trying to understand the word *privity* as a test that you can apply, you should understand it as a legal conclusion. If the relationship between two persons is such that the law treats them as the same party for purposes of preclusion, then you can say that they are in privity.

Be careful not to get carried away. Although the concept of privity has expanded over the years, it remains quite narrow. The Supreme Court recently reaffirmed this by holding that two members of the same club were not in privity with each other for purposes of preclusion, even though the second one asserted exactly the same right as the first (seeking specific information from the government under the Freedom of Information Act), and even though they used the same lawyer.[1] In Example 2,

---

[1]Taylor v. Sturgell, 553 U.S. 880 (2008).

suppose C were not a third driver, but rather a passenger in A's car. Would the judgment in case #1 preclude C from asserting a claim? Absolutely not. A and C are not the same party, and they are not in privity. It would not matter if C had been a witness in #1 or if C were A's spouse. They remain different plaintiffs. Nor would it matter if C were A's child, if A had brought the first case on A's own behalf. But if A brought the first case as a guardian on C's behalf, then A and C would be in privity, and C would be precluded from reasserting the claim.

(3) Valid and Final Judgment

The point of claim preclusion is that if a judgment is valid and final, then the parties should not get to try again. But what makes a judgment valid and final? Or to put it differently, what entitles a judgment to *recognition* as something worthy of preclusive effect?

(a) Validity

First, what makes a judgment valid? Your first instinct might be to say that a judgment is valid if it decides the case correctly. On that view, we would call a judgment valid only if it gets the facts straight and applies the law appropriately to those facts. But obviously this definition won't work. The very nature of litigation is that there are conflicting views on the facts and the law, and the objective of adjudication is to resolve the dispute as soundly as possible. If claim preclusion depended on whether the first court got it right, then every collateral attack would lead right back into the underlying dispute and would require a new trial or other proceedings to examine the facts and the law.

Validity of a judgment as a condition of claim preclusion cannot be based on the substantive merits or the outcome of a dispute. Rather, think of "validity" more as a structural and procedural notion. What entitles a judgment to recognition ultimately is the legitimacy of the court to render a decision that is binding in this particular dispute on these particular parties. This, of course, brings us back to personal jurisdiction and subject matter jurisdiction.

If a court lacks personal jurisdiction over a party or if adequate notice has not been provided, then the judgment does not bind that party. That, in one sentence, sums up the basic point of Chapter 2 of this book. Remember, though, how easy it is to waive objections to personal jurisdiction and notice. If a party appears to litigate an action without preserving the objection to jurisdiction or notice, then the party will be unable to challenge the validity of the judgment in a later action. If the court in the first action rejects the party's jurisdictional challenge, then the court's jurisdictional determination will be binding in a subsequent action. This means that, in general, a subsequent challenge to the validity of a judgment based on personal jurisdiction or notice can come only from a party who defaulted in the first action.

In Chapter 1, we saw that a court must have subject matter jurisdiction to adjudicate a case. You might think that this would mean that if the court lacks subject matter jurisdiction, then the judgment would not be entitled to preclusive effect, but it turns out to be more complicated than that. According to the Restatement (Second) of Judgments, a judgment from a court that lacked subject matter jurisdiction may nonetheless be given preclusive effect, with a few exceptions. One exception is for default judgments — if a defendant does not appear in the first action, then the defendant later can challenge the validity of the judgment by showing the first court lacked subject matter jurisdiction. Another exception is for cases in which the first court abuses its authority or substantially infringes on the authority of another court. One author suggests the example of a traffic court that enters a judgment granting a divorce and awarding child custody.[2] If a party later sought to enforce the traffic court's judgment, the judgment's validity could be challenged for lack of subject matter jurisdiction.

(b) Finality

For a judgment to be entitled to finality, it must be "final." Talk about circular logic! Preclusion is all about giving "finality" to judgments. So it may seem rather empty to say that for a judgment to be entitled to preclusive effect, it must be a final judgment. But the finality requirement is not as meaningless as it may seem at first glance.

Litigation often proceeds for quite a while before adjudication ultimately resolves the dispute. During that time, the court may make many decisions in the litigation. The court may deny a motion to dismiss, resolve discovery disputes, grant partial summary judgment, rule on the admissibility of evidence, and so forth. Such interlocutory orders—decisions by the court during the course of litigation—do not finally resolve the action. Because they remain subject to modification, interlocutory orders are not considered final enough to be given preclusive effect.

Suppose a trial court enters judgment in a case after trial, summary judgment, or some other adjudication that resolves the case. It sure seems like a final judgment. But now the losing party files an appeal. Is there a "final judgment" for purposes of preclusion? Or suppose the trial court enters judgment, and no party has yet filed an appeal but the time for filing an appeal has not expired. The question is whether finality means at the trial court level or whether it means the unavailability of further review.

Example 4: A sues B. At trial, the jury rejects A's claims, and the court enters judgment for the defendant. A files an appeal. While the appeal is pending, A files another lawsuit asserting the same claims as in the first action. B moves to dismiss the second action on grounds of claim preclusion.

#1 A → B
■ Judgment for B
■ A appeals

#2 A → B

---

[2]David L. Shapiro, Civil Procedure: Preclusion in Civil Actions 28 (2001).

Is case #2 claim precluded? That depends on whether a judgment is considered "final" pending appeal. In the federal courts and the majority of state courts, a judgment is considered final even if an appeal is pending. In these jurisdictions, A's second action would be claim precluded. The reasoning is that most cases are affirmed on appeal, and a trial court's judgment is entitled to respect unless it is actually reversed or vacated. Treating a judgment as final pending appeal also meshes nicely with the final judgment rule of appealability, discussed in Chapter 10, which states that in general a decision can be appealed only if it is a final judgment.

In California and several other jurisdictions, however, a judgment is not considered final for purposes of preclusion until after appeal or the time for appeal has passed. In this minority of jurisdictions, A's second lawsuit would not be claim precluded. As a practical matter, a court faced with such a situation could stay case #2 until the appeal in case #1 is completed, at which point case #2 could be dismissed on grounds of claim preclusion.

(4) "On the Merits"

Many cases and authorities on preclusion state that claim preclusion applies only to a judgment "on the merits." Claim preclusion is meant to prevent litigants from relitigating their dispute after the dispute has been resolved. If parties have received an adjudication on the substantive merits of their dispute, a dissatisfied party should not be permitted to try again for a better result. If, on the other hand, a lawsuit is dismissed on a threshold procedural issue, and if the procedural flaw in the first action can be repaired, then there is no good reason to prevent a litigant from refiling the same claim.

Example 5: A and B have a business dispute, giving rise to state law breach of contract claims as well as a federal antitrust claim. A sues B in federal court, asserting the state law contract claims. There is no diversity of citizenship and no federal question, so when B moves to dismiss for lack of subject matter jurisdiction, the court grants the motion and dismisses A's case. Subsequently, A sues B again in federal court, this time asserting the claim under federal antitrust law.

#1   A → B
   ■ Federal court
   ■ Breach of contract claim (state law)
   ■ Judgment for B — lack of subject matter jurisdiction

#2   A → B
   ■ Federal court
   ■ Antitrust claim (federal law)

Will the court in case #2 throw out A's claim on the ground that it is claim precluded because of the judgment in case #1? Of course not. Even assuming that the antitrust claim arose from the same transaction as the contract claim and thus would be considered the same claim, the first judgment simply was not on the merits. The court dismissed for lack of subject matter jurisdiction. That dismissal means that in the absence of diversity of citizenship or some other basis for federal jurisdiction, A's breach of contract claim did not belong in federal court. It means that A should go to federal court only if the court's limited jurisdiction permits it to adjudicate A's claim. Therefore, it makes perfect sense that A would be allowed to come back to the federal court in order to assert the federal antitrust claim.

Note that if A had returned to federal court to file the same state law contract claim rather than the federal antitrust claim, then the court would dismiss A's complaint again for lack of subject matter jurisdiction.

Here's a similar example, but looking at personal jurisdiction rather than subject matter jurisdiction:

Example 6: A sues B in Oklahoma. B is a New York company that lacks minimum contacts with Oklahoma, so the court grants B's motion to dismiss for lack of personal jurisdiction. Subsequently, A sues B on the same claim, but this time files the suit in New York rather than Oklahoma.

#1   A → B
   ■ Oklahoma court
   ■ Judgment for B—lack of personal jurisdiction

#2   A → B
   ■ New York court

The court in case #2 will not dismiss on grounds of claim preclusion, even though A had previously filed the exact same claim against the same party and had received a final judgment. The judgment of dismissal for lack of personal jurisdiction was not on the merits. Ask yourself what the Oklahoma court really means when it dismisses for lack of personal jurisdiction. It is saying, "Don't sue B here. We don't have any power over this defendant. If you want to sue B, go do it in New York."

If a case has been tried to a jury verdict and the court enters judgment based on the verdict, or if a court enters judgment after reaching findings of fact and conclusions of law in a bench trial, then naturally the judgment is "on the merits" for purposes of preclusive effect. Similarly, if a case is resolved on summary judgment or judgment as a matter of law, the judgment is "on the merits."

A more difficult question is whether a judgment is "on the merits" when a court grants a motion to dismiss for failure to state a claim upon which relief can be granted. Rule 12(b)(6), you will recall, allows a defendant to move to dismiss a complaint if the allegations in the complaint fail to state a valid claim. If a court dismisses an action for failure to state a claim, should the plaintiff be permitted to try again? Well, that depends.

Example 7: A sues B. B moves to dismiss for failure to state a claim, under Rule 12(b)(6). The court grants the motion and dismisses the action. Subsequently, A sues B again based on the same dispute, but with more extensive factual allegations in support of the claim.

#1   A → B
   ■ Judgment for B—failure to state a claim

#2   A → B
   ■ Same claim, but with additional allegations in complaint

The question is whether A's second action is claim precluded. It is the *same claim*, brought between the *same parties*, and it resulted in a *valid, final judgment*. But was the judgment *on the merits*? That depends on why the court granted the motion to dismiss in the first case.

Suppose the court granted the motion because A's claim simply has no basis in law (recall the example from Chapter 5 in which a plaintiff sued because the defendant ignored a friend request). In that case, the dismissal reflects the court's determination that A has no meritorious claim, and there is no reason to allow A to bring the same claim again. Therefore, claim preclusion should apply. To make this clear, the court might state in the order of dismissal that the dismissal is "with prejudice."

Now suppose the court granted the dismissal because of A's failure to plead adequately. Perhaps the allegations in the complaint fail to meet all of the elements of the claim, but leave open the possibility that A has a valid claim but simply forgot to include all of the necessary allegations. Or perhaps it was a technical pleading error, such as failing to include a demand for judgment as required by Rule 8(a). In that case, the dismissal does not reflect a determination that A has no meritorious claim, but rather the court's determination that this complaint has not been drafted properly. Recall from Chapter 5 that the goal of modern pleading, as embodied in the federal rules, is to attempt to resolve disputes on the merits rather than on the technicalities of pleading. Under modern pleading theory, it would not make sense to apply claim preclusion to a dismissal that was intended to tell the plaintiff to get the pleading right, rather than to tell the plaintiff that she had no case. To make this clear, the court might state that the dismissal is "without prejudice" or "with leave to amend."

What if the court dismisses the claim but the order does not state whether the dismissal is "with prejudice" or "without prejudice"? What if the order simply says "dismissed"? In the federal courts, the answer may be found in Rule 41(b), which states: "Unless the dismissal order states otherwise, a dismissal . . . — except one for lack of jurisdiction, improper venue, or failure to join a party under Rule 19 — operates as an adjudication on the merits." In other words, if a dismissal order does not specify that it is *not* on the merits, then the dismissal is considered an adjudication on the merits and is entitled to claim preclusive effect. Two caveats: First, although the federal courts and most state courts follow the Rule 41(b) approach, a few state court systems take the opposite approach; in those state courts, a dismissal is considered to be without prejudice unless the court specifies otherwise. Second, in *Semtek v. Lockheed Martin*,[3] the Supreme Court called into question whether Rule 41(b) really means that the default rule is to consider a dismissal to be on the merits unless the court states otherwise. In that case, the Court expressed concern about whether it would violate the Rules Enabling Act for a federal rule of civil procedure to govern the law of claim preclusion. The Court concluded that the "upon the merits" language of Rule 41(b) means only that the same claim cannot be filed in the same court, and does not govern whether the same claim can be filed in a different court. You'll

---

[3] 531 U.S. 497 (2001).

encounter *Semtek* again later in this chapter, in the section on interjurisdictional preclusion.

So far, our examples have presented situations in which you can figure out claim preclusion by asking yourself whether the judgment was "on the merits" in the everyday sense of those words. Claim preclusion naturally applies to a judgment based on a trial verdict or a dismissal based on a determination that the plaintiff's case is legally without merit. Such judgments go to the merits of the lawsuit. And claim preclusion does not apply to dismissals for lack of jurisdiction, improper venue, or technical pleading problems. But our next example proves that "on the merits" is a term of art, and you have to be careful about applying it.

Example 8: A sues B, and B seeks discovery from A. A refuses to comply with B's discovery requests. B moves to compel discovery, and the court grants the motion. A refuses to comply with the court order and instead tries to conceal information. Finally, the court grants discovery sanctions under Rule 37, and because of the extent of A's misconduct, the court imposes a severe sanction—dismissal of A's action. Subsequently, A files a new complaint asserting the same claim.

#1   A → B
   ■ Court grants B's motion to compel discovery. A fails to comply.
   ■ Court grants Rule 37 sanction of dismissal against A.
   ■ Judgment for B—discovery sanction

#2   A → B
   ■ Same claim

In the second action, B argues claim preclusion. It's the same claim between the same parties, and there is a valid, final judgment. But A argues that claim preclusion applies only to judgments on the merits, and the dismissal in case #1 had nothing to do with the merits of A's lawsuit. Although A's argument sounds logical, you can see that if A's argument were to prevail, it would render the Rule 37 dismissal meaningless. For the sanction of dismissal to have any teeth, it must be given claim preclusive effect, even though the judgment is not based on the actual merits of the lawsuit.

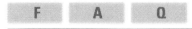

Q: Does claim preclusion apply even if the first court got it wrong?

A: The point of claim preclusion is finality, not certainty. If parties could relitigate claims whenever they don't like the result, there would be nothing left of claim preclusion. If a party thinks the court got it wrong, the proper course is to challenge the judgment on direct appeal. In rare extenuating circumstances, as discussed later in the chapter, parties can move to reopen a judgment. But in general, parties cannot avoid the preclusive effect of a final judgment merely by showing that it was erroneous. As the Supreme Court has explained, "an 'erroneous conclusion' reached by the court in the first suit does not deprive the defendants in the second action 'of their right to rely upon the plea of res judicata.'"[*]

---

[*]Federated Dept. Stores v. Moitie, 452 U.S. 394 (1981) (quoting Baltimore S.S. Co. v. Phillips, 274 U.S. 316, 325 (1927)).

If someone brings or considers bringing a lawsuit after there was an earlier lawsuit about a matter, and you are trying to figure out whether the second action is claim precluded, here's how your analysis might go:

Claim Preclusion Analysis

- To determine whether claim preclusion applies, analyze whether the cases involve the <u>same claim</u>, whether they are between the <u>same parties</u>, and whether the prior judgment was <u>final</u>, <u>valid</u>, and <u>on the merits</u>.
  I. Does the new lawsuit involve the "same claim" as the prior action?
  - ☐ In federal court and most state courts, apply the transactional test: Do the actions arise out of the same underlying factual situation?
  II. Is the new lawsuit between the same parties or those in privity with them?
  III. Is the judgment in the prior case entitled to claim preclusive effect?
  - A. Was there a final judgment in the prior case?
  - B. Was the prior judgment valid?
    1. Did the court have personal jurisdiction?
       - If the answer is no, then the judgment has no claim preclusive effect, but usually the only way to collaterally attack a judgment for lack of personal jurisdiction is by defaulting in the first action.
    2. Did the court have subject matter jurisdiction?
       - Even if the answer is no, the judgment may have claim preclusive effect, unless the first court abused its authority, or unless the defendant defaulted and has a meritorious defense.
  - C. Was the judgment in the first case "on the merits"?
    - Judgments for plaintiffs are nearly always on the merits.
    - Dismissals for lack of jurisdiction, improper venue, or failure to join a party are not on the merits.
    - Other dismissals are on the merits unless the court dismisses "without prejudice" or "with leave to amend."

C. Compulsory Counterclaims

Let's return to the simple two-car accident we saw in Example 1, but this time, it is B who files the second lawsuit.

Example 9: A's car and B's car collide. A sues B, claiming that B negligently caused the collision. B denies that he was negligent and argues that the collision was A's fault. The jury renders a verdict in favor of A for $20,000, and the court enters judgment. Subsequently, B files a lawsuit against A based on the same collision, this time seeking damages for personal injury.

#1   A → B
   - ■ Auto accident — negligence claim for A's injuries
   - ■ Judgment for A — $20,000

#2   B → A
   - ■ Same auto accident — negligence claim for B's injuries

In case #2, A moves to dismiss on the grounds that the parties already had a lawsuit about this accident. It sounds a lot like a claim preclusion argument, but there's an important difference. It would be a real stretch to say that B's claim against A is the "same claim" as A's claim against B. B is, after all, a different human being. Still, the policies underlying the claim preclusion rule — efficiency, consistency, finality — all weigh in favor of not allowing B to bring his claim in a separate action. The goal of claim preclusion is to encourage parties to resolve a dispute in a single action, rather than piecemeal.

That's why most jurisdictions have adopted statutes or rules — such as Federal Rule of Civil Procedure 13(a) — that require counterclaims to be brought in the original action if they arise out of the same transaction or occurrence as the original claim. Such ***compulsory counterclaims*** are not "compulsory" in the sense that they must be asserted. Defendants are free to choose whether they wish to assert a counterclaim. Rather, what makes a counterclaim compulsory is that if it arises out of the same underlying facts as the original claim, and the defendant does not assert the counterclaim in the original action, then the defendant will be precluded from asserting that claim in a later action. Federal courts and most state courts therefore would grant A's motion to dismiss in case #2 on the grounds that B's claim was a compulsory counterclaim in case #1.

Even in the absence of a compulsory counterclaim rule, some courts have dismissed claims on the ground that they should have been asserted as counterclaims or defenses in the first action, particularly if the effect of the second action would be to nullify the outcome of the first case.

D. Issue Preclusion

Whereas claim preclusion is about preventing multiple lawsuits based on the same claim, issue preclusion is about giving finality to a court's resolution of a particular issue. When a specific question has been answered in one case, issue preclusion prevents the parties from trying to get a different answer to the same question in another case. If issue preclusion applies, then the determination from the first case is taken as conclusively established for purposes of the second case.

To break down the elements of issue preclusion, a good starting point is the Restatement (Second) of Judgments §27: "When an issue of fact or law is actually litigated and determined by a valid and final judgment, and the determination is essential to the judgment, the determination is conclusive in a subsequent action between the parties." But just as we found when trying to capture claim preclusion in a single sentence, this sentence contains a number of pieces that deserve close examination. Picture the sentence like this:

> When an **issue** of fact or law is **actually litigated and determined** by a **valid and final judgment**, and the determination is **essential to the judgment**, the determination is conclusive in a subsequent action **between the parties**.

You've seen one of these underlined terms — *valid and final judgment* — earlier in this chapter in the discussion of claim preclusion. The requirements of *validity* and *finality* as prerequisites for recognition of a judgment apply to issue preclusion in much the same way as they apply to claim preclusion, so we won't revisit those concepts here. But the other four underlined terms raise issues uniquely applicable to issue preclusion:

1. How do courts decide whether a subsequent lawsuit raises the *identical issue* that was decided in a prior case?
2. What does it mean for an issue to be *actually litigated*, and how can courts tell what issues were *actually determined*, especially if there was a general jury verdict rather than answers to specific questions?
3. What makes an issue *essential to the judgment*?
4. Issue preclusion applies to subsequent actions between the same parties. To what extent can issue preclusion be used by persons who were not *parties* to the first action?

Sidebar

COLLATERAL ESTOPPEL

Older cases refer to issue preclusion as *collateral estoppel*, and that terminology is still used frequently by lawyers and judges. *Estoppel*, as a general matter, means that if someone is entitled to rely on something based on another person's acts, then the person who acted is prevented ("estopped") from claiming otherwise. Think of promissory estoppel, which you probably studied in contracts class. The notion behind *collateral estoppel* is that if a party has already litigated an issue, then the party should not be allowed to open up the same issue after it has been decided, as others are entitled to rely on the fact that the party already had its shot at litigating the question. The party is *estopped* from relitigating the issue. The "collateral" part of collateral estoppel distinguishes it from *direct estoppel*, which prevents relitigation of an issue in a subsequent action on the same claim. Collateral estoppel — which comes up much more frequently — prevents relitigation of an issue in a subsequent action on a different claim.

(1) Identical Issue

For a determination to be given preclusive effect in a subsequent lawsuit, the very same question must be at issue in both actions. Some call this the "identical issue" requirement. If the issue that was decided in the first case differs from the issue that is disputed in the second case, then issue preclusion does not apply.

Whenever you think about issue preclusion, your first step should be to define as crisply as possible the issue or issues that you think might be precluded. In the auto accident case in Example 1, it might be "Did B drive negligently?" and "Was B's negligence a proximate cause of the collision?" The issue may be major or minor, it may be simple or complex, but for issue preclusion to apply, the issue must be *identical* — not merely *similar* — in both proceedings.

(2) Actually Litigated and Determined

Issue preclusion applies only to issues that were actually litigated and determined in the first action. This makes a lot of sense since the point of issue preclusion is to avoid relitigating questions that already have been answered after adequate consideration.

Sidebar

STARE DECISIS

Don't confuse issue preclusion with the doctrine of *stare decisis*. Under the doctrine of stare decisis, a court's legal ruling may be followed in later cases based on the binding or persuasive authority of the precedent. Issue preclusion usually involves factual issues or mixed questions of fact and law, and its application is narrower and less flexible than stare decisis. As a matter of stare decisis, courts sometimes overrule their own precedents and need not always follow prior rulings. When issue preclusion applies, however, the resolution of the issue in the prior case is conclusive in the later case.

Notice the difference here between issue preclusion and claim preclusion. Claim preclusion prevents parties not only from pursuing claims that were *actually* litigated, but also those that *could have been* litigated as part of the prior action, as long as they constitute part of the "same claim." Claim preclusion tells the plaintiff: "You already had a lawsuit about this dispute. If you had other legal theories you could have and should have asserted them at that time."

It's different with issue preclusion. Issue preclusion never tells litigants: "You *could have* presented evidence about this issue in the earlier lawsuit, so now you're precluded from raising it." Rather, issue preclusion says: "This exact issue was already raised in a prior lawsuit. It has been litigated and answered. So we're going to take that answer and use it in the current action. You are precluded from relitigating the issue."

How does the court in case #2 know what issues were actually litigated and determined in case #1? Figuring out what has been *litigated* is a reasonably straightforward matter, which may involve seeing what evidence was presented at trial or in summary judgment papers.

Figuring out what has been *determined* is easy in some cases. In a bench trial, the judge is required to make specific findings of fact and conclusions of law. Therefore, it is easy to know what issues were actually determined whenever the factfinder in case #1 is a judge. Similarly, if case #1 was a jury trial in which the jury rendered a special verdict or a general verdict with interrogatories, the jury's determinations are stated explicitly in the answers to the special verdict questions or interrogatories.

In other cases, however, it's harder to know exactly what issues were determined, particularly if case #1 was a jury trial in which the jury rendered a general verdict. A general verdict reveals only whether the plaintiff or defendant prevails on each claim, and if the plaintiff prevails, then the amount of damages. General verdicts do a perfectly good job of resolving the case at hand, but they can be frustrating later on if you're a lawyer trying to figure out whether a prior judgment has any value as a matter of issue preclusion.

Suppose a plaintiff sues a defendant for negligence, and the defendant asserts an affirmative defense such as contributory negligence in a pure contributory negligence jurisdiction. The jury renders a verdict for the defendant. If a later case raises the same questions about who was negligent in this incident, can issue preclusion be used? The problem is that we simply do not know what the jury actually determined because the verdict form does not say *why* the jury found in favor of the defendant. Maybe the jury decided for the defendant because it determined that the defendant did not act negligently. Maybe the jury decided for the defendant because it determined that the plaintiff was contributorily negligent. Or maybe the jury decided for the defendant because, although the defendant acted negligently, the jury determined that the defendant's negligence did not cause the plaintiff's alleged injury. In the end, we know nothing about what the jury found, other than the outcome that the defendant is not liable to the plaintiff.

But with a bit of deductive logic, sometimes it is possible to see what the jury determined, even when the first case was decided by general verdict. The most helpful case I know for illustrating this point is a 1979 Indiana case involving a railroad crossing accident, *Illinois Central Gulf Railroad v. Parks*.[4] Jessie Parks was driving with his wife Bertha. Their car collided with a train. Bertha sued the railroad for her injuries; Jessie joined Bertha's case as a plaintiff seeking damages for loss of consortium. The plaintiffs claimed that the railroad was negligent. The railroad denied that it was negligent and asserted Jessie's contributory negligence as an affirmative defense. Under Indiana law at the time, a plaintiff's contributory negligence constituted a complete bar to a claim. The case went to a jury trial. On Bertha's claim, the jury found the railroad liable for $30,000. On Jessie's claim, the jury found for the defendant. Subsequently, Jessie brought a lawsuit against the railroad for his own injuries.

#1   Bertha (injury) → RR
     Jessie (consortium)
     ■ Indiana state court.
     ■ RR denies negligence, asserts contributory negligence.
     ■ Bertha — Judgment for plaintiff (Bertha) $30,000
     ■ Jessie — Judgment for RR
#2   Jessie (injury) → RR

Think about what preclusion arguments the parties should make in case #2. Before turning to the issue preclusion arguments, think about claim preclusion. The railroad, as you would expect, argued that Jessie should be barred from bringing the second case. Run through the elements of claim preclusion in your mind, and you'll see that in most jurisdictions the railroad would have a winning argument and would succeed in getting Jessie's second case dismissed on grounds of claim preclusion. The claim arose out of the same transaction; the railroad and Jessie are the same parties; and the prior case resulted in a valid, final judgment on the merits. Under Indiana law of claim preclusion, however, "same claim" was not defined by the transactional test, but rather by a narrower test that treated Jessie's personal injury claim as separate from his claim for loss of consortium. So the court rejected the railroad's claim preclusion argument.

Now, what about issue preclusion? Both Jessie and the railroad sought to use issue preclusion in case #2. Jessie argued that it was already determined that the railroad was negligent, and that the railroad's negligence was a proximate cause of the accident. He wanted the railroad to be precluded from relitigating those issues. Were those issues actually determined in case #1? Logically, the answer has to be yes. The jury in case #1 awarded damages to Bertha on her negligence claim against the railroad. To have found for Bertha, the jury must have determined by a preponderance of the evidence that the railroad was negligent and that its negligence was a

[4]390 N.E.2d 1078 (Ind. App. 1979).

proximate cause of the collision. If the jury had failed to find either of those elements, then Bertha would have lost on her negligence claim. Therefore, the court agreed with Jessie that the railroad was precluded from relitigating the issues of negligence and proximate cause.

But that's not the end of the story. The railroad, too, sought to use issue preclusion in case #2. The railroad argued that it was already determined that Jessie was contributorily negligent. If the jury found in favor of Bertha but against Jessie, the railroad argued, the reason must be that the jury agreed with the railroad's contributory negligence defense against Jessie. Jessie argued that it is not clear whether the jury in case #1 found him negligent, because maybe instead the jury found that Jessie had not suffered any loss of consortium damages. Logically, either finding — contributory negligence or zero damages — could have resulted in the jury's verdict for the defendant on Jessie's loss of consortium claim. The court agreed that it was impossible to determine why the jury had found against Jessie in case #1 and therefore refused to allow the railroad to use issue preclusion on the question of contributory negligence.

The upshot was that case #2 was allowed to go forward (because claim preclusion was denied). The next step would be a trial solely on the issues of contributory negligence (because the railroad's issue preclusion argument failed) and damages. At trial, no evidence would be required on the issues of the railroad's negligence and proximate cause, both of which were taken as conclusively established (because Jessie's issue preclusion argument succeeded).

Remember that the "actually litigated and determined" requirement is no mere technicality. Issue preclusion means that certain determinations from one case may be taken as conclusively established in another case, and the parties will not be allowed to relitigate those questions. The point of the "actually litigated and determined" requirement is to prevent the unfairness that would occur if parties were precluded from presenting evidence on issues that had not truly been litigated in the prior action, or that the factfinder in the prior action did not actually decide. So if the first case involved either judicial findings of fact or a special verdict with explicit jury determinations, look at those to see what issues were determined. But even if the first case resulted in a general jury verdict, don't give up on the possibility of issue preclusion. As in the *Parks* case, common sense and logic can show you what issues were actually determined, laying the groundwork for issue preclusion in the subsequent case.

(3) Essential to the Judgment

Even if an issue was actually litigated and determined, it would not make sense to apply issue preclusion if there is a significant risk that the factfinder in the first case treated the issue cavalierly rather than carefully. That's the reason for the requirement that the determination be essential to the judgment. If a determination was not necessary to the disposition of the case, then the judge or jury may not have considered the issue thoroughly. Also, to whatever extent the parties foresee that an issue will not be essential, they may not advocate their positions as vigorously as they would with regard to issues that are more likely to determine the outcome. Finally, if the determination was not essential to the judgment, then it could not have formed a basis for appeal, and the possibility of appellate review is one guarantor that an issue has been treated with care.

Example 10: A and B are involved in an accident in which both are injured and each blames the other. A sues B for negligence, and B asserts the defense of contributory negligence; the jurisdiction follows the doctrine of pure contributory negligence. In a special verdict, the jury finds that both parties were at fault in the accident. The verdict states that defendant B was negligent and also that plaintiff A was negligent. The court therefore enters judgment for the defendant because, under the pure contributory negligence doctrine, the plaintiff's negligence acts as an absolute bar to recovery. Subsequently, B sues A for negligence based on the same accident. (Please tell me that you are thinking, "How can B bring a separate action against A based on the same accident? Wouldn't that be a compulsory counterclaim in the first action?" You're right. In federal court and most state courts, it would be a compulsory counterclaim and therefore the second action would be precluded. But it makes a good preclusion illustration, so assume that this takes place in the state courts of one of the few jurisdictions that does not have compulsory counterclaims.)

#1　A → B
   ■ Negligence claim
   ■ Special verdict:
      1. B was negligent.
      2. A was negligent.
   ■ Judgment for B

#2　B → A
   ■ Negligence claim based on same accident

　　In the second action, A argues that a jury already determined that B was negligent, and issue preclusion should apply. Therefore, A contends, B should lose the second action based on B's contributory negligence. Would issue preclusion apply to the determination of B's negligence? No. Although it is the identical issue and it was actually litigated and determined, the determination of B's negligence was not essential to the judgment in case #1. The outcome in the first case would have been the same regardless of whether the jury found B negligent because the jury's finding of A's contributory negligence ensured a defense verdict. Since the finding of B's negligence was not essential to the judgment in the first case, issue preclusion would not apply.

　　Meanwhile, B is also thinking about how to use issue preclusion. B argues that that a jury already determined that A was negligent, and issue preclusion should apply to that finding. The issue of A's negligence was essential to the judgment in case #1 — contributory negligence is why A lost the first case. Therefore, issue preclusion would apply to the finding that A was negligent. The upshot: In case #2, it will be taken as conclusively established that A was negligent. Note that this does not necessarily mean that B will win the lawsuit. B still has to prove damages. Also, A can pursue the defense of contributory negligence by presenting evidence that B was negligent. But as far as issue preclusion goes in case #2, it will establish A's negligence but not B's negligence, because B's negligence was not essential to the judgment in case #1.

　　Alternative holdings present a difficult but important twist on the "essential to the judgment" requirement. Sometimes, a jury or judge makes multiple findings, any one of which would be sufficient to support the outcome. For example, in the case of

Halpern v. Schwartz,[5] a bankruptcy judge granted a petition for an involuntary bankruptcy against Evelyn Halpern. The judge made three separate findings relating to Halpern's transfer of a bond and mortgage to her son. Any one of the findings would have been sufficient to grant the petition. The court found that Halpern had transferred property with the intent to hinder creditors, that she had transferred property without fair consideration, and that she had made a preferential payment. Subsequently the bankruptcy trustee brought an action to deny Halpern a discharge of her debts, on the grounds that she had transferred property with the intent to hinder her creditors. For the denial of a bankruptcy discharge, intent would be a key issue. The trustee moved for summary judgment, arguing that issue preclusion should apply to the earlier proceeding's finding that Halpern had transferred property with the intent to hinder creditors.

#1   In re Halpern
   ■ Involuntary bankruptcy
   ■ Court's findings (bases for involuntary bankruptcy):
      1. Transfer with intent to hinder creditors
      2. Transfer without fair consideration
      3. Preferential payment

#2   In re Halpern
   ■ Action by bankruptcy trustee to deny discharge

At first, it looks like issue preclusion should apply. The question of whether Halpern transferred property with the intent to hinder creditors is the identical issue in the first and second proceedings. We know that the issue was actually litigated and determined. Unlike the jury verdict in *Parks*, the court in *Halpern* spelled out its findings in the first action. Nonetheless, the court in *Halpern* decided that issue preclusion does not apply because the finding of intentional hindrance was not essential to the judgment in the first action. Because it was one of several alternative grounds, the court reasoned, the issue may not have received sufficiently careful attention, vigorous advocacy, or appellate review.

This is an issue on which courts have reached differing conclusions. The *Halpern* court followed the Second Restatement of Judgments, which stated that alternative holdings should not be given issue preclusive effect because they are not essential to the judgment. But some other courts, including most federal courts, continue to follow the view of the First Restatement of Judgments, which stated that alternative holdings should be given issue preclusive effect. A lawyer faced with a question of whether issue preclusion applies to alternative holdings therefore must pay careful attention to how the question has been treated in that particular jurisdiction.

In trying to understand the importance of whether alternative holdings get issue preclusion, think for a moment about strategy. Plenty of lawsuits include multiple issues that could determine the outcome, whether various bases for a claim or various defenses that could defeat the claim. If courts follow the First Restatement approach of giving issue preclusive effect to each alternative holding, then litigants that are concerned about the future implications of a particular issue will want their lawyers to litigate each issue to the hilt. In the *Halpern* case, for example, even if it was clear

---

[5]426 F.2d 102 (2d Cir. 1970).

that the involuntary bankruptcy would be granted based on a transfer without fair consideration, the debtor would be well advised to litigate as vigorously as possible the issue of intent to hinder creditors. Even if, as a practical matter, the intent issue made no difference to the involuntary bankruptcy petition in the first action, she might choose to fight hard on that issue for fear that an adverse determination would come back to haunt her through issue preclusion in a later proceeding.

Be careful not to confuse the problem of alternative holdings with the more straightforward problem of nonessential determinations. Although it may look similar at first glance, Example 10—in which the jury found both the plaintiff and defendant negligent—does not involve alternative holdings. Alternative holdings are multiple determinations, any one of which could support the outcome. In Example 10, the finding of B's negligence did not support the case #1 judgment at all. It was, as the case played out, simply an extraneous finding that did not matter to the outcome. The problem of alternative hold-

ings would arise if, in Example 10, the jury in case #1 answered that A was negligent but B was not negligent, and the court therefore entered judgment for the defendant B. The two determinations—the defendant's non-negligence and the plaintiff's contributory negligence—would be alternative bases for the judgment. In that situation, whether the determinations would be given issue preclusive effect would depend on whether the court followed the First Restatement or Second Restatement approach to alternative holdings.

(4) Same Parties and the Mutuality Doctrine

The notion of "same parties" for purposes of issue preclusion resembles, to some extent, the treatment of claim preclusion. Only parties can be *bound* by a judgment, with exceptions that generally fall under the description of *privity*. But on the question of who can *assert* preclusion, we will see that issue preclusion is treated quite differently from claim preclusion.

(a) Who Is Bound by Issue Preclusion

This part is just like claim preclusion. In general, only parties are bound by a judgment, with a limited exception for nonparties who are in privity with a party. To illustrate the point, let's return to the three-car collision from Examples 2 and 3.

Example 11: A three-car collision occurs among drivers A, B, and C. A sues B for negligence. The jury does not find that B was negligent, and therefore returns a verdict for the defendant. The court enters judgment accordingly. Subsequently, C sues B for negligence in the same collision.

#1   A → B
- Auto accident
- Negligence claim
- Judgment for B—B not negligent

#2   C → B
- Same auto accident
- Negligence claim

Could B use issue preclusion in case #2? Absolutely not. If B were to say, "It was already decided that I was not negligent in causing the collision," B would encounter several problems. First, C might respond that it's not the identical issue: As a matter of tort law, whether B acted negligently toward A may be a different question from whether B acted negligently toward C. But let's assume that the collision occurred in such a way that the negligence issue was indeed identical with regard to both A and C. And assume it's clear that in case #1 the issue of B's negligence was actually litigated and determined, and was essential to the judgment. Even so, B could not use issue preclusion against C in case #2, because C was not a party to case #1. As in Example 2 with regard to claim preclusion, C simply cannot be bound by judgment #1 because C was not a party to the case. It's a due process thing. If the court in case #1 never acquired power over C because C was not made a party, then C is not legally bound by the judgment—either as a matter of claim preclusion or as a matter of issue preclusion.

Just as with claim preclusion, there are exceptions when a nonparty may be deemed to be represented by a party for purposes of issue preclusion. Recall the discussion of privity earlier in the chapter. The same analysis applies to issue preclusion. As a matter of both claim preclusion and issue preclusion, for example, a successor in interest may be bound by its predecessor's litigation, or a person may be bound by a judgment in a case brought on his behalf by a legal representative. But keep in mind the narrowness of the privity exception. The general rule is that only parties are bound by a judgment.

(b) Who Can Assert Issue Preclusion: The Mutuality Doctrine

Now we turn to what many students find the toughest part of learning preclusion—the mutuality doctrine and the rise of nonmutual issue preclusion. Nonmutual issue preclusion occurs when someone who was *not* a party to the first case uses the judgment for issue preclusion against someone who *was* a party to the first case. Most modern courts permit at least some nonmutual issue preclusion, but under more limited circumstances than mutual issue preclusion. To illustrate, let's return to the three-car collision of Example 11, but this time we'll let the plaintiff win the first case.

Example 12: A three-car collision occurs among drivers A, B, and C. A sues B for negligence. The jury returns a verdict for the plaintiff, and the court enters judgment accordingly. Subsequently, C sues B for negligence in the same collision.

#1   A → B
- Auto accident
- Negligence claim
- Judgment for A—B negligent

#2   C → B
  ■ Same auto accident
  ■ Negligence claim

This time, it is C who tries to use issue preclusion. In case #2, C argues that it was already established in case #1 that B was negligent in causing the collision. Unlike C in Example 11, B cannot use the "You can't bind a nonparty" argument, because . . . uhhh . . . B *was* a party in case #1. That's precisely what makes this *nonmutual* issue preclusion. C is seeking to bind B with the judgment from case #1, but B would not be able to bind C if the case had gone the other way (remember Example 11). So the possibility of issue preclusion does not go both directions; only one of the parties has the possibility of binding the other. It's not mutual.

The question is: Can C use issue preclusion against B? Until the mid-twentieth century, the answer would have been no. That's because courts would have applied the **mutuality** doctrine. Under the mutuality doctrine, a person could not assert issue preclusion unless that person could also be bound by the same doctrine. It had to be mutual. This meant that the only ones who could use issue preclusion were those who were parties to the first case.

Starting with the California Supreme Court's 1942 decision in *Bernhard v. Bank of America*,[6] however, the mutuality doctrine began to decline. In that opinion, Justice Roger Traynor reasoned that if a party had a full and fair opportunity to litigate an issue in the first case, there was no justification for allowing the same party to relitigate the issue against a different adversary in a later case. It took some time for other courts to follow suit. Almost 30 years after *Bernhard*, the U.S. Supreme Court abandoned the mutuality doctrine in *Blonder-Tongue Laboratories v. University of Illinois Foundation*.[7] The federal courts and a substantial majority of the states now allow at least some nonmutual issue preclusion, although several states still cling to the traditional mutuality doctrine.

F   A   Q

Q: What's the difference between nonmutual preclusion and the rule that you can't bind a nonparty?

A: Nonmutual issue preclusion is when one who was not a party to the first case tries to bind someone who *was* a party. From the perspective of due process, nonmutual preclusion differs dramatically from trying to bind someone who was not a party to the first case and who therefore was not subject to the power of the first court. With few exceptions, nonparties are not bound by a judgment.

You need to know a little bit more about the *Blonder-Tongue* case to understand the next piece of the puzzle — the difference between defensive and offensive nonmutual issue preclusion. Here's what the *Blonder-Tongue* case involved. A patent

---

[6]122 P.2d 892 (Cal. 1942).
[7]402 U.S. 313 (1971).

holder sued another company, alleging that the company had infringed its patent. The defendant prevailed in its argument that the patent was invalid, so the court entered judgment for the defendant. The same patent holder subsequently sued a different alleged infringer—call it Infringer 2.

#1   Patent Holder → Infringer 1
   ■ Patent infringement claim
   ■ Judgment for defendant—patent not valid

#2   Patent Holder → Infringer 2
   ■ Patent infringement claim

In case #2, Infringer 2 asserted issue preclusion: "Patent Holder, your patent is not valid. You already litigated that very issue, and you lost." Patent Holder's response to Infringer 2's issue preclusion argument? In a word, mutuality. "Infringer 2, you weren't a party to case #1, so you have no right to use that judgment for your own advantage. After all, if the first court had decided our patent was valid, you would not have been bound by that decision. It's just not fair to preclude us from relitigating the issue of patent validity, when you would have been free to relitigate the issue if it had come out the other way in the first case." Although there's some force to the fairness argument in favor of the traditional mutuality rule, the Supreme Court decided that the policies in favor of issue preclusion—efficiency, consistency, finality—apply even when the party asserting issue preclusion in the second action was not a party to the first action. Therefore, the Court allowed Infringer 2 to use issue preclusion to establish that Patent Holder's patent was not valid.

We know that *Blonder-Tongue* involved *nonmutual* issue preclusion, but was it *defensive* or *offensive*? Or to put it differently, was Infringer 2 using issue preclusion as a shield or as a sword? When you think of it that way, it is clear that Infringer 2 was using issue preclusion as a shield to defend itself against Patent Holder's infringement claim. Therefore, the case involved **defensive nonmutual issue preclusion**. Similarly, the *Bernhard* case in California involved defensive use.

Now let's return to Example 12 to see how the nonmutual issue preclusion analysis plays out. In Example 12, A sued B in case #1, and B was found to have negligently caused the three-car collision. In case #2, C sues B, and C seeks to use issue preclusion to establish B's negligence in causing the collision. What C is trying to do, as we already saw, is to use *nonmutual* issue preclusion. But would it be *defensive* or *offensive*? Since C is trying to use issue preclusion as a sword to establish a negligence claim against B, it would be **offensive nonmutual issue preclusion**.

Since most courts no longer cling to the mutuality doctrine, following *Bernhard* and *Blonder-Tongue*, you might think that it would be easy for C to use nonmutual issue preclusion against B in case #2. Not so. Courts are much more reluctant to permit offensive nonmutual issue preclusion than defensive. To understand why courts would find offensive nonmutual issue preclusion more troubling than the defensive version, look at some of the differences between how defensive and offensive issue preclusion play out.

First, consider the joinder incentives created by issue preclusion. Defensive nonmutual issue preclusion encourages plaintiffs to join all potential defendants in one action, which tends to promote judicial efficiency. Recall that Rule 20 allows permissive joinder of parties if the claims arise out of the same transaction or occurrence. In *Blonder-Tongue*, for example, if Patent Holder knows that defensive nonmutual issue preclusion is permitted, then Patent Holder should prefer to sue both Infringer 1 and Infringer 2 in the same lawsuit, because otherwise Patent Holder faces a one-way disadvantage. If Patent Holder brings separate actions and loses on the issue of patent validity in the first action, the result will be binding in the second action, but if Patent Holder wins on the issue of patent validity in the first action, the issue may be relitigated later against other defendants. Defensive nonmutual issue preclusion thus tends to promote judicial economy by encouraging joinder of parties in a single action so that an issue can be litigated once with finality.

Offensive nonmutual issue preclusion does just the opposite. If courts were to freely allow offensive nonmutual issue preclusion, then potential plaintiffs would prefer not to join in the first action, but rather to wait and see the outcome. In Example 12, A and C could have used permissive joinder to bring their claims against B in a single action. But if C believes that offensive issue preclusion will be available, then C would prefer to wait on the sidelines. That way, if A loses the first lawsuit, C remains free to bring a lawsuit and litigate the issue of B's negligence, and if A wins the first lawsuit, then C would use offensive nonmutual issue preclusion to establish B's negligence in a new lawsuit. This "wait and see" problem is one important reason why courts disfavor offensive nonmutual issue preclusion.

Second, consider several situations in which offensive nonmutual issue preclusion would be especially unfair to the defendant. Suppose the stakes in the second case dwarf those in the first. Maybe A sustained relatively minor damage and sued for $10,000 in case #1, but C suffered substantial personal injuries and property damage and is claiming one million dollars in case #2. Would it be fair to bind B to a finding of negligence from case #1? The danger is that B may not have defended case #1 vigorously because the stakes were low. Offensive nonmutual issue preclusion would have the unfortunate effect of forcing B to litigate case #1 as if it were for much bigger stakes, which would increase the cost to A as well as to the public. Similarly, it would be unfair to bind a defendant to an issue determination if the procedural opportunities in the first court — for example, the right to gather information through discovery or the opportunities to present evidence at trial — were more constrained than in the second court.

Another situation involving potential unfairness is when there have been multiple cases with inconsistent determinations concerning the particular issue. Professor Brainerd Currie created a famous hypothetical example. Imagine a train wreck that results in 50 lawsuits against the railroad brought by 50 different plaintiffs, each of whom was injured in the wreck. The railroad wins cases 1 through 25. In each case, the jury finds that the railroad was not negligent. But in case #26, the jury finds that the railroad was negligent, and so Plaintiff 26 wins. Can Plaintiff 27 use issue preclusion to establish that the railroad was negligent? Obviously, it would be ridiculous to permit issue preclusion to establish negligence under these circumstances. On the question of whether the railroad was negligent, the score is 25-1 in favor of the railroad. Case #26 was the aberration. Even if only one jury had found the railroad not negligent before the conflicting finding of negligence, most courts would not allow a plaintiff to use offensive nonmutual issue preclusion in the face of inconsistent determinations.

Finally, consider which party is bound by each type of issue preclusion. Defensive nonmutual issue preclusion binds the party who chose the time and place of the first lawsuit. It was the patent holder in *Blonder-Tongue*, not the alleged infringer, who selected the venue for case #1 and who controlled the timing of the lawsuit. It hardly seems unfair to hold a litigant to the decisions of a tribunal that was selected by that litigant. Offensive nonmutual issue preclusion, by contrast, would bind a party who may have been dragged into case #1 kicking and screaming.

The Supreme Court addressed these concerns in *Parklane Hosiery Co. v. Shore*,[9] and decided that in some cases, offensive nonmutual issue preclusion is permissible. In *Parklane Hosiery*, a private plaintiff brought a class action against the Parklane Hosiery Company. In a prior government enforcement action, a court had found that the company had issued a materially misleading proxy statement. The plaintiff in the class action sought to use this determination in his lawsuit. The Supreme Court acknowledged that offensive nonmutual issue preclusion often presents dangers of unfairness, but on the facts of the case, the Court found it permissible to use such issue preclusion. There was no "wait and see" problem because it would have been impossible for the plaintiff to join in the first action. The stakes in the first case were high and the procedural opportunities were thorough, so the defendant had a full and fair opportunity to litigate the issue. Finally, the issue had not been the subject of inconsistent determinations. Many courts decide whether to permit offensive nonmutual issue preclusion based on these considerations laid out by the Supreme Court in *Parklane Hosiery*.

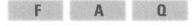

Q: Can a judgment in a criminal case have issue preclusive effect in a subsequent civil case?

A: If a criminal prosecution results in an acquittal, it is unlikely that the judgment would have any issue preclusive effect because the acquittal means only that the government failed to prove its case beyond a reasonable doubt. But if the criminal case results in a conviction, then the judgment may be given issue preclusive effect in a later civil case against the same defendant, such as a wrongful death case brought by a private plaintiff after the defendant was convicted of murder. Note that this would be a form of offensive nonmutual issue preclusion.

Even though the strict mutuality doctrine has been abandoned in most jurisdictions, you still have to think carefully about mutuality when analyzing issue preclusion because courts take seriously the fairness concerns about nonmutual preclusion, especially for offensive use. Here's what your analysis might look like when you're faced with an issue preclusion problem:

Issue Preclusion Analysis

I. First, be sure to identify clearly what issue was resolved that may be entitled to issue preclusive effect. Then ask:
   A. Is the issue identical in case #2 and case #1?
   B. Was there a valid and final judgment in case #1?
   C. Was the issue actually litigated and determined in case #1?
   D. Was the determination essential to the judgment in case #1?

---

[9]439 U.S. 322 (1979).

E. Was the party to be bound by issue preclusion either a party in case #1 or in privity with a party?

II. If the answer to any of the above questions is no, then issue preclusion does not apply. If the answer to all of them is yes, then figure out whether you're dealing with mutual or nonmutual issue preclusion.

    A. Was the party asserting issue preclusion in case #2 also a party in case #1? If so, then it's mutual issue preclusion. If not, then it is nonmutual issue preclusion, which would be prohibited under the traditional mutuality doctrine, but may be allowed under modern preclusion doctrine.

    B. If nonmutual issue preclusion, figure out whether it's defensive or offensive: Is the asserting party using issue preclusion as a shield or as a sword?

        1. If defensive nonmutual issue preclusion, then pay attention to whether there was a full and fair opportunity to litigate the issue in the first action, but most courts permit such preclusion.

        2. If offensive nonmutual issue preclusion, then courts permit it under much more limited circumstances, and with much greater attention to potential unfairness.

            ■ Could the plaintiff easily have joined in case #1?

            ■ Were the stakes or procedural opportunities in case #1 insufficient to ensure a full and fair opportunity to litigate the issue?

            ■ Have there been inconsistent determinations of the issue?

            ■ If the answer to any of these questions is yes, that may provide a reason for a court to reject offensive nonmutual issue preclusion as unfair.

E. Interjurisdictional Preclusion

What if the first case and the second case are in different courts? Not infrequently, preclusion questions arise across jurisdictional boundaries. When that occurs, must the second court give preclusive effect to the first judgment? And whose law of preclusion should apply?

This is where the Full Faith and Credit Clause comes into play. Article I, Section 4 of the U.S. Constitution states: "Full Faith and Credit shall be given in each State to the public Acts, Records, and judicial Proceedings of every other State." Each state must give respect to judgments entered by courts of every other state. Notice, however, that the Full Faith and Credit Clause says nothing about federal courts. But Congress passed a full faith and credit statute, 28 U.S.C. §1738, which adds an obligation for federal courts to respect the judgments of state courts. Neither the clause nor the statute says anything about giving full faith and credit to the judgments of federal courts, but federal common law requires that both federal courts and state courts respect federal judgments—that is, that they give federal court judgments appropriate claim preclusive and issue preclusive effect.

Internationally, the question of to what extent judgments from one country should be respected by the courts of other countries has been the subject of extensive debate and treaty negotiations. For our purposes, suffice it to say that judgments frequently are enforced and given preclusive effect across international borders, but that transnational enforcement of judgments is much more complex and uncertain than enforcement and preclusion across jurisdictional borders within the United States.

When a party asserts claim preclusion or issue preclusion based on a judgment from a case in a different jurisdiction — whether federal to state, state to federal, or from one state to another — whose preclusion law should apply? Remember that certain aspects of preclusion law vary from one jurisdiction to another, such as the definition of "same claim" for claim preclusion or the mutuality requirement for issue preclusion. What if the preclusion decision turns on an issue that would be treated differently by the court that rendered the judgment in case #1 and the court that has to decide the preclusion question in case #2? Most courts and commentators agree that the law of the first forum should generally govern the preclusive effect of the judgment.

In 2001, the Supreme Court faced a difficult twist on this question of choice of preclusion law. What made the case hard was that it involved the preclusive effect of a judgment from a state law case in federal court, and therefore implicated the *Erie* doctrine. In *Semtek International v. Lockheed Martin Corp.*,[10] the plaintiff Semtek had sued Lockheed on a state law claim. Semtek originally sued in California state court, but Lockheed removed the action to federal court based on diversity jurisdiction. The federal court dismissed "on the merits and with prejudice" based on California's two-year statute of limitations. Semtek then proceeded to file the same claim in Maryland state court, because in Maryland the applicable statute of limitations was three years, which had not yet expired. As you would expect, in case #2, Lockheed moved to dismiss on grounds of claim preclusion.

#1   Semtek → Lockheed
  ■ C.D. Cal. (federal court)
  ■ Judgment for Lockheed — statute of limitations

#2   Semtek → Lockheed
  ■ Same claim
  ■ Maryland state court

Was Semtek precluded from pursuing the action in Maryland state court after the first action had been dismissed by the federal court? It's the same claim, between the same parties, and there was a valid and final judgment. But the point of contention was whether the judgment in case #1 was "on the merits." It was a dismissal on statute of limitations grounds, which arguably does not go to the merits of the lawsuit, and under California law the dismissal would not be entitled to claim preclusive effect. But the federal court in case #1 stated explicitly that the dismissal was on the merits, and even if the court had not said so, Rule 41(b) would seem to treat the dismissal as a judgment on the merits.

The Supreme Court explained that the preclusive effect of the judgment must be determined by looking to the first case. In other words, Maryland preclusion law was entirely beside the point. But that didn't end the inquiry

---

[10]531 U.S. 497 (2001).

because case #1 was a state law case in federal court, so the question of whose law governed the preclusive effect of the judgment was really an *Erie* question! The Court ultimately concluded that the effect of a federal court judgment was governed by the federal common law of preclusion, but that federal law should incorporate state standards unless an overriding federal interest demands otherwise. Therefore, the Court held that the Maryland state court should apply the California rule that the statute of limitations dismissal was not on the merits and thus not entitled to claim preclusive effect.

F. Relief from Judgment

After an order or judgment has been entered, a party may ask the court for relief from the judgment. If the court grants the motion, then the judgment has no claim preclusive or issue preclusive effect on the party. You would expect courts to be extremely reluctant to grant such motions, and you'd be right. Rule 60(b) defines narrowly the situations in which a party can obtain relief from a judgment. For example, if the judgment was obtained by an adverse party's fraud, the court may grant relief. Newly discovered evidence does not provide a basis for relief unless it could not have been discovered in time to include in a motion for a new trial. "Excusable neglect" can provide a basis for relief, but this does not mean that parties can expect relief from a judgment simply because they or their attorneys were careless or confused. One situation in which courts are somewhat more willing to grant relief is to give defendants relief from default judgments in cases where the defendant can show good cause for defaulting, prompt correction of the default, and a meritorious defense. With the possible exception of default judgments, lawyers should not think of motions for relief from judgment as an easy way for their clients to avoid the preclusive effect of a judgment. Finality is the overriding goal of preclusion doctrines, and Rule 60(b) creates a relatively small exception to finality to avoid serious injustice.

SUMMARY

- Under the doctrine of claim preclusion, a valid final judgment on the merits precludes relitigation of the same claim between the same parties.

- Under the transactional test applied by most modern courts, "same claim" for purposes of claim preclusion means any claim that could have been brought in the first action and that arises out of the same underlying facts.

- In general only parties are bound by a judgment, but the binding effect can extend to those who are in privity with a party, such as successors in interest.

- For claim preclusion to apply, the judgment must be valid and final, and must be "on the merits" or "with prejudice."

- Under the doctrine of issue preclusion, an issue of fact or law that has already been determined against a party may be taken as conclusive in a subsequent action.

- For issue preclusion to apply, the issue must have been actually litigated and determined, and the determination must have been essential to the judgment.

■ The traditional doctrine of mutuality held that issue preclusion could apply only if both parties were also parties to the prior action. Most modern courts have abandoned the mutuality doctrine and permit nonmutual issue preclusion as long as the party to be bound was a party to the prior action and had a full and fair opportunity to litigate the issue.

■ Courts are more reluctant to permit offensive than defensive nonmutual issue preclusion. Offensive use may be rejected if the new party could easily have joined the first action, if the stakes in the first action were insufficient, or if there have been inconsistent determinations of the issue.

■ The Full Faith and Credit Clause and statute require courts within the United States to give preclusive effect to judgments from other states, and federal common law requires them to respect federal court judgments.

■ In narrow circumstances, a trial court may vacate a judgment and thereby remove any preclusive effect from the judgment.

CONNECTIONS

Personal Jurisdiction

The core idea of personal jurisdiction is that a court cannot bind a person with a judgment unless the court properly had power over that person. The law of personal jurisdiction thus operates as a check on the binding effect of judgments, and the due process principle that nonparties are not bound by a judgment constrains who can be bound through claim preclusion and issue preclusion.

Pleadings, Joinder, Discovery

Think about the logic of the broad transactional test for claim preclusion in light of the ease of pleadings, joinder, and discovery under the federal rules. It's relatively easy to plead claims under Rule 8. It's easy to amend pleadings under Rule 15. It's easy to join claims under Rule 18. And it's easy to obtain information with the broad scope of discovery under Rule 26(b). So there's no excuse if a party fails to assert a claim that arises out of the same events. The liberal approach to pleadings, joinder, and discovery set up an unforgiving attitude about preclusion. The rules are designed to get it right the first time and accord finality to the outcome.

Joinder

In the federal rules, you'll find a rule on compulsory counterclaims and a rule on permissive joinder of claims, but you won't find any rule on compulsory joinder of claims. As far as any lawyer is concerned, however, there is a compulsory claims joinder rule. It's called claim preclusion. The joinder rules (and supplemental jurisdiction) are designed to facilitate broad joinder; preclusion law encourages parties to use those joinder rules to resolve a controversy in a single lawsuit. It's no coincidence that the transactional test for claim preclusion looks so similar to the tests for compulsory counterclaims under Rule 13(a), for crossclaims under Rule 13(g), for party joinder under Rule 20, and for supplemental jurisdiction under 28 U.S.C. §1367.

Class Actions

A fundamental aspect of the law of preclusion is that a judgment binds only the named parties and those in privity with them. The single greatest exception to this rule is the class action. The claim preclusive and issue preclusive effect of a class action judgment binds all of the members of the class.

Erie

Some preclusion problems require an *Erie* analysis to determine whose preclusion law applies. If case #1 was in federal court on a state law claim, the preclusive effect of the judgment may depend on whether it is governed by federal or state preclusion law. This is the question the Supreme Court addressed in *Semtek v. Lockheed Martin*.

Trial

The procedural nature of the trial, and especially the form of the verdict, can control the issue preclusive effect of the judgment. Issue preclusion depends on knowing what issues were actually litigated and determined in case #1. What was litigated can be ascertained by examination of the trial record, but figuring out what was actually determined can be more difficult. A jury trial general verdict does not spell out issue determinations, but often they can be deduced from the claims and the outcome. A special verdict form, by contrast, identifies precisely what the jury determined and thus enhances the issue preclusive effect. Similarly, if case #1 was a bench trial, then the judge's findings of fact and conclusions of law facilitate issue preclusion.

Appeals

The final judgment requirement for preclusion resembles the final judgment rule of appealability, embodied in 28 U.S.C. §1291. Indeed, one argument in favor of giving judgments preclusive effect pending appeal is that the appealability rule presumes that a judgment is final before the appeal is taken. But the two final judgment rules serve different functions and may be interpreted differently in each context.

TABLE OF CASES

INDEX